WHISPERING JACK & PEGGY 'O'

WHISPERING JACK & PEGGY 'O'

Eugene Schmidt

Published by Tate Publishing & Enterprises, LLC
127 E. Trade Center Terrace | Mustang, Oklahoma 73064 USA
1.888.361.9473 | www.tatepublishing.com

Tate Publishing is committed to excellence in the publishing industry. The company reflects the philosophy established by the founders, based on Psalm 68:11,
"The Lord gave the word and great was the company of those who published it."

Cover design by Allen Jomoc
Interior design by Jomel Pepito

Published in the United States of America

ISBN: 978-1-62854-928-7
Biography & Autobiography / Entertainment & Performing Arts
13.12.02

ACKNOWLEDGMENT

I want to acknowledge my wife, Connie, for her tireless effort in assisting with the research, being my sounding board, and proofing the final manuscript. Without her help, I would probably still be writing the story you are about to read.

CONTENTS

Preface 11
Autumn 1918 13
Sainte-Menehould 26
Homeward Bound 43
The Good Old USA 55
Back in the Bronx 64
Merry Christmas 67
The Song Plugger 74
O'Malley's Piano Bar 80
New Year 1920 87
The Bradford Estate 94
The Agent 112
The Star Talent Agency 130
Chicago 136
Glenn Raney 140
Mrs. Bradford Meets the Family 143
The Apartment 147
The Aqua Delight 153
Radio Station WJZ 157
The Funeral 162

Radio Broadcasting 166
Let the Good Times Roll 170
The Chalmers Six 177
The B & B Company 181
The Breakup 185
Back to Chicago 195
Peggy Meets the Family 207
Buffalo, New York 214
The Weddings 224
The First Record 237
Bad News 240
Sailing Westward 244
Movies and Golf 252
An Unexpected Guest 258
Cecilia, Does Your Mother Know You're Out? 265
The Beginning of a Golden Year 270
England 279
France and Germany 287
Back to London 301
Surprise in Manchester 306
The GE Monitor 313
Peggy Returns 319
The Wow Year 326
1928 356
The Year of the Crash 378
Life Goes On 394

Hollywood 399
New York, New York 418
The Third and Final Film 425
The Dairy Farm 432
The Early Thirties 438
The Spanish Mansion 454
The Final Good-bye 462
Tying the Knot 465
The USO and Beyond 467
The Ed Sullivan Show 476
Epilogue 481
"Whispering" Jack Smith's Recordings 483

PREFACE

This story is based on the lives and times of "Whispering" Jack Smith, a famous radio broadcasting personality, and "Sweet" Peggy O'Neil, a famous stage actress. Over a number of years, the Schmidt family was close to Jack Smith and Peggy O'Neil. One family member chauffeured for and played golf with Jack Smith. Another corresponded with Peggy O'Neil for over twenty years. These close relationships resulted in stories that were passed down within the family over time. The author of this novel is a third-generation relative (great nephew) of Jack Smith. After the passing of Jack Smith, most of his personal belongings were given to the author's father. Included were 16 mm home movies in canisters with Jack Smith's annotations, a complete collection of Jack Smith's recordings on seventy-eight records, a custom-made travel case, an assortment of miscellaneous jewelry, and a cigar box full of old notes.

In 2005, the author discussed with his brothers his intent to write a novel about their Uncle Jack and Peggy O'Neil. Whenever the three surviving great nephews would meet, there would be discussion about what they remembered from the stories they had heard over the years. Additional research was done to refine the information they put together. The result is the weaving of all this information into a novel entitled, *Whispering Jack and Peggy 'O'*. I sincerely hope you enjoy this, until now, untold story.

AUTUMN 1918

THE ARGONNE FOREST

Jack thought, this place is so quiet and beautiful; can there really be a war raging on the other side of that tree line? John Schmidt, a private in the US 6th Division, 51st Infantry, Company C, had arrived three days earlier as one of the replacements to assist the French in the Great War against Germany. There was a lull in the fighting, so the more seasoned soldiers were having some fun with the new recruits. Sergeant Dutcher called all of the new men together and issued each a gas mask. Following some brief donning instructions, the group was given a thirty second time limit to put on their masks. The men watching knew that for replacements to successfully don a mask in less than one minute was a real achievement.

"Begin on my count of three," shouted Dutch.

"One, two, three." And the show was on. Schmidt had more trouble than most of the others.

"Schmidt, where did you get your training?"

"Fort Oglethorpe, sir," Jack replied.

"Well, son, you would have been choking, and well on your way to burning out your lungs." Then turning to the onlookers, Dutch beckoned for Corporal Johnson to take Schmidt aside and give him some lessons.

Corporal James Johnson had been in the army for more than a dozen years. He was a career soldier who had been promoted and busted several times because of his drinking habits. To the veteran members of Company C, he was known simply as JJ.

"Come on over here, Schmidt." JJ sat on the ground behind a large rock separating him from the enemy lines. Schmidt came over and sat next to JJ.

"What's your first name, kid?"

"Jack."

"Well, Jack, we've had mustard gas on us three or four times already and had to send a half a dozen guys off to the hospital because of trouble with their masks. The masks work okay most times. The biggest problem is getting a good tight seal around your face. Now watch how I don my mask. Always pull the two neck straps tight first. Then, pull these two head straps until you can feel it hurt a little from being too tight. Okay, you try it now."

Jack held his mask up to his face, pulling the straps over his head and adjusting them in the sequence that JJ had just shown him. It was so easy. Why didn't they show us how to do this back in Georgia?

"Thanks, Corporal. That worked so much better."

"You can call me JJ, kid. Just remember to blow out and feel for leaks around your face. If you feel a leak, try pulling the straps tighter. If that doesn't work and the gas is on us, don't remove your mask. Put one hand up to the leak and squeeze or push in to block the leak. If gas is getting into the mask, you will get a bad smell like rotten eggs. Try to get to high ground without getting shot. The gas hugs the ground, so you can avoid most of it that way."

"Where are you from, kid?"

"New York City."

"Well, kid, we're both a long way from home now. Let's go back over and hear what Dutch is saying."

William Dutcher was a seasoned veteran who had served under both Teddy Roosevelt and General Pershing. He was a descendant of the pilgrims that landed at Plymouth Rock and was extremely proud of his heritage. He was in his early forties, but had the appearance of a well-conditioned thirty-year-old.

"Men, we are going to be on the move tomorrow or the next day. We're waiting for the tanks to join up with us. General Pershing has developed maneuvers for us to work close to the tanks. When we push off, we will be strung out behind the tanks in columns of two. This will protect us from the German machine gun fire. You will have to double time to stay up with the tanks. When we get into heavy fighting, you may have to spread out behind the tanks and use whatever ground cover is available. Your squad leaders will direct you. Remember, we keep advancing until we displace the enemy from their positions. Anything short of that will increase our number of casualties."

The next morning was once again bright and pleasant. Around ten o'clock, the mechanical sound of the tanks approaching from the rear could be heard.

"I hate that sound." JJ had been in the Cavalry and still felt that horses were better suited for fighting in or near wooded areas.

Sergeant Dutcher called for the men to assemble.

"We are going over to meet with the tankers. Take a good look at the machines and the silhouette of protection they provide when we advance toward the German machine guns. One of the tank commanders will speak to us. Don't be bashful about asking questions. Doing so may even save someone's life."

Jack had seen a few tanks back at Fort Oglethorpe but never up close. They were actually smaller than he had pictured them, and he began to wonder how well two columns of men would be protected from enemy fire. One of the tank commanders came forward and talked with Sergeant Dutcher. After a few minutes, Dutcher turned to his men.

"Men, this is Tank Commander Harris. He is going to tell you some things about these tanks and what they are capable of doing in battle. Remember that these machines are most vulnerable from the rear. It is up to us to make sure there are no Germans left behind the tanks. After you hear Tank Commander Harris, we will assemble over by the tank on the left to do a few practice runs."

"Thank you, Sergeant. Men, these are Renault FT-17 tanks. They are made in both France and the United States. We operate with a two-man crew. The turret rotates three hundred and sixty degrees. The machine guns have wide sweep capability. The machine is bullet proof, but can be disabled by artillery and mortar rounds. We will be depending upon you, men, to knock out the mortar emplacements and help us with any close in artillery. When we are on smooth terrain, you will have to double time to keep up with us. Over battle scarred ground our speed is slower. If you see muzzle flashes ahead of us as we advance, you are not fully protected and may need to change your position behind us. Are there any questions?"

A replacement asked, "Will we have trouble breathing with the tank's exhaust fumes directly upon us?"

FT-17 Tank

"Son, I will gladly change places with you anytime. There are more fumes inside of this machine than you can imagine. In fact, we will be running with the hatch open and wearing these shrapnel masks until close in fire forces us to button up." Harris held up a shrapnel mask for the troops to see. "If there are no more questions, let's have the first squad line up in two columns behind the tank over to our left. Sling your weapon over your shoulder, and keep your gas masks strapped where you can readily reach them for quick donning. Once we are moving, Sergeant Dutcher will give the order to don your masks. Remember, you must keep moving and stay out of the line of fire. Shortly after hearing the gas order, you will be given another order to ready your weapons. When I turn the tank around and stop, stand at ease as we go back to get the next squad."

The exercises took over two hours with Dutch, JJ, and several of the other seasoned veterans taking turns running alongside of the men and giving them advice. Because of the tank drill, lunch was later than usual. Bread and cheese along with cool flavored water was distributed to the men as they lounged in small groups in the shade of the nearby trees. A messenger ran up and asked each group if anyone spoke German. When the messenger got to Jack's group, Jack responded that he did. The messenger asked Jack to come with him. JJ said it was okay and that he would tell Sergeant Dutcher.

The runner, Private Francis Kelly, told Jack to follow him and stay low when they were in open ground. After running for about two hundred yards, Kelly motioned for Jack to enter the end of an abandoned trench. Kelly stopped and motioned for Jack to sit and rest beside him. The trench was reinforced with timber and boards along the sides. The base was full of old puddles and mud with an assortment of discarded items. The eastern topside was strung with barbed wire and a variety of other nasty-looking objects meant to impede anyone from gaining entrance from that direction.

Francis Kelly was a slightly-built Irishman from the outskirts of Philadelphia. He had been with the company for over three months and was selected as a runner for his ability to cover ground at a very fast speed.

"Where are we headed?" Jack asked.

"About halfway down this trench there is a bunker where the top brass hang out. Two Germans were captured last night, and the brass needs someone to translate for their interrogation. Are you ready to move again?"

"Yes."

"Okay. Follow me and keep your head down. There are still snipers out there that will take a shot if they get a chance."

After another fifteen minutes of bent-over running they arrived at the bunker. Kelly reported in, and shortly after, a young captain came out of the bunker to talk to Jack.

"What is your name, Private?"

"Jack Schmidt, sir."

"And where did you learn to speak German, Jack?"

"My father was the captain of a German sailing ship. He and my mother both came from Warnemunde near Berlin and settled in New York when he stopped sailing. We spoke German as well as English in our home and the surrounding neighborhood."

"Is your German good?"

"Yes, sir. I am very fluent."

"All right, what I want you to do when we get inside is to simply translate my questions to the prisoners, and in turn, their responses back to me. Then I am going to leave you alone with the prisoners. Try to make some small conversation with them, such as about where they were born and let them know about your parents. The idea is to gain their confidence. What we really want to know is how seasoned are the German troops we are facing. Are they very young? Are they tired? What do they eat? Are their weapons in good order? Are they well-supplied with ammunition? Don't ask these as direct questions, but do try to evaluate these things throughout your conversations. Understood?"

"Yes, sir."

"I will send someone in with some bread and cheese in about ten minutes. There will be a portion for you. About one hour after that, I will again enter and ask you to translate a few questions. Then I will ask you to leave with me, and we will find a place to debrief. Okay?"

"Yes, sir."

One of the prisoners appeared to be very young. The other was probably in his thirties. Both of their uniforms were covered with areas of caked-on mud. They had not shaved or bathed for days.

The captain introduced Jack as an interpreter, and immediately started to form questions for Jack to translate into German. He started by asking if they were being treated well and then moved on to questions about troop strength, numbers of artillery pieces, the distance to the nearest town, how far away from the hospital were their lines, and so on. The answers were very evasive, and mostly meaningless or simply unanswered. Jack began to understand why the captain was counting on him to gain some meaningful information during his time alone with the prisoners.

After the captain left, the prisoners were very quiet. Jack didn't say anything until after the bread and cheese were brought in.

"This cheese is much better than what they bring to us on the line." There was no response, so Jack asked if they got meat to eat. Still no response, so he stated that if they were still here this evening, the meal would be corned beef and cabbage.

"We sometimes get sauerkraut," the young prisoner stated.

Jack told the prisoners how he loved sauerkraut, but the army never served it. He described how it was served back home in New York City. The prisoners knew of New York City. Jack told them about his parents, and how they got to New York City. Little by little, they were drawn into conversation with Jack. The younger prisoner was more open and willing to discuss things, but sometimes clammed up when the older prisoner looked his way. They both ate very quickly.

"Would you like more bread and cheese?"

They both nodded. Jack went to the doorway and asked the guard to bring more. He saw the captain give him the thumbs up signal, and within five minutes, there was more food. This time there were also some grapes and a small tin of pound cake that had already been sliced. The conversation went much smoother. The captain was right. There were many young, inexperienced soldiers on the line. Morale was not very good, and many of the soldiers were ill equipped. They knew that the Americans had entered the war, and most realized that the Germans could not win. They were simply waiting for the war to end.

The captain returned and asked to again translate some questions about German observation balloons and the location of the German aircraft. Again the answers were very evasive. The captain turned to Jack and motioned to him that they were leaving. Jack shook hands with the prisoners and followed the captain out.

They moved down the trench until reaching a wide spot with several empty ammunition crates strewn about. The captain grabbed two, and motioned for Jack to sit down.

"Jack, you did well in there. Now tell me your impression of the situation on the German line."

"Well, Captain, first, I should tell you that most of the information came from the younger prisoner. The older one was pretty much silent and sometimes looked at the other prisoner as if to be saying, 'Hold your tongue.' Toward the end of the session, the older man began to talk more, but I have a feeling that he may have been giving me misinformation. The Germans facing us are a mixed bag of a small number of very tired veterans, and a larger number of fresh young and inexperienced troops. Their food supply is poor, and sometimes they go for days without anything other than powdery bread. They seem to have adequate ammunition, and there was talk of some new armour piercing ammunition that will soon be made available to help them turn away tanks. Their biggest fear seems to be our tanks and our flame throwers. I would say their morale is very low and they appear to be in a survival mode awaiting an end to the war. I did not find out where their field hospital is located, but my impression is that it is very crowded and ill equipped, and many of their fellow wounded soldiers were ultimately dispatched back to Germany on freight trains. I think that's about it, sir."

"Thank you, Jack. We had heard about the development of armour piercing ammunition, but don't think that it has reached the front lines yet. Do you think you can find your way back to your unit?"

"I'm sure I can, sir."

"One more thing, Jack, what you just told me is to remain confidential. When you return, you simply say that you translated some stuff for the brass up in the bunker. Okay? Good luck and keep your head down."

Jack chose to return to his unit at a much slower pace. He had the opportunity to stop periodically in the trench and examine some of the discarded items that were lying around. He found a helmet with a bullet hole through the front, and wondered if someone wearing it was killed. There were shell casings and discarded food tins. He found a small mud covered leather portfolio. Jack stopped momentarily and looked at the contents. There was a hand-written letter from someone's mother along with faded photographs of brothers and sisters, or maybe a girlfriend. He decided to take it along and give it to his sergeant. The quiet was broken with the sound of artillery shells passing overhead and explosions near the German lines. Jack picked up his pace and was soon running across the open terrain. It seemed like he covered the ground faster than when he and the runner had crossed in the opposite direction. Maybe it was the artillery shells whistling overhead that made the difference.

When Jack reached his unit, everyone was huddled close to existing ground cover. His arrival was just barely acknowledged. *Good*, he thought, *there won't be any questions that I have to evade*. Soon he found out that they would be moving out at dawn. Jack felt the fear of going into combat and also an excitement that was overwhelming. JJ moved next to Jack and told him to go over his gear. Food and darkness arrived at the same time. There would be no food in the morning. Jack ate most of the beef and cabbage. He saw others stuffing leftover bread into their pockets, so he did the same. There was very little conversation, so Jack decided to pray. He had been raised as a devout Catholic and prayed that he would have the strength to get through the next day doing whatever was asked of him—even if it meant killing another human being.

Jack didn't think he would be able to sleep, but he was soon awakened by JJ signaling for him to get ready and not make any noise. JJ motioned for the men to line up in columns of two and then passed each man, whispering that the tanks would soon move up in front of them, at which time he would signal for us to fall in behind one of the tanks. The quiet was broken as the tanks started their engines and moved forward of the troops. Once again, JJ passed by each man, this time almost shouting to be heard above the tank noise for each man to stay in close and watch his signals. The tanks started forward, at the same time, artillery shells went screaming above and exploding in the German positions. Jack swallowed hard and began to run to his position. He expected a call for gas masks, but to his surprise none came. It was still rather dark and hard to see the ground, but within minutes he could see muzzle flashes ahead. He remembered the training exercise from the previous day, and altered his position slightly to the left, so no flashes were visible. The tanks slowed and opened fire with their machine guns. JJ signaled to ready our rifles. He shouted, "If you see any muzzle flashes ahead of the tanks, fire at them."

Sporadic rifle fire started. Jack saw some flashes, but found it difficult to take aim while walking behind the tanks. He noticed that JJ would stop almost instantaneously, fire and then continue moving. Jack tried stopping for a second, and found that he could acquire a target and fire. He thought, *This Browning rifle is so much better than the rifles we had at Fort Oglethorpe, I might even hit something.* It was getting brighter, and silhouettes of enemy emplacements appeared before them. The tank canons began to fire. Jack could now hear the cries of enemy soldiers as the barrage of fire took its toll. He looked to his left and right, and it seemed that there were no casualties. A few minutes later, they were on top of the enemy. JJ signaled and shouted for the men to disperse from behind the tanks. Jack's column moved to the right. He remembered that there were to be no Germans left behind the tanks. JJ signaled to take cover and fan out as they continued to move forward and toward the right flank.

About fifty yards to the left, there was a grouping of trees. Jack knew from the briefing that the French would be advancing through the trees and not to fire in that direction. He could hear bullets striking the ground nearby and tried to stay down on the ground, inching forward behind JJ. There was a shell crater a few yards in front of JJ. He motioned for everyone to move into the crater. Once in the crater, JJ counted his men and was pleased to find all present. He positioned the men along the forward rim of the crater, and told them to concentrate fire on what appeared to be a sandbox bunker about thirty yards in front of them. It appeared that an enemy mortar was firing from behind the sandbags. JJ stated that we're going to take out that mortar. Five men were to follow JJ over the top of the crater rim. The remaining men were to continue heavy fire toward the right hand side of the enemy bunker.

Jack was among the five following JJ. They stayed low to the ground, sometimes crawling, and always trying to keep cover between them and the bunker. When they reached within five yards of the sandbags, JJ shouted, "Charge!" and all ran over top of the sandbags shooting at anything that moved. With the mortar silenced, JJ signaled for the rest of the men to come forward. JJ then checked everyone. One, Private Manse, had a minor leg wound. He told Manse to stay back and wait for the medics to dress his wound. As they started to move forward, orders to don gas masks could be heard. JJ told his men the Germans were gassing their own lines and to get our masks on. Jack had no problem getting his mask on, and he felt no leaks when blowing out.

The daylight was brighter now, and the gas almost seemed to be an orange tinted fog spreading along the battleground. There was a lull in the fighting as each side regrouped. There were many dead and wounded soldiers. Most were Germans. Over close to the tree line, a group of about twenty Germans were being held as prisoners. They stood with their helmets removed, and both hands placed on top of their heads. They, too, were wearing gas masks. JJ entered the German trench in front of us, and motioned for us to take defensive positions in case there would be a counter attack.

At this point, Jack started to detect the smell of rotten eggs in his mask. He slid over to where JJ was and told him of the problem. JJ looked around and then said, "Kid, see those prisoners over by the trees? There is higher ground over there. Make your way over and stand behind a tree for cover. When the rotten-egg smell diminishes, take off your mask and smell the air. If the odor is gone, breathe in and out deeply to try and clear your lungs. Stay by the prisoners and return to the rear when they are moved. Find a medic and tell him about your situation. If they send you back up, get a new mask. Good luck, kid."

There was only intermittent gun fire now, but Jack remembered what the runner had said about sniper fire, so he stayed low and rapidly made his way to the trees. He could feel some burning in his lungs as he moved, and he started to worry about Sergeant Dutcher's warning that he could burn out his lungs. Upon reaching the trees, the gas was no longer visible, and the rotten-egg odor seemed to be gone. Jack took off his mask and was thankful to smell fresh air. He took deep breaths as JJ had instructed him.

One of the soldiers guarding the prisoners called over to Jack asking if he was all right. Jack tried to call back and discovered that his voice was gone. He gave the thumbs up signal and moved over to the guard. The best Jack could do was to manage a whisper describing his problem. The guard sent him back further to see the corporal in charge of the detail. Jack was told to stand by until they were ready to move the prisoners to the rear, and then to come along and help guard them. A short time later, the guards ordered the prisoners to form a column and move. There was some confusion, as the prisoners did not understand English. Jack wished he were able to speak. It would have been much easier to address the prisoners in their own language; however, through multiple hand signals and loudly shouted orders from the guards, the prisoners were finally marshaled along. Upon reaching the rear lines, the Germans were placed inside of a temporary compound surrounded by barbed wire.

Jack thanked the corporal and asked for directions to the field hospital tent. There were a handful of soldiers being treated at the tent. A medical officer motioned for Jack to approach him.

"What is your problem, son?"

Jack managed a whisper, "Mustard gas, sir."

The officer looked down Jack's throat while asking if there was any burning sensation in his lungs.

"Not now, sir, but my lungs were burning when I moved through the area of gas."

"I think we need to take a better look at you. I'm going to have you transported on the next truck to our hospital in Sainte-Menehould. Take a seat on the far side of the tent. Someone will be over to take care of the paper work."

"Thank you, sir," Jack whispered and then moved over to the bench along the tent wall.

An orderly arrived within minutes and filled out some forms. A tag with "Private John Schmidt, Gas Victim, 6th Division, 51st Infantry, and Company C" was strung around his neck and he was given a canteen-full of water.

"Take this along with you and drink as much as you can. It will help your throat. Stay here until the truck driver comes for you. Good luck."

Jack nodded as a sign of appreciation. It was over an hour before the driver arrived. At first, it was interesting to watch the hustle and bustle in the tent, but when more seriously wounded soldiers were brought in, Jack often turned away. He disliked the sight of blood and hearing cries from the wounded soldiers.

The driver simply said, "Follow me. You will be riding up front with me. We have six stretcher patients along with a medic in the back. We'll be on the road about thirty minutes. The only danger is from German aircraft. They like to machine-gun us. Should we get attacked, duck down because I can't stop with wounded in the back."

SAINTE-MENEHOULD

The ride through the French countryside was actually enjoyable. The truck passed through quaint, quiet villages with no signs of battle damage, and townspeople that seemingly were not concerned with the war that was so close by.

Sainte-Menehould was a good-sized town with a number of crossing road intersections. The hospital was set up in a rather large stone church. Medics rushed out to meet the approaching truck, and the litter patients were quickly taken away. The truck driver asked Jack to follow him and led him to a small entrance where his throat was quickly examined. He then was led through a long hallway to a large open room with about a dozen beds inside.

An attractive woman dressed in a nonmilitary nurse's uniform ushered Jack to an unoccupied bed at the far end of the room. Speaking in French, she told him to undress and put on a gown that was folded neatly on the bed. Jack didn't really understand much of the French language, but he felt he knew what the nurse was telling him.

A patient in the next bed said, "She wants you to take off your uniform, put on the gown, and then stretch out on the bed."

Jack thought the voice was familiar. "You're the runner that took me to translate for the captain yesterday?"

"Yeah, I remember you now, the translator. What happened? Was it gas?"

Jack was still having trouble talking, so he simply nodded.

The nurse returned with a pitcher of water, and again gave instructions in French that undoubtedly meant for him to drink a lot. After downing a glass of water, Jack turned to the runner and managed to whisper, "I haven't had much sleep, so I'm going to try to get a nap." Within minutes Jack was sound asleep dreaming about home in New York City.

Jack's father had passed away in 1915. He was quite a few years older than his mother. His mother made a decent living giving piano lessons in their home. He had a brother, Charles, who was fifteen years older and married. His brother had two sons, Milton and Charles Junior. Milton was clearly Jack's favorite, and he thought of him more as a brother than a nephew. Their houses were almost next to one another, so they spent a lot of time together except for the hours Jack was required to practice on the piano. Jack dreamed he was playing the piano and realized how much he missed the music. His goal was to someday play with a big band or orchestra. He could picture himself dressed in a black tuxedo with a white shirt and black bow tie sitting in front of a large audience. Strangely, he felt no fear of appearing in front of an audience, but rather a sense of fulfillment.

The dream ended when a nurse gently shook him awake. The nurse was accompanied by an English-speaking doctor dressed in white. The doctor asked Jack to sit up, and then placing his stethoscope on Jack's back he repeatedly called for deep breaths while moving the stethoscope around.

"How long were you exposed to the gas?"

"It was maybe ten minutes from the time I first detected the rotten-egg smell in my mask."

"What did you do after detecting the odor?"

"I moved to higher ground and removed my mask when the odor was gone. Then I took deep breaths in and out to try to clear my lungs."

"You did the right thing, soldier. Do you have any burning sensation in your chest?"

"Not now, sir, but I did experience some burning in my lungs when I was running to the high ground."

"We are going to keep you here for a while. I want you to continue to drink a lot of liquids. Your voice will get stronger in a few days. Until then, try not to talk much. The nurse will bring your uniform after it is laundered. You will then be free to move about, but stay on the church grounds, and return to your bed before eight every evening. Do you have any questions?"

"Is there a piano anywhere?"

The doctor was somewhat taken back with Jack's question, but turned to the nurse and speaking in very fluent French relayed the question. After a short conversation with the nurse, the doctor turned back to Jack and told him a nurse would show him to the piano once he was properly dressed. Jack broke into a big smile and thanked the doctor.

The doctor and nurse moved over to the runner's bed and began to examine him. After a few minutes, they moved further along the two rows of beds, checking the patients as they moved toward the entranceway. When they were far enough away to not hear, the runner said to Jack that he knew Jack was not supposed to talk, so to just give him hand signals.

"Do you play a piano?'

Jack gave him an affirmative nod, and then placed his hands together along side of his face indicating that he was going back to sleep. Once again, Jack dreamed he was back at home. His mother's house was a large, sturdy brick row home in the Bronx section of New York City. Concrete steps led to a large front porch with a heavy wooden railing across the front and between the neighboring units. There were two parlors just inside of the front door. The first was a sitting room; the second was used for piano lessons. He could picture the large upright piano where he had spent so many hours playing. He thought about his mother insisting that he practice each day. It was not fun, so why did he now miss the music so much? He pictured his nephew waiting in the adjoining parlor or on the porch for Jack to finish so that they could play stepball in front of the house. Jack was only five years older than his nephew, so he treated him more like a kid brother and thoroughly enjoyed the hours they had to play together. Milt had good athletic skills, so many of their stepball matches were pretty even. Milt had just bounced the tennis ball high off the top step and Jack had to run all of the way back across the street to get to the ball. Just as he was reaching up to catch the ball someone grabbed his arm.

"Private Schmidt, it is time for you to get up. You must try to drink more of this water. I have brought you your clean uniform. Please dress. I will be back shortly, and then take you to the piano."

Jack managed a whisper thanking the nurse. This nurse was undoubtedly French, but she spoke very good English with just a bit of an accent. Jack quickly put on his uniform while swallowing from the water glass in between movements. He was excited and wanted to be ready as soon as the nurse returned, so they could go to the piano. He was going to tell the runner, but when turning to do so, he found the bed to be empty and neatly made. Jack wondered where the runner had gone. Maybe he had been discharged and returned to the line?

"Are you ready to go? I want you to bring the pitcher and your glass. We will fill it along the way and you are to drink more by the piano".

Jack nodded. Then he picked up the pitcher and glass before following the nurse out of the room and again through a long corridor. It seemed like the church had a many hallways and corridors. Jack made mental notes of the way they traveled so that he would be able to find his own way over the coming days. The nurse stopped alongside of two heavy wooden doors that must have reached twelve-feet high. She took the pitcher from Jack and told him to wait by the doors for her return. Within a few minutes, she returned with the pitcher full of fresh water. After handing the pitcher to Jack, she moved to the doors, unlocked them with a fairly large key, and opened them inwardly. She motioned for Jack to enter. They were in a small hall with light coming in through stained-glass windows along two of the walls. On the windowless wall, there was a very old upright piano with a small bench in front of it.

The nurse moved over to the piano. "It has not been used for a long time." She had brought a cloth and started dusting the piano.

Jack whispered, "Allow me." He took the cloth and wiped away the layer of dust. Opening the keyboard cover, he dusted the keys and then playfully hit a few notes. The tone sounded pretty good. He dusted the bench and pulled it close to the piano. Sitting down he started playing old tunes from memory. The nurse came and sat next to him. She was all smiles.

"It is so nice to hear music." She poured a glass of water and passed it to Jack. "You must remember to drink. I have to return to my duties. Can you find the way back to your room?"

Again, Jack nodded.

As the nurse turned to leave, she asked, "Would you be willing to play for some of the patients this evening?"

Jack replied, "Yes."

Upon reaching the doors, she again turned and stated, "About seven tonight."

He loved the feel of the piano keys. He soon began to wonder what music he would play at seven o'clock. Would any of the patients be French? Did he know any French tunes? *Funny,* Jack thought. *I know a lot of Irish tunes but no French.* Too bad we aren't in Ireland. He started playing and simply mouthed the lyrics.

> Oh! Danny Boy the pipes, the pipes are calling,
> from glen to glen and down the mountain side.
> The summer's gone and all the roses falling …

Next he moved to,

> I'm a Yankee Doodle Dandy;
> a real live nephew of my Uncle Sam's
> born on the fourth of July…

Then,

> I'm looking over a four-leaf clover

that I overlooked before;
one leaf is sunshine, the second is rain,
third is the roses that grow in the lane.
No need explaining, the one remainin'.

Jack was amazed at how the music had returned almost instantly to him. It had been six, almost seven months since he had touched a piano. He rose from the piano bench. Many benches had hinged tops. This one was hinged. He opened the top in hope of finding some music sheets, but to his dismay, found only what appeared to be some kind of schedules written in French. He decided to ask the nurse if there were any music sheets in the church. *Water*, he thought. *I better drink some more*. Not knowing what time it was, he decided to return to his bed. He had been told the evening meal would be brought between five and six. He would eat and think about some more tunes that he might play at seven that evening.

Jack made his way through the church without getting lost, and upon his arrival found the runner sitting there. Jack whispered, "I thought maybe they returned you to the line."

"No, the doctor had the medics take me outside and do some exercises. I didn't do very well with the wind sprints, so I'll have to stay here a while longer. They want me to take long walks during the day, maybe even into town and back. Where have you been?"

It was easier to talk now, but only in a very low voice. "A nurse came and took me to a room with a piano in it. I'm going back at seven tonight to play for some patients. Maybe you can come along?"

"I would love to. Anything to get away from this bed is an improvement."

There was a large clock above the entrance to the twelve bed room. Jack checked and found it was ten past five. The food should be here soon. He again started to think about other melodies he might play. Jack was a fan of Irving Berlin's work and could recall "Alexander's Ragtime Band" and "Try It on Your Piano." The doors opened and two carts filled with a variety of food were rolled in. All of the patients in the room were capable of walking, so it was a matter of simply grabbing one of the metal trays, some utensils, and then moving over to the carts to make your meal choices. If the servers understood English, the men could ask questions. If not, you took potluck and just pointed to whatever you wanted to be placed on your tray. The food turned out to be much better than what was served on the line. Jack knew Irving Berlin was in the army and that he had written "Oh! How I Hate To Get Up In the Morning". He kind of knew some of the lyrics, but was not sure if he could play the melody. Well, I'll see how it goes tonight and maybe try playing it.

The runner had finished eating and asked if he could return Jack's metal tray and utensils along with his.

Jack nodded and said, "Thanks."

The church bells rang six times. Jack glanced back at the clock to confirm the time and then asked the runner if he would like to come along and help him get ready.

The runner quickly got up, smoothed his bed, so it looked like it was just made and said, "Let's go."

The nurse that had shown Jack to the piano was in the room, so he walked over to her and in a soft voice told her he and the patient in the bed next to him were going to the piano room to make ready.

"Good, Monsieur. I will be along at seven with some of our patients and maybe a few of the other nurses."

Jack and the runner quickly made their way through the long corridors until they reached the tall wooden doors leading into the small hall. Jack tried the doors and found them to still be unlocked. He and the runner pushed them fully open. There were several lanterns mounted along the walls and one on top of the piano. The light from the stained-glass windows was still good, but Jack knew it would soon fade with the darkness of evening, so he asked the runner to light the lanterns. He then moved to the piano, positioned himself comfortably on the bench and began testing the keys. Next he started to play "Danny Boy".

The runner moved next to Jack at the piano with a look of amazement in his eyes. He picked up on the lyrics.

...the pipes are calling
From glen to glen, and down the mountain side
The summer's gone, and all the roses falling
'Tis you, 'tis you must go and I must bide.
But come ye back when summer's in the meadow
Or when the valley's hushed and white with snow
'Tis I'll be there in sunshine or in shadow
Oh! Danny Boy oh! Danny boy I love you so.

The nurse appeared in the doorway applauding their performance. "Very good, I am going to start moving some people in, so just keep playing. It will be very informal. We are just trying to get our minds away from this terrible war for a little while."

As she left, Jack whispered to the runner, "Stay close by, and when I want to announce anything like the name of the tune, or to ask those present to sing along, I'll turn for you to bring your ear close. You in turn can tell the others."

Jack moved on to "I'm a Yankee Doodle Dandy". In less than five minutes, there were twenty-five or more people in the hall. Some were in hospital gowns, others in uniform. Many had bandaged or cast limbs. Some were supported on crutches. Most of the patients appeared to be Americans. There were even a few nurses and medics in the hall. Jack turned to the runner and whispered, "I'm going to play 'MacNamara's Band'. Tell them to sing along if they like." The runner announced the next selection with an invitation for all to sing along, and when Jack began to play, the runner actually led everyone with the lyrics.

Oh! Me name is MacNamara, I'm the leader of the band
Although we're few in numbers we're the finest in the land
We play at wakes and weddings and at every fancy ball
And when we play at funerals we play the march from Saul.
Right now we are rehearsing for a very swell affair
The annual celebration; all the gentry will be there
When General Grant to Ireland came he took me by the hand
Says he, 'I never saw the likes of MacNamara's band'

Oh! Me name is Uncle Yulius and from Sweden I have come
To play with MacNamara's band and beat the big brass drum
And when I march along the street the ladies think I'm grand
They shout 'there's Uncle Yulius playing with an Irish band'
Oh! I wear a bunch of shamrocks and a uniform of green
And I'm the funniest looking Swede that you have ever seen
There's O'Briens, O'Ryans, O'Sheehans and Meehans, they come from Ireland
But, by yimminy, I'm the only Swede in MacNamara's band.

When the song stopped, there were loud cheers and applause from the happy gathering. Someone called, "Do you know 'Alexander's Ragtime Band'?"

Jack started to play, and again the crowd joined in with the lyrics. Next came, "They Were All out of Step but Jim." Jack was just finishing "Oh! How I Hate to Get Up in the Morning".

You've got to get up; you've got to get up
You've got to get up this morning!
Oh! Boy the minute the battle is over
Oh! Boy the minute the foe is dead
I'll put my uniform away
And move to Philadelphia
And spend the rest of my life in bed.

The head nurse moved up in front of Jack and the runner. She raised her arms and asked for quiet. As the hall quieted, she stated that it was time for bed check, and all were to return to their rooms. While thanking Jack and the runner for a wonderful evening, she displayed the key to the doors and slipped it into Jack's pocket. Then turning back to the guests, she led a final round of applause and began to usher all from the hall.

Jack gave the runner a pat on the back and whispered, "Thank you. You were just great." Then he closed the piano and blew out the nearby lantern. Without a word spoken, the runner passed around the hall blowing out the rest. They closed and locked the large wooden doors, taking along the key that the nurse had slipped into Jack's pocket. Wherever they were seen on the way back to their beds, the other soldiers and staff would wave and verbally compliment their performance. Both waved back while smiling from ear to ear. It was the perfect ending to a very long day.

The next morning, Jack was awakened when he heard a loud call that food had arrived. The runner was already up. They both moved to the cart and filled their metal trays with scrambled eggs and slices of French bread. Jack motioned to their beds. They moved over, sat facing each other and broke into smiles. The runner asked Jack how he would like his coffee and slipped over by the carts to fill two cups.

Handing one cup to Jack, he asked, "Are we going to have music again tonight?"

In a low voice, Jack replied, "Let's see what the head nurse says. Maybe I will ask for permission to walk along with you into town this morning."

"That would be great, Jack. I'm a little nervous about heading out on my own not knowing many French words."

The nurse arrived as they were just finishing their breakfast. Jack took the key from his pocket and passed it to her. She did not take the key. "Private, we would very much appreciate another performance tonight. Do you think you can do it?"

Jack nodded and whispered, "I think so, as long as my friend can come along and help with the dialogue. Would it be possible for the two of us to walk into town together this morning, so we can kind of rehearse?"

"I will check with the doctor and let you know shortly." Within a few minutes, the nurse returned. "You may both walk to town. You must stay off the road. Sometimes it is difficult walking along the side, but we have had incidents where German airplanes machine gun anything or anyone that is on the road."

Jack and the runner quickly readied themselves and headed for the church entranceway. There was a guard posted. They explained their intent to walk to the center of the town and asked how to best get there. The guard said to just move down to the main road, and then turn to the right. He also cautioned them to stay off the road. The roadway had a hard clay like surface with some small stones scattered about. There was a path along the right hand side that pretty much followed the road, but at times almost disappeared into the bordering fields.

As they walked along taking in the fall scenery, Jack reintroduced himself. "My last name is Schmidt, Jack Schmidt from the Bronx in New York City."

The runner responded, "I'm Francis Kelly from a small town, Clifton Heights, which is just outside of Philadelphia. Just call me Frank."

"Well, Frank, with a name like Kelly, I now know how you did so well with the lyrics to all those Irish tunes."

"Yeah, it was kind of easy. You see, Clifton Heights is pretty much divided with the Polish living in the south end of town, and the Italians in the north. There are, however, many Irish families throughout the town. Almost everyone works at the textile mills. We Irish hang out together at work, and sometimes organize Irish get-togethers at somebody's house where we sing Irish songs all day long."

"Were you drafted, Frank?"

"Yeah, my number came up pretty quick. At first, I was kind of glad to get away from the mill, but after a week in basic training, I was wishing to be back at the mill. What about you?"

"Actually, I enlisted. I have a brother-in-law that is a general in the army. Whenever he was around, I was most impressed with his appearance in uniform, and there was something special about his military bearing. So I felt it was my duty to enlist."

"Is the general over here with us?"

"No. He was appointed by President Roosevelt to take charge of the construction of the Panama Canal and went on to become the first governor of the Canal Zone. He was discharged in 1917 and called back to active duty later in the year to serve as quartermaster. You may have heard his name, George Goethals?"

"No, Jack. I don't much follow what is going on outside of our country. I don't really know what this war is all about, or why we are over here fighting."

At this point, the path took a turn deep into the roadside field. Soon they were at the edge of a vineyard with row after row of grape vines stretching up the adjacent sloping hillside. They both stopped and just looked at the beauty of the hillside before continuing on. Field hands were working on the rows, most likely gathering the white grapes.

Jack said, "I know France produces the world's best champagne. I wonder if these are the grapes that are used."

They had been walking for almost an hour, and when the path turned back toward the road, they could see a grouping of town buildings. Soon they were next to a charming little restaurant with outdoor tables and chairs. The name read Café de Ville.

Frank said, "Let's stop and see if we can get a cup of coffee."

Jack was tired from the long walk and quickly agreed. A Frenchman with an apron tied around his waist came out and motioned for them to sit at one of the outside tables. It felt good to sit down. Jack asked the Frenchman for two coffees while holding up two fingers.

"Oui, Monsieur." The waiter went inside for a short period of time and then returned holding a tray with two cups, a ceramic pot containing hot coffee, a small glass pitcher of cream, and a small bowl of sugar. He placed everything on the table and then poured coffee into the cups. Frank and Jack thanked him, and again he disappeared into the café. Within minutes, he returned with a basket full of croissants and a small tray with a dish of creamy butter. Again, Frank and Jack thanked the waiter.

They talked about the first day of the battle, wondering how things were going. There was little information back at the church. Jack told Frank how he had trouble with his gas mask and had to leave the line. Frank said he was running a message back to headquarters when gas hit the area he was running through, and like Jack, he donned his mask quickly, but still had trouble breathing.

He delivered the message and was sent to the field tent and then on to the church in a motorcycle sidecar. Frank said the dust from the motorcycle ride was worse than the gas. It was great to sit and relax. Jack reached into his pocket and brought out a handful of coins, spreading them on the table.

"I don't know much about this French money. Do you, Frank?"

"Not really, I know the ones with the hole in the center are smaller like a nickel, a dime and a quarter would be to us. The big one is a franc. I think the smaller ones are called centimes."

Jack picked up one of the coins. "You're right, it is marked "twenty-five centimes". I don't know its true value. I remember reading on the troop ship that the value of the franc had gone down considerably since France withdrew from the gold standard and started printing a lot of money to help pay for the war."

Jack arranged the coins on the table top and motioned for the waiter to come over.

"Monsieur, we would like to pay you."

"Non, non," the waiter responded as he slid his arms back and forth over top of one another. In broken English he said, "You fight for us…for France, non charge."

Frank stood and shook the waiter's hand. Jack did the same and whispered, "Merci."

They continued walking toward the western end of the village. Very few people were within sight. At the edge of the village, there were numerous empty tables arranged in the center of a square area in the roadway. Jack commented, "This must be where the villagers have their market."

"Yeah, looks like an outdoor market. Maybe we can find out what day they have it and come to town on that day. Shall we start back to the church?"

Jack nodded, and they turned and began retracing their path back. Upon arrival at the church entrance, they found an unusual amount of activity. The guard motioned for them to come over by him, and told them that there was a big battle raging throughout the day with many wounded being brought to the church. When they entered the church, a medic asked if they could lend a hand moving the wounded on stretchers. "Yes," they both responded and followed the medic into the main church body that had been cleared of the church pews making it a large open space.

There must have been thirty or more wounded being treated by a handful of medics, nurses, and doctors. The medic led them to a seriously wounded French soldier lying on a litter. He had some bandages indicating that he had emergency treatment and was ready to be moved to another area. A young French woman appeared and motioned for them to pick up the litter and follow her. Frank and Jack followed the young woman out of the church and into another stone building. There were three rows of beds. Most were occupied with wounded. They were directed to place the French soldier in a bed and then take another out of a bed and on to the litter. This time they followed the young woman outside to a nearby field. It was at this point they realized that they were carrying a dead soldier to a marshalling area for burial. Frank and Jack continued moving litters for several hours. When things seemed to settle down, the medic thanked them and suggested they return to their assigned room.

Back at their room, things were fairly quiet. There were no nurses in sight, and the patients appeared to be taking care of each others' needs. Frank described to some, the activity throughout the church. They all speculated as to how the battle was going. At five o'clock, a young woman appeared and stated there would be no dinner this evening, but if two of them would follow her, they would be given baskets of bread and fruit to be brought back to the room.

Shortly thereafter, the English-speaking nurse appeared and moved directly to Jack.

"Monsieur, please skip the music for the next few nights. I will let you know when we can try again."

Jack nodded and in a low voice said, "I understand. If there is anything Frank and I can help with, please let us know."

"Thank you, Monsieur. I will." And she was gone.

Things were hectic for the next several weeks. Frank and Jack continued to assist the medics, and sometimes received the wounded as they were brought in on trucks. Reports were that the battle was fierce with heavy casualties on both sides. On occasion, Jack would see the English-speaking nurse; however, she never once indicated that they would resume playing music in the evening. Then as quickly as the hectic pace started, it suddenly stopped. The battle for the Argonne Forest was over. The French and the Americans were victorious. Word was that the Germans were pretty much in full retreat.

The next day, Frank was ordered to return to C Company. Jack helped him move his bags to the entrance of the church where they said their *good-byes*. Jack had a feeling of emptiness when the truck pulled away. He was going to miss Kelly. He vowed to travel to Clifton Heights near Philadelphia someday and find his wartime friend.

Later that afternoon, the English-speaking nurse found Jack and asked him if he would play music for the patients that evening again around seven.

"Yes, I will be happy to, but my friend Frank was ordered back to our unit, and I am not sure if my voice will hold up."

"I will help you with the lyrics. I think I remember most from your first performance. I shall be at the small hall early, so you need not worry about the key."

After Jack finished his evening meal, he headed for the small hall. The doors were open and the English-speaking nurse was there lighting the lanterns. There was something different about her. She was in a flowery dress and looked quite attractive. Jack had only ever seen her in a nurse's uniform with her hair tied back. Jack guessed her age to be about thirty. She had always worn a wedding band, and Jack pondered whether or not to ask about her husband.

The nurse asked, "Is there anything you would like to rehearse with me?"

Jack replied, "Come and sit next to me while I play a few tunes and voice the lyrics softly. You may sing along, if you like."

Jack found that she was quite good and quick to learn. Soon the patients and a few of the staff began to drift in. When the room was nearly full, the nurse stood up and addressed all telling them that they were welcome to sing along with the music. The hour went by quickly, and when the church bells rang eight times, the nurse holding her arms up high, asked for quiet. She thanked Jack and led a round of applause and then directed the staff to lead the patients back to their respective areas. When only she and Jack were left in the room, she extinguished all of the lanterns but one in the far corner. She then moved to the large wooden doors, closing and locking them from the inside. She approached Jack and put her hands on his shoulders.

"Jack, I have also been ordered to leave. Some of us will be moving closer to the front where another temporary hospital has been set up. I don't want to be alone tonight."

She moved to the piano bench and opening the hinged seat, withdrew two blankets and a folded bed linen. Jack could not believe what was happening.

"But your wedding band, what about your husband?"

"My husband was killed more than two years ago in this dirty war."

She placed a blanket on the floor, and as she started to spread the linen on top of the blanket, Jack knelt beside her and helped. The nurse kissed Jack gently at first, and then more passionately as they stretched out on the fresh linen.

Jack awoke with the light of dawn just coming through the stained-glass windows. He could see the nurse silhouetted against the light from the window. She was getting dressed into her uniform. *My God*, Jack thought, *I never realized how beautiful she is.* She moved close to Jack and sat beside him.

"Jack, on top of the piano you will find my name and the name of the village where I come from written on a card. The village is not far from Paris. Ask any shopkeeper, and they will be able to tell you of my whereabouts. Should you return to France after this war, I would love to see you again? We will have to leave the hall now as I must return the blankets and linen. Don't worry about your evening bed check. I took care of it. I must go now. My transportation will be here soon. I will always remember you and this special evening. Take care of yourself."

They both stood and embraced. Jack did not know what to say, and then she was gone. He quickly dressed, moved over to the piano and picked up the card. It read:

> Cecilia Lefebvre from the village of Saint Aubin Fosse Louvain.
> North and East of Paris along the border of Normandie.
> I will never forget you and your music.

HOMEWARD BOUND

News of Germany signing the Armistice of Compiegne with all fighting to stop at 11:00 a.m. on November 11, 1918 came to the hospital around noon time that day. There were cheers everywhere as the news spread throughout the old church buildings. Jack also was excited. He had thoughts of home in New York City and wondered how long it would be before he would return home. The answer came quickly. At six that evening, all were ordered to go to the main church hall. The church pews had been put back in place.

Jack found a place about ten rows back. As he slid into his seat, he glanced at the soldier to his right. *He looks very familiar*, Jack thought. Jack turned to the soldier and asked, "Are you from C Company?"

"Yes, I am. My name is Manse."

"I remember you now. You got hit in the leg on the first day when we went out behind the tanks."

"Yeah, that wasn't bad though. The medics patched me up, but a week later, I took some shrapnel in the back and ended up here. What about you?"

Jack told Manse how he got gassed and had been at the church hospital ever since. Then the hall was called to attention and a colonel with a chest full of ribbons walked to the front.

"At ease, men, the war is over for us. The ceasefire took effect at eleven o'clock this morning. Our first priority is to move all that are able from the hospitals to transport ships that are on their way to the port at Brest. By the time you get up in the morning, we will have lists posted as to your departure group. Trucks will be here before noon. I personally want to thank you for your service here in France and commend you for a job well done. You put up one hell of a fight that the Germans will not soon forget. Godspeed and provide safe journey home. I hope to be back in the states with you very soon."

The hall was again called to attention, and the colonel swiftly made his way out to a waiting vehicle.

Jack and Manse made their way out of the crowded hall. They stopped briefly in the vestibule where various notices were posted.

"I'll look for you here tomorrow morning," Jack said.

"Okay, maybe we'll be in the same group," Manse acknowledged.

They then departed in different directions. As Jack made his way back to his room, he began to wonder how the other members of C Company had fared in the battle. Jack didn't really get to know many of them, but he well remembered JJ and Sergeant Dutcher. He hoped they made it through the battle.

Morning came quickly. Everyone was busy gathering and packing their personal belongings. It was amazing how much you could cram into a duffle bag. After a quick bite to eat, Jack headed down to the church vestibule. There was a large gathering by the bulletin board. Jack spotted Manse at the far side and made his way over next to him.

"Good morning, Manse. Did you find your assignment?"

"Yes, but I couldn't remember your last name, so I'm not sure if we are together."

"Schmidt, Jack Schmidt, and here it is. It looks like Group B."

"That's my group also. So we will be together," Manse replied.

"Good. You can bring me up-to-date as to how the battle went."

They were interrupted by the loud voice of a sergeant directing all Group A members to assemble with their duffle bags along the roadway on the opposite side of the of the church entrance. The sergeant next called for all in Group B to assemble with duffle bags in front of the building adjacent to the church. Before the men could get organized into their respective groups, trucks started pulling into the driveway. Each soldier's name was checked off as they boarded the trucks. There were soldiers assisting any wounded that had trouble boarding or handling their duffle bag. When a truck was full, it immediately departed. Jack admired how well-planned and organized the whole operation was. The ride to the port of Brest was long, bumpy, and dusty, but no one complained. They arrived at the port in early afternoon. Boarding the ship was just as smooth as the departure from the hospital.

Jack read USS Comfort on the bow of the ship. He later learned that it had been a passenger service steamer for the Ward Line on the New York to Havana route. The US Navy had converted it into a hospital ship. Jack and Manse had been separated, but Jack knew they were both on the same ship, so it would be possible to find Manse later. Once onboard, the men were lined up along the deck corridors. Small groups consisting of either four, six, or eight were then led off to the cabins below the deck. Jack was lucky to be called for a small group of four. As his group of four was led through the passageways, Jack thought, This ship is so much nicer than the troopship that brought me to France.

The sailor that was leading them stopped outside of a cabin and asked if anyone had an injury that would prevent them from climbing. One of them raised his hand and said that he was recovering from shrapnel wounds to his left arm.

"What is your name, soldier?"

"Fletcher, sir, David Fletcher"

"Anybody else have a problem?" There was no further response, so the sailor said, "Fletcher, you will be in one of the bottom bunks. The rest of you decide among yourselves who gets the second bottom bunk." Then, pointing to the number on the cabin door, he told them to remember the number 343. "This will be your home for the next week. Get yourselves settled in. I will be back in an hour or so to brief you on some details, at which time I will answer your questions. Right now our priority is to get everyone onboard, so we can get underway."

Jack settled for a top bunk, and was quite satisfied with his location because he had a good view out through the single porthole.

There was a small bathroom in the cabin, but it appeared that they would have to move elsewhere for showers. It would sure feel good to get rid of the dust from the truck ride. There was little space to store anything, so Jack busied himself organizing the contents of his duffle bag for ease of access to the most used items such as toiletries, towels, and underwear. The other occupants were busy with their personal items, so he climbed up and stretched out on the top bunk.

Within minutes, he was asleep and again dreaming. This time he was with Cecilia in her small village. He imagined it to be like the village that he and Frank had walked to. Cecilia and Jack were sitting at an outside table by the café. Cecilia was ordering dinner for both of them and explaining in English what she was ordering. She was just so naturally beautiful and so smart about everything. She asked Jack if he would like some wine, to which Jack declined and went into a long tale of his father's lecturing him about the dangers of alcoholic drinks and how some shipmates under his father's command never achieved their potential because of their drinking habits. The first course of their dinner consisting of mushroom soup, fresh baked bread, and pate arrived. Jack blessed himself and reached across the table for Cecilia's hand. Holding her soft hand, he recited a short grace. They both blessed themselves with the sign of the cross and began to eat. Jack asked Cecilia if she were Catholic. Her response was that almost all of the French are Catholic, and added that at one time, the pope even resided in Avignon. Next, the waiter brought a single platter of baked fish that appeared to be flounder or trout. The waiter placed some of the fish on Cecilia's dish, and then moved next to Jack and placed some on his dish. The platter with the remaining fish was then placed in the center of the table. The fish was delicious, but Jack was not sure as to how he should dispose of the bones. He watched Cecilia and discovered that she simply removed them from her mouth with her fingers and put them on a corner of her dish. He followed suit as he wondered if his mother would approve of doing so. Just as Jack was about to tell Cecilia that he had reached his limit, the waiter arrived with a large platter of various cheese wedges. Again, he took his lead from Cecilia as she simply reached for a cheese wedge with her fingers and brought it directly to her mouth. The cheese was very good, but finally, he told Cecilia he could not eat another thing.

In his dream, Jack asked for the check, and when the waiter brought the check, he knew exactly how to read it, and exactly how to count out the right amount of francs. He left the check and the francs on the table and moved over behind Cecilia to help her with her chair. Taking her arm, they walked slowly along the street, occasionally stopping to look in the shops windows. Near the end of the street, Cecilia grasped his hand and turned him to walk a short distance up a side street and into a very neatly kept villa. Once inside she guided him up the stairs to her bedroom. Jack settled into the bed. It had been a long day, and it felt so good to stretch out. Cecilia began changing into a silky nightgown. Jack first looked at the beauty of Cecilia and then closed his eyes for a moment. Cecilia stood by the edge of the bed telling him he could not go to sleep yet and began to shake his torso.

Jack said, "Why are you shaking me?"

The sailor replied, "It's time to get up. There are some important things I want to brief all of you about."

The briefing began after the soldiers had moved out of their bunks. "Okay, what is your cabin number?"

"Cabin 343", the joint response came back.

"Good! That's one of the most important things for you to remember. The first digit is your deck number. Remember you are on a navy ship so terminology differs. The front of the ship is the bow; the back is the stern. The left side is the port side; the right side is starboard. Latrines are heads and the dining hall is the galley. You will see signs and hear loudspeaker directives using these terms, so try to remember them. There will be a wake-up horn at six every morning. If you want breakfast, roll out of your bunk and head for the galley. If not, you may sleep in as long as you want. The galley stops serving breakfast at seven thirty. There are three shifts for lunch. You men are assigned to the eleven o'clock shift. The same applies for the evening meal. You are assigned to the four thirty shift. If for some reason you miss your assigned time today, the mess checker will still allow you to enter. After today you will be required to have a written and properly endorsed slip. Are there any questions so far?"

Handing out identification cards, the sailor continued. "Keep these with you at all times. You will need them to enter the galley or go to the dispensary. The dispensary is located almost directly below you on deck two. There is a large head with showers at the stern of this deck. There will be no laundry service, so do the best you can by rinsing undergarments and socks in the shower. We will be at sea for seven days. Our arrival port is Hoboken, New Jersey. Before arrival, you will be given orders to your next base. Most of you will be sent to Fort Dix for out processing or continued medical treatment. The shipboard duty officer is located on deck five about mid ship. He will have personnel assisting him. Should you have any problems, go to the duty officer desk. Otherwise, listen for information from the loudspeakers."

There were no questions, so the sailor departed. The four roommates introduced themselves to each other and made small talk. None were from C Company, so Jack decided to try for the shower. Pulling a towel and a change of underwear from his duffle bag, he headed for the back of the ship. There was only one other serviceman in the head, so Jack enjoyed a rather long shower. The water was at least warm and not at all cold as he had anticipated. He rinsed out his underwear and returned to the cabin. The others had departed, probably to find something to eat. He hung the underwear and the damp towel over the bar at the foot of his bunk, and then checked the small bathroom. There was a mirror over the sink, so he dug out his shaving gear and proceeded to shave. He felt much better after cleaning up and decided to look for the galley. Maybe he would find Manse or someone else from C Company.

The galley was almost filled to capacity. Jack took a tray and followed the serving line. The specialty was ham and beans mixed together. After adding a couple of biscuits and a glass of water, he looked around for a place to sit and eat. There were one or two scattered seats at a large table in the corner of the galley. Jack approached one of the seats and asked if it was taken. He was invited to join the group, and soon learned that they were all from another outfit. From the conversations, Jack gathered that they had been hit pretty hard and suffered quite a few casualties. As the conversations drifted around the table, the soldier next to Jack asked him what unit he was with. Jack told him Company C, and after some small talk described in a very few words how he had become a gas victim. The food was at least warm and satisfying. He finished rather quickly and excused himself from the table, hoping to be able to make his way to an outside deck for some fresh air.

Deck four had passage to the outside walkway. Jack went out and walked part way around the deck toward the bow. There were other soldiers stopped along the deck railing just looking off into the distant ocean. Jack found a good place along the rail and also stopped to gaze out into the ocean. The sun was very close to setting, so he decided to stay and watch the sunset. His mind drifted to New York City and what it was going to be like returning home. He wondered about his brother, Charles, his nephew, Milt, and most of all how his mother was doing. He had not received any letters for probably two months. It was unlike his mother to not write, and Milt had sent at least one letter a week when Jack was stateside. *Were they all right*? Maybe it was that the mail was lost in the army system. The sun just touched the horizon. It was beautiful to watch as it slowly disappeared. Now the air seemed cooler. Most of the other spectators were making their way back inside. It had been another long, but good day. Jack also made his way back inside. It was great to be on his way home.

On the third day, there was a message broadcast over the loudspeaker, "There will be mail call today in the galley. Mail for those with last names starting with the letters A through M will be called at nine hundred hours. Mail for those with names starting with N through Z will be called at ten hundred hours. That is all."

Jack was excited. Maybe there would be some mail for him. He thought about the letter and photos he had picked up in the trench.

They were in his duffle bag. Jack ruffled through the bag until he found them. He climbed back up on top of his bunk and stretched out to read the letter. The return address on the envelope was Peoria, Illinois. Jack thought it must be someplace close to Chicago. He remembered his mother and father telling stories about the marvelous things that they had seen at the Chicago World's Fair of 1893. Unfolding the letter, Jack began to read:

Dear Joseph,

Jack thought, *Using the name Joseph instead of just Joe seemed rather formal. Probably the letter was from the mother.* The letter went on.

> From what we have been reading about the battles in France, you boys have been doing a good job. We hope and pray that the war will soon end and you will return home to us safe and sound.
>
> The corn crop is very good this year. We could certainly have used your help through the harvest, but we got through it all right. Prices are good this year. Pop has been talking about buying one of those new Ford trucks. The Johnsons got one and have been the talk of the town.
>
> I am sending along pictures of Fred and Sally.
>
> Hope they get to you all right.
>
> Love,
> Sadie

Looking at the pictures, Jack concluded that Fred and Sally were close to his age. So maybe they are brother and sister. Would a mother sign a letter "Sadie?" He didn't think so. Maybe Sadie was a girlfriend or kid sister. *Oh well*! Jack placed the letter and pictures back into the envelope and then into his pocket. He thought if he were ever to travel near Peoria, it would be nice to try to locate this family.

The loudspeaker blasted again, "The first mail call will commence in five minutes. That is all." Jack climbed out of the bunk and grabbed his towel to freshen up a bit in the cabin. His roommates were all gone. Again, he made his way to the open deck. The Atlantic Ocean can be cold in November, so he rather quickly made his way back inside and headed to the duty officer's station. Perhaps he could locate Manse. There were a couple of white hats at the station. Jack got into a short line, and when it was his turn, he simply stated that he was trying to locate a soldier with the last name of Manse. Jack spelled the name. The white hat checked a list and told Jack to try cabin 427. "Port side one deck below," the white hat bellowed and moved on to the next in line.

Jack went down to deck 4 and found cabin 427. He knocked several times, but there was no answer. Jack then decided to head for the galley where he might spot Manse. No luck in spotting Manse, so Jack decided to wait for his mail call, which would probably be within fifteen minutes. When the loudspeaker announced the second mail call, Jack went right into the galley and moved close to the table with multiple stacks of sorted mail and packages. A few minutes later, an army sergeant arrived and asked for silence. "Men, I will only call out the names on the letters and packages once. If you hear your name, raise your arm and stay where you are. Someone will bring the letter or package to you. Have your ID card in your hand, so we can verify that you are the rightful recipient. Any items that are leftover after this mail call will be brought to the duty officer's station on deck five. You may claim items there. Noonan, Matthew Noonan. Raise your hand if you are here." A soldier off to Jack's left raised his hand and immediately one of the sergeant's assistants took the letter to Noonan. It took about ten minutes until the sergeant started calling names beginning with S. "Schmidt, John Schmidt." Jack quickly raised his hand with a feeling of excitement. An assistant made his way over and after checking Jack's ID, handed him not one letter, but a packet of letters that had been tied together. *Wow, jackpot*! Jack thought as he made his way out of the galley.

Now where can I find a little solitude while I open and read these? It was close to lunch time, so Jack decided to return to the cabin and go to lunch a little late. By doing so, there was a good chance that his roommates would be gone. The cabin was empty. Jack hopped up onto the top bunk with great anticipation and untied the packet of letters. Three were from his mother, two from Milt, and it looked like one from his brother. Checking the postmarks, Jack opened the oldest letter, which was from his mother. His mother wrote wonderful letters, always upbeat and usually containing blessings or little enclosed prayers. Everything seemed to be going well at home. The next oldest letter was from Milt. He had gotten a pretty good job with Dunn and Bradstreet delivering messages, usually on a bicycle. His father gave permission to not return to school after the ninth grade. *Wow!* Jack thought, *That's a big mistake. What was his brother thinking in allowing Milt to not finish school? I'll bet Charlie got an earful from Mom.* Reading the letter from his brother shed more light on what was going on. Jack's sister-in-law, Catherine, had a serious heart problem. It appeared that the messenger job would actually give Milt more time and flexibility to help out at home. The second letter from his mother was not upbeat and confirmed what Jack had thought. Jack liked Catherine and hoped that she would get through this all right. He would keep her in his evening prayers. Milt's second letter was about his satisfaction with his job and his concerns about his mother's health. The last letter, also from Jack's mother, was a little more upbeat and talked about news at home that the war should soon be over and how she looked forward to Jack's arrival back home.

As Jack digested the news from home, he reread portions of some of the letters, and finally decided that he would attempt to contact his mother by telephone for more information when the ship docked. It was time to get to the galley before he missed lunch.

Because he was finishing lunch rather late, Jack was still in the galley when the second shift began entering. To his amazement, he recognized his old squad leader, JJ, coming through the entrance. He jumped up and started for the entrance when a white hat said, "Hey, you can't leave your tray like that on the table."

"I'll be right back," Jack responded and continued over to JJ calling, "JJ, JJ."

"Hey, kid, how are you doing? Where are you sitting?"

Jack pointed to his tray and started to move back to his seat.

"Okay, kid, I'll be over as soon as I get some chow."

As JJ approached the table, Jack noticed that his right arm was bandaged and in a sling. Jack got up and offered to help JJ with his tray and utensils, but JJ just continued to do everything on his own.

"Can't shake your hand, kid, but tell me how you have been. How did the recovery from the mustard gas go?"

Jack gave some brief details about his journey following the gas attack, and then asked what happened to JJ's arm.

"Next to last day of the battle I took two hits. One hit my shoulder; the other my arm. Both were probably from machine gun fire. Near the end of the battle, the Germans got real smart with the machine guns and would spray the field in front of them with sweeping left and right lines of fire rather than aiming at specific targets. The tanks provided little cover against this tactic and the terrain was pretty open, so a lot of us went down."

"What about Sergeant Dutcher?" Jack asked.

"Dutcher is the luckiest man I've ever known. He was always out in front, often standing up motioning for our positioning, and he never got a scratch. He'll be in France a little while longer getting our men and equipment organized for transport back to the States. The man deserves a few medals."

"Is your arm going to be okay?"

"The docs told me I'll probably heal okay, but I may not be cleared for front line duty. With the war ending, I was probably headed for a training command anyway, so I guess I'll be able to finish out my twenty. What are your plans, kid?"

"Well, I enlisted, so from what I can find out, there is no guarantee that I will immediately be discharged, but it sounds like the army plans a significant downsizing, and that people in my category will most likely be out processed either with medical discharges or honorable discharges. I'm really looking forward to returning to New York and getting started with some kind of a career in music."

JJ was finished eating, so without asking, Jack reached over and took JJ's tray placing it on his own with the utensils on top of both, and they headed out passing by the galley washing station. Jack asked about the rest of the squad and learned that probably half of them had taken hits, but to the best of JJ's knowledge, only two had died. Jack mentioned that Manse was onboard, but he had not been able to catch up with him yet, and he seemed to be pretty well healed. As they parted on deck, Jack asked for JJ to write down an address where he could be contacted. JJ promised to do so, and either give it to Jack or slip it under his cabin door.

The remaining days crossing the Atlantic were rather boring. Jack busied himself by writing letters and reading material from a small library he had located onboard the ship. JJ had delivered an address to Jack's cabin. It was for a residence in San Diego, California. Jack was surprised, as he thought that JJ was from the South, perhaps Alabama or Mississippi.

On the seventh day, the loud speakers blasted, "We should be docked by seven hundred hours tomorrow. This evening orders will be delivered to all personnel. It is therefore requested that all personnel be in their cabins between twenty hundred and twenty-one hundred hours this evening. Disembarkation will commence at nine hundred hours tomorrow. You will be called by alphabetical groups. Your group letter will be stamped on the upper right hand of your orders. When your group letter is called, proceed with your belongings to the main gangway. Personnel will be available throughout the ship to assist you. That is all."

THE GOOD OLD USA

As anticipated, Jack's orders were for him to report to Camp Dix for medical evaluation and out processing. The orders were stamped with the group letter G. *Oh well*, Jack thought. *I'm starting to get used to the hurry up and wait process.* To his surprise, G was the first group called to leave the ship. He said quick *good-byes* to his cabinmates, grabbed his duffle bag and headed for the gangway. His orders were checked by white hats several times along the way, but otherwise, departing the ship was as smooth as boarding had been. The navy had done a great job.

The soldiers leaving the ship were immediately marshaled onto buses, and as each bus filled it departed the dock. *Well, no chance to telephone home from here. Maybe I'll have a better chance at Camp Dix.* Soon they were away from Hoboken and passing through farmland. The roadway was much smoother than it had been in France.

As Jack looked out of the window, the soldier sitting next to him commented about the farms. "Looks like a lot of the farms are milk farms. You can tell by the long barns that are used for milking the cows. I would love to have me a layout like one of these."

Jack asked, "Where are you from"?

"You know those Hershey's chocolate bars we like so much. Well, I was raised on a milk farm just outside of the town of Hershey in Pennsylvania. We sell most of our milk to the Hershey's factory. I can't wait to get back home. I might try to get a job in the factory. Mr. Hershey takes very good care of his workers."

The bus stopped at the guard shack momentarily, and then moved on to a group of nearby Quonset huts. A young lieutenant boarded the bus and asked that we bring along our belongings and form in a group alongside of the bus. Once the group was formed, the lieutenant introduced a sergeant who would move us to our quarters.

The Quonset huts were fairly new but very stark. The sergeant lined the soldiers up in a single file and walked them into the hut. Cots lined each side of the long tubular interior. There were three pot belly stoves equally spaced down the center of the isle. All had fires and the hut felt comfortably warm. The sergeant stopped at each cot and asked the next man in line to take the cot. Jack was surprised that there were no real military commands used. Perhaps it was because most of the men were recovering from wounds. Jack settled into a cot about halfway down the row. Each cot was already made, and there was a wooden footlocker at the base of the bed. Once everyone had a place, the sergeant called for silence, and then asked that we organize our belongings in the footlockers. He stated that in a short time, there would be a group of orderlies arriving to gather information from our written orders, and to ask questions so that we could be given proper care while waiting further processing. We were to remain inside of the hut until told otherwise.

It didn't take long for Jack to empty his duffel bag and place everything into the footlocker in an orderly fashion. As most of the others finished unpacking, they stretched out on their respective cots. Jack did the same and quickly fell asleep. Again, he felt someone pulling on his arm. This time it was one of the orderlies.

"May I please see your orders?"

Jack handed over his orders without saying anything.

"I see you suffered from a gas attack. Can you speak okay now?"

"Yes, much better," Jack answered.

"Do you have any difficulty breathing?"

"No, my breathing has been pretty good all along. Mostly my problem was that I could only manage to whisper."

"Do you have any other wounds or anything else that bothers you?"

"No."

"Okay, you will be placed on light duty until your out processing is completed. Do you have any questions?"

"Yes, is there a telephone anyplace nearby? I would like to call my mother in New York City. She probably thinks I'm still overseas someplace."

"There are several public phones at the post exchange, which is within walking distance. Once we clear this group, you will be given free time to go to the Exchange. Welcome back and good luck." The orderly then moved on to another unattended cot.

Wow! I'm getting out. I should be home well before Christmas. Jack was too excited to lie back down, so he walked through the hut checking out everything. Jack engaged in small talk with several of the other soldiers as he made his way down one side of the hut and then back up the other.

Just as he reached the far end, a rather stern-looking sergeant entered and made his way to the center of the hut. "Listen up," the sergeant bellowed to get everyone's attention. "Those of you that have been cleared for light duty follow me outside."

Including Jack, there were five men that followed the sergeant out. He motioned for them to gather around him just a few paces away from the hut. "Men, you are the lucky ones. All of you should be home for Christmas. The men still inside will require some medical treatment before being cleared for discharge. While your paper work and arrangements for transportation are being finalized, you will be given light duty. Now, can any of you type?" One of the men held up his hand and said he could.

"What's your name, son?"

"John Walters."

"Well, John, see the green hut just three down from here. Make your way down there and tell the clerk that Sergeant Evans sent you to help with the typing."

Next, the sergeant asked if anyone knew how to tend to the fires in the three stoves inside of the hut. Jack responded that his home had a coal furnace for hot water that was very much like the hut stoves.

"Okay, son, you wait here with me and I will show you where the coal is stored. The rest of you are to report to the mess hall and tell the head cook that I sent you to help on the serving line. When you are finished with your work, you may move around the post, but return to your hut for bed check by twenty-one hundred. Son, let's go over around the side of the next hut. What's your name, soldier?"

"John Schmidt."

"Did you see much combat over there?"

"Just a couple of days and then I was hit with mustard gas."

"Are you doing okay now?"

"I'm doing pretty well. I have my voice back and my breathing is good."

"Okay, here is the coal bin." Pulling back a heavy canvas cover, the sergeant stated, "Keep it covered, so the coal stays dry. Use one of these shovels and buckets to move the coal and ashes. The ashes are to be spread on top of the street at the opposite end of this string of huts. Control the temperature inside the hut by opening a few windows if necessary, but always keep it warm for those boys. Take care."

And with that, the sergeant was gone. Jack was glad he did not get duty in the mess hall. The sergeant made it sound like the men would only be working on the food serving line, but from Jack's past experience, the head cooks had little reservation in using men for any task.

Tending the stoves proved to be rather easy, and soon Jack found that he had considerable free time. Once he had the stoves going well, he decided to walk over to the post exchange to see if he could possibly call home. It was about a ten-minute walk to the exchange. Upon entering, Jack found three pay phones mounted on the wall next to the entrance. Two were in use. He immediately went to the checkout counter and asked the young lady at the register for a dollar's worth of dimes. Jack quickly moved to the open phone and flashed for an operator.

"Number, please," the operator said.

"I want to place a call to New York City. The number is Madison 6-8696."

"Please deposit ten cents for the first three minutes."

Jack put a dime in the coin slot and waited for what seemed to be an eternity. Finally, he could hear a phone ringing at the receiving end of the line. He hoped his mother would answer and not the neighbor that shared the same party line.

"Hello," his mother's voice answered.

"Mom, It's Jack. I'm back in the states. I'm calling from Camp Dix over here in New Jersey."

"Jack, oh! My prayers have been answered. How are you, son?"

"I'm good, Mom. I should be home in a few days. How is everyone?"

"Catherine is back in the hospital. Other than that, we are all just fine. Oh! I'm so excited. I can't wait to see you. We had no idea where you were."

"Is Catherine going to be okay?"

"It's touch and go, Jack. She does pretty well for a while and then just like that she loses all of her energy. Yesterday, your brother found her on the floor when he came home from work. We are not sure if she fainted or just what exactly happened."

"How is Milt doing?"

"He has been an angel. When he is not working, he is taking care of things for his mother. He always asks about you. Sometimes I make things up and tell him that we did hear from you and everything with you is good. I didn't want him to worry more than he already does. Milt will be so excited when he hears you will be home soon."

"Listen, Mom, tell Charles that maybe I can help him with Catherine when I get home. I have to go now. There is a line of soldiers here waiting to use the phone. Love you, Mom."

"Good-bye, Jack. Thank you so much for calling."

There must have been ten or more soldiers now lined up for the phones. Jack flashed the operator. There was no money due, so he motioned to the first in line to come over as he hung up the receiver.

Jack checked the time and decided he had another hour before he needed to get back to the hut. He noticed a barber pole about halfway down the exchange corridor. Walking down the corridor, he found the shop to be without a single customer. As Jack entered, the barber waved him over to a chair and placed a large white apron around him. Jack told the barber that he was about to be discharged and expected to be home for Christmas. In a nice way he was trying to convey to the barber that he wanted a nice haircut and not traditional military close cut. They chatted as the barber worked. Jack's message seemed to have gotten through, as the barber repeatedly stopped cutting to show Jack how the haircut was progressing and to get a word or sign of approval. Inside of fifteen minutes, he was done. Jack paid the barber and gave him a twenty cent tip. It felt so nice to be well-groomed. Next, he took a quick look around the exchange in hopes of finding some things to bring home for his mother and perhaps Milt. Nothing caught his eye, so he decided to get back to the hut and check the fires.

The hut was nice and warm. Jack put a little coal into each stove, banked the fires, and refilled the bucket with coal. *Now,* he thought, *if I can get a nice warm shower my day will be complete.* The block building with the latrine and showers in it was strategically located off the corners of four huts, thereby satisfying the needs of the men in all four of those huts. Jack grabbed a change of underwear and his towel from the foot locker and walked over to the block building. One other soldier was there taking a shower.

Jack asked, "Is it warm?"

"Not bad," the soldier replied.

Jack quickly undressed, neatly folded and placed his uniform on a nearby bench, and then entered the open shower area. Pulling one of the showerhead chains, he found the water to be warm and very refreshing. "Wow, this is living!" Jack commented.

"Did you just get back from overseas?"

"Yes, and the best news is I am to be discharged and going home in a couple of days."

"Where is home?"

"New York City."

"I work in the orderly room. If things go routinely, you will be called to the orderly room to sign some documents and then sent to the paymaster station to pick up your back pay and most likely, a train ticket to the city. When did you arrive?"

"Just this morning," Jack replied.

"You should be out of here either tomorrow or the next day." The soldier was now dried and dressed. "Good luck. Maybe I'll see you in the orderly room." Then he was gone.

Nice, Jack thought. *I wonder how far it is to the train station.* He toweled off, dressed, and started back to his hut. Maybe he could find someone interested in going to chow so he would have a little company. The hut was nearly empty, so he headed over to the mess hall and entered the line. The line moved along pretty well. Most of the soldiers did not know one another, so the chatter was pretty much small talk. He picked up a metal tray and started through the serving line. As he suspected, the three soldiers that Sergeant Evans sent over here were nowhere in sight. They were probably somewhere in the kitchen either peeling potatoes or scrubbing pots and pans. To Jack's surprise, the food looked very good. He asked the servers for the hamburger steak, mashed potatoes with gravy over both the meat and potatoes, along with a serving of cooked carrots. Next, Jack picked up a glass already filled with milk and searched for an open seat. He spotted several open at the far end, and started to move in that direction when he heard someone calling, "Hey, kid. Over here." It was JJ. Jack moved toward him while JJ asked a few of the men around him to shuffle their seats so Jack could sit next to him.

"What a surprise, JJ. I didn't think I would see you again." Jack gave him a pat on the back and then sat down. "How is the arm?"

"It looks like I'll be here for maybe a month, followed by thirty days leave and then move to my next post. I'll request duty in California. You look good, kid. Go ahead and start eating while it's still hot. How are you making out?"

"Great. I expect to be discharged in a day or two and on my way back to New York." The food tasted as good as it looked. Jack didn't realize how hungry he was. "Is your home in San Diego?"

"I was born and raised in San Diego. It has the best climate in the whole world. My wife and two kids live there now on a small ranch with my dad. Someday, the ranch will be mine. When times were tough, I joined the army and kind of supported keeping the ranch going. My mother died a few years back, so it has worked out well for my family to live there with my father. It would be real nice if I can get a post close by to finish out my twenty."

"Well, JJ, you probably don't know it, but my talent is in music. I play the piano, and someday hope to be part of one of the big bands. When I'm rich and famous, I'm going to come to visit you in San Diego and take you and your family out to the best restaurant in town because I truly believe that the advice and direction you gave me about the gas mask saved my life."

"I'll be looking forward to it, kid. You take care. I've got to go. I'll see you in San Diego."

Jack was going to miss JJ, Kelly, and some of the others he met in the army, but he certainly was not going to miss the army. He finished eating, took his tray to the wash station and headed back to the hut. After giving the fires attention, he slipped into bed and thought about how nice it was going to be getting back home.

The next day was pretty routine with no call to the orderly room. Jack found the Post Library and spent time catching up with the news. The library had a good assortment of newspapers and quite a few magazines. On the third day, Jack started to become a little anxious. Why hadn't he been called to the orderly room? Maybe that guy in the shower really didn't know what he was talking about. He had a hard time sleeping and kept thinking that maybe the army was going to keep him in for the rest of his enlistment.

After getting breakfast on the fourth day, Jack returned to the hut to tend to the fires. He needed coal, so went out to fill the bucket. While he was adding coal to the fires, a clerk from the orderly room entered, but didn't really say anything. Jack was again disappointed.

He finished with the fires and moved to his cot. There was a note taped to the top of his footlocker, "Pack all of your belongings and report to the orderly room in dress uniform." In less than thirty minutes, he was on his way. He wondered who would take care of the stoves and decided to simply tell someone in the orderly room that they would need to assign a new man to do so.

There was a short line in the orderly room and it moved quickly. Before long, it was Jack's turn. There were some general questions and then documents to be signed. The clerk gave Jack his discharge papers and some other printed material in a closed envelope. Just as the soldier in the shower had told him, the next stop was the paymaster. His back pay came to over three hundred dollars. Jack felt rich. The paymaster also had a train ticket and instructions to get transportation to the train station. The ground transportation departed about every thirty minutes from an area just across from the post exchange. *Maybe I'll have time to call home*, Jack thought, as he headed toward the exchange. It was a little cold, but a nice clear day. *A good day to take a train ride*, he thought. There was no line for the phones at the exchange, so Jack had the operator dial his home. There was no answer. He checked the time on the exchange clock. It was ten thirty. *That's strange*, he thought. *Mom is usually home this time of the day. Oh well, I'll just surprise her when I get home later today.*

BACK IN THE BRONX

The neighborhood looked exactly like it was when he left. Jack dropped his duffle bag on the porch and knocked on the door. No answer, so he tried the door only to find it locked. His mother always locked the door even when she was at home. He moved his bag to the far corner of the porch and decided to walk to his brother's house. His guess was that it was around three or four o'clock in the afternoon. There should be somebody at Charlie's house. Again, there was no answer to his knocking. As he was about to leave, a young man on a bicycle rounded the corner and approached his brother's house. The rider stopped in front of the porch, dropped his bike, and ran up the steps.

"Jack, you're back! I knew you would be okay!"

They hugged each other until Jack pushed his nephew to arms' length. "Let me look at you, Milt. I think you've grown another two or three inches. Where is everybody?"

"Mom took a turn for the worse last night, so probably they are at the hospital. Come on in. I just want to freshen up a bit and change my clothes before I head over to see Mom. Maybe you can come along? Everybody will be glad to see you."

"I would love to come along. When you get done in the bathroom, let me know. I would like to use the toilet and wash up a little also. It was a long train ride."

When they were both ready, Milt complimented Jack for looking so sharp in his uniform and stated that they could catch the trolley at the corner. It would be about a ten-minute ride to the hospital.

At the hospital, Milt told Jack it was room 237 and to follow along as he knew the quickest way to the room. Milt ran up one flight of steps and then went down the corridor for a short distance. They were at the room, but no one else was around.

"Come on," Milt said as he entered the room and moved quickly to his mother's bedside. "Look who I brought, Mom. Doesn't he look great in his uniform?"

"Hello, Catherine." Jack moved over to the bed and gently kissed Catherine on the forehead.

"Oh! Jack, I'm so glad you're home safe and sound. And yes, he does look great in his uniform."

"How are you feeling, Catherine?"

"Actually, I feel okay. It's just that I get these awful weak spells and sometimes end up here in the hospital."

A nurse entered the room and stated that she had to take some pressure readings and clean Catherine up a bit. The nurse asked that Milt and Jack to move to the waiting area and that she would come and get them when it was okay to return to the room.

"We'll be back soon, Mom. Come on, Jack, let's see if anyone else is in the waiting area."

Jack waved good-bye to Catherine as they left the room and followed scampering Milt to the waiting area.

"Hey, everybody. Look who I brought."

Jack's mother jumped to her feet and ran over to hug her son. Jack's brother, Charles, moved to Jack and patted his back. George and Elizabeth Ransom also moved over to congratulate Jack. Elizabeth was one of Catherine's sisters. As things settled down, Jack went on to tell all that he was officially discharged from the army and home for good. His mother's eyes filled with tears of joy.

"I am so happy, Jack. Now if we can only get Catherine healthy and back home, it will be a true blessing for all of us."

The nurse appeared and said that two of them could go to Catherine's room to visit. Jack's mother and Charles headed for the room. George Ransom moved over to sit next to Jack, and asked Jack how he was doing and what it was like overseas. George had been the best man at his brother's wedding. He was a very colorful gentleman who had spent quite a few years in Arizona on the rodeo circuit. His cowboy name was "The Arizona Kid." He had a lot of trophies for first place in bronco and bull riding contests. George and Elizabeth had also lived with the Indians on a reservation in Arizona. He always had a lot of stories to tell and was generally the center of attention at any family gathering.

Milt listened as Jack recapped how he had been gassed and what traveling across the ocean was like and then interjected, "Uncle George, tell Jack about the farm you just bought."

Once you got George Ransom started, it was hard to stop him from talking. Milt thought Jack needed a break, and could see a sign of relief in his face as he looked Milt's way. It must have been forty five minutes before Jack's mother and his brother returned from Catherine's room.

"We are going to take Catherine home. Jack, here is the key to Mom's house. She is going to give me a hand getting Catherine settled in. George, can you give these two a ride to the house?"

"I'll be more than glad to, but I have to warn you there are no side curtains on the car."

Charles went on to state that once Catherine was settled, he would bring Mom back to her house and pick up Milt. Jack's mother said there was plenty of food in the house and gave instructions for Jack to fix something to eat. With that, they all dispersed in different directions.

MERRY CHRISTMAS

The weeks leading up to the holidays became rather a routine. Jack was up early, ate a quick breakfast, and walked over to his brother's house to help get Milt and Charles Jr. ready to leave for their jobs. When his brother was ready to leave for work, Jack would attend to Catherine. She spent most of the day either in bed or sitting in a softly upholstered chair with her feet propped up on an ottoman. Catherine liked to read, so mostly Jack was there to assist Catherine in moving about the house, and to make sure she had food and something to drink when it was time for her medications. Milt and Charles Jr. pretty much took turns returning home early in the day to care for their mother until their father returned from work. Jack's brother had a very good job working as a painter in Madison Square Garden. Jack often thought that his brother's son, Milton, had been named after the director of maintenance in the garden who also was a Milton. Milton, after all, is not really a Christian name. In any event, his brother had moved up to a supervisory position and was being very well compensated. The problem now was that Charles sometimes had to stay late at the garden and could not always be there for Catherine. Jack was proud that he could help out, and felt that the combined family efforts were in fact providing excellent care for his sister-in-law.

Usually by early afternoon, Jack was home to have lunch with his mother. If his mother had no students, he would spend hours playing the piano. *This*, he thought, *is what I want to do with my life.* Before entering the army, Jack had a semiprofessional career singing with a quartet at a theater in the Bronx. He liked singing, but now that his voice was softer, the piano just seemed to be the way to go. *But how do I get started?* Several days before Christmas, Jack and his mother were eating lunch and engaged in light conversation.

"Jack, I hear Father Dougherty is looking for someone to play the piano over the holidays, during Mass and for special gatherings. There is no pay, but this could be a good experience for you, and also give you a little exposure."

"Mom, you must be a mind reader. I have been thinking about how I might get started into a career in piano."

"Well, son, your piano is excellent. You play better than I do. I have been thinking and there really is nothing more I can teach you. Go see Father Dougherty. I think it is the right move for you at this time."

That afternoon, Jack went to the church rectory. After a short conversation with the receptionist, Jack was led back to see Father Dougherty. The pastor was delighted that Jack was willing to play for the parish. They discussed the types of music, whether or not there would be a vocalist, a choir, or both and what sheet music was available. Jack was elated when he left and headed straight home to tell his mother.

For the next three days, Jack spent all of his free time at the church practicing with the vocalist and the choir. Most of the music consisted of traditional Christmas melodies and songs. The singers were good, and by the end of the second day, Jack felt that they had a very good holiday program for the parishioners. He played at every Christmas Mass and the parishioners showed their appreciation for the performances with a hardy round of applause following each Mass. After the final Mass on Christmas Day, a gentleman approached Jack as he was putting away the sheet music and closing the piano.

"Sir, my name is Frank Murphy. I work for the Irving Berlin Music Publishing Company. You play very well, and I was wondering if you would have an interest in working as a song plugger with us."

"Well, Mr. Murphy, I was just recently discharged from the army and I can certainly use a job."

"I know you're Mrs. Schmidt's youngest son. What is your first name?"

"It's Jack, Mr. Murphy."

"Well, Jack, here is my business card. Come by and see me Monday morning and we'll see about getting you started. I'll leave word with my secretary. Come any time after nine."

"Thank you, Mr. Murphy. I'll be there on Monday." Jack could not wait to tell his mother about his good fortune.

Christmas dinner was to be at Jack's house with about fifteen family members and friends at the table, so Jack hurried home to help his mother. Jack's mother had been cooking and preparing food for several days. The turkey was stuffed and ready to go in the oven.

"Good, Jack, you're here just in time to move the bird into the oven."

Jack put on two oven gloves, picked up the roasting pan and with a loud grunt moved the turkey into the oven. "Wow, Mom, that was heavy. How many pounds is it?"

"Well the butcher said it's over twenty-five. Then add a few more pounds for the stuffing, so I guess it's close to thirty pounds."

"I have good news, Mom, Mr. Murphy talked to me after Mass and offered me a job as a song plugger. I have to see him Monday morning at his office."

"Oh, Jack, that is wonderful news. Perhaps you can play in a music store nearby. Then I would be able to buy my sheet music there."

"Who all is coming to dinner?"

"Well your brother and Catherine along with the boys are coming. The Ransoms and of course, the Schultz family will be here. Also General and Mrs. Goethals along with a few of their friends that are visiting from Panama plan to come."

"Is George Goethals still in the army, Mom?"

"I'm not sure. Catherine said he was going to take a job with the New York Port Authority."

"Well I hope he doesn't ask a lot of questions about my experience in France. I don't feel real comfortable about talking to an old army general."

"Jack, run over to your brother's and find out how they are coming along. Tell Charles that he should be here a little early because I want him to carve the turkey."

"Okay, Mom. What time will the turkey be done?"

"About three o'clock."

"I'll be back in time to get the bird out of the oven." With that, Jack grabbed his coat and was off to his brother's house. He couldn't wait to tell them about his new job.

Milt answered Jack's knock at the front door. "Jack, come on in. We're not quite ready yet."

"Your grandmother just wanted me to make sure you would be over to the house by three o'clock."

Charlie, Jack's brother, entered the foyer and replied, "We're in good shape and will easily be there by three. How many is Mom expecting?"

"I think about fifteen, and Mom wants you to carve the bird. Charlie, I have some good news. Mr. Murphy from our church has offered me a job as a song plugger. I go for an interview Monday."

Milt chimed in, "What's a song plugger?"

"Well a song plugger is a person in music store, usually up on the mezzanine level or some sort of balcony, where he plays the piano and sometimes sings the lyrics of any sheet music the customers are interested in purchasing."

"That is good news, Jack. I'll bet Mom is excited."

"Great, Jack, can I come and listen to you sometimes?" Milt chipped in.

"We'll see, Milt. Can I give you a hand with anything, Charlie?"

"No thanks. Catherine is doing pretty good today and very excited about going out."

"Well, it's pretty nice outside. Is it okay if Milt and I play a game of step ball?"

"Yes, but stay clean," Charlie responded.

At the appointed hour of three o'clock, Jack's house became a beehive of activity. It seemed like everyone arrived at almost the same time. Jack and Milt busied themselves showing the guests into the house and taking their coats. Catherine was seated comfortably in one of the large stuffed chairs and had a circle of family and friends surrounding her. The guests with the Goethals were very suntanned and almost looked out of place. Elizabeth Ransom was serving the traditional eggnog. George Ransom had corralled a few of the men and was describing his new farm out on the Island. Jack eventually made his way to the kitchen, and with Charlie's help they removed the turkey from the oven and positioned it for carving.

When Jack returned to the parlor, George Goethals took him by the arm and walked him to the side of the room. "Jack, it's good to see you home safe and sound. Catherine told me about the gassing. Do you have any lingering effects?"

"No. Actually the army took very good care of me, sir."

"Well, Jack, in a way I envy you. I have spent most of my life in the army and never saw one minute of combat. I also want to tell you how much I appreciate your looking after my sister. Catherine has nothing but praise for you. If there is anything I can help you with, please let me know."

"Thank you, sir," Jack replied, and with that, the old general made his way back to his friends from Panama. *Well, that was not what I expected. The old general really is a gentleman*, Jack thought.

"Please take your seats everyone." Jack's mother began ushering the guests to their assigned places at the table. The dinner table looked spectacular. The finest of china and silverware were placed in perfect order over a fine, handmade, lace tablecloth. There were cut crystal glasses for both water and wine. Jack's mother did not keep any kind of alcoholic drink in the house, but because some of the guests had brought bottles of wine, she quietly acquiesced allowing the drinks to be served. Just as everyone was settling, Charles arrived from the kitchen with a platter of hot turkey. Immediately behind him came Charles Jr. with a tray of mashed potatoes, stuffing, and candied sweet potatoes. One more return trip to the kitchen and all of the trimmings were on the table. Jack's mother asked George Goethals to lead them in grace. Following grace, one of the gentlemen from Panama stood and moved about the table offering to fill anyone's wine glass from a bottle he claimed to be Panama's finest. The second gentleman from Panama then stood and proposed a toast and a blessing to all. Those who did not have wine raised their glass of water and all drank to a most happy and blessed Christmas. It was a perfect meal, followed by fresh baked pumpkin pie that George Ransom claimed was made from his home grown pumpkins. As everyone finished, again one of the guests from Panama rose from his chair and moved about the table with a box full of what he said were the finest cigars that money could buy. Jack's mother quickly interceded and stated that those who are going to smoke to please move to the parlor while the table was being cleared. Jack was a nonsmoker, but he would have liked to hear some of the conversation in the parlor. Instead, he and the boys were made busy moving everything to the kitchen and following his mother's direction in getting the food put away and the pots and pans, along with the dishes and utensils, cleaned and placed back into the cupboards.

Jack managed to duck in and out of the smoke-filled parlor and determined that most of the conversation was about the operation of the locks in the Panama Canal and about some of the problems with equipment that was in use. Once his kitchen chores were over, he returned to the parlor and listened to the conversations. George Ransom had a lot of questions that were patiently being answered. The more Jack listened, the more he marveled at how gigantic an undertaking it had been to connect the Atlantic and Pacific oceans allowing the largest of ships to transit from one ocean to the other and eliminate the need to travel around the southernmost parts of South America. General Goethals and his guests from Panama seemed to know everything about the canal and how it operated. He decided that at some point in the future, he would do a little research to become more familiar with the construction of the canal that the general was very much involved with.

Jack's mother entered the parlor and announced that Catherine was going to be leaving in a few minutes. Those who still had lit cigars put them out, and the men made their way back to the dining room. Charles brought in Catherine's coat and said his good-byes. General Goethals gave his sister a long hug while speaking to her in a soft voice. The Schultz family members were busy putting on their coats and filed by Catherine wishing her the very best New Year. General Goethals and his guests thanked Jack's mother for such a splendid time as they prepared to leave. The Ransoms decided to go along to Jack's brother's house for a short while. Jack singled out Milt and told him he would fill him in about his new job after the interview. And in a very short time, the house was empty. Jack went to his mother and giving her a big hug and said, "Mom, that was the best Christmas ever."

THE SONG PLUGGER

Jack reported to Mr. Murphy's secretary at nine o'clock sharp on Monday morning. He was actually there closer to eight o'clock because Jack was not sure how long it would take riding the trolley, especially with one connection to be made. There was a café nearby, so he ordered a cup of hot coffee and waited until a few minutes before nine to enter the building. The secretary was middle aged, very attractive, and impeccably dressed in a women's business suit.

"May I help you, young man?" she addressed Jack as he entered the office.

"Yes. I am here to see Mr. Murphy. My name is Jack Schmidt."

"Oh yes, Mr. Schmidt. Mr. Murphy said you would be by this morning. Please take a seat and someone will be with you shortly."

Jack settled into one of the chairs and looked around the office. It was very clean with rather expensive-looking furniture and appointments. He thought there must be good money in the music business. Within a few minutes, a well-dressed gentleman appeared and introduced himself asking Jack to come along with him. The gentleman had introduced himself simply as Art. As they walked through a long corridor, Jack thought, *Art probably is short for Arthur.* Soon they entered a room where a piano was positioned in one corner. Art motioned for Jack to sit at the piano and then moved over to a filing cabinet where he withdrew some sheet music. He studied the sheet music momentarily and then returned some to the cabinet. With the remainder in hand, he moved over and sat next to Jack on the piano bench. Next, Art placed several sheets of music in the holder on top of the piano.

"Now, Jack, I would like you to play from the music sheets. Disregard any lyrics for now. We will get to the lyrics later. You may start whenever you feel ready."

The first selection was "After You Get What You Want You Don't Want It" by Irving Berlin. Jack played the melody with ease and felt confident with his performance. Art interrupted about halfway through and asked Jack to start over, this time singing the lyrics.

Listen to me honey dear,
Something's wrong with you I fear
It's getting harder to please you,
Harder and harder each year.
But you need a talking to.
Like a lot of people I know,
Here's what's wrong with you.

Again, Art interrupted. "Notice this next section is really for a chorus to sing. So what I want you to do is deflect your voice to make this part sound different from the first verse. Do you think you can do that?"

"I will give it a try," Jack replied.

After you get what you want you don't want it,
If I gave you the moon, you'd grow tired of it soon.
You're like a baby you want what
you want when you want it
But after you are presented with what you want you're
discontented.
You're always wishing and wanting for something,
When you get what you want you
don't want what you get.
And tho' you sit up on my knee, you'll grow tired of me,
Cause, after you get what you want
You don't want what you wanted at all.

"Very good, Jack. Now let's move on to the next song."

They spent the morning playing, singing, and talking. Art was a very good pianist, and also a good vocalist. He continued to give Jack pointers as they played. He reminded Jack that he would be working for the Irving Berlin Music Publishing Company and the goal was to sell music from the company. Art illustrated how to switch a potential customer to consider alternative music, which would be from the Irving Berlin Music Publishing Company. He stressed that it was therefore important for Jack to know the music that was available in the store and the similarities between various selections. When twelve o'clock arrived, Art told Jack he was taking him to lunch on the company, and then they would visit the music store where Jack would report for work. Art ushered Jack just around the corner to a small café where everyone in the place seemed to know Art. They sat at a table next to the street side window.

"The corned beef sandwich is very good. It's served with a dill pickle and potato chips."

"Sounds good to me," Jack replied.

Art signaled for two corned beef sandwiches and then asked Jack what he would like to drink. Jack said root beer would be fine and if they didn't have it, water would do. Art loved to watch the people and cars pass by the window and he almost always identified any passing vehicle by make, model and year.

"Do you have a car, Jack?"

"No, I don't. Maybe I will someday."

"Well it's going to be the way to travel in the future. Getting around the city without a car is fine, but when you want to go out on the Island or over to Jersey, driving is so much better. I have a Ford Model T and I'm on the road with my wife every weekend. See this one passing outside. Mine is almost like that, except I bought custom side curtains to keep the inclement weather out."

"The corned beef is great, Art. The last time I had it was in the trenches over in France. It was nothing like this."

"New York City is full of good food and good restaurants. In fact, you are going to start out working in a store over on Sixth

Avenue and Thirty-Fourth Street. I'll point out a few of the good eateries when we get over there."

When they finished, Art asked if Jack was ready to go to work. Without hesitation, Jack replied, "Let's go."

The store at Sixth Avenue and Thirty-Fourth Street was rather upscale and certainly sold more than just sheet music. Art opened the door and motioned for Jack to enter. Art immediately went to the counter and hit the top of a small bell. Within a few seconds, an attractive and well dressed woman appeared.

"Art, it is always a pleasure to see you. What brings you here today?"

"You have been asking me to bring you a song plugger. Meet Jack Schmidt, one of my best. He will be starting today. Can you show him to the piano and explain how the music is filed? I have to return to the office for another appointment. Good luck, Jack. Katie will take very good care of you." And with that, Art was gone.

"Well, Jack, follow me and I will get you situated up on the mezzanine. Do you have any questions?"

"Yes, what is Art's last name? He simply introduced himself as Art."

"His full name is Arthur Kennedy. He is the number two man in the Irving Berlin Publishing Company. For him to present you as one of his best song pluggers is a real compliment. I will expect big things from you, Jack."

Because it was still early in the afternoon, there were few customers. Jack settled in by the piano and began to look through the adjacent file cabinet drawers. Katie gave him a quick lesson on the filing system and stressed how important it was to return the music sheets in their proper order.

"Katie, is it all right for me to play without a request?"

"Yes, most certainly, the customers enjoy hearing music as they browse and sometimes will ask me to identify the song or music being played. You'd be surprised how many times just hearing a melody or song leads the customer to make a purchase. Whenever there is a specific request for a melody or song, I will call up to you. It is best that you acknowledge my request silently, simply by nodding or waving, and it is also important that you respond to the request as fast as you possibly can."

With that, Jack pulled music sheets for melodies and songs that he already knew and began playing. The filing system was simple and very easy. He was just getting comfortable and enjoying his own playing when Katie called up the first request. He abruptly but cleanly finished the tune he was playing and scrambled to find the requested piece. In less than two minutes, he was playing and singing the requested song. *Not bad*, Jack thought, and then Katie called up a second request. Not knowing whether or not to complete the first request, Jack decided to once again abruptly but smoothly finish the first request. Again, within two minutes he was playing the second request. There were more requests in late afternoon as the store became rather busy.

Jack handled them well until Katie called up a request for a song that he had played earlier. At this point, Jack realized that he had not been returning the music sheets to the file. He shuffled through the sheets he had been playing and with some luck, found the sheets he needed. When the day ended, Jack confessed to Katie his mistake in not refiling the sheets immediately after use.

"You did just fine, Jack. Go home and get a good night's sleep. I will need you here tomorrow by ten in the morning."

"Thank you, Katie. I'll see you in the morning."

That evening, Jack told his mother all about his day, including descriptions of the people he had met and the melodies and songs that he had played. He stated how impressed he was with the tremendous amount of music available and what a great opportunity it would be for him to learn so many more melodies and songs. When his mother asked how much he was being paid, Jack simply stated that he had not even asked and really didn't know. His mother told him not to worry, as the Irving Berlin Publishing Company had a very good reputation and was known for treating their employees very well.

During the first five months of 1919, Jack faithfully arrived at his job every morning before ten. He studied the music as Arthur Kennedy had suggested and found considerable success in suggesting alternative music to many of the customers. He thoroughly enjoyed what he was doing and was quite pleased with the pay from the company. Then one afternoon late in May, Arthur Kennedy visited to tell Jack how pleased they were with his work. Art went on to tell Jack that he thought it was time for him to broaden his horizons into the field of entertainment. Art explained that Mr. Berlin looked for talent to spread his music around and stated how Mr. Berlin engaged in this practice because he was a very astute businessman.

"Jack, we want you to continue here at the Sixth Avenue store for a while longer. At some point, we will be moving you to other locations where your talents may be better appreciated. In the meantime, I would like you to consider working two or three evenings a week at a nearby piano bar. It will give you a much more personal engagement with the listeners, and of course, you will have an opportunity to earn some rather attractive money. What do you think?"

"I think it sounds very exciting," Jack replied.

"Okay, Jack, here is the card of a tailor shop that is just a block away. I want you to go there after work and get measured for a tuxedo. The tailor knows you are coming and will outfit you with not only the tux, but also all of the accessories. Mr. Berlin is picking up the tab. I will come back on Friday around closing time next week and accompany you to the piano bar, so we can get you properly started."

"Wow! I don't know how to thank you and Mr. Berlin."

"Just keep up the good work, Jack. I'll see you at the end of next week."

O'MALLEY'S PIANO BAR

Jack couldn't wait to tell everyone about his new job offer. He decided to call his mother. She was very pleased and proud of her son. Jack asked if she knew what time his nephew, Milt, got home from work.

"I think he is almost always home in time for dinner," she replied.

"I'm going to go straight there tonight, Mom. I have a lot of catching up to do with Milt. If they ask me to stay for dinner, I will be home a little later. Is that okay with you?"

"Certainly, Jack, I'm glad that you want to spend some time with your brother and his family."

Jack arrived at his brother's house around six thirty. Catherine, Charles, Milton, and Charles Jr. had just begun to eat. His brother asked Jack to join them, and sent Charles Jr. to bring another plate and some silverware.

"And to what occasion do we owe this visit?" Charles asked.

As he filled his plate with the beef stew, Jack replied, "I have some good news to share with all of you. I have taken a part-time evening job singing and playing at O'Malley's Piano Bar on Thirty-Fourth Street. The Irving Berlin Publishing Company is sponsoring me, and they feel it will help develop my musical talents."

They all congratulated Jack, at which point he asked, "How are you, boys, doing with your jobs?"

Milt responded first, stating that he had moved on to a new job working on the loading dock at the Chilton Publishing Company. He said they have an apprentice program, and eventually, he would be able to move into working around the printing presses. Charles

Jr. followed telling Jack that he had been selling newspapers on the trains as they traveled in and out of the city. He stated he had hopes of becoming a conductor on the train when he gets a little older. Then Jack's brother, Charlie, chimed in, telling about his most recent promotion to an Assistant Manager's position that gave him the additional responsibilities for estimating the costs for all of the painting inside and out of Madison Square Garden, along with involvement with some other repair projects.

"Well, Charles, you hadn't even told me that," Catherine commented. "You will have to stop by more often, Jack, so I can keep up with what is going on. You are all doing so well you deserve a reward. Milt, hidden in the oven is a chocolate cake that I baked as a surprise this afternoon. Please bring it to the table, and we will all celebrate."

This is so nice being with family, Jack thought.

"You look much better, Catherine."

"I feel a lot better, Jack. And as long as I pace myself, I can do a good many things now. By the way, Jack, my brother, George Goethals, was here just two days ago and left a book for you. He said he sensed that you had an interest in the Panama Canal. The book is all about the construction of the canal from the time the French started back in the late 1800s up to the completion when George became Governor of the Panama Canal Zone. I think you will find it very interesting. It is about three inches thick and contains a lot of photographs documenting the construction phases. Remind me to give it to you before you leave."

"That is so nice of him. I was certainly amazed at the knowledge General Goethals and his friends displayed in their conversations about the canal when they were at our house for Christmas dinner. And I better head on home. I told Mom I would not be late. Thank you so much for dinner, especially the chocolate cake."

"Charlie, get the book from the bookcase in the parlor and wrap a couple of pieces of cake for Jack and Anna."

With cake and book in hand, Jack thanked Catherine and said good night to all.

Jack enjoyed the walk home. It was a nice spring evening with a full, bright moon in the sky, illuminating the houses and street almost as if it were daytime. He unlocked the front door and upon entering called out to his mother, "Mom, Catherine sent over some chocolate cake and a thick book about the Panama Canal that General Goethals left for me."

"Bring it into the kitchen, Jack. I'll pour a glass of milk for each of us. I just love Catherine's baking."

As they busied themselves enjoying the unexpected treat, Jack filled his mother in on the news about the boys' jobs and Charles' promotion. He then told more of the details about the job at O'Malley's. She was surprised to learn about the tailor-made tuxedos and commented that this might be a good time for Jack to purchase another suit or two along with some more dress shirts and ties. His mother even offered to go shopping with him, but Jack turned her down stating that he was now twenty-one years of age and that he would feel embarrassed. They finished their cake and Jack told his mother he was going to retire and read some of the book General Goethals left for him.

The book proved to be very interesting. Jack had no idea how many years it had taken to construct the canal or that the French had actually started the venture. After reading some, he paged ahead and looked at the photographs. Some of the photos dated back to the 1800s. The pictures really captured his interest and encouraged him to read more. After several hours, he decided to get cleaned up and go to bed thinking that this was a book he would want to finish. Once in bed, he began to dream. This time, the dream was about his time in France and the trip across the ocean to return home. He had visions of Kelly, the runner, and wondered what happened to him. He dreamed about the letter he found inside of the mud-caked wallet found in a trench. He dreamed about Cecelia and envisioned how lovely she looked. He thought of where JJ, his squad leader, was assigned for his next duty station. When Jack was fully awake the next morning, he decided to somehow make an effort to remember these events and people.

At breakfast, Jack asked his mother if she had the cigar box that the dinner guest from Panama had brought to the house. She said she did and had been meaning to give it to Jack's brother to possibly take to work and give out the remaining cigars. Jack asked if he could keep the box, and stated that he would put the remaining cigars in a bag for Charles. His mother said sure, but because Jack had aroused her curiosity, she asked what he was going to do with the box. Jack simply said he had some notes with names and addresses from people he had met in the army and he wanted a place to keep them all together. Before going to work, Jack returned to his room and gathered the old wallet and the various notes with names and addresses and placed them in the cigar box. *Well that's a start*, he thought.

The next week went by fast. Arthur Kennedy arrived at the store in midafternoon. He asked Jack if he had the tuxedo. Jack told him it was hanging up in the back of the store.

"Okay, Jack, come on down and change. I'll handle the piano for a while. Take your time."

Jack had been very pleased with the tux when he tried it on in the tailor's shop. Within twenty minutes, he was back. Katie saw him and commented about how handsome he looked. Art asked Katie if it would be all right if they left a little early to go over to O'Malley's.

"Of course it will," Katie replied.

They both thanked Katie and left for a short walk over to the piano bar. The owner was near the entrance when Jack and Art entered. Art introduced Jack.

"Jack, this is Mr. O'Malley. I've known Patrick for quite a few years now. He runs a first-class establishment and is a credit to our great city."

"It's a pleasure to meet you, Mr. O'Malley."

"Just call me Pat. I've heard a lot about you, Jack. Follow me and I will show you around and explain what is expected of you before the evening crowd arrives."

Art followed along with Pat and Jack. The piano was on one side of a small stage with long velvet drapes in the background. There was a fair-sized dance floor just in front of the stage. On the opposite side, there were tables covered with white tablecloths, each with a small vase of fresh flowers positioned in the middle. Jack was impressed. It was all certainly very elegant looking and a place where someone would want to bring either their girlfriend or wife.

"What do you think, Jack?"

"I'm impressed. You have a first-class establishment."

"Do you have any questions, Jack?"

"Yes. I understand there will be some requests for specific songs and melodies. Is there a place near the piano where I can keep some of my music sheets?"

"There is, Jack. You will find a break in the curtain just behind the piano bench. You may put your file just inside of the curtain, and I think you will find easy access without even disturbing the curtain. Is there anything else?"

"No, sir. I think I would like to set myself up now and start playing a few soft tunes."

"Fine, Jack. Art, how about you and I move over to the bar? I want to ask you for some advice on a new automobile I have been looking at."

With that, Jack busied himself setting up his music and becoming familiar with the piano. The nameplate indicated it was a Baldwin. *A fine piano*, Jack thought, as he tried the keys. *And well-tuned.* Slowly some patrons started to arrive. They were all very well-dressed and mannerly. The gentlemen held the ladies' chairs for them, and the ladies politely thanked them. *Nice*, Jack thought, *I shouldn't have to worry about any bar brawls here*. Jack well remembered a few not so nice places he had performed in prior to joining the army. Bar brawls were nasty and seemed to be contagious to the point that a majority of the customers somehow became engaged in the action. Jack decided to find the bathroom before he officially started playing. On his way back to the piano, Pat O'Malley slipped up beside him taking Jack's arm and asked if he was ready for an introduction. Jack responded that he was, and realized that he wasn't nervous but rather excited to be able to perform for this kind of audience. Mr. O'Malley's introduction was quite simple, introducing Jack by his name and then adding a few lines about his army experience in France. The patrons applauded probably for his service in the army.

Jack began playing. About halfway through, Jack stopped, hit a few melodramatic keys and then asked if anyone could name the tune he had been playing. A pretty young lady close to the stage responded, and identified the melody as "Blue Skies".

"Thank you, young lady," Jack replied as he continued to play "Blue Skies". *Well, I'm off to a good start*, Jack thought as he began to sing the lyrics. After a few more songs, a gentleman approached Jack and asked if he knew "Red Robin Comes Bob, Bob, Bobbin' Along." Luckily, it was a song that Jack was very familiar with, so he just started playing and soon added the lyrics. And so the evening went. There was much interaction between Jack and the patrons. Many were dancing and there were quite a few requests. About two hours into his performance, Pat O'Malley stepped up on stage and asked how everyone liked the music. There was a loud round of applause. *This time*, Jack thought, *it's for my performance and not just because I'm a veteran*. Mr. O'Malley held up his hands, thanked everyone and stated that Jack would return to play more after a short break. As they walked away from the stage, Mr. O'Malley told Jack he was doing a fine job and to keep up the good work.

Jack played two more sets as the evening wore on. He thoroughly enjoyed interacting with the patrons. Soon it became apparent that the evening was coming to a close. The waitresses began to clear the tables as people left. When there were only three tables still occupied, Mr. O'Malley once again came to the stage and announced a last call for drinks. He then walked past Jack and told him to wrap it up with a nice soft melody. Most of the employees stopped at the bar once their work was done as it was Mr. O'Malley's custom to give each a drink before they headed home. Jack was waved over to the bar and asked what he would like to drink.

"A cold glass of ginger ale will just be fine."

"Wouldn't you like to boost that with a little liquor?" one of the waitresses asked.

"No thank you. I'm not much of a drinking man," Jack replied.

Jack joined in some light conversation, and when his glass was empty, he said good-bye to all and left.

Time went by quickly, and Jack thoroughly enjoyed his time at O'Malley's Piano Bar. At the close of each night, Jack joined the other employees at the bar for what became his traditional ginger ale. Some of the employees talked about the Eighteenth Amendment to the United States Constitution that had been ratified back in January. There had been mention of the Volstead Act, sometimes called the National Prohibition Act, and how the act might impact their jobs in the near future. Mr. O'Malley told them not to worry, but then had the phrase Piano Bar removed from his sign and replaced with Fine Dining. At the end of October, the news was that the Volstead Act had passed through Congress over President Wilson's veto. Everyone expected a big change, but as the days passed by, nothing happened. Thanksgiving and Christmas were just around the corner, so the employees' talk turned to the holiday season as they put thoughts about prohibition far from their minds.

NEW YEAR 1920

The Schmidt family planned to gather at Jack's brother's house on New Year's Day as Catherine was doing much better. Jack's mother had volunteered to prepare a ham along with some side dishes so that Catherine would not have a great deal of kitchen work. Jack's job was to carry the ham and several side dishes over to Charlie's house. Because of Charlie's promotion at work, they now had a telephone, so Jack decided to call his two nephews to come over and help transport the food. Milt and Charles Jr. arrived within minutes after the phone call. They were both anxious to see Jack, as they had heard he was making his way around the city entertaining people with his piano playing. Jack fueled their curiosity by describing the upscale piano bar, the well-dressed patrons and the very pretty waitresses. He told them about the owner's custom at closing time for all of the employees to enjoy a drink at the bar. They were disappointed when Jack told them he only drank ginger ale.

"You mean you can have any kind of whiskey drink you want and you always settle for just plain old ginger ale?" Charles Jr. asked.

"That's right. And with prohibition coming, it won't be long before everyone will be drinking soda only. Now tell me how you two are doing. Is there any romance in the air? How are your jobs going? And how is your mother these days?"

"Mom is doing pretty well and the conductors say I'm doing fine on the railroad. They have been teaching me all about tickets, like how to read them and how to sell them to onboard passengers. I'm pretty sure I'll be able to get a conductor job sometime, maybe even this year. And Milt has started dating this real good-looking girl."

"Okay, Milt, let's hear about this good-looking girl."

"It's no big deal, Jack. Remember when I quit school and started work delivering messages for Dunn and Bradstreet? Well, I became good friends with one of the other message delivery guys. His name is William VonderLieth. We keep in touch and have spent some time with a few other friends out on the Island fishing, canoeing, and on some weekends camping overnight. I usually see him a few times each month and not too long ago, when I was over at his mother's house, I met his sister. She is a real nice girl and we hit it off pretty well, so the next time I was over to his house, I asked her out for a date."

"Tell me more. What's her name? How old is she? What does her father do?"

"Her real name is Johanna, but she prefers Jean. I didn't ask about her age, but I guess she is about my age. Her father died a few years ago. He was a construction worker and fell from the steel work on one of the skyscrapers being built."

"And what does Jean do?" Jack continued.

"Well, she is real smart. She went to a business school and now works in an office typing letters and such."

"Good for you, Milt. You're doing better than I am. The trouble with working late hours and weekends is that there is little time for social life, but the money is very good. So good, in fact, that I have arranged for a special Christmas present for each of you. There is a tailor shop close to where I play the piano. This tailor is very good. He made my first tuxedo, and I have been back several times to have custom-made suits. Here is a card for each of you. Just go to the shop and tell him your name. He is going to make a suit for each of you at my expense. Merry Christmas!"

They both thanked Jack profoundly and then busied themselves gathering the food to be taken to their house. Jack took the ham because it was the heaviest, but as they walked over to his brother's house he looked at how his two nephews had grown, and thought perhaps he should have let one of them carry the ham.

The family dinner at his brother's house was nearly perfect. Jack realized that he missed spending time with all of them. Charles told them there may be a new Madison Square Garden coming in a few years. He said the existing building only had a capacity of eight thousand, and with the popularity of professional boxing, they were turning away people at almost every event. Charles said he had seen some preliminary plans that would increase the capacity by ten thousand seats.

"You mean there will be eighteen thousand seats around the ring?" Jack had trouble visualizing such a large open building.

"Yes. And it will be a multipurpose building with the capability of moving large clusters of seats around and changing the floor to accommodate different sporting events," Charles replied.

"Wow, Dad. Do you think you will be able to get us any free tickets to the fights?" Milt asked.

"Anytime there is a good chance that an event is not going to sell out, I can usually get standby tickets at little or no cost. If we get to eighteen thousand seats, I should be able to get a nice selection of tickets for all of us."

Jack's mother asked how Catherine's brother, George Goethals, was doing, and was told that he was officially retired from the army and working with the New York Port Authority. Jack commented about how impressive the book about the Panama Canal was. He stated that he had finished reading the book and offered it to his nephews. They both declined with lame excuses about how busy they were and that they would not have time to read. Jack simply commented that if they ever change their minds, the book would be over at their grandmother's house.

After several hours of reminiscing, Jack and his mother departed for home. Along the way, Jack told his mother about Milt starting to date. She thought that it was wonderful, and of course, prodded Jack about when he was going to bring home a girl.

"Someday, Mom, when the time is right, I promise you will be the first one to meet her."

Catherine had wrapped some of the leftovers along with two slices of her famous chocolate cake for Jack and his mother, so they decided to enjoy the cake with a glass of milk in the kitchen. Jack talked about his concern with new prohibition laws and what impact they might have on his employment. As always, his mother listened and then told him when things change it is best to go one day at a time. She talked about how Jack's father knew it was time to stop sailing with the introduction of the steam ships. So he retired from sailing and soon found employment instructing others how to rig the old sailing ships. He no longer was away from home for months at a time, and those were among the happiest years of their lives.

Over the next six months, Jack repeatedly thought about the advice his mother had given. He did pretty much take things one day at a time, and in so doing, noticed a slow transformation at O'Malley's. The entrance door was changed with a second door installed just inside the first at the end of a small hallway. The second door had a very small opening with a sliding closure that could only be moved from the inside. The door was kept locked. Jack was given a password to speak after first knocking on the door and seeing the closure slide open. Over time, he heard the term *Speakeasy* and thought to himself *how appropriate.* The clientele were different, still very well-dressed, but somewhat more belligerent. It was becoming more and more difficult to satisfy their requests for songs, especially as the evening wore on and the customers consumed more alcohol. Closing time was no longer at a set time and the gathering of employees at the bar for a drink before heading home came to an end. At one point, Mr. O'Malley told Jack he was going to have several strippers putting on a show on Friday evenings and then asked if Jack could play burlesque melodies. Jack's response was that it was not the best type of music for a piano performance, and he would suggest hiring a small group with horns and a good drummer. Predictably, Jack's hours at O'Malley's were slowly reduced.

Then one evening in June, a pretty lady handed Jack a note that he at first thought to be just another request for a song or melody. Upon unfolding the note, he was surprised to read: "I would like to hire you to entertain my guests at an Independence Day Party. Call me. Lorie Bradford. GA7-8744." After reading the note, Jack looked over the tables and dance floor for the lady, but did not see her. Perhaps she had left. As he continued to play that evening, he thought, *Why not.* He was not enjoying O'Malley's as he did when he first started there. Maybe it was time to try something new.

Around noon the next day, Jack made the phone call.

"The Bradford residence. May I help you?" a voice at the other end of the line answered.

"Yes, I would like to speak to Lorie Bradford."

"And may I ask who is calling?"

"This is Jack Schmidt."

"Just a moment, Mr. Schmidt, I will see if Mrs. Bradford can take your call."

"Hello, Jack. I'm so glad that you called. I take it that you are interested in working the party on Independence Day weekend."

"Yes I am, Mrs. Bradford. I would like to get a little more information before committing to anything."

"Certainly, Jack. What are your concerns?"

"Well, where exactly are you located? I don't drive and I would have to see if I can get to your residence by transit."

"My estate is up on the Hudson River just outside of the city. But don't worry about getting here and back to your place. I will send my driver to pick you up and he will also take you home. Pack an overnight bag, as we will be putting you up in one of the guest bedrooms. And don't worry about money. You will be handsomely rewarded, I assure you, and if you are dissatisfied with your compensation, just tell me and I will make things right."

"Thank you, Mrs. Bradford. Your offer is very attractive, so I'm going to say yes."

"Good, Jack. Do you have a phone number where you can be reached?"

"Yes, It is Madison 6-8696. I live with my mother. Her name is Anna. Should I not be home, she will take a message and I will get back to you."

"Very good, Jack. Someone will be in touch with you near the end of this month to finalize times and other details. I'm counting on you, so please don't let me down."

"Don't worry, Mrs. Bradford, I won't let you down, and I'm very much looking forward to the opportunity of entertaining your guests. Thank you so much for asking me. Good-bye, Mrs. Bradford."

"Good-bye, Jack."

Jack was excited after the call. He thought he should have asked how much Mrs. Bradford was going to pay, but after her comment about being handsomely rewarded, it just didn't feel right to ask. He knew his mother was going to ask about the pay, so maybe he thought, *I will just make up a number to satisfy her.* Jack wondered what the estate would be like. Maybe his mother knew something about the Bradford name. *Well,* Jack thought, *I will be home for dinner with Mom tonight, so maybe she will have some advice for me.*

At dinner that evening, Jack filled in his mother about the changes occurring at O'Malley's. When he mentioned the strippers, his mother was taken back and told her son that he had done the right thing in refusing to play burlesque music for strippers. She also felt that maybe it was time to move on to something new. She wasn't sure, but had heard of a Bradford Industries, a large manufacturing company in New York City that made industrial machinery and equipment. They both thought it best for Jack to stay on at O'Malley's for a while until he had a better handle about what he was moving onto. It would be easy for him to reduce his days at O'Malley's. His mother suggested that when he gave final notice that he was leaving, he should contact the man that had placed him in O'Malley's and explain the situation. Jack concurred, and as always, felt reassured in his actions after discussing them with his mother.

THE BRADFORD ESTATE

Jack was just finishing his breakfast on Thursday morning the twenty fourth of June when the phone rang. His mother answered and then said it was for Jack. When Jack answered, the person on the phone identified herself as Mrs. Bradford's secretary and stated that she was calling to finalize Jack's travel details for Independence Day weekend.

"Mr. Schmidt, we plan on sending a driver to pick you up at seven in the morning on Saturday the third of July if that is okay with you? And I will need an address to give to our driver."

Jack replied that seven in the morning would be fine and gave the secretary his address. There were a few more details, including things like he should bring a tuxedo to wear when he is entertaining, a suit with shirt and tie if he planned to attend church on Sunday. Jack asked if it was a Catholic Church and when the secretary replied that it was, he said he would attend. He thanked the secretary, and after hanging up the phone, he thought, *Well it looks like I'm all set for my new adventure.*

At exactly seven o'clock Saturday morning, a rather large enclosed sedan pulled up in front of the house. Jack was sitting out on the porch with his bag. He went down the steps and asked the driver if he was from the Bradford Estate. Jack said he would get his bag, but the driver would not allow him to do so and instead opened the rear passenger door for Jack to enter. The driver then went up on the porch, retrieved Jack's bag, and placed it in a special storage trunk at the back of the car.

"Is that everything?" the driver asked.

"Yes it is. Thank you," Jack replied as he thought this driver must have parked around the corner in order to arrive exactly at seven o'clock. "Did you have any trouble finding the house?"

"No, Mr. Schmidt. I have a very good map of all the city streets. My name is James. It is about a forty-minute drive to the estate. The windows on the doors will crank open if you care for more fresh air. Make yourself comfortable and feel free to ask me about anything as we drive along."

"Thank you, James, and please call me Jack. Mr. Schmidt makes me feel kind of old. Will we be passing the Army's West Point Academy along the way?"

"No, Jack. It is a little farther to the north.

The driver pointed out things of interest as they drove along and asked Jack about his experience in the war. James had a son fighting in France and was so glad to have him back home safe and sound. Jack wasn't able to determine if James' son had been in the same theater of operations as he had, so he kept his comments and answers to questions very general. In a short time, Jack decided that he liked the driver and hoped that all of the employees at Mrs. Bradford's Estate were as nice as James.

The estate was on a hill overlooking the Hudson River. A cluster of magnificent-looking buildings were located at the end of a long driveway that was lined on both sides with evergreen trees. There were no neighboring properties in sight, and the fields were cut and trimmed like a golf course. As they drew closer, Jack could see that the main building had columns that reminded him of pictures he had seen of the Capitol Building in Washington, D.C. The entire building was surrounded with flowers that were in full bloom.

"Who takes care of the lawn and all of these flowers?"

"We have a gardening crew that keep things green in the summer and remove the snow in the winter. When they are not busy with gardening chores, Mrs. Bradford keeps them occupied with small repairs and painting. She is a very good manager."

As soon as the car stopped, the driver was out and opening the passenger door for Jack.

"If you will wait on the porch, Mr. Schmidt, I will bring your luggage and show you to your room."

Once on the porch, Jack looked around to the surrounding area and thought to himself, *So this is what an estate looks like.* James was soon by his side and asked Jack to follow him. They passed through a tall entranceway with double screen doors and then across a marble floored, lobby-like room with large paintings and portraits displayed along the walls. At the far side, there was a winding staircase. James continued along carrying the bag up two flights of stairs like he was an eighteen-year-old with Jack following a step behind. At the top, they went down a rather long carpeted hallway to the guest room that had been prepared for Jack.

"I will be back in about thirty minutes to guide you to the dining room where Mrs. Bradford will join you for breakfast. There is a bathroom behind the door to your left where you may freshen up."

"How should I dress?" Jack asked.

"You are dressed fine for now. I'm sure Mrs. Bradford will go over the details for this evening's gathering."

"Thank you, James. I will see you in a half an hour."

When Jack arrived at the dining table, Mrs. Bradford asked him to be seated and promptly dismissed James.

"Good morning, Mrs. Bradford."

"Good morning, Jack. I have taken the liberty to order your breakfast. I hope you will like a cheese omelet with rye toast and coffee."

"That sounds good to me, ma'am."

"Now, Jack, you must have a thousand questions about this evening. Let me just tell you what we are doing and how you fit in. The guests will start to arrive around midafternoon. They consist of business associates, old friends, a few politicians, and our pastor. As the guests arrive, they will be handled by my house staff. A few will be overnight guests just as you are. The house staff will serve cocktails and hors d'oeuvres. You can see the piano in the far corner. I want you to arrive at the piano in your tuxedo at four o'clock. Here is a listing of some of the melodies and songs that I would like you to play. You may start playing the soft melodies as soon as you are set at the piano. Should anyone have a specific request, it is all right for you to satisfy them. When dinner is served, stop playing and then leave the piano after the pastor says grace. If you are hungry, just go to the kitchen, and the cook will fix a platter for you. You can use your own judgment about when to return. I would say it should be when the house staff removes the dishes after the meal and the guests start to mill around again. At this time, we will need music that they may choose to dance to. When dusk arrives, we will all be moving out onto the terrace to enjoy our private display of fireworks. You are most welcome to join us at this point. After the display, I expect most of the guests will start to say their good-byes and depart. If I feel that we need more of your music, I will let you know. Otherwise, you are free to mingle with the guests. Do you have any questions?"

"You've explained things very well, ma'am. My only question is about attending church tomorrow?"

"I will make sure that you are up in plenty of time and you may ride along with me to Mass. When we finish breakfast, feel free to roam around the estate. I think you will find it to be a very interesting place."

"Thank you, Mrs. Bradford, and I must say that the omelet was very good."

As Mrs. Bradford moved the napkin from her lap to the table, Jack took that as a signal that breakfast was over, so he rose from his chair and moved to assist Mrs. Bradford with her chair.

"All right, Jack, I will see you back here around four o'clock."

"I'll be here, ma'am." As they departed, Jack decided to go outside, as the weather was just perfect. He exited at the rear of the manor house and sighted a garage nearby with at least ten garage doors. Two of the doors were open, and as he approached the first, he found James inside polishing a very large sedan.

"So this is what you do when you're not out driving."

"Hello, Jack. Come on in and I'll show you around. Just let me finish buffing this fender."

The nameplate on the car read, *Packard*. Jack was amazed at how big and luxurious this vehicle was. It was painted black with a brilliant metallic grill and lots of shiny metal trim.

"This Packard is Mrs. Bradford's favorite. It is a very powerful and comfortable vehicle. It has an electric starter, so there is no need to hand crank the engine."

"It certainly is a beautiful car. Is that a race car down near the end of the garage?"

"Yes it is, Jack. Mr. Bradford had several race cars. This is almost identical to the one he was killed in while racing. It was very tragic. A tire came off and the car went completely out of control and ended upside down. Mrs. Bradford was in the stands watching the whole accident unfold. These were built in California and are actually very good machines. Mr. Bradford's accident was very unfortunate."

"When did it happen?"

"It was about four years ago."

"What a shame. It must have been very hard on Mrs. Bradford."

"It was, Jack, but she is a tough lady. She immersed herself in the running of Bradford Industries and has done a tremendous job of keeping the business going."

"Well, from my time at breakfast with her, I was very impressed at how organized she is and the pleasant manner in which she conducts business. I can readily understand that Bradford Industries is doing well."

"Walk along with me, Jack, and I'll show you some of the other cars."

As they walked, James named each car and described their good and bad features. Some were more than ten-years-old, but they were all cleaned and polished to look like new. At the opposite end of the garage, James introduced Jack to the mechanic. He had an engine disassembled and was doing an overhaul. Jack marveled at the fact that someone could put something like that back together again. It was lunch time for James and the mechanic. They asked Jack to join them in the kitchen of the manor house. When they entered a side room off the kitchen, there were a half a dozen other estate employees seated around tables engaged in casual conversation as they enjoyed sandwiches that had been prepared and placed on a tray in the center of each table. Jack followed suit, helping himself to a sandwich and a glass of iced tea. It was a very pleasant and engaging gathering. Once James told the others that Jack had been in the war, there were a lot of questions and the people went out of their way to please Jack. When the workers started to return to their chores, Jack returned to his room and freshened up. He then spent the next several hours reviewing his music. He wanted very much to please Mrs. Bradford and her guests.

Dressed in his tailor-made tuxedo with white shirt and black bow tie, Jack made his way to the piano a few minutes before four o'clock. He had selected several nice soft melodies to start his performance. The guests were still milling around and played little attention to the music. In fact, it was more like they were thankful that the music did not interfere with their conversations. He worked in some of the melodies that Mrs. Bradford had selected and then moved on to a few soft vocals. When he got to "Blue Skies", the room became silent with the guests turning toward Jack and intently listening. Mrs. Bradford sensed the dramatic change and quietly made her way to the piano. When Jack finished "Blue Skies", she moved next to Jack signaling for him to pause.

"Everyone, I would like to introduce to you a very special, young talent from the Bronx, Mr. Jack Schmidt. He recently returned from the Great War in France. We discovered him playing in the city a few months back and enticed him to come here for your listening pleasure on this very special weekend." Following a round of applause, Mrs. Bradford finished by saying, "If any of you have a specific request for a song or melody, simply tell Mr. Schmidt and he will do his best to satisfy you. And now if you will all please take a seat, Father York is going to lead us in grace."

Jack took his cue and remained quiet until the blessing was over and then very quietly slipped away from the piano and into the kitchen. He settled at a table in the far corner, and when one of the waitresses asked if she could bring him anything, Jack settled for an iced tea, stating that he would try a platter later. He thought that anyone spending much time around this kitchen would most assuredly gain weight. Jack guessed that it must have been at least a five-course dinner by the number of different dishes that the waiters and waitresses were moving in and out. After thirty minutes or so, he waved for one of the waitresses and asked if there was any soup. She responded that they had delicious chicken soup, so he settled for that as his dinner. He thought, *This is better, as it is rather tough to perform on a full stomach.*

After finishing his soup, Jack moved to a chair where he could see most of the large dining table. Soon the dishes were being cleared and some of the guests had vacated their chairs, so Jack quietly moved back to the piano. He looked for a signal from Mrs. Bradford to resume playing, but when none came, he decided to use his own judgment and once again started to play a low-key melody. On his second number, he noticed that the guests had moved much closer to him. A gentleman looked at Jack and raised his hand. Jack acknowledged the gentleman and received a verbal request for "I'm a Yankee Doodle Dandy".

"A very fitting selection for Independence Day, sir," Jack responded as he began to play and sing. On the second verse, he invited the audience to join in. Jack thoroughly enjoyed working a crowd. At the end of the selection, he immediately moved on to "You're a Grand Old Flag". The next selection was "The Caissons Go Rolling Along". Jack could pretty much pick out those that had served in the military just by their reaction to the song. Another hand was raised, this time by a very attractive lady.

Jack pointed to the lady and said, "Yes, ma'am."

"Can we please have some dance music?"

"How about," and he started into "Let Me Call You Sweetheart". There was a small round of applause, mostly from the ladies. The dance floor filled rapidly, and without stopping, Jack moved to "Daddy's Little Girl" followed by "You Belong to Me" and the "Joe Turner Blues".

The sun had gone down and Jack could see that the sky was getting pretty dark. Mrs. Bradford again came up next to the piano and signaled for everyone's attention.

"We are about ready to start the fireworks. If you will all follow me out of the door next to the kitchen, we can get under way."

Jack playfully began the "Colonel Bogey March" and the guests fell into a column, marching in tune with the music. When everyone was out, Jack followed. Many of the guests gave Jack a pat on the back or a handshake with comments like, "Nice job, son" or "It was truly a pleasure listening to you."

The fireworks were spectacular with ground displays of the flag, a ship, tanks, and cannons. There were numerous rockets streaking into the black sky and then bursting open into patterns of multicolored streamers. The crowd and Jack were in awe and thoroughly enjoyed the display. There was a grand finale with multiple rockets streaking into the dark night seemingly all at the same time. When the booming noise stopped, all that remained to be seen was the wispy smoke in the sky. The people began to return to the manor house with Jack again following along as he conversed with some of the guests. Mrs. Bradford was right when she said the guests would most likely depart after the fireworks. It seemed inappropriate for Jack to return to the piano, so he just stood by and kept an eye on Mrs. Bradford for a possible signal that he should resume playing. The house staff had cleaned away all of the dishes and glasses. It even looked like the dining table had a fresh tablecloth. Mrs. Bradford had worked her way toward the front entrance as many of the guests were seeking her out to thank her and say good night before they departed. In less than thirty minutes, there were only a half a dozen people remaining, and it turned out that four of them were overnight guests. Mrs. Bradford directed the staff to see the overnight couples to their rooms and then moved over to Jack, taking him by the arm and leading him into a smaller room that appeared to be either a library or a study. She asked one of the staff to bring two glasses of iced tea and then dismissed the staff for the remainder of the evening.

"Jack, I hope you don't mind sitting with me for a while. I like to relax and unwind after an evening of practicing my social etiquette."

"I don't mind at all, ma'am." Jack went on to explain how all of the employees used to gather at the bar in O'Malley's before calling it an evening and heading home. He said things had changed with the emergence of the prohibition laws and he kind of missed those evening gatherings.

"Jack, you did a marvelous job this evening. My guests were very impressed with your talent and your performance. I have something in mind that might help you, but first I want to learn more about you. Do you mind telling me some things about yourself?"

"No, ma'am, I don't mind at all. Where would you like me to start?"

"Tell me about your mother and father, your neighborhood and friends, and I would like to hear a little about your experiences in the Great War."

Jack started with a brief description of his parents and how they had come to America. He found talking with Mrs. Bradford to be a very relaxing and enjoyable experience. She occasionally interrupted him and asked for more details or maybe wanted to know how he felt about a specific situation. She held his arm tightly when he talked about the Great War, and he could sense that she was horrified about the killing and maiming of so many. After almost an hour of conversation, Mrs. Bradford told Jack that she had a close friend who is perhaps the best agent for entertainers in New York City. She asked if it would be all right for her to set up a meeting between Jack and the agent, perhaps again with a small gathering at her estate, so the agent might hear Jack play and sing.

"I've never had an agent, ma'am. And if he is the best in the city, I'm really not sure that I can afford him. I'm still kind of sponsored by the Irving Berlin Music Publishing Company."

Jack continued on, explaining how he and his mother had discussed the situation at O'Malley's and had decided that before giving Mr. O'Malley notice that he would be leaving, he should first visit with Arthur Kennedy at The Irving Berlin Music Publishing Company to explain his situation and his reasons for leaving.

"My compliments go to you and your mother for being so considerate. I certainly agree with your approach. However, you should understand that working under contract with an agent will not cost anything in upfront money. Instead, the agent will work for you to better your career. Typically agents collect a percentage of the money you are paid for your performances. The more popular you are, the more your agent will be able to charge for your performances. So you see it is in the agent's best interest for you to advance in your career, thereby increasing the amount of money he receives."

"Well, that does sound pretty good. Let me sleep on it before I give you my answer. Okay?"

"Certainly, Jack, but please try to let me know before heading back home so that I can make the proper contacts and arrangements. It is getting late, so I think we should retire for the evening. I understand you are going to Mass with James and me in the morning. We will be leaving here at nine. I will have my staff ring you at eight. And Jack, I would like you to stay over tomorrow evening. If that works for you, we will go directly to the country club for breakfast following Mass and then from there, I would like to ride out to the plant where I need to sign a few papers and then I can show you around a bit. Can you do that?"

"I would love to. I'll call my mother sometime tomorrow and tell her not to expect me back until Monday. And thank you for taking an interest in my career and for the advice you have given to me."

At exactly eight o'clock the next morning, Jack's room phone rang with a wakeup call. Jack had actually been up since about six thinking about Mrs. Bradford's suggestion that he sign on with an agent. He usually discussed moves like this with his mother and relied heavily upon her input. *But hey*, he thought, *I'm twenty-two-years-old and an army veteran*. I guess it's about time for me to make some decisions on my own. He felt very uncomfortable with the thought that he would go home first and then let Mrs. Bradford know his answer. She would see immediately that he had to talk it over with his mother. *Okay*, he thought, *unless something happens today to change my mind, I'm going to say yes and thank Mrs. Bradford very much for taking an interest in me.*

Jack headed downstairs at about ten minutes before nine. James already had the car parked in front of the manor house. Jack thought about going out to talk to James, but just then he heard someone on the staircase. He waited and sure enough it was Mrs. Bradford.

"Good morning, Mrs. Bradford, you look very nice this morning." Jack took her arm and escorted her to the side of the car where James was holding the door open.

"Good morning, Mrs. Bradford, and good morning, Jack. I trust you both had a good night's sleep."

James motioned for Jack to sit next to Mrs. Bradford at the back and then closed the door before moving around to the driver's seat. Jack was amazed to hear the electric starter engage and then the engine roar to life. All of the cars that he had been familiar with had to be cranked by hand.

"I really like the way this car starts. I have shied away from hand cranking ever since my brother broke his thumb starting his car. The last thing I need is a hand injury."

"The electric starter is much better," Mrs. Bradford replied. "We have three cars now with electric starters, and of course when I choose to drive, I always take one of those three."

Wow, Jack thought, *what a woman*. She even drives her own cars! It took about thirty minutes to get to the church. James stopped in front of the church and moved to each side of the car, first assisting Mrs. Bradford and then Jack. Mrs. Bradford told Jack to come along as they moved to enter the church. Many of the parishioners knew Mrs. Bradford and greeted her by name as they moved into the church. Mrs. Bradford moved all of the way up to the first pew. Again Jack was amazed. He thought she must really know her religion otherwise we would be further back in the church. The celebration of Mass was done very well. The choir was not only good, but also easy to understand. The service was short and to the point. *Just the way it should be on a hot summer morning*, Jack thought.

Mrs. Bradford introduced Jack to some people on the way out of church when they were waiting for James to pull forward in the line of vehicles in front of the church.

Once back in the car, Jack said, "I enjoyed the service very much. The choir was good and the pastor kept the Mass short as it should be on a hot day."

"Excuse me, Jack. James, I would like to go directly to the country club."

"Yes, ma'am," James replied.

"Yes, Jack, our pastor does a good job all year round. We are very lucky to have him. It is only about fifteen minutes to the country club. Are you hungry?"

"Yes, I am, ma'am. I'm used to eating an early breakfast on most days."

As they turned off the main road, Jack sensed that the country club was actually part of a golf course. Mrs. Bradford told him it was in fact a nine-hole golf course and that there was more than enough acreage to expand the course to eighteen holes. It was apparent that she had a financial interest in the club. At the club entrance, James again assisted both from the car. Mrs. Bradford then dismissed him, telling him to return in about an hour and that they would then drive to the Bradford Plant. Inside of the dining room, the maitre d' made a fuss over Mrs. Bradford and escorted them to a table by the window overlooking the ninth hole. Jack ordered a club special from the menu, which consisted of scrambled eggs, bacon, toast, pancakes, and coffee. After doing so, he thought maybe he should have been a little more reserved, but Mrs. Bradford seemed pleased to see that Jack had such an appetite. When the coffee arrived, Jack told Mrs. Bradford that he had given a lot of thought to her suggestion about getting an agent and his answer was *yes*. By her expression, Jack could tell that she was very pleased that he had accepted. The hour went fast. Jack did finish all of his breakfast, and before they knew it, James was standing next to the table awaiting further orders.

"I am just going to freshen up in the ladies' room and then we will be right out, James."

Jack decided to visit the men's, room and indicated to James that he would meet him out front in just a minute. The ride to the Bradford Plant was quite pleasant with both James and Mrs. Bradford pointing out sites of interest along the way. There was a guard house at the entrance gate. James stopped and the guard came out to greet Mrs. Bradford. He quickly opened the gate and waved the car through. Near the front of the complex there was a low brick building that appeared to be an office. James parked in front of the building, and as he assisted Mrs. Bradford, she told him they would be several hours and suggested that he return for them around four o'clock.

Jack followed Mrs. Bradford into the building and down a corridor to an office with lettering on the door that read, L. Bradford, President. She stopped at the door for a moment and told Jack that the door lettering used to read, Lawrence Bradford, President.

"Jack, as you probably already know, the business world is very much a man's world. With my first name being Lorie, I decided to change the lettering on not only the door but also some of our stationery. To this day, many of our business associates still think the company is being run by a man. I don't want to be a revolutionary woman; I just try to do what is best for Bradford Industries. There are some important papers here for me to review and sign. Please make yourself comfortable while I attend to them, and then I will give you a tour of the plant."

It only took Mrs. Bradford about fifteen minutes to handle the paperwork. When she finished, they left the office and moved to the far end of the office corridor and then through a side door that opened into a very large industrial building with a variety of big machines. Machined parts were neatly arranged in rows, as far as one could see.

"Wow, Mrs. Bradford, I can see this is a very large operation."

"Yes it is. Come this way, Jack. We make a lot of industrial machines like these internal and external grinders, many of which are used to manufacture electric motors and even the starter in our car. Business has become very competitive in recent years, so I have been toying with the idea of selling the newly manufactured machines at my cost or even slightly below and concentrate on making our profit on the spare parts that we sell to keep the machines operating. Some of these units are set up in assembly line fashion at various companies. When one of the machines goes down, the whole assembly line stops. We provide support, but it sometimes takes weeks to get the required parts manufactured and shipped. My idea is to actually stock a wide range of spare parts here. We know from past experience which parts are most likely to fail. The one problem that I have not yet solved is how to communicate enough information to the user so that they can analyze the problem and order the correct part to accomplish a rapid repair, and dramatically reduce the assembly line down time."

"Mrs. Bradford, remember me telling you about my nephew, Milton. Well, just last week I spent some time over at his house and he was showing me some of the material he is studying and working with in his apprentice program at the Chilton Publishing Company. He is going to become a compositor when he finishes the program. Apparently, his responsibility will be to lay out the page format in technical manuals. Some of the manuals he showed me had exploded views of all of the parts that go into a truck engine. I'm thinking that maybe the Chilton Company can help you with your ideas."

"That is very interesting, Jack. Do you think you can get your nephew to bring those manuals here for me to see? Perhaps he can come along with you when I get things set up for the agent to be here?"

"I'm pretty sure I can arrange that. I'll go see Milt as soon as I get back to the Bronx."

They spent several hours walking through the plant. There was no one else there. Mrs. Bradford said she and her husband would often come to the plant on the weekends and spend time examining the equipment and the environment. Their goal was to improve the operating process, thereby creating more efficiency and always to keep the employee foremost in mind when considering any changes. Bradford Industries is a non union plant, and the way to keep it that way is to make a workplace that the employees enjoyed coming to. She explained what each machine was used for, often in such detail that Jack was lost. He was impressed with the workplace. He had imagined that many of the manufacturing plants were real sweatshops. Maybe some were, but the Bradford Plant truly looked like a nice place to work. Soon it was time to meet James, so they made their way back to the office.

The return ride to the estate was short and uneventful. When they reached the manor house porch, Mrs. Bradford stopped, thought for a moment, and then asked Jack if he would like to join her at the pool. She would have one of the staff bring a pitcher of iced tea, some sandwiches, and fresh fruit. She told him he would find a robe in his room to wear and to meet her at the pool about seven. It felt like it was going to be a hot, muggy evening, so Jack readily accepted the invitation.

When Jack arrived at the pool, it was already getting dark. Mrs. Bradford was in the pool swimming laps. Jack did not have a swimsuit and had simply put the terry cloth robe over his underwear. He sat in a chair at the side of the pool.

"Jack, come in and join me."

"I don't have a swimsuit, ma'am."

"Well at least move over to the edge where you can put your feet in. The water is very refreshing."

Jack did, and found the water to be just right.

"This will be my last lap. Will you be kind enough to bring my towel and robe to the other end of the pool? Then we will partake of some of the refreshments. And Jack, the staff knows not to disturb me at the pool. When we are alone together, please call me Lorie. Ma'am and Mrs. Bradford are so formal."

"Okay, ma'am. I mean okay, Lorie."

Jack arrived at the end of the pool just as Lorie touched the edge. As she exited the pool, she asked him to wrap the towel around her and dry her back. It wasn't until then that Jack realized she had no bathing suit on. He managed to maintain his composure and tried to keep his hands from touching any part of her body that would be inappropriate. She certainly was a beautiful woman.

"Bring the towel around the front of me. Don't be afraid to touch my breasts. Women love to have a man's hands touch them at the appropriate time."

Her breasts were soft and firm at the same time. "Lorie, you are such a beautiful woman. I really don't know how to react."

"Just relax and let me lead you through the rest of the evening. Help me get into my robe and we will go over to the table and have something to eat."

The sandwiches and fruit were excellent. Jack felt himself relaxing somewhat as they engaged in casual conversation. Lorie asked if there had been any woman in Jack's life who so impressed him that he wanted very much to see her again. His response was that there was a woman over in France, and he went on to tell Lorie about his experience with Cecelia. He said it was painful to think about her not knowing whether she even made it through the war. Lorie playfully rubbed her leg against Jack's under the table and told him she was going to help him forget Cecelia at least for this one night. She went on to tell Jack that he had seen her as a hostess and as a business woman and now she wanted him to see her simply as a woman.

"I know I am a good twenty years older than you, Jack. But I still have the innate passions of a sensuous woman. I need to have more in life to look forward to than another day at the office or another weekend with guests at this beautiful estate. I want to spend time with a man like you. I want to put my arms around you and whisper sweet things into your ear. I realize there can never be anything permanent between us, but I so want to live for the moment with you."

Jack reached across the table and held both of Lorie's hands. "Lorie, you are such a beautiful and smart woman. I can't believe

I am here with you like this. I too need something more than just playing the piano and singing. Can we start with a simple kiss?"

"Yes we can," Lorie replied as she shook off her robe and dove into the pool. "Take your underwear off and come and get that kiss."

Jack followed and put his arms around her, gently kissing her lips. It felt so good to be with her. They playfully teased each other for a period of time until Lorie said it was time to get serious and make their way back to the bedrooms. Along the way, Lorie told Jack that she would open the door connecting their two bedrooms once she had finished bathing and was ready for him to come and spend the evening with her as he had done with Cecelia. Jack also bathed and anxiously waited for the connecting door to open. When the door finally opened, Lorie came to Jack and took him by the hand leading him to her bed. She was wearing a silk nightgown and smelled just wonderful. The lights were dimmed just as Cecelia had dimmed them that night in France. Lorie sat down on the side of the bed and patted a spot next to her where she wanted Jack to sit. She gave him a gentle kiss and then told him she had been a teacher before marrying Lawrence. She then told him to lie back and relax. Lorie was about to teach him how to pleasure a woman so that she would never, ever forget him.

Lorie was shaking Jack. As he opened his eyes he could tell it was morning.

"What time is it?"

"It's ten o'clock, young man. That was quite a night." Then she playfully bent over and kissed him. When Jack reached to put his arms around her she said, "I'm sorry, Jack, but there is no time for that. I have a luncheon I must go to at the club with several business associates. I'm going to have to ask you to go back to your room. You may sleep more if you like. If you want breakfast, just stop in the kitchen and they will take care of you. James knows that you will need a ride back today. You can usually find him in the garage. I loved every minute of our time together last night and you have given me something precious to look forward to. I'll be in touch, and when you come next time, please plan to stay at least two nights."

With that, she kissed him several more times and then pulled him from the bed and patted him on the behind as she ushered him through the connecting door.

THE AGENT

While riding back home, Jack kept going back over his weekend at the Bradford Estate. *Unbelievable*, he thought, and the worst part was that he would not be able to tell anybody about his personal time with Lorie. He had not told anyone about Cecelia until last night. Lorie was such a unique person. *Why am I so attractive to older women*? Cecelia was at least ten years older and now Lorie is twenty. He loved the good life at the estate, and wondered if he would ever be able to attain such wealth and status in his lifetime. Well, it was certainly nice to get a taste of high society, but now back to the Bronx. Arriving at his house, he told James that there was a good chance he would be returning to the estate in a week or two and he hoped to see James again.

Things at home were the same. Nobody was beating down the door to offer him engagements. He thought more and more that he had made the right decision to get involved with an agent. Now the hard part would be to break the news to his mother. Up to this point, she had always been involved in his decisions. At dinner that evening, Jack gave his mother a pretty detailed description of the Bradford Estate and the Bradford Plant. He told her how his performance was and that it seemed to be well received, and finally, he told her about Mrs. Bradford's offer to line him up with sort of an audition before one of the top agents in the city. To Jack's surprise, his mother was not at all upset that he had made his decision to go ahead with the audition without first consulting her. In fact, she seemed to be proud of the way he had handled himself. Jack had not mentioned anything about trying to get Milt to bring some of the Chilton Publishing material to the estate for Lorie to look over. He decided some things are best left unsaid. Maybe Milt won't be able to do it anyway.

"Mom, I'm going to go over to Charles' house when we finish. There is a great golf course at the estate that I want to tell Milt about."

"Before you go, Jack, I have some homemade soup in the kitchen that I want to send to Catherine. I'll put some in a covered pot for you to take. Tell Catherine it is all right to keep the pot until I next see her."

Well, that went smoother than I thought it would. It felt good to be home, and Jack was looking forward to visiting his brother's family. Maybe there is a way that I can get Lorie to arrange for Milt and me to play a round of golf? That would certainly entice Milt to make the trip.

Everyone was at his brother's house when Jack arrived. They were just finishing dinner and invited Jack to join them for a dish of chocolate pudding. Jack told them about his weekend at the estate. The boys listened very intently, and on occasion, asked Jack to give more details. It was obvious that Charles Sr. and Catherine were also impressed. Then he decided to tell them he was planning a return engagement and might even be able to take Milt along for a round of golf.

Milt was smiling from ear to ear. Catherine said she supposed that it would be all right. And then the conversation drifted to things his brother's family had been doing. After the dishes were cleared, Jack took Milt aside and talked to him about the publications from the Chilton Publishing Company that he had shown Jack. He described what he had observed in the Bradford Plant and stated that the president of the company was very much interested in the type of parts illustrations that were in the Chilton Manuals. Jack told Milt if he could bring some of the manuals to the estate along with the names of the right people to contact at Chilton, he might be able to steer some business to Chilton and we should be able to get a free round of golf. Milt indicated that as long as it would be on a weekend, he could do it.

"I'll make a call and let you know for sure. It will probably be this coming weekend or the next. Keep it mum until I find out for sure."

Around noon the next day, Jack called Mrs. Bradford and left a message with her secretary that he would be able to bring the exploded parts diagrams on the weekend of either the tenth and eleventh or the seventeenth and eighteenth of July. He further indicated that he would be at home that evening should Mrs. Bradford care to call back. Following dinner that evening, Mrs. Bradford did call. Jack answered the phone so there was no need to explain anything to his mother. Lorie told him she was still working with the agent and it would most likely be the weekend of the seventeenth and eighteenth. She teased about how much she missed his gentle touch, but would just have to wait a little longer to see him. Jack mentioned that he kind of bribed his nephew into coming by telling him they might be able to play a round of golf at the club.

"Consider it done, as soon as I confirm a date and time with the agent, I'll set up things for you at the club. I will personally call you when I have details. I can't wait to see you. Good-bye, love."

Well, Jack thought, *that was easy.* He then decided to spend a little time practicing at the piano. After all, the real purpose of this little adventure was to get his career on track and break away from O'Malley's. His mother heard the piano and made her way through the house until she was next to the piano.

"Jack, I have seldom heard you sing like that. Your voice has improved. Please sing some more for me."

He played and sang tunes from "The Merry Widow" and "Babes in Toyland", both of which he knew by heart. His mother was impressed and told Jack so.

"Son, you are definitely ready to move on to better things. When do you perform for that agent?"

"It looks like the weekend of the seventeenth. And I hope to take Milt along with me, so we can enjoy a round of free golf at the country club."

"Keep practicing, Jack. You know the old saying, 'Practice makes perfect'. I'll pray for you."

"Thanks, Mom, I'm going to give it my best shot."

On Thursday, the phone rang around noon. Jack answered in anticipation that it was Lorie calling with detailed information. Instead it was Mr. O'Malley calling to see if Jack could cover both Thursday and Friday evenings, as the three piece group scheduled for Friday had canceled. Jack didn't much care for Friday evenings anymore because the clientele now wanted to stay at the speakeasy until the early hours of the morning and became more demanding as the night wore on. He reluctantly agreed to cover Friday, but told Mr. O'Malley that if the crowd started to get unruly, he was going to leave. Mr. O'Malley concurred, and said he also missed the good old days before prohibition. After hanging up, Jack thought it would have been a good time to give Mr. O'Malley a hint that he would be leaving soon. Then he thought, no, it would be better to stick with the plan he and his mother had discussed.

Thursday's performance at O'Malley's went smoothly, and Jack found himself once again enjoying the interaction with the crowd. Friday was another story. The evening started out fine, but by the time midnight rolled around, there were customers at three of the tables who were obviously drunk, very loud, and often using offensive language. Jack finished the melody he was playing and went over to the bar without announcing a break or stating that he would be back in a few minutes. Two male customers accompanied by a rather wild-looking woman came over to the bar and started harassing Jack.

"Bartender, put some whiskey in this boy's drink."

"No thank you, sir. I don't drink when I'm working."

The wild-looking woman grabbed the bottle from the bartender's hands, and while attempting to pour some into Jack's drink, she splashed whiskey all over his hand and the sleeve of his tuxedo. Jack attempted to walk away, but the second man grabbed him by the arm.

"Don't do that," Jack said.

"What are you going to do about it, punk?"

As Jack pulled his arm free, the first man attempted to grab him up near his collar. Jack snapped, and his army training seemed to automatically take over. With the palms of his hands open, he smacked the attacker as hard as he could, square on both ears. His assailant fell to the floor screaming. Jack turned just in time to find the other man running at him with a whiskey bottle raised high in the air. Jack kicked him hard in the groin and brushed the bottle swinging arm to the side. Next, the wild woman jumped on his back and started scratching at his face. Jack grabbed both of her wrists and slung her against the bar where she slithered to the floor. He then turned, brushed himself off, and walked directly out of O'Malley's.

After such an encounter, one's nerves finally catch up with them. Jack was no different. He walked for a couple of blocks, but could not stop shaking. Jack decided to hail a cab and head for home. By the time he was home, the shakes were pretty much gone. It was late, so his mother was not up. The first thing Jack did once inside of the house was to examine his face in the mirror. Sure enough, the wild woman had left a few marks on his one cheek and along his neck. He got cleaned up and went to bed thinking that he would sort this whole experience out in the morning.

At breakfast, his mother noticed the scratches right away. Jack explained what had happened, and his mother instantly went to the medicine cabinet to retrieve a small jar of Vaseline. She told him to hold still and then gently applied the jelly over the scratches.

"Put this on a couple of times a day and try to keep it away from your shirt collar. The scratches are not deep and should disappear in a few days. Jack, I think it is time for you to visit Mr. Kennedy as we discussed and tell him about last evening and that you have decided to leave O'Malley's."

"I agree, Mom. I'll call Monday morning and see if I can schedule a meeting with him next week. In any event, I have made up my mind to no longer play the piano at O'Malley's."

Around nine o'clock Monday morning, Jack called for an appointment with Mr. Kennedy. The secretary told Jack that Mr. Kennedy was in and asked in a very professional way how much time would be needed. Jack thought no more than fifteen minutes and told the secretary so.

"Mr. Schmidt, if you can be here by eleven thirty, I can squeeze you in for a short meeting with Mr. Kennedy."

"Thank you very much, ma'am, I will be there in plenty of time."

Jack arrived at eleven fifteen and was surprised when the secretary said he could go right in.

"Good morning, Mr. Kennedy."

"Good morning, Jack, and please call me Art. What brings you here today?"

"Well, Art, I intend to give notice at O'Malley's that I will no longer be working there, and I felt that I owed you the courtesy of being informed first. Also, I want to thank you for all that you have done for me." Jack went on to describe the changes that had taken place since the implementation of the Volstead Act and his bad experience Friday night at O'Malley's. He mentioned his intention to sign on with an agent in the near future and his outlook of being reasonably assured of gainful employment for the foreseeable future.

"I'm sorry for your unfortunate experience. Yes, times are changing, Jack, and there are things that many of us dislike about some of the change. However, the music goes on. We have so many wonderful new songs and talented entertainers. I certainly agree with your decision to leave O'Malley's. And remember, if there is ever anything we can do for you here at Irving Berlin Publishing, don't hesitate to let us know. Thank you for coming in and letting me know of your intentions. Good luck to you, Jack."

Art walked out of the office with Jack. They shook hands and after Jack was gone, Art turned commenting to his secretary, "Now that young man is going places."

Normally, Wednesday was payday at O'Malley's, so Jack decided he might as well go in to pick up the money due to him and tell O'Malley that he was leaving. Jack knocked on the office door and heard Mr. O'Malley tell him to come in.

"Good morning, Jack. I have your money here for you. I got a call from Art yesterday, so I know you're leaving. I can't blame you after that fray on Friday night. Everyone is still talking about how you handled yourself. In fact, a couple of the people said I should hire you as a bouncer. I put a few extra bucks in the envelope to pay for the cleaning of your tux."

"Thanks, Mr. O'Malley. And thanks for giving me the opportunity to gain some experience playing at your place. I managed to escape Friday with a few scratches on my face, but it could have been real nasty."

"I know, Jack. I've had a serious talk with my security guys and we are going to try and prevent any reoccurrence of what you experienced. I want to wish you luck in your new endeavor, and I hope you stop by to see us from time to time."

"Thanks again, Mr. O'Malley, I'll try not to be a stranger. So long."

They shook hands and Jack left. It felt good to be outside of the speakeasy knowing that he would not have to return to work there again. Jack had some time to kill, and because it was such a beautiful day, he decided to walk over to the Sixth Avenue music store where he started out as a song plugger. He hoped that Katie would be there. She was a nice lady and kind of fun to talk with. Katie noticed Jack as soon as he entered the store.

"Jack, hello. I can't believe how handsome and mature you've become. I've heard a lot about you, including your fight with the lowlife at O'Malley's this past weekend. How are you?" She moved close to him and gave him a big hug.

"I'm doing pretty well, Katie. I just gave notice at O'Malley's, so I may not get by this way for a while. How are you and how is the sheet music business doing?"

"Some days we can't keep up with the customers, and on others, the store is nearly empty like today. Overall, we're making money and keeping Mr. Berlin happy. So what are you going to do now, Jack?"

"I'm scheduled to meet with an agent, and if I get signed, I expect he will be able to keep me busy. I hope to stay clear of the speakeasy clubs and maybe get some engagements that will advance my career."

"Well, Arthur Kennedy speaks very highly of you, Jack, and he is a good judge of talent. So you just keep working hard and you'll get your break."

"Thanks, Katie, I've got to run along. I'll keep in touch."

Thursday evening, Lorie called and once again Jack answered the phone so he would not have to explain much to his mother. Lorie was excited. She had everything set for the weekend. James was to pick Jack and Milt up at seven on Saturday morning and take them directly to the country club. Their instructions were to be sure to wear long pants and shirts with collars. The personnel at the country club would fit them with golf shoes and have sets of clubs and golf balls for them to use. They would each have a caddie. The round of golf was completely free including the caddie fees. And should they order any food or drink at the club to just tell the help to put it on Mrs. Bradford's tab. Following golf, James would bring them to the manor house and usher them to the same guest room that Jack had used previously. They were to get cleaned up and meet Lorie in the library. There would be several hours available to go over the material Milt was bringing. Whenever they would finish in the library, Milt and Jack were to go to the kitchen to eat. James would then take Milt back to the Bronx. There would be a small group of guests for Jack to entertain later in the evening. He was to wear a suit rather than a tuxedo. The agent would be among the guests, and Lori would introduce him to Jack near the end of the evening. There was a possibility that the agent would also stay overnight.

"Wow, Lorie, you certainly did cover everything. I can't wait to see you and hate that I have to be a complete gentleman until late in the evening."

"I'll make it up to you, love. I think about you a lot and how we are going to share two nights together. Will Milt be disappointed leaving early?"

"No, in fact, he'll be happy. He has a girlfriend in the Bronx who he sees on most weekends."

"Okay, love. I'll dream about you tonight."

"Good night, Lorie. Me too, and I'll see you soon."

Saturday came quickly. Milt was excited about playing golf and seeing the Bradford Estate. James arrived exactly at seven o'clock. Jack quietly commented to Milt that he didn't know how this driver manages to arrive exactly at the appointed hour. The ride to the country club was routine with most of the conversation between Jack and Milt. Jack wanted to know how things were between Milt and his girlfriend, and of course, Milt didn't want to discuss much about his romance. Once at the club, they were treated like very important guests. It was a fun round, after which they enjoyed sodas and sandwiches in the club.

"Now this is living, Jack."

"It sure is, and how about those caddies? I'll bet I shaved five or ten strokes off my score just by following their advice. I hope that material you brought for Mrs. Bradford is good enough to get us a return round."

"Mrs. Bradford? I thought it was for the president of the company."

"She is the president of the company and a darn good one from what I have seen. Well, are you ready to see the manor house? I'll ask them to give James a call to come pick us up."

James parked in front of the manor house and gave Jack a room key while telling him they should both go to the same guest room he last stayed in and get freshened up. When they were ready, they were to immediately go to the library. Jack indicated that he knew where the library was as they gathered their things and headed up the staircase. Milt was very impressed with the house and the guest room.

"Is this the room you stayed in on your last visit?"

"Yes, pretty nice, isn't it? And you can even have breakfast brought to the room."

"Wow, this is living, Jack."

"Okay, let's hurry up. You can have the bathroom first. Mrs. Bradford is not a woman who likes to be kept waiting."

When they entered the library, Mrs. Bradford was sitting at the table looking at mechanical drawings spread out on the table.

"Hello, Jack. It is so nice of you to have come. This young man must be the nephew you have been telling me about."

"Hello, Mrs. Bradford. Yes, this is Milt."

"Nice to meet you, Mrs. Bradford, and thank you so much for our round of golf at the country club."

"You are quite welcome, Milt. Bring your manuals over and put them here on the table. I would like you to show me how the various parts of a component are displayed."

"Well, ma'am, I brought two manuals for a fire engine. The fire engine is a rather complex piece of equipment with built in pumps and motors and an assortment of controls." As Milt flipped through several pages, he stopped periodically and commented, "Now here you see an illustration of the truck's engine. Notice how various sections of the engine are exploded into individual parts, each with a specific part number. Let me show you in the next manual the text and illustrations that explain in what sequence to disassemble the engine and how to inspect various parts for defects. The next several pages explain how to reassemble the engine and specify measured tolerances that are acceptable. Is this what you had in mind, Mrs. Bradford?"

"Milt, this is exactly what I had in mind. Can your company develop manuals for heavy industrial equipment in this fashion?"

"I don't know why not, ma'am. Jack asked me to bring along the names and phone numbers for some people at Chilton who may be able to help you. Please understand that I am only an apprentice and really unable to go much further than showing you these typical manuals."

"Can you leave these with me for a while?"

"Yes, ma'am, but eventually, I'll need them back to return to the company."

"Well, I want to thank you for taking the time to come along with your uncle today. He has explained to me that you are anxious to return home as early as possible. James is parked out front and waiting for your arrival so that he can transport you back home. I will be in touch with the people at Chilton Publishing, and in so doing, I'll put in a good word for you."

"Thank you, ma'am, and good-bye."

"I'll walk out with you, Milt. Mrs. Bradford, I'll be right back."

Jack and Milt walked out of the manor house, chatting along the way. When they reached the car, Jack said he would catch up with Milt in the next week, and then explained to James that Milt lived just a few doors down from Jack's house. Jack felt excited as he returned to Lorie. It was hard to keep up his guard and use "Mrs. Bradford" rather than "Lorie" when speaking to her and to stay at least arm's length away from her when all he could really think about was hugging and caressing Lorie.

"Jack, I am very pleased with the material your nephew brought. I will meet with my managers next week and see if we can get started developing manuals for our equipment.

Come sit next to me on this side of the table. How was your day?

"It has been great up to now. It was fascinating being with Milt and watching his reactions as we indulged in living the life of the wealthy. We really enjoyed the round of golf, and I'm glad that Milt's material may be of some benefit to you".

"But, Jack, you said 'up to now'. What's bothering you, Jack?"

"I guess I'm a little nervous about performing for the agent later." Then, talking in a very low tone, "But mostly I have trouble with acting so proper. Lorie, more than anything right now I want to hug you and kiss your beautiful lips. It's very hard to suppress my real feelings until sometime later."

"I know, Jack. I feel the same way." Then rubbing her leg against his. "I'll make it up to you later. I promise. Now let's talk business. I want you to look sharp tonight. Dress in your suit and plan to arrive at the piano by four thirty. The agent will be in the small group of dinner guests. I will introduce you to him after you have finished playing. I'm not sure as to what he may want you to do at that point. I know your talent is real, Jack, so just act natural and perform as you did at our Independence Day gathering. Now I have to check with my staff to see if everything is nearly ready. I suggest that you go to your room, relax, and then dress up for me. I can't wait to see you after all have gone." Then squeezing his hand, Lorie stood and headed off to the kitchen.

Jack was at the piano a few minutes before four thirty. Lorie came over and told him to play some soft melodies until the group was seated and ready for a blessing of the food. At that point, he was to go to the kitchen for a quick meal. He was to stay no longer than twenty minutes before returning to the piano. At some point after that, when the time was right, Lorie would come next to the piano and introduce Jack to the group.

Jack looked over all of the guests as they arrived, trying to guess who amongst them the agent was. He enjoyed playing soft melodies. In fact, it was a good way to warm up before singing a vocal. Lorie was a master at greeting the guests and marshaling them about the dining room. Jack looked at his watch and predicted to himself that everyone would be seated at the dining table and ready for the blessing by five o'clock. He was sure Lorie had the kitchen staff briefed and ready to start serving food around five. When everyone was seated, he again glanced at his watch. It was four fifty-five. He wondered if the agent would be seated close to Lorie, but after looking at the guests so seated, Jack discounted that thought. The men sitting close were rather dull-looking. He imagined that the agent would be a rather vibrant-looking individual. Oh well, he would just have to wait for his introduction. At that point, Lorie signaled that they were about to say grace, so he brought his music to a nice smooth stop, and quietly moved from behind the piano and over to the kitchen.

Jack had an iced tea and just a half of a sandwich in the kitchen. He didn't feel like he was at his best singing after eating a lot. At the appointed time, he slipped back to the piano and waited for Lorie's introduction. After about five minutes, Lorie rose from her seat and moved over next to Jack asking for everyone's attention.

"Ladies and gentlemen, for those of you who were here with us to celebrate Independence Day, you will remember Jack Schmidt. He is a very talented young man with an endless repertoire of music. We were very fortunate to have him return this evening for our listening and dancing pleasure. Should any of you have a favorite tune or song, just ask Mr. Schmidt and he will do his best to accommodate your request." Then gesturing toward Jack, she said, "Take it away, Mr. Schmidt."

Jack thanked Mrs. Bradford and then started singing a few songs that were nice for dancing. There were quite a few requests, all of which he was familiar with and readily accommodated. Jack felt good and knew that he was putting on one of his best performances. He forgot all about the agent until the group started to break up and say their good-byes. At that point, Mrs. Bradford came back to the piano with a well-dressed gentleman that Jack guessed to be in his early forties.

"Jack, take a break for a while. I want you to meet Mr. Stanley Schuman. Mr. Schuman is the founder and president of the Star Talent Agency in New York City."

"It's a pleasure to meet you, Mr. Schuman. I've heard of your agency."

"I hope everything you heard was good, Jack. I must tell you that I was very impressed with your performance this evening. Mrs. Bradford has told me quite a bit about you and indicated that you might be in a position to now have an agency represent you."

"Yes, I am interested in working with an agency."

"Well, Jack, I won't take any more of your time this evening. What I would like you to do is come to my agency next Wednesday around nine in the morning and we will get started in bringing you into our fold. Wear a suit and tie. Also bring along your tuxedo, as we will be taking a lot of photos. We can work with or without a written contract. I prefer a written contract and I'll give you documentation on Wednesday to take home and review. I think Mrs. Bradford will vouch for me and tell you I am a fair and reasonable man who will always have your best interests in mind. Here is my business card. Please call me if you have any questions before Wednesday."

"Thank you, Mr. Schuman. I'll be at your agency Wednesday morning. And thank you, Mrs. Bradford, for taking an interest in my career."

With that, Lorie then walked along, chatting with Mr. Schuman as she escorted him to the front porch. When she returned, her eyes had a dazzling brilliance to them and she was smiling from ear to ear.

"I knew it, Jack. He definitely likes you and thinks he can make you into a star performer. I'm so excited. Let's change into our bathing suits and enjoy an evening swim. I'll meet you at the pool."

"Okay, I'll show you my appreciation at the pool."

When Jack arrived at the pool, Lorie was already swimming laps. *Now how did she get here so fast?* This time he looked closely and to his surprise found that she was wearing a bathing suit. He waited until she finished several laps and then dove into the pool. Lorie dove under the water and swam directly over to Jack. She burst out of the water right next to Jack, and reaching out, gave him a bear hug. Jack started to say something, but Lorie sealed his mouth momentarily with her hand and then gave him a very long and passionate kiss.

"Now, is that better?"

"Much better, Lorie, but I'm not sure if I can wait until we return to the house to make love to you."

"You devil, grab your robe and your towel and follow me. I know a nice secluded spot just a short distance from here." She led Jack down a footpath into a small cluster of evergreen trees. In the center of the cluster there was a small grass covered clearing. Lorie took his towel, and then placed both towels on the ground. Lying down, she motioned for Jack to do the same. She was instantly kissing him, and told him there was nothing a woman liked more than her man wanting to make love to her. In less than a minute, both bathing suits were on the ground and their two bodies blended together. They were in the tree clearing for almost two hours talking and laughing and then embracing again. Finally, Lorie told Jack that they must return to the house before daylight. He laughed as they gathered their things and donned their robes. Lorie whispered that she could not wait until he was in her bed for the evening.

On Sunday morning, James drove them to church and back to the manor home. They had breakfast served in the library where there was some degree of privacy. It was the beginning of another perfect day. The weather was just beautiful, so Lorie suggested that they go sightseeing. She would have the staff prepare a picnic lunch and told Jack she would do the driving. Lorie asked Jack where he would like to go, and to her surprise, his answer was to the West Point Academy. Jack went on to tell Lorie that he had a lot of respect for the officers whom he had contact with while in the army, and he just felt that it would be good to see the academy that produced such leaders. Lorie knew the way to the academy and because it was Sunday, she thought that visitors would be allowed on the grounds. The scenery along the Hudson River was breathtaking. As they drove along, Lorie questioned Jack again about his experience in the Great War. He didn't often talk about the war, but found it rather comforting that someone he was now very close to wanted to know more about his past. Jack told her about the conditions on the battlefield and the ever increasing number of casualties arriving at the Sainte-Menehould field hospital. When he talked about carrying stretchers with dead soldiers on them, Lorie gasped. Jack decided it would be better to tell Lorie about less gruesome things, such as finding the leather portfolio with family pictures and a letter. He described Francis Kelly who he befriended at the hospital and JJ, who literally saved his life by telling Jack what to do when his gas mask failed. Jack went on talking about the mementos that he had placed in a cigar box at home and his intentions of sometime in the future looking up these people and meeting with them to see how their postwar lives were. Lorie wanted to hear again about the French nurse and the night that Jack spent with her. Blushing, Jack described in great detail the music and singing in the church hall that evening. His description of his private time with Cecilia, however, was very limited. Lorie seemed to respect that and was satisfied.

At the academy, they were stopped at the gate by two soldiers and then given permission to proceed to the parade grounds. There were picnic tables near the parade grounds, so it turned out to be a perfect place to have lunch. Lorie was very interested in watching soldiers and their families move about the campus. She wanted to know if Jack had wished he could have attended the academy. Jack said that he didn't think that he would have made a very good military leader. He went on to talk about his father and the stories he told about the responsibilities of being a ship's captain. Jack kind of wrapped things up by telling Lorie that he was doing exactly what he had always dreamed of. Lorie smiled and squeezed his hand then gently kissed Jack on the cheek telling him how proud she was of him. They visited the chapel and then moved on to the artillery pieces facing the Hudson River. Next came a short drive through the town, and then they headed back to the estate. Lorie dominated the conversation talking about her plans for Bradford Industries and how she was going to make more money selling the parts for her equipment. She envisioned setting up factory training for her customers and expanding the roles of her sales reps to include the technical expertise to satisfy her customers' needs to absolutely minimize downtime on any of the Bradford Industries machinery. Jack found it hard to get her to stop talking business. They approached a sign indicating there was an overlook ahead off the side of the road. Jack suggested that they stop. The overlook was high above the Hudson with great views of the expansive landscape and the winding river. There was only one other vehicle parked at the overlook, so Jack and Lorie found time to embrace in each other's arms. Lorie playfully told Jack what she was going to do to him when they settled into her bedroom for the evening. Jack loved her playmaking, and just relaxed enjoying the moment with great anticipation for what was to come later. *This*, he thought, *is living*.

The alarm sounded at six on Monday morning. *Oh no*! Jack thought, *It can't be time to get up*. But yes, it was. Lorie was out of bed and getting ready to head to the factory.

"Come on, young man. Last night was fabulous, but today is a work day." Pulling on his arm, she said, "Time to move back to the guest room. You can sleep as long as you want. The staff will make breakfast for you and James knows to drive you home whenever you are ready. I loved our time together yesterday, and especially the last two nights. Now give me a kiss and scoot. And don't forget to let me know how things go on Wednesday."

Reluctantly, Jack returned to the guest room. He was amazed out how quickly Lorie switched from lover to business woman. He didn't want to spend more time at the estate, so he readied for breakfast and his ride home. As he entered the kitchen, Lorie was just leaving for the factory.

"Good-bye, Mrs. Bradford, and thanks for everything." Jack winked at Lorie.

"Good-bye, Jack, and I wish you luck on Wednesday." And she returned the wink.

The ride back home with James was routine. Jack decided to ride up front with James and they talked a lot about James's son. At times, Jack sensed that James knew that he and Lorie were lovers. It was kind of the way he phrased things like a father protecting his daughter. Jack simply let things pass and always agreed that Mrs. Bradford was a wonderful person. He made a mental note to make mention of this to Lorie.

At dinner on Monday evening, Jack briefed his mother about his audition and being scheduled to visit the Star Talent Agency on Wednesday. She was very proud of Jack, and commented about the maturity he had shown throughout this process of getting to an agent. His mother did, however, say that she would pick out the suit, shirt and tie for him to wear on Wednesday.

THE STAR TALENT AGENCY

Jack was up bright and early Wednesday. He wanted to look his very best, so he shaved nice and close, dressed in the outfit his mother had selected, buffed his shoes to a brilliant shine, and spent a little extra time combing his hair. His mother was pleased with his appearance, and after making a slight adjustment to his tie, she told Jack he looked just great. He carefully placed his tuxedo in a special traveling bag, gave his mother a kiss on the cheek and was off to the Star Talent Agency. Jack knew his way around the city and preferred using the public transit system. It took about forty-five minutes to get to the agency. Because he was early for his appointment, Jack decided to stop for a cup of coffee. He loved to watch the New Yorkers scurry back and forth to their jobs. He could see the entrance to the agency across the street. There was no one going in or out. Jack began to wonder, *Is this a really good agency*? Maybe it is too early in the day for most clients and customers, but how about the employees. Jack looked at his watch. It was eight forty-five. *Time to go*, he thought. Walking out of the coffee shop, Jack felt more nervous than when appearing before an audience. *Calm down*, he told himself. The audition is essentially over. This is just the next step in the process. He entered the agency and moved over to the receptionist. She was a very attractive, well-dressed, young lady.

"Good morning. Are you Mr. Schmidt?"

"Yes, I am and good morning."

"Mr. Schmidt, I have some paper work for you to complete." As the receptionist passed a clipboard with several papers attached, she continued, "There is a table and chair just off to your right. You may take these over there, and when you have completed them please return to me."

Looking at the form, Jack thought, these seem *pretty routine.* He started filling in the forms with name, address, phone number, person to contact in event of emergency. On the third sheet, it became more difficult to complete some of the questions. What is the name of your physician? I don't really have one. I better just leave this one blank. Do you have any relatives living in foreign countries? If so, please list their names, approximate ages and country. I can't answer this. Maybe Mom can help? Jack finished as much as he could and then returned to the receptionist.

"Ma'am, there are some questions here that I really can't answer, so I have just left them blank."

"That's fine, Mr. Schmidt. Should we require more information, someone will be in touch with you. Now if you will please follow me, I'll show you to Mr. Schuman's office." At the office door, the receptionist knocked. There was no answer, so she opened the door and escorted Jack in. "Take a seat, Mr. Schmidt. Mr. Schuman will be along shortly." She then turned and exited the room, leaving Jack there by himself.

About ten minutes passed before Mr. Schuman arrived.

"Good morning, Jack."

"Good morning, Mr. Schuman."

Jack stood and they shook hands. The agent asked Jack to come over and sit in the chair next to his desk. He told Jack to address him simply as Stan, and then asked Jack to think of him as a father because he was going to ask Jack to do some things that might seem strange, but were really necessary if they were going to successfully launch Jack's career.

"Now, Jack, I've given a lot of thought as to how we should best proceed to make you a star. You have the talent, young man, which is the primary ingredient. What we need to work on is your image. Are you with me?"

"I think so, sir."

"Okay, first, I want you to change your last name to Smith. Schmidt immediately labels you as a German, and there is considerable anti-German sentiment in our country. We will prepare all of the necessary documents. All you will have to do is finalize the name change at the municipal building. Can you do that?"

"I guess so. My mother may not be happy though."

"Good. I also want to dress up your name a little. It's like giving you a stage name. We know you were gassed in the war and the gassing had some effect on your voice. So my people came up with the name of 'Whispering' Jack Smith. How does that sound to you?"

"That sounds pretty neat."

"Jack, you are still living at home with your mother. I admire you for wanting to stay close to her, but in this business, it is important that you have your own apartment, preferably in Manhattan. This doesn't mean you can't spend time with your mother. It's more of a front, but you will have to frequent the Manhattan apartment. I have a sponsor that will set up the apartment for you. It will be completely decorated and furnished in good taste. There will also be a piano in the apartment. Management of the apartment building will provide a cleaning service for you at no additional cost. You will be responsible to pay a very modest rent, which our agency will handle for you simply by deducting the amount of rent from your earnings. Can we do that?"

"It sounds too good to be true."

"Now the third area that we have to work on is exposure. I can book you at a lot of weddings and private parties, which are good for producing income, especially because you are a one-man show and don't have to split your fee with anyone. However, such events don't really gain the kind of exposure we are looking for. So I want to also book you with a small band where you will be given one or two solo vocals during a performance. The money won't be as good, but the exposure can be invaluable. There is also a brand-new medium coming whereby music will be sent into American homes by radio. I've been privileged to see some demonstrations of this new medium, and I am convinced that if we can get you on radio at some point in the future, your career will soar. How does everything sound to you so far?

"It all sounds good to me, sir."

"Stan, just call me Stan. Now let's talk money. This agency works for you at a flat rate of 15 percent. In other words, if you have an engagement that pays one hundred dollars, the agency collects the fee. We give you eighty-five and we keep fifteen. If we book you out of town, our agency will make and pay for all of your travel and lodging arrangements. These expenses are then simply deducted from your pay. If you prefer to make your own travel and lodging arrangements, that too is fine. We also will establish a fund for you whereby we automatically invest 5 or 10 percent of your earnings for you. You can tell us how to invest the money or we can give you recommendations to follow. In most cases, you can withdraw this money whenever you so choose. Do you have any questions on the money end of this business?"

"No, I follow you for the most part, Stan. It will take a little time for me to fully digest everything."

"Okay, so here is where we are. You've got the talent, but you have to keep working on it. We are going to change your name and set you up in a Manhattan apartment, thereby enhancing your career image. Our people will start immediately to book you in a combination of performances that will maximize both your income and your exposure. In a short time, you should see a dramatic increase in your income, and if you so choose we can further increase your earnings with some smart investments. When you leave today, Janet the receptionist will have a packet of material for you take home. Look through it. Talk it over with your family and friends. If you choose to sign the contract, fine. If not, I am willing to work with you for a period of time on a handshake. Now I'm going to walk you down the hall to meet Ted. Ted is going to take a lot of pictures of you and set up a portfolio that we can present to potential customers."

The agency did not finish with Jack until after six o'clock. He found a public telephone, and called home to tell his mother he was running late and for her to not wait dinner for him. Jack then thought about calling Lorie, but decided that she may not be home from the factory yet. He would need more change anyway to call long distance, so he decided to get a bite to eat in a nearby café where he could most likely also get some more change. Upon entering the café, Jack heard someone calling his name. It was Arthur Kennedy from the Irving Berlin Music Publishing Company.

"Come over and join me, Jack. What have you been up to?"

Jack was glad to see Art and sat down at the table with him. "Well, Art, I have actually been doing pretty well. I did a couple of private parties and made more money than I would have in a month at O'Malley's. How is the corned beef sandwich here?"

"It's great. Order the corned beef special. They top it with coleslaw and put a special Russian dressing on it."

Jack ordered and then filled Art in about signing on with the Star Talent Agency. Art knew Stanley Schuman and highly recommended Mr. Schuman and the agency, stating they were the best in the business. As the conversation drifted, Jack asked if Art knew much about radio broadcasting.

"It's brand-new, Jack. I've seen demonstrations of the technology. It's going to be great, but first a network of broadcasting stations has to be developed, and considerable marketing effort will be necessary to get the population to buy and place radios in their homes. We are about a year or two away, but once it starts, it is going to do incredible things for our music business. If you have any extra cash, I recommend investing in some American Telephone and Telegraph stock."

"Thanks for the tip, Art. I'll keep it in mind."

"I have to run, Jack. It was great talking to you."

Taking both checks, Jack says, "This one is on me in appreciation of all you have done for me. So long, Art."

With a pocket full of change, Jack headed for the phone booth at the back of the café. He got through to the Bradford Manor House and after identifying himself, only had a brief wait until Lorie was on the phone. Jack started to tell Lorie about his day at the Star Talent Agency and also about his chance meeting with Arthur Kennedy, when the phone operator interrupted stating that he would have to deposit more coins to continue his call. Lorie quickly asked if there was a number on the public phone. Jack read the number to her and she said to hang up and she would call his phone. When the phone rang, Jack continued with the description of his day.

"Tell me again about the Manhattan apartment. That sounds so exciting. Will I be allowed to visit?"

"Of course you will be allowed to visit. I'll be able to play and sing privately for you and call you Lorie or Love without worrying about who might be listening."

"Oh, Jack, I am so excited for you."

"Lorie, when do you think we can see each other again?"

"Soon, I hope. What do you think your mother would say about meeting me? I mean as a business sponsor, not a lover. If you like, I can drive to your house and either have dinner at home with your mother or we can drive to a restaurant. I'm sure we can work in some private time after that."

"Now, that sounds like a good plan. Let me pass it by my mother."

"Okay, lover, and try to plan my visit for a Saturday or Sunday."

"Good-bye, Lorie. I miss you."

CHICAGO

The agency wasted little time in scheduling Jack for a variety of performances. He did a wedding reception three days after his visit to Star. Someone had cancelled and Stan had just happened to have a new talent available to fill in. There was a short stint for an office birthday party on the following Tuesday. On Wednesday, Stan called and asked if Jack could travel to Chicago for a Friday, Saturday, and Sunday performance at one of the classy downtown hotels. Stan said Janet would start on the travel arrangements immediately. Jack said okay, but asked that Janet hold up on his return trip, as he may want to come by way of Peoria, Illinois. Later, Jack called Janet and asked if she would look at a return trip for him on Monday with an overnight stay in Peoria, Illinois. Jack simply said he wanted to look up an old army friend. After getting off the phone, Jack went to his bedroom and retrieved the cigar box containing his memorabilia. He removed the leather portfolio, reread the letter, looked at the photos and then placed everything on his bed to be packed for his trip. Jack called Janet again and asked if he was scheduled for anything on the Sunday following his return from Chicago. The answer was no, so he asked her to keep that date open for him.

At dinner that evening, Jack told his mother about the pending engagement in Chicago and then went on to talk a little about Mrs. Bradford, who he described as his sponsor. He mentioned inviting her to their home, maybe for dinner. Jack's mother was quite receptive to the idea and did not want to hear of going to a restaurant. She would prepare a fine meal for them. Jack mentioned that because Mrs. Bradford had already met Milt maybe they could also invite Milt and his girlfriend to come.

"What a splendid idea, Jack. I have been hearing little bits and pieces about Milt's girlfriend. It would be an opportune time to meet her. You let me know if Mrs. Bradford can make it and then I will set up Milt's coming. I'll work through Catherine. That way Milt will not have a chance to say no."

"Thanks, Mom. I'll call Mrs. Bradford tonight."

The next day, Jack was on the train to Chicago. *Wow*, he thought, *things happen fast when you're with an agency*. Jack had brought along the Star contract to study on the train. After an hour of reading, he kind of surrendered and realized that some of the language was very difficult to interpret. He thought, *I have two recommendations from very reputable and trustworthy people telling me that Stan is the best in the business and assuring me that he would never do anything to harm me. Stan already has me booked making more money than I ever have and even traveling*. With that, Jack closed the contract and put it away, deciding he would sign and return the document to Star upon his return to New York. The train ride reminded him of his ride to Fort Oglethorpe in Georgia. He dozed off and pictured the people he had met while in the army. He could even picture the two German prisoners that he had helped interrogate. What happened to them? Where are they now? Did JJ get the duty assignment he wanted? Was the runner, Kelly, back working in the mill? And beautiful Cecelia, did she make it through the war okay? Where is she and what is she doing? Then he visualized the pictures in the leather portfolio that he had picked up in the trench. I wonder if the soldier who carried that portfolio made it home from the war. If so, maybe I'll get to meet him in Peoria.

"Chicago, Chicago, we'll have a one hour layover here." The conductor's voice woke Jack.

Okay, let me look at the directions that Janet gave me. Looks simple, take a cab from the station to the Alexandria Hotel. Upon arrival at the hotel, identify yourself at the check in desk as "Whispering" Jack Smith, their weekend entertainer. Should there be any questions, have them contact Star. What a pleasure having someone like Janet take care of all of the details.

Check in at the hotel went very smoothly. He was shown to a nice room and told that one of the managers would be in touch within the hour to go over the program planning. Basically, it amounted to playing and singing in the ballroom. Jack asked if anyone was performing that Thursday evening and was told no. He then asked if it would be all right for him to play some tunes and sing some songs this Thursday evening. The manager said he thought it would be okay, but to first let him check and make sure there wasn't a group meeting that might warrant a quiet atmosphere. The manager called a little later and gave Jack the go ahead, but also reaffirmed that there could be no charge for his Thursday performance.

When Jack arrived at the ballroom, there were only a few people present. Jack was dressed casually, and as he moved to the piano, those present simply thought it was a hotel guest who wanted to play a little piano. After about ten minutes, there were couples dancing. After thirty, the floor was getting crowded. Eventually, someone had a request that Jack acknowledged and played. To Jack, it felt pretty much like his time at O'Malley's except on a much larger scale. Soon one of the hotel employees brought out a microphone and placed it close to Jack. It was fun to sing with the microphone, and Jack could see that the crowded ballroom guests were enjoying his performance. He played and sang for more than two hours before announcing a break. He asked if they would like him to return and was rewarded with a long round of applause. *This*, Jack thought, *is fun*.

The weekend at the Alexandria was very enjoyable. His performances were pretty much like his impromptu Thursday night performance. He did a little sightseeing and shopping in his free time. Jack wanted presents to bring back for his mother and for Lorie. What do you buy for a woman who has everything? He settled on two very nice handmade clutch purses. The saleslady told Jack that these were very popular with the ladies and even gift wrapped each at no additional charge.

On Monday morning, Jack was back on the train. He arrived at the Peoria Station just before noon. The station master showed Jack where to store his baggage until he returned for his train to New York on Tuesday. Again Jack read Janet's instructions. To his surprise, the instructions directed him to the local post office and said to ask about transportation to the address written on the envelope Jack had found back in France. Well, Janet has been right up to now, so why doubt her? The post office was within walking distance. At the post office, Jack displayed the address on the envelope and asked how he might get transportation there. To his surprise, the postal clerk said the mail delivery truck would be heading out on that rural route at one o'clock and Jack was welcome to ride along with the mailman. Now how did Janet find that out? Jack thanked the clerk and said he was going for a bite to eat at the restaurant across the street and would return before one o'clock.

The mailman was also a veteran of the Great War having served in the battles of Northern France. There were frequent stops along the way to both deliver and pick up mail. At one of the stops, the mailman asked if he could look at the contents of Jack's envelope. He thought from Jack's conversation he might know something about the family Jack was about to meet.

"Yes, sir, just as I thought. This has to be Glenn Raney's family. His sister Sadie used to live here until about a year ago. Glenn lost an arm over in France. I think he was in the fight down where you were. He has an artificial arm now and does right good with it running his farm. I think it's the right arm."

"Well, I'm sorry he lost his arm, but relieved to know that he made it through the war."

"Here we are. Do you want me to wait a minute for you?"

"Do you come back past this way on your return to town?"

"Sure, I can do that. It'll be about an hour and a half from now."

"Okay, thanks very much. If I'm hung up for a ride back to town, I'll be out here waiting for you. If you don't see me, just keep on going."

GLENN RANEY

Jack walked along a long dirt driveway to a farmhouse with several outbuildings, including a fairly large barn. The house seemed to be well-kept, but the barn and other outbuildings were in various states of disrepair. Jack knocked at the door and a rather attractive, wholesome-looking woman of about thirty years answered.

"Hello, ma'am. My name is Jack Smith. I'm a veteran of the war in France, and I think I have some things that belong to Glenn Raney."

"Please come in. My name is Dixie. I'm Glenn's wife. Glenn is out in the fields now, but should be back soon. Can I get you something to drink?"

"Yes, ma'am, a glass of water will be great. The ride out here with the mailman was kind of dusty. Oh, here is your mail. I thought I would walk it up for you."

"Come and sit in the kitchen, please. Did you know Glenn in the war?"

Jack went on to say he really didn't know Glenn, and further explained how he had come upon the leather portfolio at the bottom of a trench in France. He told Dixie that his work took him to Chicago last week, so it seemed like a good time to visit Peoria and try to find out what happened to the soldier who lost the portfolio. Jack went over what the mailman had told him and expressed his relief to find that Glenn had made it through the war. Dixie was very excited. She said Glenn would be so happy to see someone who had been over there in France when he was. She wanted to know if Jack could stay for dinner. Jack explained about the mailman offering a ride back to town.

"Nonsense. We will get you back to town. When do you have to be there?"

"My train leaves at ten in the morning."

"Well then, Jack Smith, you will have dinner with us and be our overnight guest. We will get you to the train station well before ten tomorrow morning."

"Thank you, ma'am. I will sure welcome some home cooking after all that hotel food in Chicago. While we are waiting for your husband, maybe you can look at this letter and tell me a little about your family."

Dixie looked at the pictures and then read the letter, telling Jack that the letter was from Glenn's sister, Sadie. The pictures are of Sadie's two children, Fred and Sally. My husband's first name is Joseph, but everyone knows him as Glenn. Sadie is about the only one who calls him by Joseph. Sadie lost her husband a few years back, so she and her children lived with us for a while. They live just a few miles down the road now.

"Well that makes sense. I kind of thought it was from a soldier's mother and the pictures were of brother and sister."

At that point, Dixie heard the back screen door and told Jack that was probably Glenn. She excused herself and returned in a minute excitedly introducing Jack to her husband. Glenn shook hands with his left, so the mailman was correct when saying Glenn had lost his right arm. Glenn was a tall, strong-looking, well-tanned man. They sat at the kitchen table while Glenn downed a few glasses of water and talked about their tours in France. Dixie had to leave to meet their children at the school bus stop. Jack met the children when they arrived back home, and then he and Glenn moved to the front porch to sit in the rocking chairs while Dixie busied herself preparing dinner. It seemed like Glenn was wounded a few days before Jack arrived in France. His arm was amputated at the hospital in Sainte-Menehould. Jack talked about Company C's attack using tanks for cover and how the Germans put mustard gas on the battlefield. He described how his gas mask began to leak and he also ended up at Sainte-Menehould. It was amazing how much common experience they shared. They both returned to the States on the same troopship and both were out processed at Fort Dix. Before long, Dixie was calling them to come to the dinner table.

"Dixie, you won't believe how Jack and me were pretty much in the same places over in France and even returned home on the same troopship."

After a little general conversation, Dixie asked, "What kind of work were you doing in Chicago?"

"Well, Dixie, I play the piano and sing. My agency had me booked at a hotel to entertain the guests in the hotel ballroom."

Hearing this, Glenn stood up and said, "Now I know who you are. You used to play music for us at the hospital every evening for about an hour. We all sang a lot of those Irish songs. It was great. We all looked forward to the evening songs. Jack, I am so glad you came by today. I want to thank you for those evenings. It was a time when all of us took our minds off our personal problems and actually enjoyed ourselves. Too bad we don't have a piano. Dixie, you and the kids would have been in for a real treat."

"I'm glad you enjoyed the songs. It was fun to do it."

Eventually, Dixie put the children to bed. Jack and Glenn returned to the porch rockers and talked into the early morning hours. It was good to reminisce. At breakfast the next day, Jack asked if it would be okay to keep just the envelope that he had found in France. Dixie told him he certainly could and went to retrieve it.

"Thanks, Dixie. I just want something to keep with my memorabilia from France. I will make some notations to go inside of the envelope on my train ride back to New York."

MRS. BRADFORD MEETS THE FAMILY

The train ride back to New York City was uneventful. Jack had a sheet of stationery from the Alexandria Hotel that he had taken as a souvenir. He turned it over and made notations about Glenn Raney and his family before folding the sheet and placing it into the envelope from France. *There*, he thought, *I'll return this one to the cigar box with closure.* He only had several hours of sleep at the farmhouse, so it was easy to doze off on the train. Again, he dreamed about France and the people he had known there, but this time Lorie took the place of the French nurse. Jack was awake shortly before the train arrived at Central Station. As he looked out the window, Jack thought, *It is nice to be back in the city. Farming is not for me.*

Dinner was late with his mother. Jack filled his mother in about his time in Chicago and Peoria. His mother told Jack that going to see Mr. Raney was a wonderful thing to do. She then went over all of the details for the coming Sunday dinner with Mrs. Bradford, Milt, and his girlfriend.

"Milt's girlfriend's name is Jean. Catherine says she is very pretty and very smart. She studied at a business school and now has a good office job. She has been a big help to Milt while studying for his apprenticeship."

"Mom, do you know if Mrs. Bradford is going to be chauffeured to our house?"

"Her secretary said she will be driving herself and wanted to know if there was parking in front of our house."

"Thanks for doing this for me, Mom. Mrs. Bradford has really done so much to jump start my career, it only seemed proper to honor her request to meet some of my family."

"Well don't be surprised if Catherine and your brother show up on Sunday when it's time for dessert. Catherine's curiosity is getting the best of her."

Milt and his girlfriend, Jean, arrived first on Sunday. As Catherine had said, she was a very attractive young lady. Jack told them about the Star Talent Agency, his trip to Chicago and then Peoria, and that Mrs. Bradford was also to join them for dinner. Milt reflected on his time at the country club and the Bradford Estate. Jack asked Jean about her family, but before she could give much of an answer, there was the sound of a motor vehicle parking in front of the house.

"Excuse me," Jack said. "This is probably Mrs. Bradford. I'll be right back."

Jack returned in a few minutes and introduced Mrs. Bradford. He then went to the kitchen to tell his mother Mrs. Bradford had arrived. She immediately followed with Jack to the parlor.

"Mom, this is Mrs. Bradford, the lady I have been telling you about who has been helping with my career."

"It is so nice to meet you, Mrs. Schmidt. You have such a lovely home. Sometimes I wish I lived closer to the city like this."

"Thank you, Mrs. Bradford. Now please excuse me. I must return to the kitchen or we will have a burned dinner. When it's time to bring the food out, I'll call. Milt and Jean can give me a hand bringing everything from the kitchen."

Jack's mother had her finest china and silverware set on the table over a fine linen tablecloth that her husband had purchased in a foreign country. She called from the kitchen for Milt and Jean. While they were gone, Jack—speaking very softly—told Lorie how beautiful she looked. The aroma of the food arrived just before the food. The main course was a center cut roast of beef with mashed potatoes and gravy along with an assortment of various vegetables. There was also a bowl of salad and a basket of fresh-baked biscuits. Jack had the honors of cutting the roast. Everything was so delicious that conversation was held to a minimum as everyone ate.

"Milt, I must tell you that the information you brought to me has been most helpful. We have met with several people from Chilton Publishing and are well on our way to having manuals for most of the machinery manufactured by Bradford Industries. I want to again thank you for getting us started."

"It was my pleasure, Mrs. Bradford. I kind of thought you were making progress because some of the company executives have stopped by to talk to me and personally thank me for my involvement."

"So, Milt, did they give you a raise yet?" Jack asked.

"I don't think they can with our union rules. However, I have been assured that I will have a position in the Compositing Section as soon as I finish my apprenticeship."

"I have been told that a lot of the credit goes to Jean for the hours she has devoted to homeschooling you," Jack said.

"Jean has been a big help, Jack, and I am deeply indebted to her. Thank you, Jean."

"Now, Jean, just before Mrs. Bradford arrived, you started to tell us about your family."

"Well, I think you already know that Milt and my brother both started working as messengers for Dunn and Bradstreet at about the same time."

Once again Jean is interrupted with knocking at the door. Jack excused himself to answer the door and immediately returned with Catherine and his brother Charles in tow. Catherine had baked a chocolate cake, and of course, had perfectly timed delivery. Jack made the introductions as Catherine and Charles joined them at the table. They talked for more than an hour, during which time Lorie was quite surprised to learn Catherine's brother was the famous George

Goethals and that Charles was so deeply involved in the planning of a new Madison Square Garden. Jack's mother talked about the days when her husband was the captain of a German sailing ship and about some of the sailings on which she had accompanied her husband. Lorie was indeed very impressed with Jack's family. Jack finally inserted into the conversation that he had promised to show Mrs. Bradford where the Star Talent Agency was and to drive past a few of the places where he had recently performed. He wanted to go before the daylight was gone. Mrs. Bradford thanked Jack's mother for the delicious meal and a wonderful visit as she and Jack said their good-byes and left.

"Do you want to drive, Jack?"

"I wish I knew how. Maybe someday I'll learn."

"You know, Lorie, I tried to learn a little about Jean. But each time she started to tell us something, we were interrupted."

"Well she certainly is a pretty young lady with perfect manners. I think she is well-suited for your nephew. Incidentally, I have already seen the agency. So young man, I am taking you straight to a small hotel just on the outskirts of the city."

"Can you drive a little faster?"

THE APARTMENT

The Star Agency kept Jack busy throughout the remainder of the year and into 1921 Jack had pretty much mastered the use of the microphone, and requested that one be provided whenever possible where he performed. The money he made was very good. In addition to investing in American Telephone and Telegraph stock, Jack took Mr. Schuman's advice and invested equal amounts in a soda company called Coca Cola. Early in the year, Mr. Schuman asked Jack to stop at the agency and plan to spend about half a day with him. Stan was excited when Jack arrived. He spent a short time going over the details of their contract and showing Jack how his money was being accounted for. He told Jack he was impressed with the progress Jack was making. Stan said they were sometimes getting specific requests for "Whispering" Jack Smith, which attested to the fact that he was becoming a known talent. Then Stan deflated Jack's balloon a little by stating they still had a long way to go. He stressed the need to expand beyond New York City. And finally, he told Jack that his local image had grown to the point that it was time for him to move out of his mother's house and into the Manhattan Apartment they had previously discussed.

"In fact, Jack, the apartment is ready. I want you to take a ride out to Manhattan with me this afternoon for a visit. We know you don't drive, so we placed you in a location where you will have ready access to a parking space for visitors. Should you start to drive, a private space will be assigned to you. You also have easy access to the transit system. Are you ready to go?"

"You bet I am, Stan."

Along the way, Stan informed Jack about the protocols for dealing with the doormen, the elevator operators, and the clerk at the reception desk. He went on to inform Jack that the apartment had all new furniture and drapes, fresh paint, and that a piano had been located and should also be in place. When they arrived, the doorman gave Stan directions to park. It seemed to Jack like the doorman knew Stan. Maybe the Star Agency has other clients placed here in the same apartment building. They signed in at the reception desk and Stan received a key. There were several elevators. One had the door open with the operator standing by ushering Stan and Jack into the elevator.

"Floor please."

"Eleven."

At the eleventh floor, the elevator came to a very smooth stop. Stan and Jack thanked the elevator operator and exited. Stan led the way indicating that he must have been here before.

"I must say, Stan, the employees here look sharp in their uniforms and they acted very professionally."

"This is a class act. We have three other clients currently staying here. One of these days maybe we can get all of you together to meet. Here we are at eleven zero seven. That's kind of easy to remember."

Stan unlocked the door and they both entered.

"Wow! This is nice." Jack immediately moved to the upright piano in the parlor. "It's a 1914 Steinway 'K' piano."

"I was told it is a very good piano. We were fortunate in that someone was moving out of the building, so we only had to have the piano moved a short distance. Piano movers want an arm and a leg for their services. Come over here and check this out, Jack." Stan moved over to a brand-new RCA Aeriola Radio with a horn speaker. "This is what I was telling you about. There are not many stations broadcasting yet, but that's going to change in the very near future."

Jack tried the radio and then moved on to the kitchenette. Opening some of the cabinet doors, he found it to be well-equipped with dishes, pots and pans, and even food staples like coffee and sugar. On the opposite side of the parlor there was a small hallway leading to two bedrooms and a full bathroom. He found great views of the city from most of the windows.

"Who set this place up so beautifully?"

"One of the rules at Star, Jack, is that we never reveal the identity of a sponsor."

"Well at least pass my wholehearted thanks along."

"I can do that for you, Jack. Will you need any assistance in moving your things?"

"No, I have two strong nephews and my brother has a big Buick. So we should be able to handle it okay. This place is so well-furnished that all I really need to bring is my wardrobe and some toiletries."

"Well take your time and look around. I'll be in the parlor when you're ready to leave."

Jack knew he would have to tell his mother he was moving to an apartment. It was going to be painful. The only extended absence from his mother's house had been his time in the army. It was good that his brother's family lived close by. When he returned home late in the afternoon, he surveyed his wardrobe, trying to visualize which items to move and which to leave behind. After all, he was not going to become a stranger to his mother and he would still stay overnight here on occasion.

At dinner that evening, Jack talked to his mother in detail about how things had changed since signing on with the Star Agency. He mentioned how some of his pay was now automatically being invested in two highly recommended stocks. He said changing his name from Schmidt to Smith was not something he wanted to do, but working with an agent is something like working with a lawyer. You are paying for his expertise and should therefore follow his advice. He stressed that his career seemed to be on the right track, and related that the agency was sometimes getting requests for him to perform. Next, he worked in Stan's talk about developing an image that agency customers can readily identify with and accept. Jack then dropped the bomb about the apartment in Manhattan that had been set up for him. He mentioned his visit there earlier in the day, and the fact that there was a 1914 Steinway "K" Upright Piano in the apartment parlor. To Jack's surprise, his mother seemed to be one step ahead of him.

"Jack, Manhattan is not that far away. I knew you would eventually be moving out of this house. But you will be close by and I will still see a lot of you. You know some of my friends have sons and daughters who have moved as far away as California. That is very hard. They almost never see their own children again. So I thank God for having you and Charles close by. You will have so much more opportunity to practice with your very own piano. I am very proud of how you have handled yourself these past few years. You are truly mature now and no longer need your mother telling you what to do. I'll always be here for you, son. So, just promise me that you will not become a stranger to this house and let's move on with our lives."

"Thanks, Mom." Moving around the table, he gave her a big hug. "You always know exactly the right things to say to me. And you know I'm addicted to your cooking. So, I guarantee that you'll continue to see a lot of me. I'm going to ask Charles and maybe one of the boys to help move some of my wardrobe this weekend. Maybe you can come along to see the apartment."

"I would love that, Jack."

On Saturday morning, Charles and Milt arrived in the Buick. Jack went out and waved for them to come in. His mother had coffee waiting to be served along with some fresh baked biscuits.

"What's the name of this apartment high rise?" Jack's brother asked.

"It's the Chelsea Arms."

"I know exactly where it is. That's a pretty classy place and in a great location. How did you find it?"

Jack told his brother and Milt more about his involvement with the Star Talent Agency and how the agency really set the apartment up for him. When Jack told them how much his monthly rent would be, they were amazed at how low it was. Jack said it was all rather complicated between being involved with both the agency and an unknown sponsor and that he didn't really understand how everything worked.

"Well, you've got a great deal, Jack. Now what do we need to carry over?"

Jack led his brother and Milt to his room where he had everything packed and ready to go. In no time at all, everything was moved to the Buick. The interior of the Buick was very spacious, so there was plenty of room for all to be comfortably seated. As Charles started the engine, Jack commented about the marvel of the electric starter.

"No more broken thumbs for me. The broken thumb darn near cost me my job at the garden."

It was a short and pleasant ride to the Chelsea Arms Building where the doorman escorted Mrs. Schmidt to a seat in the lobby while the others began to offload the Buick.

"They are fine-looking men, ma'am. Are they all from your family?"

"Yes, two are my sons and one is a grandson."

"Well, have a nice day, ma'am, and if there is anything that I can do to further assist you, please don't hesitate to let me know."

Jack checked in at the desk. He listed the names of his guests and then signed the register. Jack was surprised when the clerk immediately passed him a key for 1107. *How did the clerk know my apartment number without me telling him?* The clerk then hit a buzzer twice and in less than a minute, one of the elevator operators appeared.

"Please take the luggage cart to 1107. When the rest of the guests arrive, I will send them up." Then he turned to address Jack. "Sir, when the rest of your party arrives, just go to the elevators and one of the operators will see you to your apartment. Should you need anything, simply dial the desk."

Jack went over and sat next to his mother while they waited for Charles and Milt.

"I have not seen such professional and courteous service since I last sailed with your father."

"It's going to take me a while to get used to it, Mom. Maybe that's part of the reason for the agency wanting me here?"

When the elevator arrived at the eleventh floor, Jack told the operator he knew the way to the apartment and there was no need for him to leave the elevator. They quickly moved Jack's articles into the apartment, and while Jack started to organize his clothes in the dressers and closets, the others explored the niceties of the apartment. Jack's mother tried the piano, playing a few soft tunes.

"Very nice, Jack. I think one or two of the keys might be off slightly. Give it a little use and then decide if it needs tuning."

Milt wanted to know if he could come and stay overnight sometime. Jack told him as soon as his membership in York Country Club went through, he could come and stay so they could get an early start on the golf course.

"Jack, are you really going to be a member?"

"Yes, it's another one of the perks the agency is working on."

"Wow! I can't wait."

Charles had a great interest in the radio with the horn speaker. Jack showed him how to turn it on and tune stations. Jack told Charles that the horn speaker was an option that allowed everyone in the room to enjoy the radio. He explained that there were not many stations available yet and some had a considerable amount of static, but two of his contacts in the music business had seen demonstrations of what is to come and claim that radio broadcasting will soon reach almost every household. Charles wanted to know how much a radio cost. Jack didn't know, but said he would try to find out. Jack said he would finish organizing his things later, and suggested that they all go to lunch at a restaurant.

"It will be my treat."

"Sounds great to me," Charles said. "There's a new place over near the garden that has great food and a unique backdrop behind the serving bar."

THE AQUA DELIGHT

The Aqua Delight was a restaurant in the daytime and a speakeasy at night. It was within easy walking distance from Madison Square Garden. Charles said he had been there for lunch and several times after work for working meetings. Charles parked the Buick behind the building, and they all entered from a back door leading to a long inside corridor that ended at the coat room and the maitre d' station. The maitre d' recognized Charles, and immediately made a big fuss about meeting his family and seating them at one of the best tables. Once they were seated, Charles directed their attention to the large plate of glass behind the serving bar. He said that in a little while, the tank behind the glass would be illuminated and they would be able to see fish and sometimes even mermaids swimming across in front of them.

"Mermaids. You're kidding, right, Dad?"

"Well, it is a little early. But you can bet they will be in the tank for the evening crowd."

"What will they think of next," Mrs. Schmidt commented.

The menu was extensive, at least ten pages long. Mrs. Schmidt took great pleasure in looking through the selections. Jack thought to himself he should make an effort to take his mother out for dining more often. Jack and Milt had quickly settled on sandwiches. Charles and Mrs. Schmidt were selecting from the platters. When the waitress appeared, they ordered four ginger ales. Jack knew his brother would prefer a beer, but probably did not want to upset their mother.

It was good to be together. They reminisced about old times and told stories about their father, the old sea captain. Milt was delighted to hear about his grandfather and the adventures that his grandmother had shared with her husband sailing around the world. Jack inserted that if he got the chance, he would like to return to Europe. He said it was beautiful in France, and he would just love to be there in peacetime.

Charles was right. The food was certainly delicious. Just as they were finishing, the fish tank was illuminated. Milt was amazed and moved over close to the serving bar for a better look. There weren't any mermaids, but there was a multitude of multicolored fish swimming about.

Returning to the table, Milt said, "That is truly unbelievable. I never knew there were fish tanks that big."

"Would anyone care for coffee or dessert?"

"Do you have chocolate cake?" Milt asked.

"Yes we do. Fresh baked this morning."

Mrs. Schmidt ordered coffee and Milt ordered cake. Jack and Charles passed.

When it looked like his mother was done with her coffee, Charles suggested that they walk over to the garden. He would show them his new office and some of the alterations that were recently completed within the building. Everyone thought it would be a nice thing to do. Jack settled the check, and Charles asked the maitre d' if it would be all right to keep his car parked at the back lot while they took a short tour of the garden.

"Certainly, Mr. Schmidt, and please walk back through the restaurant on your return. Your son may just see a mermaid."

It took less than five minutes to get to the garden. Charles approached the security guard at the entrance, and after showing some identification, he waved for everyone to follow him. They had all been inside the garden at one time or another in the past, but it was still surprising to see the inside of a building open all of the way around and capable of holding eight thousand people. Charles ushered them through an inside door to a staff only elevator and then up to the level where his office was located. The office was only a short distance from the executive offices.

"This is quite nice, Charles," his mother told him.

Milt wanted to know what all of the drawings posted on the wall were. Charles told them these were artist renditions of what the new garden would look like. Remember I told you it will be large enough to hold eighteen thousand spectators for our boxing matches.

"That's more than twice the size of this building. What do you think, Mom?"

"I am always impressed with the construction of these big and modern buildings. You are very fortunate to a part of such an endeavor."

"Now, let's go down into the spectator side of the building and I will show you some of the work I have been involved with."

Charles took them back down the elevator and into the box seat area.

"These are the most expensive seats. They are five to ten times the cost of a general admission ticket. What we are going to do is expand this box seating area and build in a box seating section on the side opposite from us. Now look up at all of the overhead structural beams. That's what my painters are working on now. As you might imagine, it is very difficult to position the painters so high up and to keep them supplied with paint. We are about half done at this point. Once construction on the new garden commences, we will simply maintain things here, which will basically be touch up painting. I will probably have to lay off half of the crew."

They walked all of the way around the interior of the building as Charles continued to point out different things and then exited on the side closest to the Aqua Delight. Charles led everyone back into the restaurant as the maitre d' had suggested, and sure enough, there were two mermaids swimming across the fish tank from opposite directions. They were very pretty women with specially fitted suits that enclosed the lower part of their bodies into fish-like tails. Milt was happy that he had gotten to see the mermaids. Mrs. Schmidt was not impressed. Jack thought it was a good theatrical trick to bring in new customers, especially being located so close to the garden. They watched for a minute or two and then headed through the building toward the parking lot. As they passed the maitre d', Charles thanked him.

RADIO STATION WJZ

Lorie was anxious to see Jack's new apartment, but there always seemed to be a conflict between their schedules. Finally, they both had a weekend free, so Jack made arrangements for her parking at the apartment and he had a variety of groceries delivered. Jack thought it will be so nice this one time to not have to be someplace. He planned to play and sing songs for Lorie. He was anxious to show her the radio, and most of all, Jack wanted to display his recently acquired culinary skills. His alternative plan was to take her to dinner at the York Country Club where he now had an official membership. Lorie was to arrive sometime Friday evening, and had promised to call as soon as she could break away from the factory. The phone rang around five fifteen in the afternoon.

"Hello, Jack, love, I'm about to leave the office now. I packed an overnight bag. Is it all right if I get cleaned up and changed at your apartment?"

"Certainly, Lorie, I'll even help scrub your back."

"I can't wait to see you, Jack."

"I've missed you too, love. Don't stop to eat anything. I am preparing a special candlelight dinner for you. What time do you think you will get here?"

"I think it will be between six and six thirty."

"Okay, I'll be in the lobby. Just pull up by the doorman. I'll get our parking instructions and meet you out front. One other thing, what name do you want me to use when I list you on the guest register?"

"My maiden name is Rogers. So, let's use Rogers."

"Okay, see you soon."

Upon entering the apartment, Lorie told Jack everything looked just perfect. She was very impressed.

"I'm so proud of you, Jack." They shared a long embrace and passionate kiss until Lorie pushed Jack back saying, "Okay, I'm going for a quick bath and a change of clothes. You work on dinner. I'm really starving."

Jack had a small roast of pork and some whole potatoes cooking in the oven. He had some biscuits ready for the oven and a pot of carrots simmering on top of the stove. Jack also had a bottle of wine for Lorie. He still followed his father's advice and abstained from drinking any alcohol. The table was nicely set with a small bouquet of flowers in the center and candle sticks off to each side. *Everything should be ready in about thirty minutes*, he thought. If Lorie is really hungry, she should be back here just in time. Jack checked the biscuits and found them to be browned just right. At that moment, Lorie came into view. She was wearing a shiny, silky white sleep set with long slacks and a very revealing overblouse.

"Wow, you look so beautiful." Once again they embraced and enjoyed another long passionate kiss. "Please sit here, so I can concentrate on our dinner. Would you like a glass of wine?"

"No thanks, Jack. I'll settle for a nice cold glass of water."

Jack brought Lorie the glass of water and then busied himself removing the food from the oven.

"Can I help with anything, Jack?"

"Yes, you can light the candles and if you know how to work the radio, maybe you can find some soft music for us. Sometimes I get some stations and sometimes it is all static."

In a few minutes, Jack cut the roast and set the pork on a platter with the potatoes and carrots positioned around the edge. The biscuits were wrapped in a white linen towel and placed in a basket. Jack dimmed the lights. Lorie had little success in tuning a station, so Jack told her to give up and come eat while everything was still hot. Lorie was impressed with the appearance of the food on the table. They held hands saying grace before filling their plates.

"Oh, Jack, this is delicious. I may want to hire you to work with my kitchen staff."

"No thanks. I find cooking to be very relaxing and enjoyable on a small scale. I would be lost trying to prepare a big meal. I sometimes wonder when my mother has a large number of guests for dinner, how she manages to get everything to finish cooking at the same time and stay hot."

When they finished eating, Jack excused himself from the table, telling Lorie he would be right back. He returned with a small package and placed it on the table in front of Lorie.

"It's just something I picked up in Chicago when I was thinking about you."

Opening the package, Lorie exclaims, "Oh, I love it. It's beautiful, Jack. How did you know I needed a clutch purse?"

"Well, I asked the saleslady what would be an appropriate gift for a woman who has everything. Her reply was that women can always use another clutch purse." Reaching for Lorie's hand, Jack says, "That top you are almost wearing is driving me crazy. We'll do the dishes later. Right now let me show you one of the bedrooms."

Later, when they finally returned to the kitchen, Jack once again tried the radio. This time he was successful. The station broadcast was clear. Music was playing, which both Lorie and Jack thought must have been from some kind of recordings. As they washed and dried the dishes, a voice on the radio identified the station as WJZ New York and signed off for the evening, thanking the listeners for having tuned in.

"Stan told me that radio was going to revolutionize the music industry. I believe he is right. Well, if the radio isn't going to give us any more music, let me sing a few of my favorites for you. Come sit with me at the piano."

Jack played and sang "I Ain't Got Nobody", "You Belong to Me", "Let Me Call You Sweetheart", "I'm Always Chasing Rainbows", and "A Good Man Is Hard to Find". This time, Lorie took Jack's hand and led him to the bedroom.

Melting into his arms, Lorie says, "Jack, I think this is the best night of my whole life."

Jack woke up Saturday morning smelling bacon. Lorie was already out of bed and in the kitchen preparing breakfast.

"Well, it's about time, sleepyhead."

"Lorie, you wore me out last night." Then playfully embracing her, Jack says, "But, I still have a little life left in me."

"Save it for later, lover. Right now I have made your favorite breakfast, bacon and eggs. Please take a seat. Would you also like a cup of coffee?"

As they ate breakfast, Jack asked if she would like to take in a vaudeville show that evening. Lorie thought it would be a fun thing to do. Jack went on to suggest they drive over to his new country club in the afternoon for an early dinner and then return to park at the Chelsea Arms. He went on to explain that it was much easier to take the transit line right down to Broadway.

"You must promise not to let go of me while using the transit system. I would be absolutely lost here in the city."

"I promise. I am anxious to see the venue of a typical vaudeville performance. Stan has been talking about getting me a spot on one of the shows. He says we have to be careful because the show consists of many unrelated performances, and it is important to be sequenced in a spot where the audience is ready to be entertained with music. Stan gave another example of a singer once giving a great performance, which was then followed by a standup comic. The comedian chose to poke fun at the singer's performance, thereby getting laughs, but at the undeserving expense of the singer. I am so glad you got me started with Stan, Lorie. There are so many potential hidden pitfalls in this business. It really is beneficial to have someone like Stan looking after my best interests."

Lorie loved the York Country Club. Jack sensed that even though she never mentioned anything, Lorie had her business mind engaged and was evaluating things that might possibly work well in her own country club. They enjoyed a great meal and then returned to Jack's apartment to freshen up before heading downtown.

Jack had been told that vaudeville at the Palace was always good. The billboard in front of the theater was certainly enticing. The acts included several comics, magic, an animal trainer, two singers, and a short theatrical play.

"What do you think, Lorie?"

"I like it. Let's go in."

Jack purchased two tickets and they proceeded into the theater. It felt good to be able to treat Lorie after she had done so much for him. They sat close to each other as Jack held Lorie's hand and told her in a very soft voice how much he appreciated her coming for the weekend. The entertainment was good. Jack and Lorie both thought they could have eliminated the animal trainer and perhaps had more music. The comics were good, but as Stan had told Jack, they did poke fun at the expense of other entertainers or well-known people. Following the theater, they stopped in a small café for coffee and pastries before returning to the Chelsea Arms. Jack turned on the radio and once again music was being broadcast.

"I didn't change the tuning dial, so this must be that WJZ station."

They relaxed enjoying the music and talking about which church they should go to in the morning. Once again, a voice on the radio thanked the audience for listening to WJZ and signed off for the evening.

"Well, lover, this was a perfect day. Sing some more songs for me like you did last night and I'll reward you as I did last night."

THE FUNERAL

It sometimes feels like when everything is going just right, God lets us experience a tragedy just to remind us of how mortal we are. For Jack's close knit family, it was the loss of Catherine. Catherine died in her sleep when her weak heart just gave out. Jack learned of her passing from his mother's phone call. He immediately called Janet at the agency and asked her to keep his schedule clear for the next few days until his sister-in-law's funeral arrangements were finalized. He thought about calling Lorie, but then decided he should not trouble her with his family problems.

Jack went to his mother's around noon and then they both went to his brother's house. Charles Sr. and his two sons, Milt and Charles Jr., were all home. Jack and his mother hugged each and passed on their condolences. Mrs. Schmidt had a short private conversation with her son, Charles, and then effectively took charge of setting up the viewing and the funeral. Jack offered to stay with Milt and Charles Jr. while Mrs. Schmidt and Charles went to the funeral parlor. Jack tried to make light conversation keeping the boys' minds off such a troubling time. He remembered when his own father had passed away and the anxiety he had experienced. He talked about his father's death, and told them that only the passing of time eased the pain that he had experienced. He asked them how they were doing in their jobs and what was going on with their girlfriends. They had not eaten for a while, so Jack suggested they walk to the local delicatessen and he would treat them to a sandwich. By the time they returned from eating, Mrs. Schmidt and Charles were back.

"We have settled on Thursday for the burial of your mother," Charles said. "The viewing will be here in our house just before Mass. I'm going to the rectory now to see what times can be arranged for the viewing and Mass. Please listen to your grandmother and try to do as she says so we will be ready on Thursday."

"Well, let's start with you bringing your suits to me. If you don't have a clean white shirt, bring one that needs washing. I'll clean and press your shirts, and if your suits need pressing I'll take them along also. The next thing we need to do is clean the house. There will be a lot of guests coming both before and after the funeral. Jack, you can be in charge of getting everything spotless. Tomorrow, Jack and I will go food shopping. I'll be here Wednesday to prepare some of the food. I don't think we will have any overnight guests unless George Ransom and his wife decide to stay over. Jack, please set up a guest room just in case. I think it will be all right for you to go to work until Thursday. Tell your supervisors about the funeral arrangements as soon as you get to work and let them know you will be back to work on Friday. Okay, go check your clothes."

As the boys headed upstairs, Jack commented, "Mom, you would have made a great sergeant."

"Well, private, go check the cleaning supplies in case we need to pick up any at the store."

Thursday came fast. There had been a number of visitors to Charles's house. Some brought flowers; some brought meals. All remembered Catherine as a wonderful person and truly grieved her passing. The viewing was set for nine to ten on Thursday morning and was to be followed by an eleven o'clock Mass. Internment was to be at Saint Raymond's Cemetery in the Bronx. Milt was driving now, so he was to drive his father's Buick, first to church and then to the cemetery. His father, his brother, his grandmother, and Jack would ride along. Just before going to church, Milt asked his father if he could keep his mother's gold initial ring. Milt knew that the ring had been made with a lock of his mother's hair enclosed inside of the gold band. Charles was moved by his son's request, and told Milt that he would make sure the ring was removed from his mother's finger before the casket was closed.

Catherine was well known, partly because she was George Goethals's sister. The viewing line seemed to be endless. To Jack's surprise, Lorie appeared in the doorway. Jack went to greet Lorie and then stayed with her as the line moved toward the immediate family members.

"Mrs. Bradford, it is so nice of you to come. How did you learn of Catherine's passing?"

"Stan had Janet at the agency give me a call. You have such a nice family, Jack, you should have called me."

"I thought about calling, but I know how busy you are during the week and I just didn't want to trouble you."

As they reached the immediate family members, Mrs. Bradford very graciously spoke her condolences. When Jack introduced her to George Goethals, she surprised him by telling him she thought he had done a wonderful job with the Panama Canal. Jack's mother was truly glad to see Mrs. Bradford and thanked her very much for taking the time to come. Jack marveled at Lorie's social skills and vowed to himself that he would learn to improve his own skills from Lorie's example. Jack waited behind the open casket for Lorie and then walked with her to the car.

"Can you give James directions to the church? We will attend Mass, but not go on to the cemetery. Jack, please let me know if there is anything I can do."

Jack gave directions to James and then thanked them both very much for coming.

The church was packed for Mass and the procession to the cemetery was very long. Saint Raymond's Cemetery was at the northern edge of the Bronx. Jack's father was buried there.

He thought if time permitted he would go to his father's grave and pay his respects. As it turned out, when they were departing the cemetery, Jack's mother asked Milt to drive to his grandfather's grave. They all exited the car and joining hands by the gravesite, they said a prayer.

The ride back to Charles's house was quiet and kind of sad. At the house, Mrs. Schmidt took charge again, as there undoubtedly would be guests arriving. Jack ushered the boys into the kitchen to organize things, so they could easily serve refreshments. He told both of them that should they need anything in the coming days to not hesitate to call. Jack stressed that it would be good to stay close to their father for a while. Try to be home for evening meals with him and go to church with him on Sundays. Jack said he would be by more often and would see if their grandmother would be good enough to occasionally cook a Sunday dinner for all of the family.

George Ransom and his wife were the first guests to arrive. Charles was truly glad that they came back to the house. To Jack's surprise, quite a few executives from the garden came to the house. He couldn't remember seeing the executives earlier in the day, so maybe they cut work short and came to pay their respects. One of the executives had seen Jack perform and engaged him in a conversation.

"My name is George. I saw you perform about a month back. You put on a damn good show, Jack. Charlie tells me you want him to change his last name to Smith."

"Well, I did ask him, George, based on advice from my agent. I've been told there is still a lot of anti-German sentiment from the Great War and my stage name should be more American."

"Were you in the Great War, son?"

"Yes, sir, I fought in France."

"Well, consider the name change done, Jack. I'll put a little squeeze on your brother."

Jack stayed until most of the guests had departed. He was amazed at how many of them knew about his budding career. When his mother was ready to leave, Jack walked her back home and decided to stay for the evening. He thought his mother could also stand a little company.

RADIO BROADCASTING

As the months passed by following Catherine's death, Jack's brother and his nephews seemed to be adjusting. They all kept very busy with their jobs, and it seemed like the boys tried to spend a fair amount of time with their father. Jack continued to see Lorie. She loved visiting the apartment, as her time there completely took her mind away from running both the estate and Bradford Industries. On Lorie's most recent weekend visit, Jack told her Stan had discussed the possibility of him playing piano for a singer on the very same WJZ radio station that they sometimes listened to. Lorie wanted to know why Jack couldn't both play and sing. Jack explained that, as he understood things, the vocalist was under contract. He went on to relate Stan's take on the situation.

"Stan says the vocalist has a drinking problem and has been known to go off on a bender for weeks at a time. Stan's plan is to put me on piano, and the next time the vocalist doesn't show up for work, I'm to just pick up the singing along with the piano playing. Stan says the pay is not that great for playing the piano, but if and when I take over as the vocalist, he will negotiate a very attractive contract for me. What do you think?"

"Stan is a smart man. I think he is right about radio broadcasting being a boom in the near future. It will certainly give "Whispering" Jack Smith wide exposure. The only negative is waiting for the current vocalist to go on his bender."

"Okay, Lorie, I'm going to do it. All I needed was a little reinforcement from you."

One week later, Stan had Jack go to the WJZ station building for an interview and to meet the vocalist, Greg Richards. Jack didn't recognize the name and kind of thought his voice was a little too high. They did a few songs together, and the WJZ people seemed pleased. In fact, they wanted to talk about contract terms. Jack politely assured them that he was very dependable, but that any contract would have to be negotiated through the Star Talent Agency.

The next day, Stan called, "You're in, Jack. You start tomorrow morning. Be at the radio station around eleven. The broadcast is scheduled to start at noon. And if Richards doesn't show up any day, do as I told you and also call me immediately after the broadcast."

Working at the WJZ Station turned out to be very enjoyable for Jack. The commute was easy and the hours were great. Greg Richards was easy to get along with, and the managers at WJZ were great to work with. Most days, Jack was out of the station building before five in the afternoon. He frequently stopped at his mother's house to join her for dinner. On occasion, Jack went over to his brother's just to see how they were getting along. Sometimes, Stan scheduled him for an evening performance someplace in town. Sundays were usually free, so he often golfed at the country club. He had ample time to practice at the piano in the apartment. Lorie continued to visit, usually on a weekend. Overall, life was very good.

The big change came about three months after Jack started at WJZ. As predicted, Greg Richards did not show up for work one Monday. Jack started the broadcast on time by playing a few tunes and then began singing and playing old-time favorites. Jack had pretty much mastered the use of the microphone, so he embellished his performance by telling the radio audience not only the names of the songs, but also some short history about things, such as who wrote the lyrics, when the song was first published, whether or not recordings were available, and if so, on what type of media. He played and sang for three hours nonstop. The WJZ managers were very impressed. At the end of the day, their only question was could Jack repeat his performance on Tuesday should Greg Richards not show up.

Jack's answer was, "I'll be here ready to go."

When leaving the building, Jack stopped at one of the lobby phone booths and called Stan.

Janet answered very excitedly, "Hello, Jack, you were marvelous. We received a phone call earlier today to tune in to WJZ. Stan is very excited. Hold on and I will try to find him."

After a minute or two, "Hello, Jack, great job, kid. Do you think you can keep it up?"

"Sure, Stan, I love broadcasting that way. My only problem is going three hours without stopping is a little rough."

"Okay, I'll handle getting you a break, say, every twenty minutes. Some of the stations are broadcasting local news events every hour on the hour. Others insert commercial advertising.

I'm sure WJZ will want to stay competitive, and you set them up beautifully to solicit advertising money from the record companies. When you open and close your broadcast tomorrow, be sure to announce yourself as "Whispering" Jack Smith. Hang in there, Jack. I smell a big contract coming your way. Just keep things under your hat until I get everything nailed down. I'll be in touch."

"Thanks, Stan. I'll do my best."

Jack wanted to tell Lorie and his mother about the broadcast, but took Stan's advice and simply returned to the apartment. At the apartment, he practiced some songs for Tuesday's broadcast. Jack knew music and music history. All of his practice, his time playing as a song plugger, and his ability to recall the names of writers, vocalists, publishers, and dates had culminated in a super broadcast performance. He selected music sheets to take along to the station on Tuesday, and formulated a mental schedule of how he would perform at the station. Jack found it all to be fun. *What a beautiful day this has been*, he thought. *Thank you, God.*

Greg Richards was missing again on Tuesday. Before the broadcast started, the WJZ managers sat down with Jack and told him how they appreciated what he was doing to keep the broadcast going. They talked about breaking on every hour when someone would broadcast news from another microphone. Additionally, they would signal Jack about every twenty minutes through the broadcast to end a song. At that point, someone would pick up the broadcast verbally with either a sponsor's advertisement or a special service announcement. He was to take about five minutes and watch for a hand signal to come back on at his microphone. *Well,* Jack thought, *Stan got everything we talked about. I wonder how the money is going to turn out.*

Except for one short delay when switching broadcasting between microphones, Tuesday's program was great. Jack had good feelings for what he was doing. He put great effort into delivering a memorable performance and then signed off.

"You have been listening to your old-time favorites with 'Whispering' Jack Smith. Tune in the same time tomorrow for more listening pleasure."

Jack finally felt like he was a star.

LET THE GOOD TIMES ROLL

On Thursday morning, Stan called.

"Jack, I have a contract for you with WJZ Radio. If you can stop by the agency this morning, I'll go over it with you. It's a good one, so I would like to get it finalized with signatures before anyone at the radio station wants to make changes."

"I'll be there in about an hour. Thanks, Stan."

Jack skipped breakfast and headed right to the Star Agency. Janet was all smiles when he entered the agency.

"Congratulations, Jack. You knocked them dead the last two days. Everybody has been talking about your broadcasts, and the phones are ringing off the hooks with requests for bookings. It looks like you are going to be quite busy for a while."

"Thanks, Janet. I'm glad the broadcast went well. Stan said to come in this morning to go over a contract."

"He's expecting you. Go right in."

Jack entered Stan's office and they looked through the contract together. The money was very good at forty-five thousand dollars base salary per year. It also had incentives that had to do with the number of commercial advertisers and Jack's personal appearances promoting WJZ Radio. Broadcasts on the weekends were not to be the norm, and if ever performed there would be extra compensation.

As they went through the multi-paged document, Stan pointed out a few important forbidden items and some allowable items. Jack was not to be allowed to promote any product or service without the written permission of WJZ. He was forbidden from broadcasting from any station other than WJZ. On the plus side, Jack was allowed to book performances as long as there was no conflict with his duty hours at WJZ. And the one that Jack liked the best was at the conclusion of each four-week period of radio broadcasting, Jack would be given one full week off.

"The four-week break is important, Jack. I put it in for several reasons. We don't want you to burn out, but more importantly, we want the radio listeners to miss you and want to hear you again. What do you think so far?"

"I love it, Stan. I've never made that kind of money and the time off is beautiful."

"Okay, now some fatherly advice. I don't want you acting like a drunken sailor with this windfall of money. You are going to have taxes to pay, and as always, I suggest you continue to invest a nice portion of your earnings for your future years. We will estimate what tax you will be liable for and put that money aside in the bank for you."

"It sounds good to me, Stan. Where do I sign?"

On the way out of the agency, Jack gave Janet a big hug and a kiss.

"The next time I visit, I'm going to bring you flowers."

"I wish all of our clients were as happy as you. Good luck, Jack."

Jack stopped at the café where he and Arthur Kennedy had eaten on several occasions. He wondered if he should inform Art of his good fortune, but decided Art's connections were so good that he would probably find out before my own family. Jack had time to call his mother before going to the radio station. His mother picked up the phone as always after the second ring.

"Hello, Mom. I'm on my way to work and I have great news to share with you. I just signed a contract for radio broadcasting with WJZ. It's for big money, Mom."

"Oh! That's wonderful, Jack. I knew you would get a break one of these days. Congratulations, son."

"Listen, Mom. Don't tell anybody yet. I'm going to try and get Charles and the boys to go out to dinner with us this weekend. I'll call you about the weekend plans."

Next, Jack looked through his billfold for his brother's phone number at the garden. *I'm going to have to organize these numbers and addresses a little better*, he thought while thumbing through the folded slips of paper. *Ah! Here it is.*

The phone at the garden rang at least five times, and just when Jack was going to give up, Charles answered.

"Hello, Charles Smith, Madison Square Garden. How may I help you?"

"Charlie, It's Jack. I'm trying to get everyone together to go out for dinner on Sunday. It will be my treat. Mom says she is available. Can you and the boys make it?"

"I'm good anytime after Mass, and I think Milt will be okay, but we may have to bring his girlfriend along. Charles is low on seniority with the railroad and works a lot of the weekends, so he may not be available."

"Okay, get as many as you can, and I'm okay with Jean coming along. Let's shoot for two in the afternoon. Mom and I will walk down to your place. I'd like to go to my country club, so if we get there a little early there won't be a problem getting a table."

"I'll see you and Mom Sunday."

"And Charlie, did I hear right? You answered the phone Charles Smith, not Schmidt. Thanks, brother."

Jack made one more call back to his mother to give her the two o'clock time on Sunday and then headed over to the radio station.

Thursday and Friday went pretty smooth at the radio station. The staff and management at WJZ were treating Jack like he was truly a star celebrity. Word must have leaked out as to how much his salary was. Before broadcasting, coffee was brought to him, and again at each break someone would bring a glass of water or soda. Everyone was overly friendly. The managers talked to Jack about golf and suggested that they get together to play a round. They were impressed when finding out Jack already belonged to a country club. It seem like the managers at WJZ all belonged to the West Chester Golf Club. When Jack told them he frequently played with his nephew on Sundays, two of the managers challenged him to a match sometime in the near future. Jack said he would check with his nephew and get back to them. Jack thought, *Wow, what a difference one week can make.*

Dinner at the York Country Club was great. Milt's girlfriend, Jean, came along. Charles Jr. couldn't make it because of work. Jack waited until after they had all ordered before announcing he had signed a contract with the WJZ Radio Station. He described the salary as being a very substantial amount, and then went on to tell about his days off and other benefits. Of course, his mother already knew about Jack's signing, but the others were genuinely amazed.

Milt asked, "When do you broadcast?"

"Mondays through Fridays from noon until four o'clock," Jack answered.

"Jack, I've never even heard a radio broadcast," Milt exclaimed.

"Well, that's the other piece of good news. Do you remember seeing the radio in my apartment when you visited? Charles, you asked me how much one cost and I said I would try to find out. I did find out, and then decided to buy one for your house and one for Mom's. Now you will be able to enjoy radio. The store where I purchased them will send someone out next Saturday to set up the radios and show you how to operate them. The most important thing to remember is to be sure the radio is turned off when you are not using it. They are battery powered and over time, the batteries will need to be replaced."

They all thanked Jack. Jack went on to tell Milt to be sure and invite Jean to the house, so she can also hear the radio. Then turning to Jean, he said, "Jean, the radio will have a special amplifier and horn-shaped speaker attached, which means that anyone present in the room will be able to hear the broadcasting. Many of today's radios require the listener to wear a headset. And, young lady, the last time we were all together, you continually escaped telling us anything about yourself. Milt tells us little or nothing, so now seems like a good time for you to fill us in."

"Well, I think you all know I met Milt through my brother. They both worked as messengers for Dunn and Bradstreet a while ago. Milt and my brother, William, remain very close friends. One night, William brought Milt for dinner at our flat and before leaving, Milt said he would like to see me again. So, we have been dating for almost two years now." My last name is VonderLieth. My parents came together from German to this country. My father is dead now. He had a fall at a construction site and never fully recovered. My mother is a hard worker and managed to get me through business school, so I now have secretarial job. That's about it."

"Where in Germany did your parents come from?" Mrs. Schmidt asked.

"They both came from Hannover."

"Yes, I know Hannover. It is very nice there. Do you understand German?"

Jean replied in German, and then everyone at the table briefly switched to German.

The waitress arrived with their food, so they changed back to speaking English. Jack and Charles were sitting next to one another, with Charles at the end of the table. Charles lead them in saying grace and when finished, he motioned for Jack to lean close.

"How much did those radios cost?"

"In a very low voice," Jack replied. "They were priced at sixty-five dollars each without the horn speakers. I purchased a total of three. One is a present for Mrs. Bradford for all of her help. So, they gave me a break. I think it worked out to about sixty-dollars each with the horn speakers. And when I get a chance, I'm going to take Mom shopping for new parlor furniture. It's nice to have money to spend."

"Wow! That's a lot of money, Jack. It's almost enough to buy a car. I certainly appreciate what you're doing."

The following Saturday, Jack visited with his mother in the morning. He didn't want her to be upset by the intricacies of the radio when it was set up in her house. The installation was all done by ten o'clock. Jack learned a few things himself when the installer explained the purpose of each dial and how to tune for clarity of sound on each station. His mother was still a little apprehensive, so Jack promised to show her later until she became comfortable with it. He then told his mother that the real purpose for his visit was to take her to Macy's to pick out new parlor furniture. She was very excited and must have thanked her son a dozen times.

"Come on, Mom, we are going to eat lunch at Woolworth's."

Jack knew his mother loved to go to the Woolworth's luncheon counter, and it was close to Macy's department store. He wanted to get back to the apartment before six, as Lorie was coming for the evening. The selection and purchase of a new sofa, wingback chair, and ottoman went faster than Jack thought it would. Apparently, his mother had been to Macy's several times over the past few years looking at parlor furniture, but always walking away feeling that she could not quite afford to buy it. The store would deliver the furniture and take away the old pieces. After leaving the store, Jack walked his mother to the transit stop and waited until she boarded the trolley before heading for his apartment.

Lorie arrived around six fifteen. Jack went out and rode along with her to their parking space.

Walking back to the lobby, Lorie commented, "I have a bone to pick with you."

"And what can that possibly be?"

"You know darn well what I'm talking about, Jack. You can't afford to be spending that kind of money on radios. Had I been at home when the installer came, I would have sent it back."

"Do you like it?"

"Jack, I really do. It's in the study and it sounds just wonderful."

"Let's get you signed in, Miss Rogers, and then I'll tell you the rest of the story about the radio."

Once in the apartment, Lorie wrapped her arms around Jack and gave him a long passionate kiss.

"That's part of my thank you. Now tell me the rest of the story."

"Well, Miss Rogers, the big story is I hit pay dirt at WJZ. I am now playing the piano and singing the vocals. Stan worked out a very nice contract for me that guarantees a minimum of forty-five thousand a year."

Lorie grabbed Jack again kissing him very hard and said, "I knew it, Jack. I just knew you would make it big someday. Oh! This is so wonderful. Will I be able to hear you sing on the radio?"

"Yes, you can listen to me most weeks, Monday through Friday from noon to four o'clock. That is as long as you don't send the radio back."

"Thanks, Jack. I can't wait until I hear you on the radio. Right now I'm going for a bath. I'll call you when I'm done, so you can come dry my back."

THE CHALMERS SIX

Radio broadcasting spread like wildfire in 1922. "Whispering" Jack Smith became a household name in New York City and his fame spread as the broadcasting signals reached further and further. Jack put a lot of effort into his broadcasting preparation and was justly rewarded.

One day, the WJZ managers reminded Jack about the golf match that they had discussed and pointed out that soon it would be too cold to play. Jack responded that his nephew normally is available on Saturday mornings and stated he would see about the coming Saturday. They decided to play at the West Chester Country Club.

That evening, Jack went to see Milt.

"How is your golf game, Milt?"

"It's about as good as ever. What's up?"

"These two managers down at the radio station have been after me to play a round of golf at the West Chester Country Club. I told them I would check with you and see if we could put a match together. From hearing them talk, I think their games are a little better than average. I would love to beat these guys and get them off my back."

"Jack, West Chester Country Club is a very classy place. I would love to play there. They will have the advantage, as the course is new to us. However, if we get good caddies, we should be okay."

"Do you think you can get the Buick to drive there?"

"Probably, I'll check with Dad and let you know for sure."

"Okay, plan to pick me up around six this Saturday. I'll be in touch."

On Saturday morning, Milt arrived at Jack's apartment as planned, and after loading the golf bags they started out to the West Chester Country Club. Along the way, Jack told Milt he was thinking about buying a car. Jack mentioned that he liked what he had read about the Chalmers Six. Milt didn't know much about the Chalmers other than it was an expensive automobile.

"Well, if you're thinking seriously about buying a car, Jack, you're going to need some driving lessons. Why don't you ask Dad if he is willing to let me give you some lessons in the Buick? Dad may prefer to teach you; however, he has been so busy at work that he probably won't have time to do it."

They were not disappointed upon arriving at the country club. A long, winding driveway led up to a very elegant looking clubhouse. They were well ahead of the time Jack had agreed to meet with the WJZ managers.

Milt and Jack were on the practice putting green when the WJZ managers arrived. After introductions were made, they headed for the first tee. Milt thought it odd that the WJZ players had no warm-ups other than a little stretching. The match was close through the first nine holes, during which Milt and Jack developed a lot of respect for the knowledge of the course their caddies displayed. It paid off on the back nine as they each followed the recommendations of their caddies and made some great shots. The WJZ players conceded on the fifteenth hole.

Back at the clubhouse, Jack gave each of the caddies a very handsome tip. Milt then noticed out of the corner of his eye that Jack was collecting a handful of bills from the WJZ players. On the drive home, Milt asked Jack if he had bet on the match.

"Normally, I don't gamble. But these two guys were almost insistent. It was a big bet and it was great to win. I loved your shot over the tree. I've never seen you try a shot like that."

"Jack, I was planning to go around the tree and just get an open shot to the green, but the caddy handed me the sixty degree iron and just pointed over the top of the tree, so I went for it. I really enjoyed playing that course. Do you think they will invite you back again?"

"No, I think we've seen the last of those two as golfers. They must be pretty cheap or something for the caddies to dislike them so much. What did you think of them?"

"They were okay, but I wouldn't want to spend a lot of time around them. How do you get along at the radio station?"

"You know me. I get along with most anybody. But like you said, Milt, I don't want to spend a lot of time with them either. Anyway, we won enough for me to make a down payment on a new Chalmers." Then Jack passed several bills to Milt, "Here, this is for you to treat Jean to something special tonight."

The following Monday morning, Jack called Arthur Kennedy.

"Hello, Jack. Congratulations on your radio show. You're doing a magnificent job. What can I do for you?"

"Art, I'm thinking about buying an automobile and I wanted to get your thoughts about a new Chalmers Six."

"That's an excellent choice, Jack. They have been making automobiles for over ten years. I've driven the Chalmers Touring model. It has a very smooth ride. The engine is powerful and the handling is very impressive. The car is expensive, Jack. I think the Chalmers Six is priced around thirteen hundred right now. I have a friend at the Carl H. Page Company at Broadway and Fiftieth Street. They sell Chalmers. Let me give him a call and I'll get back to you. Maybe I can save you a few bucks."

"Thanks, Art. I have to head over to the radio station soon, so maybe it will be best for me to call you tomorrow morning."

"Okay, Jack, I'll talk to you tomorrow."

Jack called the next day. Art told Jack that he could get a very good price on a new Chalmers Six. The price would be between one thousand and eleven hundred. Art went on to say that the Chalmers Company was having financial difficulties and there was a possibility that they will discontinue manufacturing the Chalmers automobiles sometime in the near future. Art said he would not let that news stop him from purchasing one of their cars. His recommendation was to take advantage of the steeply discounted prices. Jack thanked Art and decided to check with Milt to see if they could meet at the Carl H. Page Company on Saturday.

Milt and Jack arrived at Broadway and Fiftieth Street within five minutes of each other. They were to see a Mr. Gifford. There were two Chalmers Six automobiles on the lot along, with six other Chalmers models. Mr. Gifford was very pleasant to deal with. He spent considerable time going over the features of the Chalmers Six while opening the engine panels and folding the top down.

Once he understood that Milt was an experienced driver, Mr. Gifford offered the car to Jack and Milt to drive and show it to Jack's mother and brother. Jack's mother and his brother were quite impressed with the car and went for a short ride. Charles told Jack he didn't think he could get a better deal anyplace for a large automobile like the Chalmers, and suggested that Jack be sure to get side curtains for the inclement weather.

Back at the automobile dealer, Jack inquired about the side curtains. Mr. Gifford responded that the side curtains would be included at the price he had quoted to Jack. That sealed the deal and Jack bought his first automobile.

Over the next few weekends, Milt spent his time teaching Jack to drive. Jack was well coordinated and picked up on handling the automobile rather well. The strange thing was that unlike Milt, who loved to drive, Jack found driving to be more of a chore than a pleasure. However, they both thoroughly loved the Chalmers Six.

The Chalmers Six

THE B & B COMPANY

Jack called Lorie after he mastered driving the Chalmers and asked if she would be at home on the weekend. He had not seen her for quite some time. Lorie was excited to hear from Jack and said she would be at the estate all weekend. Jack said he had a ride out on Saturday and that it would be nice to see her. He promised not to interfere with any social functions that might be in progress. Lorie responded for him to just come, and stressed that her evening was definitely free, so to please plan on staying over.

When Saturday arrived, Jack gassed up the Chalmers and headed out North on Broadway toward the Bradford Estate. He liked driving on the open road, although it was a little chilly in the morning without the side curtains in place. Upon arriving at the Bradford Estate, he found little activity, so he pulled around to the garage area and parked in a space that did not block access to the garages.

Jack entered through the kitchen and found James and the mechanic seated eating lunch. One of the staff recognized Jack, and when greeting him asked if he would like something to eat.

"Well, yes, thank you, I am a little hungry. Can I have a ham sandwich and an iced tea? I'll be sitting over with James and the mechanic."

"I'll bring it to you in just a few minutes, Mr. Smith."

Jack went over and said hello to James and the mechanic. He asked if he could join them, and after some small talk, Jack announced that he had bought a Chalmers Six, which was parked out by the garage.

"You must be doing very well, Jack. That's a rather expensive automobile, James said."

"I got a very good price. It seems that Chalmers is having financial difficulties and is therefore offering steep discounts."

The mechanic asked, "Would you mind if I look it over when I return to the garage? I've never seen a Chalmers up close. They sure are beautiful automobiles."

Jack nodded affirmatively while James asked, "Are you here to see Mrs. Bradford, Jack?"

"Yes, she knows I would be stopping today, but she doesn't know that I bought a car and that I can now drive. I wanted to surprise her."

"Well, Mrs. Bradford is in the library with a couple of gentlemen from another company. I'll have one of the staff give her a note advising that you are here and will be out by the garage with us."

"Thanks, James. I promised I would not interfere with any of her activities, so a note should be just fine."

After finishing lunch, they headed out to the Chalmers Six. James and the mechanic were obviously impressed. James settled in behind the wheel while the mechanic opened the engine side panels and examined the engine. James asked if it would be all right to fold the roof down. Jack agreed, and after the roof was down, James excused himself indicating that he was going to get his camera. They were taking picture as each of them posed next to the driver's door when Mrs. Bradford arrived with her two business guests.

"Hello, Jack. Is this your car? I can't believe you bought a car. It is just beautiful, Jack. You'll have to promise to take me for a ride. I would like you to meet two of my business associates, Mr. Francis Brady and Mr. Fredrick Siegel."

As they shook hands, Mrs. Bradford added that Jack was an entertainer who had performed at the estate several times before his popularity soared.

"You may have heard him as "Whispering" Jack Smith on the radio."

Mr. Brady commented, "We listen to you in the afternoons at the office. You have a very nice broadcast, young man."

Then the two businessmen excused themselves, stating to Mrs. Bradford that they would be in touch. Mrs. Bradford also excused herself as she started to escort the guests to their automobile.

She then turned back and told James not to put the camera away, stating she would be back to get her picture taken with the new car.

When Lorie returned, James took a picture of her and Jack next to the Chalmers, and then James and the mechanic kind of drifted away. Lorie sat in the car and again told Jack how beautiful it was.

"You will take me for a ride, won't you?"

"Better than that, Lorie, I'll let you drive."

"Oh! You're going to need a special reward for that. But first let's go to the library. I have so many things to tell you."

In the library, they sat close enough to hold hands and touch each others' legs. Lorie asked if he would like a drink from the kitchen. Jack explained he had just finished lunch with James and the mechanic.

"Jack, I've missed you like crazy. But I'm engaged in a rather large business deal that will merge Bradford Industries with another company that manufactures electric motors, some of which are components of my machines. The Mr. Brady who you just met is the owner of the electric motor manufacturing company. The other gentleman is his business lawyer."

"I've missed you too, Lorie. We have both been kind of busy lately, so let's take advantage of this time we have together. How about a nice drive up along the Hudson?"

"I would love that, Jack. Just let me change my outfit quickly, and then I'll tell you more about my business deal as we drive."

Lorie amazed Jack. She simply got behind the wheel of the Chalmers and started driving like she had owned the car for years.

"Oh! I like this car, Jack. It has a lot of power and handles almost like a race car."

They drove north along the river toward West Point as they had done before. Lorie told Jack more about her business venture. She mentioned how Milt's help with the Chilton Company manuals had really put them on a path to improving profitability. Bradford Industries now had a Service and Spare Parts Department. They stocked 90 percent of the parts that might be needed to repair any of the Bradford manufactured machines. What was not in stock could easily and rapidly be made in one day or less. She went on telling Jack about the number of technicians she had training personnel at companies that had purchased her machines. She then talked to Jack nonstop about her plans to merge Bradford Industries with Brady Electric Motor Company. As Jack understood what he was being told, the Brady motors were used exclusively in the Bradford machines, so by combining the two companies there were considerable cost savings that would improve the overall profitability for both owners. The new company was to be named B & B Industries.

Jack interrupted Lorie, "There's the sign for Lookout Point. Let's pull in and park for a while. I'll put the top up and install the side curtains so the ride back will be a little warmer."

There were no other cars at the lookout, so Lorie parked over to the far side and then embraced Jack, giving him a very wild and passionate kiss.

"I really miss kissing you, Jack. Come on, I'll help you with the top and the curtains."

Sitting inside of the Chalmers with the curtains in place gave a comfortable feeling of privacy. Lorie and Jack became very passionate, kissing and touching each other until another automobile entered and parked at the far end of the lookout.

"Wow, Jack, I can't wait to get you in bed. Let's head back and stop along the way at the Country Club for dinner. After that we can retire early."

"When I drove out this morning, I thought maybe it would be nice to take you out for dinner. Right now I think we should head straight back, raid the kitchen, and retire early."

"Straight back it is, love."

THE BREAKUP

Throughout the next year, life was very good for Jack and his family. He didn't see Lorie as often. She seemed to be very involved with her business merger. His brother was also tied up at the garden getting ready for the 1924 Democratic National Convention. Jack's mother was doing very well and kind of enjoying a semiretired status. She still gave some piano lessons. Charles, Jr. was a full-time railroad conductor and had a girlfriend whom Jack had not yet met. Milt and Jean were very much in love, and it looked like there would soon be a wedding. The New York Port Authority announced the construction of a new bridge to be named in honor of George Goethals. Jack remained very much involved and active in radio broadcasting. When the Star Talent Agency booked him for outside engagements, it was always with very attractive compensation. As Arthur Kennedy had predicted, the Chalmers Company merged with Maxwell Automobile Manufacturing Company and stopped production of the Chalmers line of automobiles. Jack had been following his agent's advice about both investing and saving a good portion of his income. He took very good care of his mother and spent some money on his wardrobe and on some niceties for himself, such as cameras and jewelry.

One day, Milt called and told Jack he would like to get together with him on the weekend to talk about some problems Milt was having. They met at Jack's apartment the following Saturday.

"Jack, I hate to bring my problems to you, but Dad is so busy these days I hardly see him and I'm not sure if he can help me with this situation."

"Okay, Milt, tell me what the problem is and let's see if I can help."

"Well, I've asked Jean to marry me. She said yes, but she is not a Catholic. So I went to see Father Dougherty to see about making arrangements for the wedding. I thought that it would not be a big deal because Jean is a Christian, just not a Catholic. Father Dougherty told me it is a big deal, and that we would have to apply for a dispensation."

"First, let me congratulate you, Milt. Jean is a lovely girl and I think you two are well-suited for each other. I know the church does not encourage marrying outside of our faith. Tell me more about what Father Dougherty said."

"Well, he said the dispensation process is very costly and that I would have to pay before the church initiated the process. When I asked how much money I would need, I was shocked. Jack, I could buy a new car with the kind of money Father Dougherty is talking about. I have enough money saved, and I'm not here to ask you for money. It's just that it makes me so mad at Father Dougherty and the church. I don't know what to do. I'm a good Catholic, Jack, but maybe I should change to Jean's Protestant faith and get married in her church. What do you think?"

"Would Jean be willing to convert to Catholicism?"

"Maybe, after we are married. She is very upset about the whole issue right now. You have to understand that she and her family are very religious. They read the Bible all of the time and attend services at their church. It is very hard for them to understand the resistance from our Catholic Church."

"You don't want to marry outside of the Catholic Church. If you do, the church will not consider you to be married and you will be living in sin. Did Father Dougherty say how long the dispensation would take?"

"No, he didn't, but I got the impression it could be quite a while. He made me feel like I was the one causing this big problem. I was very disappointed. I always thought a priest was someone you could go to for help."

"Are you and Jean in any hurry to get married?"

"No, we can wait, but I would like to be able to at least plan ahead for our wedding."

"Okay, Milt, here's what I think you should do. Tell Father Dougherty that you want to go ahead with the dispensation. Pay the church as he requested in advance. If you need help financially, I will help you. While this is going on, ask Jean to attend Mass with you, so she can get a better understanding of our faith. Explain to Jean that even if she does not become a Catholic, you will be required to bring your children up as Catholics. Jean is a very intelligent young lady, but make sure she understands what will be required of her. If Jean accepts these things, go ahead and plan the wedding. If not, you have a serious problem and should seek more counseling from the church. Should more counseling be needed, perhaps I can arrange for you to meet with the pastor at Mrs. Bradford's parish? I talked with him on occasion at Mrs. Bradford's Estate when I was entertaining there and he seems like a very reasonable man."

"Thanks, Jack. Why didn't Father Dougherty explain these things to me?"

"Maybe he was having a bad day. Hang in there, I'm sure things will work out for you and Jean. And pass along my congratulations to her."

"Thanks again, Jack, and please keep this under your hat for a while."

A few months later, Jack was having dinner with his mother when she told him that his brother was thinking about getting married again.

"Wow! Who is the girl? I didn't even know Charles was dating."

"I don't know much more than she is a widow who works at the Aqua Delight where we all had dinner together a few years back. Her name is Jane and she has a daughter. Charles promised to bring her by to meet me, but he has been very busy getting ready for the Democratic National Convention."

"I wonder how the boys will handle this. Do they know?"

"Charles told me he is going to have a talk with them, but I don't know if he has done it yet. I told Charles that the boys could move in with me if necessary. I don't give many lessons anymore and it would be nice to have some company here at home."

"Do you think it's okay if I call Charles tomorrow and talk about this?"

"Yes, Jack, I think it would be good for him to talk to you about his plans. He is not trying to hold back anything from us. It's just that he is so busy with the coming convention that he is never around."

Jack did call his brother at the garden the next morning. Charles was excited to talk about his lady friend and thoughts about marriage. Jack learned that the widow's daughter's name was Gladys and she was married to a gentleman named Joe O' Neil. The daughter and her husband lived in New Jersey. Jack asked what plans his brother had for living arrangements after he married. Charles told his brother that he and Jane had been looking at a property in Valley Stream out on Long Island. It was a three-year-old single house on a nice piece of property. He could buy it at a very attractive price because the owner's spouse had recently passed away.

"Have you told the boys yet?"

"No, Jack. I was hoping to tie up some of the loose ends before telling them. I don't want them to think I am kicking them out of the house to fend on their own."

"When I talked with Mom last night she mentioned that she would be happy to have them come to live with her. I think that's a pretty good idea. We will have someone looking after Mom, and the boys will have a nice place to stay where they will get plenty of home cooking."

"I kind of like that idea, but I'm not sure how Milt and Charles will feel. Jack, if you are free this Saturday, how about meeting me at the Aqua Delight for lunch. Jane will be there in midafternoon. I would very much like you to meet her, and perhaps we can discuss some options that will work for all of us."

"Okay, I'll see you Saturday. But you should plan on telling your sons very soon. It would not be right for them to find out from someone other than their father."

When Saturday arrived, Jack drove over to the Aqua Delight and went inside. Charles was not in sight, so Jack told the maitre d' that he planned to meet with his brother for lunch and would just wait at the bar until Charles arrived. The maitre d' remembered Jack and complimented him on his radio broadcast. Jack thought, *how can he remember me*? It has been over two years since I was here. Oh well, I guess remembering people in this business is important. Jack sat at the bar and ordered a ginger ale. He was looking at the glass enclosed tank behind the bar when the bartender asked if he had ever seen mermaids swimming in the tank.

"I was here a couple of years ago in the late afternoon when a mermaid started swimming across, but we were just leaving, so I really didn't see much."

"The mermaids usually start around three. There are actually two. They look very much alike dressed in their mermaid swimsuits. Most people think there is one swimmer going back and forth in the tank. Actually, one swims across and stops while the other swims in the opposite direction. It is very entertaining."

At that point Charles arrives. "Hello, Jack. Let's grab a table at the back, so we can have some privacy."

Charles and Jack shook hands, and then Charles signaled the maitre d' indicating they were going to sit at the back. Jack had not seen his brother for some time, and was pleased that they were going to have lunch together. He wondered what Jane would be like when she arrived to join them. Charles stated it might be a while before Jane showed up and she probably would not be eating, so they should order now. They talked about the Democratic National Convention at the existing garden and construction of the new Madison Square Garden scheduled to open in 1925. Charles was indeed overwhelmed with work. Jack suggested that maybe his brother should hold off on the wedding until things slowed down a bit at work. Charles responded that would probably never happen, and added that Jane was in a bit of a bind with her current living arrangements.

"Jane lost her husband about a month before we lost Catherine. She kept things going by working two jobs. Her daughter recently married and now lives in New Jersey. Jane could not really afford the house rent, so she moved to an apartment. Jack, the apartment is a real zoo. I worry about her living there and can't wait to get her out of there. The house we looked at in Valley Stream is available for immediate occupancy and will just be perfect for us. I'm thinking of buying the house now and letting Jane live there until we marry."

"Well, I think you should take time out to tell your sons what is going on before purchasing a new home. They deserve to meet your intended bride, and you both need to explain your plans to them. If you don't do that, Charlie, you may be chasing them away from you for a long, long time.

"It's really not all that complicated. You just need to slow down a bit and start to include Milt and Charles Jr. in your decisions. Have you met Jane's daughter and her husband?"

"Yes, they are a wonderful couple. I think they both are very much looking forward to see Jane and I marry."

"Well, Charlie, Mom also deserves a chance to meet Jane and get to know her. Maybe you can put a deposit on the Valley Stream house. That will buy you some time. In the meantime, bring her to at least meet Mom. We will have to work on catching the two boys together at the same time, so Jane can meet them. Maybe I can work something out for you."

"Thanks, Jack. I'm supposed to be the older brother giving advice, but everything you said is right." I'll make some time to get better organized and do this thing right."

"One other thing, are you going to ask George Ransom to be your best man again?"

"No. In fact, I was planning on asking you. Will you do it?"

"I will be honored to be your best man, Charlie."

Just as they finished eating, Charles caught a glimpse of Jane coming in from the front of the building.

"Excuse me, Jack. That's Jane. I'm going to get her and bring her back here."

Jane was an attractive woman with a rather nice figure. She was almost as tall as Charles. She was probably about the same age as Charles and in very good shape. After Jane's introduction, she joined them at the table. Jack found her to be very nice to talk with. She seemed to have a good sense of humor. Jane knew about Jack's radio broadcasting, but simply mentioned it and did not dwell on the subject. Charles announced that Jack had agreed to be best man.

"Oh! That's wonderful. Charlie told me he was going to ask you. My daughter has agreed to be maid of honor, so we will have to try and all get together soon."

Jack asked how his brother and Jane had met. Charles told him he was grabbing a quick bite to eat one day at the Aqua Delight when Jane arrived a little early for work and sat near him at the bar. After a little light conversation, they each discovered that they had lost their spouses almost at the same time. Jane commented that it was like her prayers were answered when she and Charles met. She related that most people don't realize how your life changes when you lose your spouse and then changes even more after your children are grown and off on their own. She said she was very lonely and sometimes depressed before she and Charles met. Jane explained that they now had reason to plan for the future once again and look forward to sharing new experiences. They talked for almost an hour before both Charles and Jane said they had to get to work. To Jack's surprise, Jane was scheduled for mermaid duties. He had kind of assumed that she was one of the waitresses. Jack told his brother he would be in touch, and headed out to the parking lot. As he sat in the Chalmers, Jack thought, *Now what have I got myself into?* Well, time to get back to the apartment. Lorie was coming for the evening. He was very much looking forward to seeing her. Maybe she would have some advice about how to get things better organized for his brother's wedding and at the same time keep all concerned happy.

When Lorie arrived, she was very excited. She had brought readymade meals from the estate and asked Jack if he would warm the food while she took a quick bath and changed. Jack had the radio tuned in to station WJZ. The reception had improved considerably from the time he first moved to the apartment. The broadcast was recorded music and actually sounded very good. Lorie entered the kitchen just about the time Jack was going to call and announce the food was ready. She was wearing the same shiny, silky white sleep set with long slacks and a very revealing over blouse that she had worn their first night together in the apartment.

"Oh! Wow! That outfit looks familiar. You sure know how to drive a man crazy."

As Lorie gently kissed Jack, she whispered, "I want this to be a very memorable night."

Putting the food on the table, Jack said, "I still have that same kind of wine from our first night together here. Would you like some tonight?"

"Yes, thank you, I think I will have a glass this evening."

After Jack filled Lorie's glass, she raised it in a toast and said, "Here's to all of the wonderful times we have shared."

Jack acknowledged the toast, and then went on to tell Lorie about Milt's problem with the church in getting permission to marry a Protestant. Lorie thought it would work out in time and volunteered to solicit her pastor's help if needed. After listening to the details of the recommendations Jack had made to his brother concerning his brother's marriage, Lorie told Jack that he had handled the situation beautifully. She congratulated him on being selected to be best man. Jack then told Lorie about some recent conversations he had with Stan Schuman about the recording business. Stan had predicted the coming of radio broadcasting and now he's excited about the recording of songs.

"Stan tells me the industry has agreed on a standard format for recording on a twelve-inch disc at a speed of seventy-eight revolutions per minute. He said up to now there were too many different formats, speeds and types of media to really commercialize the recording industry. He predicts that within twelve months, most homes will have a record player. Stan wants me to get in on the ground floor. He is working on lining me up with a recording studio. Once records are cut, multiple copies are produced and then sold in music stores much the same way as sheet music is now sold. And here is the sweet part, for every one of my records sold a percentage of the sale goes to my account. What do you think?"

"I think that's wonderful, Jack. Just trust Stan and follow his advice. He is an amazing agent. I'll be your first customer."

"No, I will automatically send you a copy of every record I ever produce. I at least owe you that much."

"Okay, deal. Now let's clean up the kitchen so we can go over to the piano. I want you to play and sing for me like you did on our first night here."

As they washed and dried the dishes, Lorie updated Jack on the status of the merger between her company and the electric motor manufacturer. She was very excited about the initial results. She and the owner of the other company were getting along great. The new company was named B and B Industries. Profits were better than they had anticipated and the capacity of the plant had almost doubled. As they finished, Lorie told Jack she would tell him more in the morning.

Their evening together was even better than that first night in the apartment. Lorie just loved when Jack sang to her. She couldn't keep her hands off him, and kept gently kissing his cheek and whispering sweet things into his ear as he played the piano.

"Oh! Jack, you have meant so much to me these last several years. You gave me something to live for, something to look forward to. I will always love you, Jack. I just want you to know that, no matter what happens."

Jack stopped playing and said, "Lorie, you know, you too will always hold a special place in my heart."

He kissed her very passionately, got up from the piano bench, swept Lorie into his arms and headed for the bedroom.

The next morning, they were both worn out. Jack snuggled up to Lorie and suggested they sleep in, go to late Mass and have brunch at the country club. Lorie agreed, provided they made love one more time before going back to sleep.

Lorie suggested they drive both cars to the country club. That way she could get an early start on her drive back to the estate. The brunch was good, but Lorie had a very unsettling look about her.

"Jack, I have to talk to you very seriously. Last night and this morning were just perfect. I will always remember them, but they have to be our last. I wanted to tell you last night, but it would have spoiled our evening. Frank, the owner of the company I merged with, has asked me to marry him. He is a widower with two young boys that I thoroughly adore. We have dated, but have never been intimate. We do get along fine and enjoy each other's company, but realistically, I know it will be a marriage of convenience. In any event, you know me, Jack. I am a one-man woman. I'm going to accept his proposal and I'm going to miss you like crazy, but that's the way it has to be. Please don't be mad at me, Jack."

"Lorie, I could never be mad at you. Do you realize that we have never even had an argument? I think we both knew our relationship had to end at some point. I respect you for telling me now. I too will miss you very much. I hope we can remain friends, but distant friends. I will busy myself in my work and see what the future has in store for me. I sincerely wish you all of the best in your coming marriage. Now let's walk out to the cars, have one last parting kiss, and go our separate ways."

BACK TO CHICAGO

Several months passed before Stan called Jack to ask if he could take an engagement in Chicago during his upcoming one week break from WJZ. Jack would be performing in a semi-vaudeville setting in the downtown section, and his hotel room would be in the same building as the performance. Stan said one of the acts had dropped out unexpectedly and the producer needed a fill in for one week.

"You will have about forty-five minutes to fill in each evening and two performances on Saturday. You can pick whatever songs you want. The hotel room will be provided at no cost and the money is very attractive. If you can handle it, I may even be able to negotiate a little better deal when I call back. Janet will make all of the arrangements for you. You will go out on the train Saturday and return on the following Sunday. What do you say?"

"It sounds good to me, Stan. I can use a little time away about now."

"Good, Jack. I'll make the call and Janet will get back to you with all of the particulars."

The train ride to Chicago was boring as it had been on his first trip. Jack kept thinking about Lorie and the times they had spent together. What a woman! It's going to take a little time for me to get over her. Then his mind wandered to the pending family weddings. Milt was still waiting for the church to approve his marriage. Milt and Jean were optimistic and planning a June wedding, but not making firm commitments until the church rendered its decision. Milt was probably still mad at Father Dougherty and not going to Mass. Jack thought, *He'll get over it in a while.* Jack's brother had taken his advice and arranged to bring Jane to their mother's house on Sunday. *Let's see, that's tomorrow.* I hope Charlie brings the boys over too. I'm kind of glad I won't be there. It's really up to Charlie and Jane to do the right thing now and keep harmony in the family.

Jack dozed off and dreamed about his mother and father. Before leaving the apartment, Jack had taken the Chicago World's Fair Pin from the cigar box and packed it in the suitcase. In this dream, he had visions of his parents at the fair witnessing the birth of electricity and other marvels that are now taken for granted. *What an exciting time to have lived in*, he thought. If he had a chance, Jack planned to visit the old fair grounds and kind of retrace his parents' steps.

The vaudeville theater in downtown Chicago had a fresh new look, but Jack later learned it was really from renovations, some of which were ongoing in the attached hotel. Jack checked in and went to check out his room. It was adequate with a double bed, chair and table, and a good-sized individual bathroom. Jack remembered staying one time in a hotel where the bathrooms were placed in between the rooms and each room had a door accessing the bathroom. When using such bathrooms, you locked the door on your neighbor's side, thereby preventing an unexpected intrusion. Jack's unpleasant experience was his neighbor forgot to unlock Jack's door, thereby preventing his access to the bathroom.

He decided to walk outside for a bit and find a nice restaurant for his evening meal, then retire early. Returning to his room, Jack got directions to the nearest Catholic Church. His plan for Sunday was to go to Mass, have breakfast and visit the old fair site. Sunday brought rain. Jack managed to get to Mass, but the rest of the day was pretty much a washout.

About ten o'clock that evening, there was a loud *bam-bam* at Jack's door. Opening the door, he found a very frightened young lady in her nightgown.

"Please! Please help me! Somebody was in my room! I don't know what to do!"

Jack tried to calm the young lady with little success. He got her out of the hallway, and she finally settled down enough to answer some basic questions.

"Tell me what happened."

"I had just gone to bed! The door opened and this big man in dark clothes came in! I screamed and he ran! I don't know what to do!"

"Okay, settle down. You're safe now. Did you have your door locked?"

"I don't know! I think so! It doesn't work right all of the time! I called the desk last week and they said they would fix it. But it still doesn't work right. What am I going to do? I don't know what to do!"

Picking up the chair in his room, Jack attempted to demonstrate to the young lady how she could prop the chair under the door handle in her room and effectively prevent the door from opening.

Waving her arms in the air, she continued her frightened ramblings, "I can't do that! What if it doesn't work? I won't be able to sleep! I don't know what to do! Can't you please help me?"

Jack grabbed hold of each of her wrists and planted a heavy kiss on her lips.

"What did you do that for?"

"Well, I couldn't think of any other way to get you to stop talking. Do you feel better now?"

"I do, but I can't go back to that room."

"Okay, you can stay here for a while."

"Listen, Mister, I really need to get some sleep. What's your name?"

"My name is Jack and you can trust me. My door lock works fine. So here's what we are going to do. I have a double size bed, so you are going to sleep on one side and I will be on the other. We'll get this thing straightened out with the hotel first thing tomorrow morning."

"Okay, Jack, but no fooling around or I'll scream so loud that the whole hotel will be in here."

As they both gingerly positioned themselves in the bed, the young lady asked, "Where did you learn to kiss like that?"

"It's a long story. Just go to sleep."

"Okay, but just give me a gentle good night kiss. Your kiss really calms me down."

Jack gently kissed the young lady and said, "Thanks for that comment. Most women want a kiss to excite them. Now, no more talking and try to get some sleep."

With the lights out in the room, there was just a sliver of light coming from the almost-closed window drapes. He looked at the young lady next to him. She had fallen asleep almost immediately. Her face was really quite attractive. I wonder who she is. I wish I could tell Lorie that I found a woman who tells me my kisses have a calming effect. He gently rolled away from the young woman, almost to the edge of the mattress. He thought, *If I accidently touch against her in my sleep, she probably will scream and bring the whole hotel here.*

When Jack awoke the next morning, the young lady was gone. He wondered if she was all right. She probably returned to her room at daybreak. He thought, *I should go check on her, but I don't really know which room she came from and I don't know her name. So I can't ask the desk what room she is staying in.* Jack had to meet with the show producer at nine o'clock, so he busied himself shaving and dressing. He didn't know how long the meeting would be and he wanted to get some breakfast before the meeting. Maybe the young mysterious lady would be in the hotel dining room. There were only a few people in the hotel dining room. Most were dressed in suits and looked like businessmen. Jack ordered bacon and eggs with coffee. He was about halfway through his breakfast when a gentleman approached his table.

"Are you Jack Smith?"

"Yes, I am."

"I'm George Finn, the producer. Do you mind if I join you?"

"Not at all, Mr. Finn, please sit down."

"I know our meeting isn't until nine, but I wanted to get a cup of coffee and a quick bite to eat. Do you mind talking business here at the table?"

"Go right ahead, sir."

"Well, your agent probably told you about the bind we are in for the second performance segment of our show. I thought about canceling the second segment, but our audiences are pretty smart and will certainly feel as if they are being cheated. Do you mind if I call you Jack?"

"No, not at all."

"Well, Jack, I've actually heard you over the radio. So, when your agent said he might be able to send you to help out, I was very excited. Is there any possibility that you can stay longer than one week?"

"No, I'm sorry, sir, but I have a contract with the radio broadcasting station in New York."

"Okay, I understand. At least I'll have some time to line up someone else for the remainder of our shows. After we finish here, we'll walk over to the theater so you can see the setup. Can you think of anything you will need?"

"As long as you have a piano and a microphone, I'm all set. Just give me the cues to enter and to wrap up."

They walked over to the theater and Jack found the arrangement to be to his satisfaction. Jack asked Mr. Finn what time he wanted him to report behind the stage. The first segment started at six o'clock, so Mr. Finn's response was to just be backstage before six. They shook hands and parted. Jack thought that maybe he had time to visit the old fair grounds, but when he stepped outside of the hotel, it was raining again. Back in the lobby, he picked up a newspaper and a magazine and returned to his room thinking maybe he would write a letter to his mother. She loved receiving mail.

Jack was backstage by five forty-five. There was a beehive of activity underway. He learned that the first performance was by a comic. *Well, that's good*, he thought. Stan had told him it was bad to have a comedian follow your performance. I'll bet Stan checked this all out before booking me. It sure is good to have a sharp agent. Finally, the Master of Ceremonies located Jack and went over the specifics of his introduction.

"I will say, 'And now ladies and gentlemen, all the way from New York City, you have probably heard his golden voice on your radio, it is my pleasure to present Whispering Jack Smith.' I will turn and move my arm toward you. At that point, you enter, move to center stage, bow, and then move to the piano. Any questions?"

"Yes, is there a cue for me to wrap up?"

"I will be in the wing opposite you. You will see me raise both arms with my palms open and facing you, that's your wrap up cue. If you don't see me or if I raise one arm with my finger pointing up and continue to move it in a circle, that means we are having some kind of difficulty and to keep on playing. Your exit will be back to center stage, bow, and then move to my position in the wing."

"Okay, I'll see you on stage."

Jack's performance was flawless. He went through a series of songs before pausing to ask the audience if they recognized the melodies. He would play a few notes and sing a few lines of the previous series until he heard someone in the audience identify the music. At that point, Jack would tell the audience something about the particular selection, just as he did on his radio broadcasts. The audience loved it. Once he had the audience engaged, he asked if anyone had a request. The spotlight gave him some difficulty locating individuals in the audience, but overall, the interaction with the audience went very well. His performance was frequently laced with applause. After playing three or four requests, the Master of Ceremonies appeared in the wing with his arms raised and palms open. Jack ended the song he was playing and thanked the audience for their appreciation. He moved to center stage, bowed, and then headed to the wing. The audience stood and the applause grew louder. The Master of Ceremonies signaled for quiet, but obviously they wanted a curtain call, so he asked if they would like to hear Jack play one more number. The applause was nearly deafening. The assistants in the wing ushered Jack back to the opening and asked him to return to the stage. Things quieted down when Jack reached the piano. Jack told the audience that he had been working with a song writer on a new song entitled "Cecilia" and this would be the first time it was performed for an audience.

"This song is dedicated to a French nurse who cared for me at a hospital in the Great War. Before the war ended, she was moved very close to the front lines. I never found out if she lived through it all. Her name is Cecilia and I still pray for her every day. I hope you like it."

At the end of "Cecilia", there was another deafening, standing ovation. Jack waved in appreciation to the audience, bowed several times, and exited. *Wow! I don't remember ever having such a spirited reception.* As he passed backstage, the personnel there repeatedly congratulated Jack. He was anxious to get some breathing room, so he made his way to the room in the hotel. He sat for a moment to reflect on his performance, said a quick prayer of thanks and changed out of his tuxedo. Next, Jack headed for the hotel lobby. It was no longer raining, so he decided to find a restaurant someplace nearby on the street. It felt good to be out in the open air.

His mind wandered as he walked. He wished his mother and maybe Lorie could have been there to see his performance. He thought about Cecilia and wondered what had happened to her. He found a nice-looking restaurant that did not seem crowded. Jack went in and had a light meal before heading back to the hotel. It was close to eleven o'clock and the hotel was very quiet. He enjoyed a nice warm bath and had just slipped into his pajamas when, *bam-bam*, the same knock came at his door. He quickly put on his robe and answered the door. Jack wasn't surprised to find the same young mysterious lady outside of his door. This time she was calm, fully dressed, and holding an overnight bag behind her back.

"Well, hello, Bam-Bam. I was wondering what happened to you."

"Hello, Jack, I came to apologize about last night and to thank you for being so understanding and helpful."

"Listen, I was glad to be of help, but you left without telling me, and I was rather concerned about you this morning. Come in out of the hallway."

"Jack, I just finished working and I dread the thought of sleeping in that room again. Can I impose upon you one more time to stay here? I felt so safe last night and had my best night's sleep for quite a while."

"Okay, Bam-Bam, but you have to promise me you won't scream out in the middle of the night if I accidently touch up against you. I kept waking up last night thinking I might be too close to you."

"Why do you call me Bam-Bam?"

"I'm sorry. I don't know your name and I guess I identify you to the noise you make knocking at my door. Where is your room anyway?"

"My room is one down to the left on the opposite side of the hall. Is it all right if I get cleaned up in your bathroom and change into my sleepwear?"

"Sure, help yourself."

Jack had not yet written to his mother, so he thought this would be a good time. From his experience, women took a very long time bathing and fixing themselves up. He was kind of glad he had not written earlier because he could now tell his mother about his first night's performance. He had just finished the letter and was addressing the envelope when Bam-Bam returned from the bathroom.

"Were you writing to someone?"

"Yes, my mother."

"Where does she live?"

"She lives in New York City. Have you ever been there?"

"Oh yes, many times."

"What is your job, Bam-Bam?"

"I work with the vaudeville group over at the theater. What do you do, Jack?"

"I'm working over at the theater also."

"Jack, did you happen to hear the singer in the second act? The way he enunciated all of the lyrics and rolled his *R*'s was truly marvelous. And he was so knowledgeable about all of the songs. I was backstage and couldn't see him, but tomorrow I'm going to try to find a place out by the audience to watch some of his performance."

"Yeah, I thought he was pretty good. I understand he does a radio broadcast from New York City. Listen, would you be interested in going with me tomorrow to see a part of Chicago where the World's Fair was held back in 1893?"

"Sure, I don't have anything to do until the evening performance. What's at the old World's Fair location that interests you?"

"I'm really not sure what's there now. My parents were there at the time of the fair, and they have told me so many stories about the things they saw back in those days. It's just something I would like to do. Here, look at this. It's a pin my mother gave me."

Jack passed his mother's pin. It was almost as big as a silver dollar with letters seemingly suspended from the inner circle that read: World's Columbian Exposition Chicago 1893. There was a cutout of Columbus's sailing ship set in the center above a globe with the year 1492 attached.

"Oh, this is beautiful, Jack. So this World's Fair was in honor of the four hundredth anniversary of Columbus discovering America."

"Yes. And the interesting thing is that so many inventions were on display. My parents talked about demonstrations of electricity, horseless carriages, steam engines, building innovations and many other things that we take for granted today. I'm pretty sure some of the buildings are still standing, and there is probably a display in one of them with photos and paintings of the fair. Okay, let's go to bed and remember you promised not to scream if I accidently touch you."

"Yes, Jack, and can I have one of those gentle good night kisses?"

"Okay." After a pause, Jack says, "I think you were kissing me back that time."

"No, I wasn't. Well, maybe a little bit. Go to sleep and thanks again for putting up with me."

The next morning, they had breakfast together and then traveled by taxi to the old fair site. The cab driver was pretty familiar with the site and gave them some tips about where to start and what to look for. It seemed that there was a building that served as a museum where many of the original items from the fair were on display. The driver said there might be a small charge for admission. Jack thoroughly enjoyed walking about the site and Bam-Bam rather enjoyed being in Jack's company. She wondered what his job was at the theater, and then dismissed the thought as not being important. After about an hour at the site, they were walking side by side when Bam-Bam gently reached over and held Jack's hand. It was very natural for both of them, almost like they had been friends for a very long time. The displays and pictures inside of the museum proved to be of interest to both of them. This time as they moved about, Jack reached out gently to hold her hand. When they reached the end of the wall of the photos and paintings they had been looking at, Jack reached over for her other hand. Holding both hands and turning Bam-Bam to be directly in front of him, he just looked at her for a moment.

"What, what are you looking at, Jack?"

"I'm looking at you. You certainly are a very pretty young lady. In all of the excitement the past two days, I guess I never took the time to really look at you. Are you going to tell me your real name yet, or do I have to continue to go on calling you Bam-Bam?

"Not yet, Jack. When the time is right, I promise to tell you. Besides, I kind of like Bam-Bam."

"Okay, let's find a place to have some late lunch and then head back. I have to be in the theater before six."

At the hotel, Bam-Bam gathered her things from Jack's room and moved to the door.

"Thank you for a wonderful day, Jack. I really, really enjoyed being with you."

"Thanks for coming along. I enjoyed your company also. Maybe we can do something tomorrow."

"Tomorrow is no good for me. I have to be in the theater when rehearsal is going on."

"Well, stop by my room tonight. I'll leave the door open, so you don't even have to knock."

"Thanks, Jack. I'll be here."

Jack's second performance was every bit as good as the first. There was another curtain call, and this time there were calls from the audience for him to sing his new song, "Cecilia". *Jack thought, News about new songs sometimes travels fast.* After finishing "Cecilia", Jack followed his routine to get a light diner and then retire to his room. In the bathtub, he wondered if it was smart to have had left the door unlocked. It was still a little early, so he put the thought out of his mind and enjoyed the hot bath. He decided to shave before bed. *I guess I want to make a good impression on Bam-Bam if she shows up.* Dressed in his pajamas and robe, he stretched out on the bed, going back over the events of the day in his mind. *Today was a very good day*, he thought, and then dozed off. He didn't hear the door to his room open, and then suddenly there was a gentle slap to his cheek. It was Bam-Bam.

"What was that for?"

"You know what! Why didn't you tell me you're 'Whispering' Jack Smith? I feel like such a jerk."

"Come here. I'm sorry."

Jack reached up and put his arms around her, pulling Bam-Bam into the bed and kissing her very hard. This time she definitely kissed back.

"Wow! That kiss kind of makes up for it. When are you going to tell where you learned to kiss like that?"

"Not until you tell me your name."

"Okay, Jack. My name is Peggy, Peggy O'Neil."

"Not 'Sweet' Peggy O'Neil, the singer and actress in the main performance? I should have known. I just knew there was something familiar about you. The day I first arrived here I was looking at your poster outside of the theater. Now I feel like the big jerk."

They both laughed and embraced while exchanging kisses. Peggy told Jack she was definitely staying with him for the night, and to please not fall asleep while she got cleaned up in the bathroom.

The rest of the week flew by. Peggy and Jack spent as much time as possible together. Jack thought being with Peggy was so much different than being with Lorie. He enjoyed every minute with Peggy. There was no pretense in front of people. They had so much in common to talk about. Jack felt a growing attachment toward Peggy and sensed that she felt the same way. Near the end of the week, they discussed the future. Jack was returning to New York City; Peggy had two more weeks with the Peg O' My Heart production in Chicago and then she was booked for an engagement in New York City. Perfect, all they had to do was to wait for two weeks and they would be able to see each other again. Jack gave Peggy his address and phone number, telling her his Manhattan apartment had two bedrooms and she was most welcome to stay there. She teased that she would be afraid to stay in one of his bedrooms by herself. She wanted to know his broadcasting schedule, and promised to call him every day. On Jack's last day in Chicago, they arranged with the hotel to switch rooms so Peggy would have a door that always locked.

And then Jack found himself on the train heading back to New York City. He had pleasant dreams on the return trip, and as the train drew close to New York City, he took a small piece of paper from his pocket, drew an "X" across it and attached it to the World's Fair Pin. He thought, *This one goes back into the cigar box, mission completed.*

PEGGY MEETS THE FAMILY

Peggy came to Jack's apartment on a Saturday morning early in April of 1924. Jack signed her in as a continuing visitor under the name of P. O'Neil, hoping that her celebrity status would remain unknown. Peggy just loved the apartment. She said her clothes would be in the second bedroom, but she preferred sleeping in the first. They spent the first afternoon together at the piano playing and singing songs together until hunger pangs set in.

"Come on, we'll go over to my country club and have dinner. When do you start work?"

"Well, we don't open for another two weeks, but we have some new cast members, so there will be a rehearsal Monday afternoon and probably every afternoon through the first week."

"That's just great. We should have a lot of time together. I want to show you around and get you to meet some of my family. Are you ready for that?"

"I would love that, Jack."

Just as in Chicago, they thoroughly enjoyed every minute of the time they shared together. Jack made arrangements with his mother to have a family dinner at her house for the following Saturday. Everyone indicated that they would be there except his brother. He was still tied up at the garden, but said he could possibly get away to meet Jack for lunch on Saturday at the Aqua Delight. When Jack told him he was bringing a lady friend, Charles responded that he would definitely meet him for lunch. They settled on a time of twelve o'clock, which in all probability meant his brother's fiancée would not be there to meet Peggy. The big surprise was the news that Charles, Jr. now had a lady friend and he was bringing her on Saturday to dinner.

Jack and Peggy arrived at the Aqua Delight around eleven forty-five on Saturday morning. Charles was not in sight, so they settled in at the bar to await his arrival. They both ordered glasses of ginger ale. Peggy knew that Jack did not drink alcoholic beverages and was thankful for it. She had seen her share of lushes around show business who literally destroyed their careers because of their drinking. Peggy did not exclude alcohol and occasionally enjoyed a glass of wine or a mixed drink.

"Peggy, in the evenings they actually have mermaids swimming across this fish tank. In fact, my brother is going to marry one of the fishes."

"You're kidding me, aren't you?"

Jack went on to tell Peggy more about his brother, his brother's family, the loss of his wife, and his involvement with work at Madison Square Garden.

"You know, Jack, sometimes I'm not sure if you are putting me on."

At that point, Charles arrived and moved over to the bar. Jack introduced Peggy and they moved to a table at the back of the restaurant. Charles didn't know that Peggy was "Sweet" Peggy O'Neil, the singer and actress, and Jack left it that way. He wanted his brother to meet the woman, not the actress. They got along just fine. Charles filled them in on his wedding plans. He had recently bought the house out in Valley Stream and his fiancée was living there now. The wedding date had been set for the first Saturday in June. After the wedding, Milt would stay at their Bronx home and pay the rent. Charles Jr. was to move in with his grandmother. The boys had been out to Valley Stream and loved the house. They had met Jane and were okay with their father remarrying. If all went as planned, Milt and Jean would be married late in June. They planned to stay in the Bronx house for a while and eventually find a place of their own.

Peggy talked about her upbringing in Buffalo. Jack learned some things about Peggy that he had not been aware of. Her father left home before she ever knew him, and her mother died when she was in school. Her mother's sister looked after Peggy. She actually was an orphan attending Saint Patrick's Catholic School in the Buffalo Diocese. Jack thought, How in the world did this young lady rise to stardom? I'm going to have to pry more out of her later.

Following lunch, Charles, having learned that Peggy had never been in the garden, offered a short tour. Peggy was impressed with the building and the preparations being made for the National Democratic Convention. As they walked through the building, Charles was interrupted twice by workers seeking direction on their work tasks. Jack sensed their visit was interfering with his brother's work, so he told his brother they really had to go. They exchanged pleasantries and headed for the exit close to the Aqua Delight.

"He really is very busy with his job. Sometime after the convention is over, I'll bring you back here and we can spend some time with Charles touring the old building. He knows every nook and cranny inside of the place and a lot of the history about the building and the events held there."

"I would like that, Jack. What shall we do now?"

"I think we should return to the apartment, have a nice afternoon nap and then freshen up for our evening dinner at my mother's house. And by the way, you told Charles things that I never knew about you."

"Well, sweetheart, my grand plan is for you and me to take a trip to Buffalo sometime in the near future, and I promise I will tell you everything there is to know about me before we get there."

"Okay, that's a deal."

Peggy enjoyed riding through the Bronx to Jack's mother's house. She commented on how well-built the homes were, and she liked the fact that all of the houses had large front porches. The streets were very orderly and clean. Jack told her that the residents were very proud of their neighborhood and sometimes even gathered together to clean the streets and sidewalks. It was a nice sunny day, and Jack's mother was sitting out on the porch when they pulled up and parked in front of the house. Jack and Peggy exited the Chalmers and climbed the steps to the porch. His mother seemed very excited and was now standing awaiting an introduction. Jack seldom brought friends home.

"Hello, Mom. I want you to meet a very good friend of mine, Peggy O'Neil."

"Hello, Peggy, it is such a pleasure to meet you. I am a very big fan of yours and have been following your career for years. Come, let's go into the house."

As they entered the house, Jack thought, *Now how did Mom instantly recognize Peggy as the actress and singer?*

"Mom, I want to ask a favor of you. When the others arrive, please don't let on that Peggy is Peggy O'Neil the actress. And how did you know?"

"Being around the music business all of these years, how could I not know who 'Sweet' Peggy O'Neil is. Her pictures are displayed in many of the music stores and even on some music sheet jackets. And Peggy, you are even more beautiful than your pictures. Why don't you want the others to know?"

"Thank you, Mrs. Schmidt, and I must tell you that you have done a wonderful job in training Jack to play the piano. Jack just feels that should I be introduced to your grandsons as an actress, most of the conversation will be about me and we really want to learn about them."

Mrs. Schmidt responds, "Fair enough, but you won't be able to hide your identity very long."

Peggy was helping Jack's mother in the kitchen when the others arrived. Jean looked pretty as ever, and the young lady with Charles Jr. was also very well dressed and attractive. Jack called for his mother and Peggy to come from the kitchen. They were there in a moment and introductions were made all around. Charles' new lady friend's name was Mamie and she was originally from Allentown, Pennsylvania, but now working in New York City. Mamie had an accent quite different from the way New Yorkers spoke, but also very nice.

"Jack, see if you can get anyone a glass of soda or iced tea while Peggy and I handle things in the kitchen. Dinner will be ready in about fifteen minutes."

Once back in the kitchen, Mrs. Schmidt asked Peggy if she was performing in New York City.

"Yes, we are rehearsing with new cast members now and should open next weekend at the Astor Theater."

"Which show is it going to be, Peggy?"

"It will be *Peg O' My Heart* which was very popular in Chicago. I hope the New York audience receives it as well."

"Well, I'm going to see if I can get Jack to take me to see you."

"I'll work on him too. Between the two of us and a couple of free tickets from me, we should be able to get you there."

"Thank you, Peggy. I'm so thrilled to have you here in my house. It's going to be hard to not slip up and let the others know who you really are. Okay, let's put the food out. You take those two big platters and I will bring the rest."

The others had moved to the front porch to see Jack's car and enjoy the beautiful day. When they were all back inside and seated at the table, Jack's mother lead them in grace and then they started to pass the platters around the table. It was a simple meal consisting of meatloaf, mashed potatoes, carrots, and fresh baked biscuits. The food was delicious and very elegantly presented on the serving platters. They talked about Milt and Jean's wedding plans. Milt and Jean were still not sure if approval from the church would be given in time, and because the church review was so costly, they were not having a reception and probably would not go on a honeymoon. All were concerned, but Jean dismissed the subject by simply saying to get married was the most important thing and everything else would be taken care of in time. Jack made a mental note to explain to Peggy later about Jean's father being deceased and her family being very poor. Charles and Mamie were very upbeat and pleasant. Mamie worked as a sales clerk at Macy's Women's Department.

From the way she was dressed, Mamie obviously was very good at her position. Charles' position with the railroad was now permanent and he seemed to be very happy with his employment. When they finished eating, Mrs. Schmidt asked the ladies to help bring the dishes to the kitchen. She told the men to relax on the porch, and once things were cleaned up they would call them back to the table for homemade chocolate cake and coffee. After a short time, Mrs. Schmidt and Mamie carried the cake and desert dishes to the table. Jean and Peggy were to follow with coffee, coffee cups, and saucers.

Jean whispered to Peggy, "You're Peggy O' Neil the actress, aren't you?"

"Yes, I am, Jean, but please don't tell the others. Jack wanted everyone to just meet me as I am. How did you know?"

"Oh, Peggy, you are so beautiful and refined, I just knew. Can I tell Milt later after we leave?"

"I think it will be all right then. Everyone is going to find out eventually. Mrs. Schmidt knew right away and promised not to 'let the cat out of the bag' this evening. Okay, we better get this coffee out to the table."

They spent another hour at the table, mostly talking this time about Charles' and Jane's new home and their wedding plans. Everyone was not aware that Jack was going to be the best man. Jack got a lot of congratulations and some kidding about whether or not he would sing at the wedding. Jack promised to have a toast prepared that he would sing rather than speak. It was just a great evening together. Peggy thoroughly enjoyed herself and was glad Jack kept her actress identity a secret, at least for a little while.

On the way back to the apartment, Peggy said that it was just terrible that Milt and Jean were having so much difficulty with their wedding plans. Jack explained that some time back, her father had a fall from a new building that he was working on and died a short time after as a result of the injuries. He told Peggy that Milt and Jean both had good jobs, but with the church's dispensation investigation being very costly and Jean's mother needing some financial support, they really didn't have many other options.

"She is really a wonderful young lady, Jack. When we were in the kitchen, she told me she knew I was Peggy O'Neil, the actress, and promised not to tell the others. I told her it was okay to tell Milt on their way home. Maybe we can figure out some way to help them."

"Maybe, but first let's see what time brings. I have next week off from the radio station. What does your schedule look like?"

"I should be off until our final rehearsal on Friday evening. Now that I have met your family, would you like to ride up to Buffalo with me and see where I grew up? We can leave late tomorrow or Monday and return to be here not later than Friday afternoon."

"That sounds good to me. I'll tell the agency to keep my schedule clear and check the train schedules. It will probably take twelve to fifteen hours. Would you like to go overnight if I can get a sleeping compartment?"

BUFFALO, NEW YORK

Jack arranged for a sleeping compartment on the train departing Penn Station at nine fifteen in the evening and arriving at the Exchange Street Station in Buffalo at twelve thirty Monday afternoon. Peggy had used the New York Central several times and was happy to have a sleeping compartment. Otherwise, it was a long time to sit in a coach. The return would get them into Penn Station Friday morning around ten, so Peggy would have plenty of time to get ready for rehearsal.

Sunday turned out to be a beautiful day. Jack and Peggy went to Mass at his mother's church, but did not find any of Jack's family there. They decided to go for brunch at the country club. While driving to the country club, Jack attempted to give Peggy strict instructions to pack light, as they were only going to bring one suitcase. Of course, he was fighting a losing battle. At the club, Peggy became rather serious.

"Jack, do you remember when I told that before we got to Buffalo, I would tell you all about my past?" Jack nodded affirmatively. "Well, I think I should start now. There is quite a bit you should know."

Peggy asked Jack if he remembered her saying she was an orphan at a very young age and her mother's sister helped to raise her. Jack remembered and told Peggy so. Peggy continued on, asking Jack if he remembered her talking about Saint Patrick's School in Buffalo. Again Jack remembered and nodded.

"Well, I was fortunate to get parts in the school plays at Saint Patrick's. In a short period of time, I starred in all of the school plays. My mother died when I was in school, but my aunt looked out for me and insisted that I continue my education at Saint Patrick's. I will forever be indebted to my aunt for what she did for me. Without her help and support, I would not have made it to the theater."

Peggy hesitated for a minute and then went on, "Before I became a well-known performer, I fell in love with and married a handsome young man who worked in a family run carriage repair business. Our first year together was perfect. Then I began to get offers for minor roles in various theatre productions away from our home. I had a supporting part in a musical comedy playing for several weeks in nearby Rochester, New York. The last week of the show was cancelled without notice. I immediately headed back to Buffalo, and upon entering our house, I found my husband in bed with one of the girls from the carriage repair business. I was horrified! I screamed and left the house, never to return. My aunt let me stay with her for a few days. She even went to my house and gathered personal belongings for me. Three days after finding my husband like that, I visited a local lawyer and instructed him to negotiate an immediate divorce. I was making good money, and my agent had told me I would be making much more in the near future. So I simply told the lawyer that I had no interest in the house, its contents, or any support from my husband. He kind of cautioned me against following that action, but went ahead and finalized the divorce as I had requested. It was clean and easy. I had no real ties to Buffalo, so I hit the road with one performance following another. It felt good to be free, and I didn't miss my husband one little bit. The only question that still bothers me to this day is, What did I do to deserve his infidelity?"

"Peggy, what your husband did was inexcusable. You should never blame yourself for his actions. In a way, he did you a favor. By being cut free from him, you were given the liberty to advance in your career and become a star."

"Oh, I don't know. I was really kind of lucky, Jack. My big break was in Chicago a few years ago when I was unexpectedly given the lead in *Peg O' My Heart*. I poured my heart and soul into the show and have been at the top ever since. Did you know I've also had several parts in the movies? My agent has me lined up to do two more this year. Movies are fun to do, but I really prefer the theater."

"I hate to ask you this, Peggy, but how old are you?"

"My birthday is coming up soon. I was born on June 16, 1894. But for professional reasons, I sometimes give my birth year as 1898. Now turnabout is fair play. How old are you Jack?"

"I'll be twenty six on the thirty first of May. Maybe we can celebrate our birthdays together. And I guess it's time for me to come clean. I promised to tell you about how I learned to kiss and make love. The woman I occasionally spent time with was about twenty years older than I am."

Jack went on to tell Peggy about Lorie Bradford and how she took an interest in his career after seeing his performance in a piano bar. As Jack told his story, he eventually described Lorie swimming without a bathing suit in the estate pool and asking him to bring a towel to dry her as she exited the pool. When Jack stated he didn't know Lorie was swimming naked, Peggy exclaimed, "I'll bet. What man would not know that a naked woman was in front of him?"

"Well, it was kind of dark and I wasn't thinking about romance or anything."

Jack continued on, finally telling Peggy about how he and Lorie broke up and stressed how happy he was when Peggy entered into his life.

"Well, Jack, it sounds like you have a little bit of a gigolo in you. But I must say, I really do love you, Jack. You have brought happiness into my life that I have never known before. And now that we have both explained our past years, let's go back to the apartment and make love as we look forward to our future together. We have several hours to kill before heading to Penn Station, and don't think you're going to sleep all of the way to Buffalo."

Later, they headed off with two suitcases to Penn Station where Jack signaled for a Red Cap to take the bags. Their compartment was suitable, much better than coach seats. After getting situated, Jack asked if Peggy would like to go to the dining car for a bite to eat. They ordered sandwiches and sodas and then took in the scenery as the train traveled toward the northern parts of New York. Peggy said the clickity-clack noise from the rails always made her sleepy and she appeared to be anxious to return to the compartment.

Back in the compartment, Jack readied the bed while Peggy changed into her sleepwear. Jack expected that she would be sound asleep in less than five minutes. Two hours later, he realized she meant what she said earlier when she told him not to think about sleeping all of the way to Buffalo. Jack felt something very special about this woman. He thought, *So this is what love really is all about. But I wonder if we can really make it work. With our careers, we will often be traveling in different directions and working different hours. Oh well, as I advise others, we should wait for a while and see what the passing of time brings.* Jack dozed off and only remembered the conductor announcing arrivals at Albany and Syracuse before he felt Peggy gently shaking him awake. She was completely dressed and looking very pretty. Peggy gave Jack a gentle kiss and asked if he would like to go along to the dining car for some coffee and breakfast before they arrived at the Buffalo Station.

"Sure, sweetheart, just give me a few minutes to freshen up and put some clothes on."

There were not many passengers in the dining car. They ordered breakfast with juice and coffee. The scenery was just magnificent in the early daylight. Peggy described to Jack how things changed dramatically in the winter months when the heavy snowfalls hit the area. She pointed out some of the vineyards along the way and stated that the New York wines were building quite a nice reputation for taste and quality. Jack talked about how he had walked past the vineyards over in France when he was at the hospital recuperating from being gassed. Peggy asked some questions about the war and about the effects of being gassed.

"War is horrible, Peggy. I was only in action for a short while before the Germans put gas on us. My mask malfunctioned and I picked up traces of the gas smell. My squad leader told me exactly what to do and where to go. I owe him dearly for that. Initially, I lost my voice. I don't think my lungs were damaged at all and my voice slowly returned. The armistice was signed while I was still at the hospital, and I was almost immediately shipped back home. But, Peggy, some of the things I saw in the hospital were just terrible. I hope I never have to experience war again."

"Do you think it affected your singing voice?"

"Maybe a little bit. I was singing with a quartet in the Bronx before going into the army. I probably don't have as much volume as I had then, but with the use of a microphone, I think I'm actually much better now."

"Next stop Buffalo," the conductor called out.

They returned to their compartment and placed the remaining items into the suitcases. Jack asked Peggy if she knew how far away the Statler Hotel was. She knew it was pretty close, but thought they should use a taxi.

"The hotel should be nice, Peggy. It just opened last year."

"I did hear about the construction. It should be very close to Niagara Square."

The taxi ride was only minutes, and they found the hotel to be a magnificent high rise comparable to those in New York City. At the room, Jack tipped the bellboy while Peggy started to unpack the suitcases and organize things. Peggy informed Jack that she was going for a nice hot bath before they started out on their day in Buffalo.

"If it's a big tub, leave the door open and call me when the water is ready."

As they took turns washing each other's backs, Peggy suggested they attempt to hire a driver for the day so that she would be able to show him some of the highlights of Buffalo.

"Jack, did you know that the Jenny airplane flown in the Great War was manufactured right here in Buffalo at the Curtiss Aeroplane and Motor Company. My uncle works there. And you know those beautiful Pierce Arrow automobiles we see once in a while, they are built here also. We can visit both companies if you like. I think they have displays and tours for visitors."

"I would like that, but don't you want to visit your aunt?"

"Yes, I think we can do that later this afternoon or tomorrow. I also want to stop by Saint Patrick's School for a short visit. The school and my aunt's house are in the same neighborhood." As Jack finished drying Peggy with the hotel towel, she commented, "Okay, that's enough. If you keep on doing that we will end up right back in bed."

Jack called the hotel desk and inquired about hiring a car and driver for the day. The clerk said he would call back in a few minutes and when he did, Jack was informed that the driver would meet them in the lobby in thirty minutes. They went to the Curtiss factory first. There was a Jenny on display inside of the factory. Peggy asked if Jack had ever seen one over in France.

"Maybe. I saw several planes in the sky, but they were pretty far away and all kind of looked alike."

There was a short tour, so they decided to go through the factory. Their driver, George, joined them on the tour. George knew a lot about the Curtiss factory and filled in a lot of facts the tour guide did not cover. It was amazing to see airplanes being built kind of on an assembly line. After the tour, George drove them to the Pierce Arrow Automobile Plant. At Pierce Arrow, there was a spectacular showroom filled with both old and new Pierce Arrows. They were very expensive automobiles. Perhaps that's why Peggy and Jack liked them so much. There were no factory tours offered, but there was a large window on one side of the showroom where the assembly of new cars could be observed.

It was well past lunch time at this point, so they asked George for his recommendations. One of the places George suggested was close to Saint Patrick's, so they agreed to go there. The name of the restaurant was McKenna's. Like many of the establishments, beer and alcoholic drinks were available. Jack invited George to join them. They all passed on alcohol and settled for sodas and three corned beef special sandwiches, which George had highly recommended. The sandwiches came with chips and dill pickle slices. The food was excellent. George tactfully verified that Peggy was Peggy O'Neil the actress, and then asked when she was going to give a performance in Buffalo. Peggy's response was not this trip, but maybe in the near future. She asked George about the Abbott, the Circle and the Sattler Theaters. Were they still open and for what kind of performances? Peggy was somewhat disappointed to learn that one of the theaters was now showing motion pictures only. Peggy asked George to drive past the theaters if they were close to the route they were taking.

After the late lunch, they headed for Saint Patrick's School. George parked and stayed with the car while Jack and Peggy entered the building. Peggy knew her way around and led Jack right to the Administrative Office. There were several people in the office. One was a priest. After a minute or two, they realized that they had visitors, one of whom was their own Peggy O'Neil. They all immediately moved to Peggy, and individually hugged her as they exchanged greetings. Almost as an afterthought, they stood aside giving Peggy the opportunity to introduce Jack as her good friend, Jack Smith. She didn't quite get away with the limited introduction, as one of the women sensed that Jack was also an entertainer and asked if he could be the "Whispering" Jack Smith whom they sometimes hear on the radio. Once Jack verified that indeed he was "Whispering" Jack Smith, all of the attention momentarily switched to him. Out of the corner of his eye, Jack could see Peggy taking the priest's arm and leading him slightly away where she then passed an envelope to him. Jack thought, *I'll bet there's a very nice donation inside of the envelope. He decided it was really her business and he would not ask about it.* They reminisced for almost an hour before Peggy stated that it was time for them to leave as she wanted to visit with her aunt. Peggy promised to let them know if her schedule brought her back to Buffalo to perform, and Jack promised to dedicate one of his radio broadcast songs to his friends in Buffalo.

Peggy gave George directions to her Aunt Cara's house on Front Avenue, and within a few minutes, they were parked in front of the house. Peggy led Jack up to the house and knocked.

"Oh my God, Peggy, it's so good to see you! You should let me know when you're coming."

"Aunt Cara, I want you to meet a very good friend of mine, Jack Smith."

"Hello, Jack. Thank you for bringing my little Peggy."

Aunt Cara called for them to come in and then disappeared into the kitchen while she continuously carried on a conversation with Peggy and Jack. In a very short time, she was back with a pitcher of iced tea, cookies, and glasses on a tray.

"There now, let's sit over here while I catch up with what you have been doing."

Peggy reviewed the shows and the cities where she performed over the last six months or so. Aunt Cara then wanted to know all about Jack. Peggy described Jack as a radio entertainer who played piano and sang songs that were broadcasted to many of the major cities, including Buffalo. Aunt Cara went for pencil and paper so she could write down the radio station identification and tuning band. She promised Jack she would listen for his broadcast. Aunt Cara said her husband was working the late shift and would not be home until after eight o'clock. She asked if they would like to stay for dinner. Peggy declined, telling her aunt that they had just enjoyed a great corned beef special at McKenna's and also had a driver waiting for them in the car outside. She told her aunt their plans were to go to Niagara Falls tomorrow, and should they have any time left in this short trip she would try to stop by for another visit.

Back in the car, Peggy asked George if buses still ran between Niagara Square and the Falls.

George told them he thought the buses ran about every hour starting around seven in the morning through about ten in the evening. He said the hotel clerk would have the bus schedule. George took a route back that went by the Circle Theater. When Peggy saw the theater, she asked George to stop. Peggy exited the car, telling both Jack and the driver that she would be back in a few minutes. She entered the theater and was gone for about ten minutes. Returning to the car, she told Jack and the driver how the theater had not changed at all since she last performed there. Peggy went on talking about her performance and how the theater was always packed. She said there were no better audiences than those right there in Buffalo. To Jack, it was obvious that this young actress thoroughly enjoyed performing in the theater. At the hotel, they both thanked George for a great job. Jack paid him and included a generous tip.

The next morning, they picked up the Niagara Falls bus schedule from the hotel desk and headed for the dining room to have breakfast. The buses did run on an hourly schedule, so they decided to just enjoy their breakfast and walk to Niagara Square for the next bus. The bus ride was only about thirty minutes. Jack had never seen the falls. Peggy had been to the falls several times, but still looked forward to seeing them again. Jack was amazed when the falls came into view.

"I can't believe how high they are. I've read about some of the people who went over in barrels, but never imagined how dangerous it must have been."

"Listen to the roar, Jack. Can you imagine how powerful that water is? I would love to go on the Maid of the Mist boat ride again. The boat goes behind the stream of water cascading over the falls. They will give us raincoats to keep dry. It is just spectacular to see everything up so close. What do you say?"

"Well, I guess you'll peg me a coward should I say 'No', so let's go for it."

The ride was just as Peggy had described it. They both got drenched with water, but for the most part, stayed dry under the raincoats. They hugged each other each time Peggy let out a little scream and then laughed until the next splash hit them. Following the boat ride, they decided to do the tour of the power generators close to the top of the falls. During this tour, Jack realized that the generation and distribution of electric power was why industry had blossomed throughout the nearby areas. On this tour, they had the option of departing the tour on the Canadian side of the falls. They decided to do so and have lunch in Canada. After lunch, Peggy headed straight for the shops. She really didn't shop for herself, but rather for her friends and associates. Jack decided to pick up a few souvenirs for his mother and two nephews.

"Peggy, stick to small items. There isn't much room in the suitcases."

"Oh, don't you worry, Jack. I always manage to find a way to bring things back."

It turned out to be just a perfect day for Jack and Peggy who were obviously very much in love with each other. They had no need to be aware of their celebrity status at the falls. No one even asked for an autograph. They flirted with each other and laughed, enjoying their surroundings to the fullest. They almost hated to return to the hotel and waited until the next to the last bus on the schedule arrived before heading back.

They slept in late on Wednesday. Every time Peggy got out of bed, Jack coaxed her back in. Jack imagined it was like being on a honeymoon. On Thursday morning, Peggy told Jack she was going to visit with her aunt for a few hours. She would go by taxi and be back for lunch. Then they would pack and get ready for the train ride back to New York City.

THE WEDDINGS

Time seemed to fly once Peggy and Jack returned to New York City. *Peg O' My Heart* at the Astor Theater was an instant hit with sellout audiences every performance. With Peggy working evenings and Jack days, they didn't have much time to share together. Jack often had dinner with his mother where he kept up with family news. Milt and Jean were to be married on the seventh of June. Jack's brother Charles was to be married on the twenty-eighth of June. It was going to be a busy month. Jack had his work schedule kept open for both wedding days and also for the week following Milt and Jean's wedding.

Jack's agent, Stan, called to ask Jack about the week he was keeping open following the first wedding. Stan had an opportunity to book him into the famous Ritz Carlton Hotel in Atlantic City for outstanding money. Jack told Stan he would give it some thought and get back to him the next day. When Peggy returned from her performance that evening, Jack talked about the Atlantic City offer.

"Peggy, if you can get off that same week, I have been thinking that we might be able to work something out to take Milt and Jean along with us, so they can have a meaningful honeymoon."

"You are a genius, Jack. I will definitely get the week off. You tell Stan that you will take the offer if he can negotiate two connecting suites at the Ritz Carlton, and throw in that 'Sweet' Peggy O'Neil is willing to give two or three guest appearances during your performances."

"Thank you, sweetheart. You know, you do so many nice things for me. Maybe that's why I love you so much. Wouldn't it be nice if we could get married?"

"Is that a proposal? No, I know my divorce is a big problem. Jack, in Buffalo on the day I went by myself to visit my aunt, I also stopped to see Father McNaulty at Saint Patrick's. He said I can try for an annulment and told me he would help me with submission of the paperwork."

"Well, that sounds great. The day the church approves it, I will be on my knees in front of you with the biggest diamond ring you have ever seen."

"Oh, honey, I love you so much. Okay, I'm going to write to Father McNaulty and see what can be done."

Stan had no trouble negotiating the Ritz Carlton performance. He told Jack that with the addition of Peggy's guest appearances, he was able to not only get two free connecting suites, but also more money for the package deal. He did caution Jack to have Peggy inform her agent as to what she was up to and to state that the guest appearances would be without compensation.

Jack eventually got in touch with Milt and told him about Atlantic City. He made Milt promise not to tell Jean until after the wedding and to just make sure that she took the week after the wedding off from work.

Milt and Jean were married early Saturday morning on the seventh of June. It was a small wedding on a gorgeous day, and Jean looked like a movie star in her wedding gown. Following the ceremony, which was performed in Milt's church, everyone was invited back to Jack's mother's house. She had been cooking and baking all week so that her grandson and Jean would have something like a reception. At the reception, Peggy and Jack gave Jean an envelope, insisting that she open it. Inside of the envelope was a printed invitation to stay for one week at the Ritz Carlton Hotel in Atlantic City. She first tried to share the news with her new husband, and then realizing that he already knew, she turned to Peggy and Jack with tears running down her cheeks and hugged each of them.

"Thank you. I don't know what to say. Thank you both so much."

Peggy responded, "Don't worry about a thing, Jean. Jack and I are going to be staying at the Ritz Carlton also. Just be sure to bring a bathing suit. We are going to have a good time together."

Milt asked Jack what time would they be leaving. Jack told them he had an eight o'clock performance, so he thought they should be on the road between two and three that afternoon. Jean was so excited she ran over to show her mother and brother the printed invitation. Her brother, Bill, offered to take Jean back to the house, so she could pack a suitcase.

The gathering at Mrs. Schmidt's house was very festive. Her son, Charles, had brought beer and wine. The food was all presented buffet style with the guests helping themselves. Because the weather was so nice, many of the guests moved out onto the front porch. Jack's Chalmers Six was all cleaned and polished for the occasion with a small streamer of tin cans tied to the back bumper. Milt's bag was already in the car. Jean was back just before two o'clock. Milt immediately took her suitcase and loaded it onboard the Chalmers. Milt and Jean then made their way about the guests until they had thanked them all. Sensing it was a good time to make a getaway, Jack started the Chalmers and playfully called out, "All aboard, next stop Atlantic City."

After driving several blocks, Jack pulled over and parked. Milt and Jack removed the trailer of noise making cans from the back of the car. Peggy exited the front seat and sat with Jean at the back.

"Let's let the men handle the driving and worrying about which roads to take. You and I will just enjoy the scenery along the way."

Peggy then went on to explain how Jack had them set up with adjoining suites. She talked about Jack's evening schedule and about her being a guest on stage for some of the shows. She told Jean that there would be plenty of time to enjoy the beach and the boardwalk.

"Oh, Peggy, this is like a dream come true. Milt and I will forever be indebted to you and Jack for making this all possible."

At the Ritz Carton, they quickly checked in and were shown to their suites. Both suites had windows overlooking the boardwalk and ocean. As Jack departed from Milt and Jean's suite, he said, "We'll get back together again in about two hours and decide about dinner." Then turning to Peggy, "They need some private time and I think we do too."

"I agree. I'm going for a nice refreshing bath. The door will be open."

The four of them ate in the Ritz Carlton dining room and then moved on to the ballroom. Jack went backstage for a short time. He returned with one of the managers who escorted them to a front row table just off to the side and close to the stairs leading up to the stage. Peggy, Jean, and Milt were seated and Jack once again went backstage. One of the shapely cocktail waitresses dressed in a very skimpy outfit brought a bottle of wine and said it was on the house. Shortly thereafter, the Master of Ceremonies moved to center stage from behind the right side of the curtain.

"Ladies and Gentlemen, tonight we have a couple of special treats for you. First, from New York City, the voice you have all heard over the radio, 'Whispering' Jack Smith, accompanied by our own RC Orchestra."

The orchestra began to play as the curtains were drawn open. There was a grand piano center stage. After about a minute of orchestra music, Jack entered from the right wing of the stage and moved to the piano. He acknowledged the applause and then picked up the microphone and began to engage the audience.

"How is your radio reception here in Atlantic City? I had trouble with mine in New York City. I live on the top floor of a high rise in Manhattan, and until last week, static continued to be a problem. I had several technicians look at my equipment to no avail, but then as luck would have it, I mentioned my dilemma to the elevator operator. The next day, he walked to my apartment with me and dropped a spool of wire out of a window and then hooked one end up to the radio. From that day on, my reception has been crystal clear. So for those of you living here at the Ritz Carlton, whenever you are having a problem, talk to your elevator operators."

Jack moved to the piano and started to play. After a minute or so, he stopped and asked the audience if anyone knew the name of the tune. He had the audience engaged and continued on playing and singing, sometimes with the RC orchestra and sometimes solo. He always added a lot of dialog about the history of the music and songs. The audience loved it, and the applause grew louder and louder. About halfway through his routine, Jack moved over to the orchestra leader and asked him to play "Sweet Peggy O'Neil". Next, he moved to the front of the stage and asked the audience to join in with the lyrics. With everyone singing, Jack moved to the side of the stage and then down to Peggy's table where he helped her with her chair as she stood and took his arm. The two of them climbed the stairs back onto the stage and moved close to the piano. At this point, Jack picked up his microphone and announced, "Ladies and Gentlemen, I am honored to present to you Miss Peggy O'Neil." The applause was deafening as the orchestra continued to play "Sweet Peggy O'Neil."

Jack and Peggy kidded back and forth about why she left Broadway for Atlantic City, and then settled into a short session of songs starting with "Peg O' My Heart". Jean's eyes were watery with tears of happiness. She had never seen such a performance, and to know the stars was just amazing. Milt was more composed, as he often chauffeured for Jack and had seen and heard many of his performances, just not from a front row table. Peggy returned to the table after about fifteen minutes, but the audience wouldn't settle for that and continued to stand applauding until Jack once again went to Peggy's side and escorted her back on stage for one more song.

The next day, Peggy and Jean were up early for a brisk walk on the boardwalk. Neither of them had ever been to Atlantic City, so it was fun to explore the multitude of shops and attractions along the boardwalk. They stopped for coffee and doughnuts at a small café near Steel Pier. Jean said she had read about Steel Pier and would like to go there on one of the evenings. Peggy talked about when she and Jack first met in Chicago. She explained to Jean about Jack wanting to go to the old Chicago World Fair Grounds and inviting Peggy to go along.

"I didn't know he was 'Whispering' Jack Smith and he didn't know I was Peggy O'Neil. We were just two people staying in the same hotel and working with the vaudeville group at the theater. He wanted to tour the old site because his parents had been there when it was open. There was a museum with photographs and artifacts that was very interesting. I remember a picture of the Ferris Wheel that looked very much like the one e saw on Steel Pier. The Chicago Ferris Wheel was described as being the first ever in the entire world. Before we leave Atlantic City, I'm going to ask Jack to take me on the Ferris Wheel."

"Well, I would love to do that also. I'll ask Milt."

After several hours, they returned to the hotel only to find the men still in bed. Peggy suggested they change into their swimsuits and tell the men they would be on the beach. Milt and Jack reluctantly got out of bed and promised to come to the beach after getting some breakfast. The weather was perfect. The ladies had rented two umbrellas and were thoroughly enjoying themselves stretched out on towels in the shade of the umbrellas. When Jack and Milt arrived, they talked briefly before the men walked to the edge of the water. Within minutes, they were back. Jack told them the ocean water was very cold. With the exception of several breaks to get food and drinks from the boardwalk vendors, they spent most of the day on the beach. Peggy had the evening off, but Jack had to be on stage by eight, so they decided to get changed and go to Steel Pier before Jack's performance. Jack would leave the pier in time to do his show. They all rode on the Ferris Wheel and exclaimed it was an experience they would never forget.

The week went by fast. Peggy performed four times instead of three. The audience went wild over her appearances. Milt and Jean went to the shows whenever Peggy was to perform. On the last night that Peggy performed, they learned that the guests at the table next to them that night were Al Capone, the Chicago crime boss, Lucky Luciano, a New York City mobster, and Nucky Johnson, an Atlantic City political racketeer, along with their lady friends. Jean had trouble keeping her eyes off them. Peggy and Milt handled the situation a little more diplomatically. Then without any warning, Jack had the orchestra playing "The Wedding March". He was at their table and soon escorting Jean and Milt up onto the stage.

"Ladies and gentlemen, I just want to take a moment to tell you that this has been a fabulous week for me. You have been just a great audience. And I wanted you to meet my other special guests, Jean and Milt. Milt is my nephew. He and Jean were just married this past Saturday."

There was a long, loud round of applause with calls for, "Speech, speech." Jack passed the microphone to an embarrassed Jean.

"I... I don't know what to say. This has been the best week of my entire life. Milt and I love Atlantic City and hope to return here for every one of our anniversaries. Thank you so much for treating us so nicely."

There was another long, loud round of applause this time with calls for *Kiss*. Milt and Jean entered into a long embrace and kiss and then returned to the table as the orchestra struck up "The Wedding March" once more. At the table, the mobsters and their lady friends had moved over to congratulate the young couple. There were hugs, handshakes, and gentle kisses to Jean's cheeks.

"Thank you so much. We will never forget your kindness."

On the drive back to New York City, Jean couldn't stop talking about her Atlantic City experiences, especially about Al Capone and his friends and how they seemed so nice.

Everyone returned to work on Monday with only two weeks to go until the second wedding. Because of Jack's brother's involvement with Madison Square Garden, the wedding plans were a little more elaborate with a rather large reception. The wedding Mass was to be performed Saturday morning followed by the reception at the Aqua Delight. The garden had an evening boxing schedule, so the reception would fit in nicely.

Jack's agent called midway through the week and asked Jack if he remembered the conversation they had a short time ago about recordings. Stan went on to tell Jack he pretty much had him set up to do one or two recording sessions.

"Jack, the idea is to get a jump out of the starting gate. You give them about two hours in the recording studio and we'll end up with two songs on individual records. It's going to cost us a few bucks, but then we'll be in a position to have the recordings reviewed by several experts for their constructive critiques. We can take or leave their suggestions. The object is to get the best possible marketable recording. We can return to the recording studio and cut the same songs with any changes we want to incorporate or try entirely new selections. I would like to end up with two records that I can push for mass marketing. There's a lot of money to be made if we do this right, Jack."

"Okay, I'm game, Stan. My mornings are free for the next several weeks. Will you be coming along with me or do you just want me to show up at the studio?"

"I'll go with you, kid. Let me set something up and I'll call you back. You think about which songs you want to record and put a little practice in on them."

When Peggy arrived back at the apartment that evening, Jack told her about Stan's call and asked her to help him with selecting the songs to record. He told Peggy that he felt comfortable with six songs and asked if she would listen as he played and sang. They would then try to pick the two best songs. Jack started with "Cecilia" and then moved through "I'm Knee Deep in Daisies", "I Care for Her and She Cares for Me", "Feelin' Kind of Blue", "I Wanna Go

Where You Go", "Then I'll Be Happy" and "Are You Sorry?" Peggy loved all of them, but told Jack that when he sang "I Care for Her and She Cares for Me" and "Feelin' Kind of Blue", she felt like he was singing directly to her, and so her vote was for those two.

"Thanks, sweetheart, I'll start with them. Now let's go to the bedroom and have some fun before we go to sleep."

Stan called the next morning. They were set for the following Tuesday at eight o'clock in the morning. Jack told Stan what songs he had selected and Stan concurred. Following the phone conversation, Jack went to the piano and began to practice. After the third time through "Feelin' Kind of Blue", he felt a bump as Peggy sat down next to him on the piano bench.

"Oh! Sorry, honey. I forgot all about you sleeping back there."

"It would be so much easier if you had a Peggy song."

Jack playfully starts with "Sweet Peggy O'Neil". Peggy removes her nightgown and wraps it around Jack's head. She then runs for the bedroom.

Running behind her, Jack exclaims, "It looks like I might be a little late for work."

The process at the recording studio went pretty smoothly. Jack felt it to be very similar to his radio broadcasting. They did several takes, and then the two operators in the control booth asked Stan to step into the booth. About five minutes later, Stan was out of the booth waving for Jack to come.

"We're done, kid. Actually, your first recording was good. The guys in the booth don't usually experience easy sessions like that, so they had you do two more just to be sure. I'll pick up the recordings next week and get the review process started. Things will probably be slow moving, so don't be disappointed if we haven't heard anything for a while. Our goal is to have records in the stores by early next year."

"Thanks, Stan. Give me a call if you need anything else. I have to get over to the radio station for my afternoon broadcast."

The rest of the week was spent getting ready for his brother's wedding, which was just a few days away. Peggy was very excited because she just loved weddings. She told Jack that she did send a letter to Father McNaulty in Buffalo about starting the church process to annul her first marriage. Jack gave her a bear hug and told her they were going to have the most magnificent wedding ever seen in the Bronx. The wedding attire for Saturday was simply dark suits with white shirts. Jack's brother was supplying all men in the wedding party with identical ties. Peggy was having trouble deciding what to wear. Jack was not concerned because in her ever expanding wardrobe there had to be something that would be just perfect. Peggy actually looked stunning in everything she wore.

"Peggy, I need some help with words for the toast to the bride and groom. I promised to sing it and I'm finding that it's a little hard to get something together as a song."

"Okay, what do you have so far?"

Jack moves to the piano and starts to play.

To my brother, Charles and his lovely bride, Jane
In days gone by when our father passed
on into the big blue sky
Neither Mom nor I knew how we would get by
Like a knight in shining armor on his big white horse
Charlie came to the rescue and removed our remorse
We were never hungry or cold for he was,
but one block away
I'll never forget my big brother's efforts to this very day.
Years later, both Charlie and Jane lost
a much loved soul mate
But then as time passed, they magically started to date
Until this special wedding day we now celebrate
So join in and raise your glasses as we wish them a life full
of happiness and cheer
Should you ever need my help, Charlie,
I will always be here.

"Jack, that's perfect. You don't need to change a thing. Before you started, I thought you might slip in one of your comments about Charles marrying a fish, which would not have been very nice."

The week flew by, and before they knew it, Charlie's and Jane's wedding day arrived. Jack and Peggy got an early start and stopped by Jack's mother's house before going to the church. Mrs. Schmidt was very excited.

"Peggy, can you imagine nothing exciting happens and then all at once we have two weddings in the same month. Now if I can only get my boy, Jack, settled. Are you working on him, Peggy?" Mrs. Schmidt asked.

"Yes, I am, and if things go well, you may have another wedding to attend before this year is over."

"That would be wonderful, Peggy. You keep after him."

They talked for a while and then headed over to the church. Once again, it was a beautiful June day. Everyone looked like they had just stepped out of a magazine clothing advertisement. Peggy moved close to Jean, and when the time was right, she engaged her in conversation to see how married life was going. Jean said it was just perfect; they were going to move into Milt's childhood house the following week. Charles Jr. was moving up the street to stay with his grandmother, and sometime within the year, Jean's mother would also move in with Milt and Jean. Peggy told Jean she envied her having such close family contact. It was the one thing missing from Peggy's life. The church had filled and it was close to time for the wedding Mass to begin. Before taking his position, Jack told Peggy there were a lot of people in attendance that he didn't know. He asked her to use her skills later to find out who some of these guests are. He and Peggy were masters at engaging people in conversation.

"We'll compare notes later tonight when we're all alone."

Then he was whisked away to take his place in the wedding party. The wedding Mass was very nice and brought tears to the eyes of some in attendance.

Following the ceremony, most of the guests headed over to the Aqua Delight. A large portion of the dining room had been strategically separated from the tables closer to the bar and fish tank. The area was decorated very nicely, and a staff of waiters and waitresses stood by to assist the arriving guests. In spite of the prohibition laws, alcoholic drinks were being freely served. There was a grand piano in the front corner with a microphone set up next to it. Members of the wedding were seated at a very long table that had been covered with a floor length white tablecloth. A banner written in dark blue and red letters was strung just in front of the white tablecloth. It read, Wishing Charles and Jane The Best Always.

Peggy, Jean, and Mamie sat at a table just in front of the wedding party. The reception started off on a traditional note with the serving of a delicious four-course meal that included two choices of fish, two of steak, and chicken. The atmosphere in the room was rather calm and sophisticated with an occasional chiming from utensils striking against the glasses, which would continue until Charles kissed his bride.

At the end of the meal, it was time for Jack to toast his brother. Jack moved to the piano and striking a few notes attracted the attention of the audience. He played the piano, singing the toast he had written for his brother. At the end of the toast, there were calls of "Here, here." Next, Jack asked his brother and Jane to move to the dance floor. He played and sang the "Anniversary Waltz". Halfway through, Peggy went to Mrs. Schmidt and escorted her to the dance floor. Just as Jack's mother arrived at the dance floor, he masterfully directed his brother to join Mother and dance. Peggy, in the meantime, brought Jane's son-in-law to the floor to continue dancing with Jane. It was all very smoothly done as Jack and Peggy had prearranged between themselves. Jack then moved on to several more slow songs that were well suited for dancing. When he had the floor pretty well filled, Jack struck a few odd notes and asked the guests if they were ready for some fun. Peggy moved to the dance floor, and then again, as the two of them had prearranged, Jack began playing the Charleston. Peggy assumed the lead dancer's role while Jack verbally badgered anyone attempting to leave the dance floor. It was truly a lot of fun. Jack continued with upbeat selections for about fifteen minutes and then called for a drink break.

During the brief intermission, Peggy moved over close to Jack who had stood up and moved to the opposite side of the piano. Almost instantly, Peggy and Jack were surrounded by an assortment of guests. There were a few autographs but mostly a lot of conversation. Peggy and Jack would very tactfully steer the talk so that they learned about the guests. It was obvious that there were a lot of well-heeled people in attendance. Most mentioned both the existing Madison Square Garden and the one under construction. There was some talk about the up and coming Democratic National Convention. Jack began to realize how well his brother was connected.

There followed more songs and dancing. A good time was had by all, and as the celebration wound down, Peggy and Jack received invites to continue the party at varied residences. They were both a little tired and anxious to return home where they could compare notes about those in attendance and just relax, so they respectfully declined the invitations and returned to their apartment.

THE FIRST RECORD

Late in 1924, Jack received a call from his agent, Stan Schuman.

"Jack, we are getting close to releasing your first record. The recording will be on the RCA Victor label. 'I Care for Her and She Cares for Me' will be Side A with 'Feelin Kind of Blue' on the back. I have what I think is a very attractive contract. You will get a percentage of the price of every record that is sold."

"It sounds good to me, Stan. Do you want me to drop by the agency?"

"Not just yet. By contract, we are required to go to the recording studio to listen to both sides of the record and give our seal of approval for RCA to proceed with the production of records for distribution to the music stores. I'll try to set something up for us to go to the studio early in the morning one day this week or next. We can probably finalize the contract at the same time. I'm very excited about this, Jack. If everything falls into place, we should be able to move you on to bigger and better things in no time at all."

"Thanks, Stan, I'll be waiting for your call."

When Peggy returned to the apartment that evening, Jack told her about Stan's call. She was very excited, and also thought that the release of Jack's record could open more opportunities for him.

"Now Peggy, I want you to look through some literature I have on a Bell and Howell movie camera and projector. You and I have been very fortunate in getting to travel to many places. I thought it would be nice to have a visual record of some of what we see and also be able to show others where we have been. You have already been in a number of movies, so you probably know all about this stuff."

"Yeah, Jack, right! I can't even remember the names of some of those movies, let alone anything about movie cameras. You know I made my first movie in 1913. I played the part of Nell in a movie entitled *The Penalty of Crime*."

Then, silently counting on her fingers, Peggy went through an exercise of remembering all of her movies. The grand total was ten. Jack couldn't believe she had already been in ten movies. Jack commented that he wanted to see all ten of her movies. Peggy appeased Jack by looking through the Bell and Howell brochure and then begged off, telling Jack she really knew very little about technical things, but she thought his idea was very good.

The following week, Jack and Stan met at the recording studio around eight o'clock on Thursday morning. They were both impressed with the sound qualities on both sides of the recording. Stan asked if there was a record player similar to one that could be found in someone's home available in the studio. He then asked if they could hear the record on the home record player. Stan went one step further and requested that he be allowed to place the record on the player and follow the studio employee's instructions to start the player. Jack thought, This is why I need an agent. I would have never thought of doing this. The sound quality was good, but not quite as good as it had been on the studio equipment. Stan was satisfied and told the studio people he would get back to them on Friday.

They headed to a café nearby the studio and over a cup of coffee, Stan reviewed the details of the contract with Jack. Stan explained each section of the contract in lay terms and emphasized to Jack that it was a fairly long-term contract; therefore, it was necessary that they get it right. Like most contracts there were pros and cons, but for the most part, they both had a feeling that it was a good one. The contract not only covered the record about to be released, but also covered pricing options for all future recordings for a number of years. They both affixed their signatures. Then Stan shook Jack's hand, wishing him a good and long career in this new venture.

Jack had been singing "I Care for Her and She Cares for Me" several times a week at the radio broadcasting station. On occasion he also sang "Feelin' Kind of Blue". He made a conscious decision to play and sing "I Care for Her and She Cares for Me" at least twice a day and "Feelin' Kind of Blue" once. Stan had told Jack it was okay to plug the songs by stating that they were soon to be released under the RCA Victor label and would be available in most music stores.

The Christmas and New Year's holidays came and went very fast. To Jack's surprise, Peggy had given him a complete Bell and Howell Sixteen Millimeter Home Movie System. Jack was fascinated with his Christmas gift from Peggy and spent a good bit of his free time trying to learn how to operate the camera and projector. Jack and Peggy were very busy making the rounds to the homes of friends and of course, Jack's family. Peggy loved to visit with Jack's family. It seemed to help fill the void that many orphans feel throughout their lives.

In February of 1925, Jack's first record hit the music stores. It was an instant hit. Because of the demand for the recording, the RCA Victor people asked Stan to have Jack record additional songs. Stan, being the ever vigilant business man, responded to RCA with a stall tactic saying that he would contact his client and get back to them. Stan then called Jack.

"Hello, Jack. The record is doing great. Sales are through the roof and the RCA people want more recordings. I want to stall them, Jack. In the past, I have seen new things take off only to become quick flashes in the pan. I think we have an opportunity here to build up a little demand for you to put out more records. You are in the unique position of being on the radio, so your songs can be sampled. My target would be to hold off more releases until the summer. What do you think?"

"Well, I'm happy about our first record's sales. As for delaying more recordings, whatever you think is best is fine with me, Stan. You have not given me a bum steer yet."

"Okay, kid. I'll handle things and keep you informed. If anyone wants to talk to you about more recordings, just refer them to me."

"Right, Stan. Thanks."

BAD NEWS

When Peggy arrived at the apartment that evening, Jack was anxious to tell her about the RCA Victor request for more recordings and the delaying approach that Stan had recommended. Peggy looked rather sad, and before Jack said anything, he could see that she had been crying. Jack immediately went to Peggy, wrapping his arms around her.

"What's the matter, babe?"

"It's bad news from Buffalo, Jack." She then took a letter from her purse and passed it to Jack. "The Archdiocese of Buffalo did not approve the annulment of my marriage."

Holding one arm firmly around Peggy, Jack read the letter. It basically stated that Peggy's husband denied any infidelity and there had been no evidence to the contrary.

"It's my own damn fault, Jack. I'm always in such a hurry to get things done. I should have listened to my divorce lawyer when he recommended filing for cause rather than convenience. Then I would have had documented proof of his damn infidelity. What are we going to do now?"

"Listen. This is only a piece of paper. It's not going to change the love we have for each other. I'm going to love you forever no matter what happens. I can't imagine life without you. Remember me telling you about Milt's problem in getting the church to approve his marriage to a non-Catholic and how the cost of the process wiped out all of his savings. Well, what I haven't told you is that Milt is still mad at the church and no longer attends Mass. I don't want that to happen to us. I don't want to lose you and I don't want us to lose our religion, so we are going to continue to live together and confess our love as being sinful. God knows of your husband's infidelity, and God will have the final judgment. At some point, maybe the church will change their decision. If they do, we will celebrate with our own marriage."

"Oh, Jack, I love you so much. You always know the right thing to say. I feel so much better now. I do have some good news. My agent has me lined up to make three movies out on the west coast in which I will be cast as Peggy O'Neil. When I get some firm dates, do you think you might get a couple of weeks off and come along with me?"

"Now you're talking. I would love to see how your movies are made. Maybe the experience will help me with the Bell and Howell equipment. You get me the dates and I'll see what can be arranged."

During the next several months Peggy was busy with her Broadway show and Jack with his radio broadcasting. In anticipation of the pending trip to the west coast, both were lining up options for an extended period of time away from New York. As Jack thought about the trip, he contemplated the possibility of travelling on a steamship passing through the Panama Canal. He got some preliminary information and thought it was entirely feasible. They would be able to board a ship in New York Harbor and dock on the west coast at either San Diego or Los Angeles. He would love to see the canal that Gen. George Goethals was so involved in, and maybe there would be a way to check on his old army squad leader, JJ. Jack knew Peggy disliked the long train rides, so he put together a planning document that he intended to present to Peggy when the time was just right. Jack decided the opportune time would be on Peggy's birthday, the sixteenth of June. When the sixteenth arrived, Jack quietly dressed and departed the apartment to pick up some fresh flowers and a box of Peggy's favorite chocolate candy. Peggy almost always slept late due to her evening performances. Jack, very quietly, reentered the apartment and went about setting the kitchen table for an elaborate breakfast, including Peggy's favorite crumb cake with birthday candles. Another of Peggy's favorites was scrambled eggs, so Jack pre mixed a bowl of eggs, set up the frying pan and then headed to the bedroom to gently awaken his birthday girl. She was out like a light, sleeping stomach down as she often did, so he laid down beside her and began to gently rub her back.

"Oh, Jack, that feels so good. What time is it?"

"It's time for the birthday girl to get up and enjoy a very special breakfast that I am preparing."

Jack kissed her gently several times and then departed for the kitchen. Peggy rolled out of bed and freshened up by splashing water on her face, brushing her teeth and simply fluffing her hair. She was just naturally beautiful and did not require a lot of makeup and grooming to look her best. Realizing that this truly was her birthday, she bounced into the kitchen in anticipation of the special breakfast Jack was preparing.

"Oh! Jack, the flowers are just beautiful. They weren't here last night. Where did you get them? And a birthday card. And a cake with candles. There better not be too many candles on that cake. Oh! It's my favorite crumb cake. Jack, you are just too much."

Jack moved to Peggy, giving her a big kiss and nudging her close to her place at the table and then helping her into the chair.

"Happy birthday, kid. Let me get these eggs started, and then after we eat, I have one more surprise I want to show you."

They laughed and kidded each other as they ate and drank coffee. Jack lit the candles and sang "Happy Birthday" to Peggy. After the crumb cake, Peggy said she was ready for the surprise. Jack went into the sitting room, and then immediately returned with a folder and a rather thick book.

"Now, my dear, you know how you always complain about those long train rides. Well, Jack boy has the perfect solution."

Jack began to spread pictures of a steamship and described a very relaxing and pleasant journey to the west coast via the Panama Canal. He talked about George Goethals and flipped through some of the photo pages in the book that General Goethals had given him. Peggy seemed to be very interested.

"You know, Jack, I have always dreamed of crossing the ocean in a passenger liner. I never thought about the Panama Canal, but why not? If we can work out the dates, I'm game."

"Okay, the tickets will be my birthday present to you. Happy birthday, love."

"Now, Jack, I know you have to leave for the radio station soon. So leave the kitchen for me to clean and come along. I want to show you my appreciation in the bedroom."

When Jack returned from work that evening, he took the cigar box from his bureau drawer and withdrew the paper with J. Johnson's address. He looked at the address briefly to verify it was in the San Diego area and then folded and placed the paper in his billfold. *Maybe*, Jack thought, *I can work a visit in with old JJ when we dock in San Diego.*

SAILING WESTWARD

Peggy's date to report to the movie set was on a Wednesday, the fifth of August. Jack was able to get booking on the *MS New York* Steamship departing from New York City on Saturday, the twenty-fifth of July. Both Jack and Peggy arranged for three weeks of time away from New York City. Jack was to be back on the radio starting Monday, the seventeenth of August. He made arrangements to return home by train. Peggy's agent kept her return trip open pending how the work on the movie set progressed.

As their departure date neared, Jack packed a suitcase. Laundry service was available on the steamship, and he was sure he could find cleaning services on the west coast. Peggy, on the other hand, had a large travel trunk delivered to the apartment to pack a multitude of shoes and clothes that she thought might be needed on the trip and on the movie set. The *MS New York* would be in port for six to seven days in order to refuel with coal. Coaling time for a ship normally took four days and created a lot of coal dust which had to be cleaned from the ship prior to boarding any passengers. Arrangements were therefore made to have Peggy's trunk and Jack's suitcase delivered to the ship two days prior to departure.

They were both very excited as they started on their new adventure. Upon boarding the ship, they found their cabin to be very luxurious with a large bathtub and quite a bit of furniture, including a table and chairs for in the cabin dining. Peggy's trunk and Jack's suitcase, along with the luggage that they carried to the ship, were already in the cabin and set up for quick access. They met the cabin attendant and were politely briefed as to what services were available. The attendant suggested they start with a light lunch in the dining room and then move to the outside deck as the ship sailed out of port.

The *MS New York* departed port with the help of a couple of tugs and then blasted the ship's horn as the tugs detached. It was a beautiful sun filled day as Peggy and Jack stood at the deck railings taking in the magic of the harbor with the passing boats and the scenic shoreline. When the ship passed the Statue of Liberty, Jack became a little nostalgic as he talked to Peggy about how his own father must have passed here many times. Peggy embraced Jack and told him how happy she was that they were actually traveling on an ocean liner.

"Jack, you know you are the man of my dreams. Everything you do with and for me is just perfect. I would have never thought about sailing to the west coast and here we are on our way. I love you, darling. Please don't ever change."

"I love you too, sweetheart. Now, how about we find a couple of deck chairs and just sit and watch the ocean go by."

The trip south along the east coast was very smooth until they passed the Florida straits where the waves were much larger. Jack and Peggy thoroughly enjoyed the opportunity to relax. The weather was good, so they were often out on the deck chairs. The ship had an extensive library and both enjoyed reading. On the third evening, they were invited to dine at the captain's table.

The captain had learned of their celebrity status and was quite anxious to meet with Peggy and Jack up close and personal. It turned out to be a very enjoyable evening, with Jack and Peggy promising to sing a few numbers the following evening for the guests around the dance floor.

On the fifth day, the ship neared the Panama Canal. Most of the passengers were on deck with binoculars and cameras. Peggy and Jack situated themselves on the foredeck with an excellent view of the canal's locks. Jack had read and reviewed the book on the Panama Canal, so he explained to Peggy how once the ship was towed into the lock, the huge gates would be closed, and water from the lake would then be allowed to fill the lock, thus raising the ship. The gates in front of them opened and the ship moved into the next lock repeating the same procedure.

"Pretty amazing, isn't it, sweetheart? Tomorrow we will sail across the lake and through the man-made cut in the hills until we reach the set of locks that lets us back down to sea level at the Pacific Ocean. Today we are going to be tendered to the shore and transported to the cross country railroad. We will then have a tour of the Canal Zone where I understand there is a statue of George Goethals."

"I've never been on a small boat."

"Don't worry, babe. You're with the son of a sea captain. I'll hold onto you and make sure you don't fall."

The tendering to shore was uneventful, but the train ride across the isthmus was quite an adventure. The sides of the cars were completely open and there were many local passengers in with the tourists. Two seats up from Peggy and Jack there was a woman sitting next to a beheaded chicken that was strung up to the overhead luggage rack. For the most part of the ride they could see parts of the canal and ships moving along the lake. There were times when they passed through sections of the tropical jungle. Each time they did, Peggy snuggled very close to Jack and away from the open part of the railroad car except when the guide pointed out animals called sloths in the trees. The coloring of the sloths made them difficult to see because they kind of blended in with the tree trunks, but after several sightings, Jack and Peggy did see one. It took about forty minutes to get to the Canal Zone where the guide had all of the tourists depart the train and gather together, so he could give them a briefing about where they were going and what they would see. Next, they boarded an open sided bus and began a tour of the Canal Zone. The guide walked up and down the aisle in the bus pointing out things of interest and running a continuous dialog about the history of building the canal.

The bus parked in an open area where Panama City could be seen across the water. There were vendors with various bright-colored items of clothing and various handmade souvenirs. Peggy immediately headed for the vendor displays while Jack sought out the guide.

"Excuse me, sir. Will we pass by the statue of George Goethals?"

"Yes, in about ten minutes. Do you have a special interest in the statue?"

"Well, my brother was married to George Goethals's sister, so I have met the general on several occasions, and I truly amazed at what he accomplished here."

"What is your name, sir?"

"Jack Smith."

"Well, Mr. Smith, I will have the bus stop at the statue, so you may get out and snap some pictures if you so choose."

"Thank you. I appreciate that very much."

When Peggy returned with a bag full of merchandise, Jack told her that the bus would stop at George Goethals's statue and he was going to ask either the guide or one of the other tourists to take one or two pictures of them posed in front of the statue. The stop was brief, during which the guide made a big fuss over having one of General Goethals's relatives on the bus. Back on the bus and pulling away from the statue, they found the Canal Zone to be very active as the workers and family members moved about. They passed by the housing section, the general store, the post office, a church, and finally, they stopped for a bathroom break. Following the break, they returned to the train and headed toward the Atlantic Ocean to rejoin the *MS New York.*

Back onboard, Peggy told Jack that she had a wonderful day and showed him each of her purchases while stating who would be the recipient of each item. It amazed Jack to see how Peggy was always thoughtful of her friends and coworkers. They enjoyed a delightful five course dinner, and then settled into deck chairs to just watch as the ship slowly moved through the passageway toward the Pacific. The sunset was beautiful, and then as darkness set in a variety of electric lights came on and grew brighter in the darkness of the night. Peggy reached over to hold Jack's hand.

"I love you, Jack Smith."

When they returned to their cabin, Peggy sat at the desk and began to write a letter.

"Who are you writing to?"

"I like to keep in touch with my aunt, and I sometimes write to Jean. Our time at the Panama Canal was just so amazing and beautiful I feel like I should be sharing it with others."

"I haven't seen Milt or Jean for a while. How are they doing?"

"Shame on you, Jack. They are doing just fine. Jean's mother has moved in with them and they all get along great. She tells me your brother is very busy with the opening of the new Madison Square Garden, so they seldom see him. They do, however, occasionally stop at your mother's house to check on her and sometimes take her to their house for dinner. Your mother and Jean's mother love to get together and speak in German about the old country."

"You're right. I'll have to try and spend a little more time with everyone when I get back. I'm turning in. It has been a great but long day. Good night, Love."

"Good night, Jack. I won't be up long."

The next day, there was a five-hour port call at Acapulco, Mexico. They both went ashore where Peggy managed to purchase another bag full of items. There was one last port call at Cabo San Lucas, Mexico, and then they headed to their destination. The ship was to dock in the early morning on the third of August. San Diego was a large port where there were a considerable number of navy as well as commercial ships docked. Jack decided it was time to tell Peggy about his plan to try to contact his old army squad leader, whom he credited with saving his life during the war. Peggy fully understood Jack's feelings and wanted to accompany Jack if he managed to find his friend. The remainder of their travel in California would be about one hundred miles by train to Edendale. The ship's company took care of the luggage and gave Jack a telephone number to call when they were ready to have the luggage moved to either a hotel or the train station.

It took Jack a while working with the telephone operators to locate a good number for his old army friend. When he got through on the phone, JJ answered and instantly remembered Jack.

"How are you, kid? I've been listening to you singing over the radio, and I've told my wife all about you when we were over in France."

"I'm great, JJ. I'll be here in San Diego all day and was hoping we might get together for a bit."

"Where are you now?"

"We came in on the *MS New York* and just docked at pier 11. I have a lady friend with me. How would we get to your place?"

"You just sit tight, kid. I'm only about twenty minutes away. I'm going to come over in the car and pick you and your friend up. I'll be there around nine o'clock and meet you at the gangplank."

"Great, JJ. We'll be looking for you."

When Peggy learned that JJ was going to pick them up, she discreetly put two of her purchases into a separate paper bag and placed the bag for an easy pick up to carry along. JJ was right on time. He and Jack shook hands and hugged each other for a minute before Jack introduced Peggy.

"You're Peggy O'Neil, 'Sweet' Peggy O'Neil, the girl the song is all about?"

"Yes, Mr. Johnson, I'm afraid I am."

"You're even prettier than I imagined, ma'am, and just call me JJ. Come on and get in. We're going for a short ride out to my ranch. I can't wait for my wife to meet you all."

The ride to the ranch was quick. JJ pointed out landmarks of interest and talked about his retirement from the army and taking over operation of the family ranch. When JJ turned off the main road, they had almost a mile to go on a kind of rough dirt driveway leading up to the ranch house. His wife was awaiting their arrival on the front porch and immediately came to the car. She was very excited to have company.

"Jack and Peggy, meet my wife, Jodie. Jodie, you're not going to believe this, but Peggy here is the 'Sweet Peggy O'Neil' from the song."

"I certainly do believe it and you've got those pretty blue eyes just like in the song to prove it. Now come on along into the house. I made some fresh iced tea to wash our driveway's dust out of your throats."

"Jack, I'd offer you something a little stronger, but after I came home from the war, I quit drinking. So we don't keep anything in the house."

"The tea is just fine, JJ. I don't drink any alcohol and Peggy only occasionally has a glass of wine."

Jodie invited Peggy along to show her around the house. JJ and Jack stepped outside where JJ pointed out the features of his ranch and explained to Jack how he made a lot of money off the livestock. After an hour or so, Jack stated that a long time ago, he had promised himself to visit San Diego, so he could take JJ and his family out for dinner. Jack then asked if there was a nice restaurant nearby. There were several, so they told the ladies of their plan. Everyone freshened up a bit and then they were off and on their way to Fred's Family Restaurant. It was kind of hickey for Peggy and Jack, but the place was clean as a whistle and the food was excellent. Peggy commented that there were no restaurants like this in New York City, and that she was thoroughly enjoying the change of atmosphere and the good food. Jack asked about Sergeant Dutcher and found out that he had been awarded some high decorations in Washington, D.C., but after that, JJ never heard anymore about him. JJ and Jack reminisced for a while about the Great War and then it was time for Peggy and Jack to head for the train station. Before they left the dinner table, Peggy took two small bags from her purse, giving one to Jodie and the other to JJ.

"We picked these up in Panama and I thought they might serve as a nice remembrance of our visit to your beautiful ranch."

Jodie opened her bag very excitedly and was amazed when she found a fine handcrafted lace kerchief. JJ's bag contained a very colorful bandana. They were both thrilled with the gifts and offered sincere thanks. Jack told them to thank Peggy, as she was in charge of shopping. At the station, Jack told JJ he was really glad to see he had fully recovered from his war wounds and was doing so well as a rancher. They promised to stay in touch, each knowing it probably would not happen, and then Peggy and Jack were boarding their train.

Onboard, Peggy said, "They seemed like a very nice couple."

Jack responded, "Peggy, he was one of the best fighting men this country ever had. I'm so happy to see he is doing so well. I feel like I should have done more for him than just take them out to dinner. And thank you so much for bringing along the two gifts."

Jack then brought out his billfold and removed a small paper. He drew a large 'X' across the paper and returned it to his billfold. Taking notice, Peggy asked Jack what he was doing.

"From my time over in France I began collecting items related to the people I met over there. One was a letter I found in an abandoned trench. On the return from my first trip to Chicago, I went by way of Peoria, Illinois, and met the soldier and his family. He had lost an arm, but otherwise, was doing well. It just did my heart good to see that he was okay. I kept the envelope, but not the letter or picture and put an 'X' across the front indicating closure. The one I just crossed out was JJ's address. When I get back to the apartment, I'll put JJ's paper back into the old cigar box where I keep these things. Before my life is over, I hope to have closure on everything in that cigar box."

"Jack, you never cease to amaze me. Maybe that's why I love you so much."

MOVIES AND GOLF

It was close to midnight when the train arrived at the Los Angeles Station. Jack arranged for the trunk to be sent to their hotel and then called for a Red Cap to bring the suitcases out to the taxi stand. It was about a fifteen-minute ride to the hotel in Edendale. The hotel was located right next to the movie studios, so it would be very convenient for Peggy. When checking in, Jack asked the night clerk about golf courses in the nearby area, and to his delight, was informed that there were numerous courses that he could play. They were both dead tired from a long but rewarding day. Peggy was not due to report to the movie studio for another day, so they simply went to bed for a good night's rest.

The next morning, they cleaned up, sorted out their clothes, setting some aside for the hotel laundry service, and then made their way to the hotel dining room. It was after ten o'clock, yet the dining room was a beehive of activity. Peggy spotted some of the bigger-named movie stars and discreetly pointed them out to Jack. Jack had kind of forgotten that Peggy had been making movies for a number of years. At that point, an older well-dressed gentleman approached their table.

"Peggy, it is so nice to see you again."

"Hello, Mr. Johnson. I would like you to meet my very close friend, Jack Smith."

"Whispering Jack, I presume? I've heard you over the radio, young man. Very impressive."

"Well thank you, sir. Would you care to join us?"

"Yes, but just for a few minutes. I have to get over to the studio."

Peggy and Jack ordered breakfast while Mr. Johnson settled for a cup of black coffee. Jack soon learned that Mr. Johnson was the famous film director, Emory Johnson. In fact, he was to direct *The Non Stop Flight* movie that Peggy was to act in. Jack managed to mention that he had recently acquired a home movie set and had hoped to pick up a few pointers about using his camera. He later mentioned trying one or two of the nearby golf courses, and that quickly Jack had a filming instructor and a golfing partner.

"I have to get over to the set now. Jack, you come over with Peggy tomorrow and stay behind me. I'll give you some pointers on how to get good film shots. Are you any good at golf?"

"I'm a nine handicap."

"Well, if you care to partner with me, there are a couple of actors that I would love to beat on the course. Peggy, you won't mind giving up Jack for an afternoon or two, will you?"

"I'm used to giving him up for golf. No, I don't mind at all, Mr. Johnson."

When Peggy reported to the studio the following day, Jack went along and stayed behind the film director. It was really very interesting how Mr. Johnson moved the actors and actresses about while calling for a variety of camera shots. He sometimes had all three cameras filming at the same time and maybe would call for number two to cut while one and three continued to run.

Eventually, without looking around for Jack, Mr. Johnson told Jack to pay attention to the lighting.

"Jack, it is most important to have good lighting. Stay away from shadows, and if you are filming outside always try to have the sun at your back. Now watch the camera operators. See how they pan their equipment very slowly. If you move the camera too fast, the images will blur. I have us set for our golf match at the Wilshire Country Club. When we finish shooting this morning, we'll all ride over in my car. The pro shop will fix you up with a set of clubs and anything else you may need. We can grab a quick bite to eat at the club. You're with me, aren't you, son?"

"I'm with you, Mr. Johnson. I just hope I don't let you down."

"Outside of this studio just call me Emory. If you have any questions about what's going on here, just ask me later when we are in the car and I will try to answer them for you."

With that, Mr. Johnson called for all cameras to 'cut', and then he moved onto the set, positioning the actors and actresses while demonstrating the moves and emotions that he wanted in their performances. It was all very interesting, and Jack began to get an appreciation for the amount of work that went into producing a movie. Peggy was not in the next scene, so she moved off the set and came back to stand next to Jack. He told her about agreeing to play a round of golf that afternoon.

"That's fine, Jack. I have to come back to the studio this afternoon anyway in case the cut and paste team in the film room need a close up retake. Emory will come back to the screening room this evening and review everything. He usually makes some additional changes or decides on different inter-titles or maybe changes the dialog that is printed out for the audience. He likes for us to sit in on these progressive screenings. You can probably come along if you want."

"I very much want to. So I'll catch up with you at the hotel room when we return from playing golf."

The ride to the Wilshire Country Club was short, but rather interesting. The two actor golfers were introduced as Knute and Frank. They were rather self-centered individuals and summarily dismissed any knowledge about radio broadcasting. Jack did have a few questions for Emory, but each time he started to ask something either Knute or Frank would jump in with their comments and interpretation of what Jack was trying to ask. Emory allowed the actors to ramble on and then sometimes ended the discussion point with a, "This is how it really is".

When they arrived at the country club, Knute and Frank headed for the locker room. Emory stayed behind with Jack.

"Now you see what I have to deal with, Jack. Those two are so full of hot air. Before we get out on the course, I want to give you a heads up. We have to watch these two birds. They have a tendency to forget some of their strokes. If you see one of them turn around and look back toward the tee we just hit from while counting, I can almost guarantee you that a stroke or two will be forgotten. Pay attention to their game and politely challenge any scoring discrepancies you see. Once they know we are paying attention, their counts will become more accurate. I will have some money bet on the match, so I want the counts to be honest."

"Emory, I know exactly what you are talking about. We have some New York golfers with the same problem. I will pay attention and not hesitate to challenge a bad count."

Once Jack was set up with clubs, balls, and tees, Emory suggested they grab a quick sandwich. Jack declined, saying he was not hungry and would prefer to hit a few drives on the range before the match started. They agreed to meet on the first tee in fifteen minutes.

As the match progressed, it became obvious that Knute and Frank were in trouble. Emory was much older than the others and didn't hit his shots quite as far, but he was very accurate and his short game around the greens was excellent. By the fifteenth hole, Emory was only two strokes behind Jack. Emory and Jack all but had the match won. Jack was well on his way to scoring less than eighty when the thought occurred to him that he should let Emory finish with the best score. It would certainly be more satisfying for Emory and the scoring was kind of meaningless to Jack. So he intentionally missed several putts and when they finished on the eighteenth green, Emory's score was one better than Jack's.

Back at the hotel room, Jack told Peggy how he intentionally missed a few shots near the end of the match so that Emory could finish with the best score.

"You are such a good-hearted man, Jack, but a little wet and smelly from sweat right now. So get in that bathroom and take a nice refreshing bath. I'll be waiting in the bedroom for you. We have an hour or two to kill. Maybe you'll be able to think of something for us to do."

At the film screening that evening, Mr. Johnson was in a very good mood. He quickly reviewed the film's progress to date, directed a minimum of changes, and then dismissed most of those in attendance. He waved for Peggy and Jack to move next to him, and then asked Jack if he would be available the next afternoon for a round of golf at the Hillcrest Country Club. Jack first looked to Peggy for a sign and then responded in the affirmative. Mr. Johnson went on to describe the course.

"The course we played today was designed by Norman MacBeth. It's a good course, but I think you're going to find this next course to be outstanding. Both are par seventy-one courses. The Hillcrest Country Club opened in 1920, just one year after the Wilshire course. Hillcrest was designed by Wille Watson and is just a tremendous layout."

"It sounds good to me, Mr. Johnson."

"Okay, tomorrow we will be playing with another actor, David, and one of my cameramen. They are both good guys. Come over to the studio around noon. Now I want to better answer some of the questions you posed earlier in the day. You asked about who developed the inter-titles and the dialog that is sometimes printed on the screens. Most studios use professional title writers. In my opinion, it is very important to have good title writers. They can make or break a picture. The boys misled you a little today about the piano and organ music you hear in the movie theaters. Good movies provide a music cue sheet with the film. The intent is for the pianists or organists to follow the cue sheet. Our problem is that some musicians place their own interpretations into the music, giving some of the scenes emphasis when no emphasis is intended. I personally prefer an orchestra score. There is little room for individual interpretation and the score carries the director's intent. *The Non-Stop Flight* is to have an orchestra score. And the story line is not as complicated as my actors were telling you. It is a straight forward adventure melodrama whereby Lars Larson is forced to become a smuggler after his wife's kidnapping. He gets involved in the United States Navy's non-stop flight from San Francisco to Hawaii. We are going to have some great shots of the navy seaplane. Is there anything else I didn't cover?"

"No, sir. Thank you for taking the time to enlighten me. And I'm sorry to say I won't be able to play golf with you after tomorrow. I'll be on my way back to New York. Please take good care of Miss O'Neil for me and don't keep her out here any longer than necessary."

AN UNEXPECTED GUEST

Jack's return to New York City amounted to a long and boring train ride. He missed Peggy like crazy and wondered how the movie was progressing. Whenever the train made station stops for any length of time, Jack searched out a newsstand and bought papers and magazines to both catch up on his reading and to keep his mind occupied as the train traveled along.

Jack was back at his apartment before noon on Saturday. *Good*, he thought, *I won't need to check in with the radio station or the agency until Monday morning. Maybe I'll visit Mom and see how everyone is doing.* He unpacked and organized his clothes while trying to decide whether or not to shop for some groceries or eat at the club that evening. Saturday evenings were not the best time to show up as a single guest at the club. He decided to check on the Chalmers. It started right up, so Jack drove over to his mother's house. She was home and anxious to hear all about Jack and Peggy's voyage through the Panama Canal. They spent some time catching up, and then Jack invited his mother to ride along to the delicatessen.

"Yes, Jack, I need a few things. Give me a moment to freshen up and get my purse."

"Okay, Mom, but it's going to be my treat, so you can leave your purse at home."

When they got to the store, Jack thought, *I was only away for a few weeks and how I missed the New York rye bread, the pickles in the barrel and the assorted deli meats and cheeses. There is no place like New York City.* His mother knew everyone in the place, and of course, had to tell them her son had just returned from a voyage through the Panama Canal and a visit to the movie studios in California. They were quite impressed. Back at the house, his mother asked Jack to stay for a while, but he begged off telling her he still had a few things to do and he still needed to prepare for the Monday radio broadcast. On the return drive to his apartment, Jack thought, *Maybe I should have stayed a little longer with Mom.* She seems a little lonely at times, but I really should get things ready for work. At the apartment, Jack made himself a sandwich and then put the food away. He tried the radio to see what WJZ was broadcasting, and to his surprise found they were covering a Yankees' baseball game. He left the game on and started to look through his sheet music in preparation for the Monday broadcast when the phone rang.

"Hello."

"Hello, love. I've been lying here in bed dreaming about you and waiting for you to call."

"Peggy! I'm sorry. What time is it there in California? I thought you would still be sleeping."

"It's a little after ten now. I miss you something terrible, Jack, so I guess that's what wakes me up. How was your trip back to New York?"

"I miss you too, sweetheart. The train ride was boring and uneventful. It was nothing like our great trip out to California. I did catch up on my reading of current events. I just returned from Mom's house. I took her to the deli and we both picked up some food. I plan on eating in tonight and getting my routine ready for work at the station on Monday. How is the movie coming along?"

"I had a long talk with Emory yesterday, and he says we are done shooting most of the scenes from the studio. We will be going over to the navy base to do some outdoor filming. Some of the shots will be in and around the seaplane. I'm kind of excited about that. When we return to the studio, Emory wants to start shooting some scenes for his next movie, *The Gosh-Darn Mortgage*. He said I may be able to complete the shots at the Edison Studio over in New Jersey at some point later on."

"Well, that sounds great. Maybe you'll be back sooner than we thought."

"I hope so. I think I can now force myself out of bed and go get some breakfast. Call Monday evening if you can. I should be here. Good-bye for now. I love you, Jack Smith."

"Good-bye, babe. I love you too and I promise I'll call on Monday sometime after my broadcast."

Jack returned to the sheet music and made some quick notes on his prep sheets. He really enjoyed radio broadcasting and was looking forward to returning to the station on Monday. The Yankees were winning in the baseball game. He thought about the times he and Milt went to the games together and made a mental note to try and get some tickets for a home game before the season was over. How many to buy was the problem. Would Milt want to bring Jean along; would Peggy be back and able to go along? Maybe he would just get a half a dozen or so, and whoever could come along would be fine. He could always give away any leftover tickets at the radio station. Jack was more than halfway through his broadcasting preparation when the phone rang again. *Wow*, he thought, *maybe Peggy's calling back.*

"Hello."

"Hello, Jack. It's Lorie."

"Well hello, Lorie. How are you?"

"Jack, I need to see you. I have a big problem and I think you are the only one that can help me."

"Do you want me to come to your place? I can be there in an hour or so."

"No. It would be much better if I come to you. Jack, are you alone?"

"Yes, as a matter of fact, I am. I just got back from California. Do you want to tell me what the trouble is?"

"I'd rather not discuss it over the phone. I can be at your place in about two hours, so maybe you can meet me in the lobby?"

"Okay, I'll be there."

This is not like Lorie, Jack thought. *She is always so in control of everything. I wonder what her problem can be*. He checked the time. *Okay, I better be in the lobby by seven o'clock*. He returned to his prep sheets, made a few more notes and placed the sheet music along with the notes into his attaché case. Next, he straightened up the apartment and cleaned the few soiled dishes. He chilled a bottle of wine just in case she would want a glass. If she has not eaten, I can easily make a sandwich for her. Checking his watch, he still had thirty minutes to go before moving to the lobby. The Yankees' broadcast was over and he had not heard the final score. The radio broadcast was now for international news. He sat and listened for a while, thinking that WJZ had really come a long way since he first started with them.

He moved to the lobby, and within ten minutes, Lorie pulled up and parked. Jack immediately went out and got in on the passenger side of Lorie's car.

"Hi, Lorie. Just pull up straight ahead and then park in any spot on the right."

"Okay, Jack. Will you please bring along the bag from the back seat once we're parked."

Grabbing the small suitcase, Jack asks, "How do you want me to sign you in?"

"Use Lorie Roberts, please."

Jack responded affirmatively and moved to the desk. He thought Lorie was rather quiet and she smelled as if she had been drinking. He wondered what was in the bag. Maybe it contained something to do with her problem. They moved to the elevator. The operator took them to Jack's floor. Lorie didn't say a word the whole time. Once inside the apartment, Lorie let go. She grabbed a hold of Jack and in a sobbing voice told him that she didn't know what to do and the only thing she could think of was to come to him.

Gently holding Lorie in his arms, Jack said, "All right, just try to calm down a little and maybe you can tell me what has you so upset."

"It's that bum that I married. Do you have anything to drink, Jack?"

"Sit here on the sofa, and I'll bring you a glass of wine."

Lorie continued to talk, sometimes slurring her words, "Jack, he's not half the man that you are. He's lousy in bed and guess what I found out he was doing? A good friend of mine came to me with a story about my husband's behavior at a bachelor party. My friend's husband was at the same party. Francis got smashed and ended up in bed with a whore. Jack, please bring the wine bottle and fill my glass. I really need a few drinks. I tried to teach him how to make love to a woman, but he is so 'macho' he thought he knew it all and our sex life has suffered for it. Jack, you know I'm a good lover. How could he turn to a whore for satisfaction? Then when I confronted him with it, he broke down like a little baby and asked my forgiveness. How do you forgive something like that? Everything else in our lives is fine. We are great business partners and I really love his two sons. I didn't know what to do, so I threw him out of our bedroom and told him I would think about it. The more I thought about it, Jack, the more I told myself that the only way to take Francis back is to get even with him. Jack, do you have any more wine?"

Jack excused himself and went to the kitchen to open another bottle. When he returned to the sofa, Lorie had her eyes closed. She held out her glass to be filled and then continued.

"So here I am, lover. I brought my sleepwear that you always liked so much. I want to spend the night making love to you, Jack. I want you to take me over and over again just like we used to do it. In the morning, I'll return to the estate and tell Francis how things are going to be between us in the future. If he is willing to make our marriage work under my terms, I'll take him back, but he is going to have to beg to get back into my bedroom. Fill my glass one more time, Jack, and then let's go to bed."

Jack filled Lorie's glass one last time and waited until she finished the wine. He then helped her to her feet and guided her into the bedroom and onto the bed.

"Here, let me help you out of your clothes."

"See what I mean, Jack, you know exactly how to treat a lady."

"You look every bit as lovely as I remember you, Lorie. Here, stretch out and let me put this pillow under your head."

Jack sat on the edge of the bed and gently stroked Lorie's hair. Within minutes, she was sound asleep. He returned to the living room, opened the small suitcase and brought the sleepwear back to the bedroom. Jack arranged the sleepwear on the bed to appear as if it had been removed in the heat of passion. He then picked up Lorie's clothing and shoes, turned out the light and returned to the living room, carefully folding and placing the clothes on a chair.

Jack spent the night sleeping on the sofa. He checked on Lorie several times during the night and again at daybreak. She slept right through, hardly changing her position in bed. What will I do when she finally gets up? Well, let me start by setting the table and organizing some things for a quick breakfast. Most of all she is going to need some good hot coffee. Jack made the coffee and started to fry some bacon. Lorie must have smelled the coffee and bacon, because when he looked up there was Lorie dressed in her sleep wear and looking pretty bad.

"Good morning, Jack, and thank you for last night. You are the best love maker in the whole world. I feel so much better. That was just what I needed, except for this headache. Do you have any aspirin?"

"Here, sit down and let me pour you a cup of coffee; then I'll go get a couple of aspirin for you. Are you hungry?"

"Well, the bacon smells so good. Can you just fix me a piece of toast and put some bacon on a plate with it? I really have to get back to the estate. I want to try and make the eleven o'clock Mass."

"Coming right up, and how about a little more coffee?"

"Thanks, Jack. As soon as I finish here, I'm going to freshen up and then get on my way. I hope you don't mind. I owe you big time for last night."

"I don't mind, Lorie. The important thing is keeping your marriage intact. I hope you will be able to work things out."

Lorie headed to the bathroom, and Jack stayed in the kitchen making like he was cleaning up. *Wow*, he thought, *she thinks we spent the night in bed together*. Well, whatever works for her is fine with me. I just won't say anything. In fact, I won't be able to tell anybody about it. Why do these strange things always seem to happen to me? When Lorie returned from the bathroom, she filled her small suitcase and then gave Jack a hug and kissed his cheek.

"You need not come down with me, Jack. Thank you again for last night. I'll try to keep you posted on how things work out."

With that, Lorie was gone. Jack returned to the kitchen, poured himself a cup of coffee, and sat down to go back over in his mind the weekend's events. He scratched his head and thought, *Oh well, I too have time to make it to the eleven o'clock Mass in the Bronx.*

CECILIA, DOES YOUR MOTHER KNOW YOU'RE OUT?

The remainder of the summer in 1925 went by very quickly. Jack was knocking the listeners dead with his radio broadcasting. Peggy had returned from California and was rehearsing for a new show on Broadway. Jack and Peggy took a tour of the new Madison Square Garden with Jack's brother and both were amazed at the immensity of the building. Milt, Jean, Jean's brother Bill, Charles, Peggy, and Jack went to a Yankees-Red Sox game. The Yankees won, making all happy. And most importantly, Jack received a phone call from his agent informing Jack that things were set up for his recording of "Cecilia" on the Victor label.

"This is our big opportunity, Jack. I want you to sing "Cecilia" two or three times each day on your broadcast. Be sure to tell the listeners that the song will be available under the RCA Victor label in September. If everything goes as I expect it to, the music stores will probably not have enough stock of the record to meet demand. If the stores run out, that is not necessarily bad. The pent-up demand will make the recording even more popular. You may end up with a song in the top ten and even a golden record."

"I hope you're right, Stan. I'll give it my best shot. When do we record?"

"Next Tuesday morning. I'll meet you at the studio at eight."

When Jack and Stan arrived at the studio, their experience was totally different from their prior visit. It was more like receiving red carpet treatment. They were offered coffee and pastries and had all kinds of assistance in setting up to record. Stan told Jack that the people there could smell when they had a winner. Jack sang and played for three separate recording sessions. All three takes were good and Jack thought all three were pretty much identical. Stan led the way in reviewing what had been recorded and requested that each session be played back at least twice. He was happy with the results of all three, but settled on the second recording as the one to be passed to Victor for production. Jack agreed and they were back out of the studio before ten o'clock.

Outside, they headed for a nearby café and settled into a booth. After ordering, Stan asked Jack about his travel to California. It was obvious to Jack that Stan's interest was in the movie business. Jack told him about how the director took time to show Jack what to do to get good home movies. When Stan heard that Jack had played golf with the director, his eyebrows really went up.

"Jack, you actually were on the golf course with Emory Johnson?"

"Yes. He asked me to partner with him, so he could beat a couple of his actors on the course. We won and Emory was very pleased."

"Do you call him Emory?"

"He told me inside of the studio to call him Mr. Johnson; outside call him Emory. He is a real nice man, Stan."

"I would love to have a connection with the movie people, Jack."

"I only played two rounds of golf with the man, Stan. I'll talk to Peggy about your interest in making a connection with the movie people. She has made a lot of movies and will be doing some work over in the Edison, New Jersey studios. Maybe I can get a name for you."

"Okay, kid, whatever you come up with will be great. Do you have any interest in getting into the movies?"

"Not really, Stan. I wasn't impressed with what I saw in the studio out in California. Broadcasting is much more exciting. It's real time. Out there, if they don't like how a film shooting turns out, they just do it over. And the reviews are really boring."

"You were at a review!"

"Yeah, Emory asked me to come along one evening with Peggy."

"I am so jealous, Jack. Well, I've got to run. I'll keep you informed about the record. It should be in the music stores by mid September."

When the weekend rolled around and Jack had some time to spend with Peggy, he told her about his conversation with Stan.

"What's his interest?"

"He didn't really say, but I assume he would want to send actors or some of his professional entertainers with well-known names to appear in the movies. When Stan sniffs out money to be made, he goes after it."

"I'll ask around the next time I'm over in Edison."

Jack went on to tell Peggy about the recording session.

"Stan says the record will hit the music stores in mid September and he thinks it will make the top ten. Come sit with me at the piano, and I'll play and sing it for you."

"Very nice, Jack. I like it and I think it will certainly make the top ten. What's on the flip side?"

"It's "I'm Knee Deep in Daisies". Now, how about a little "Sweet Peggy O'Neil?"

As Jack starts to play and sing, Peggy pulls him away from the piano by the ear.

"That's enough of that. I haven't seen you all week. Come along with me to the bedroom and I'll show you the real 'Sweet' Peggy O'Neil."

"Cecilia" hit the music stores the third week of September and was an instant success. As Stan had predicted, some of the stores ran out of the record. Jack received a lot of calls congratulating him on his hit record. When he received congratulations from his old friend, Arthur Kennedy, from the Irving Berlin Publishing Company and also from Katie at the music store where he started as a song plugger, Jack began to truly believe he had a hit. These two definitely knew music. By early October, "Cecilia" had moved up to number twelve on the charts. By the end of the October, it hit number nine. Stan called and congratulated Jack.

"You did it, kid. Now the next step is to line up the songs that you like the most. Give me a list of at least a dozen. It doesn't matter if they are old or new or popular or not. Just pick out what you like and what you can really sing. Your name is out there now in the top ten. Music fans and collectors will be looking for more recordings from 'Whispering' Jack Smith and we're going to give them some. I would like to get a couple more out this year and a bunch more in 1926. Can you do it?"

"I think so, Stan. Give me about a week. I'll give a lot of thought to the songs I broadcast and select a dozen for you that I really like. I'll drop the list at your office next week."

"Good, Jack. In the meantime, I'll start to set up things with the studio and the RCA Victor gang."

As Jack went through his broadcasting the next several days, he made mental notes about his preference of songs worthy of recording. At home in the evenings, he would play and sometimes sing them a time or two. When he really liked a selection, he added it to the list being prepared for Stan. He thought if time permitted he would try them out on Peggy. When he wrote in the twelfth song title, he read through the list one final time to be sure he had written the titles correctly and that he was truly satisfied.

1. I Wanna Go Where You Go Then I'll Be Happy
2. Are You Sorry?
3. Poor Papa
4. Don't Be a Fool
5. I Don't Believe It, but Say It Again
6. I'd Climb the Highest Mountain
7. To-Night's My Night with Baby

8. When the Red, Red Robin Comes Bob-Bob-Bobbin' Along
9. I'm Tellin' the Birds that I Love You
10. Clap Yo' Hands
11. Me and My Shadow
12. You Won't See Me, If I See You with Anyone

Peggy was very busy, so Jack just took the list he had written the following Monday morning to drop it at the agency. Stan was not in, so he started to explain to Janet what the list was intended for. She cut Jack off short.

"I know all about the list, Jack. Do you mind if I look at it?"

"No, not at all."

After a minute, Janet told Jack that she thought the selections were very good. She also told him "Cecilia" had reached number seven in the top ten.

"You're doing just great, Jack. I'll make sure Mr. Schuman sees the list as soon as he gets here."

Jack said good-bye and headed to the nearby café. He ordered a light breakfast with coffee and then just sat there thinking about all that had happened over the last few years. It was hard to believe that he was actually a well-known entertainer and broadcaster. And to have Peggy O'Neil as his sweetheart, wow! He wondered what was going to happen next.

THE BEGINNING OF A GOLDEN YEAR

At Christmas time, Peggy and Jack made the rounds in Jack's family. She thoroughly enjoyed doing so. Jack knew it had a lot to do with Peggy being raised as an orphan, so he put a lot of effort into keeping her involved in his family's events. One of their visits was to Milt and Jean's house. Near the end of their visit, they were completely surprised when Milt invited them to come back for a New Year's Eve celebration.

"Sure, we can make it," Jack responded. "What can we bring?"

"You just bring Peggy, Jack. You two have done so much for us we will never really be able to repay you. Dad has the booze lined up through one of his contacts at the garden, and we have taken care of everything else."

Peggy and Jack were elated. They asked who else would be coming. It turned out to be just about everyone in the family, plus a few of Jean's relations and some from Jane's side of the family.

When Jack and Peggy returned to the apartment that evening, Peggy told Jack that it would not really be proper to show up at the party empty-handed.

"We pretty much know who will be there, so why don't we make a list of names. I'll call Jean during the week and find out how good our list is. I just love talking to her, Jack. We have become very close friends. She sometimes sends me short letters and I sometimes write to her. I almost feel like she is my sister. Anyway, once we have the list finished, we can decide on kind of a common gift that will please everyone. What do you think?"

"Whatever you say, babe. I'm one 100 percent with you. Just tell me how much money you want."

Peggy did call Jean during the week and nailed down the names of those who would be at the New Year's Eve party. She then reviewed the list multiple times, trying to decide on nice token gifts for all. Should there be one gift for ladies and another for men? It was tougher than she thought. When Jack arrived, he asked what all the paper and notes were for.

"Jack, I'm totally confused. I have a complete list of the people going to Milt and Jean's, but I don't know enough about everyone to come up with a good gift idea."

"Why don't you keep it simple, like tickets to a musical on Broadway?"

"Jack, you are a genius. *Mercenary Mary* is in town and should run for the next six or eight weeks and I think I can get a very nice discount on show tickets. Thank you, dear. I will take care of the rest. I know where to get very cute ticket jackets. We'll put the right number of tickets into the jackets and annotate the names of the recipients, so they will be easy to distribute. I'll let you know what the damages are."

The party turned out to be great. The big news was that Milt's brother, Charles, was engaged to Mamie, and Jean's brother, Bill, had just become engaged to a very nice young lady, Eloise. Bill was a great guest to have at a party. He was very outgoing and continued to crack one joke after the other. There was always a circle of guests surrounding him. Peggy singled out Jean and told her how happy she was about her brother's engagement.

"Peggy, are you having any luck with your annulment?"

"I'm afraid not. The priest that I have been working with in Buffalo has told me we have exhausted all options. I've been thinking about contacting one of those gangsters we sat next to in Atlantic City and put a 'hit' on my former husband."

"Well, that should work! I'd try the one that controls New York City first. What was his name?"

"Yes, the one with the steel-blue eyes that looked right through you. I think his name was Lucky Loosey or something like that."

"It was Lucky Luciano, Peggy. A gangster could never be called Lucky Loosey. I've seen his real name in the newspapers sometimes."

"Well if I were to have a 'hit' put on my ex-husband, it would certainly get me a one-way ticket straight to hell. So, I guess Jack and I will just have to continue living in sin."

They were both having a good laugh when Jack moved next to them.

"What's so funny?"

"Oh, it's just ladies' talk, Jack. You wouldn't appreciate it."

Peggy said, "Let's make the rounds and distribute the tickets." Then turning to Jean, she leafed through the ticket jackets until she found the one for Milt and Jean. "Happy New Year, Jean."

Jean quickly opened the jacket and then exclaimed, "Mercenary Mary, I can't believe it." She quickly hugged both Peggy and Jack while thanking them, and then excused herself from their company as she went to find Milt.

"I'm not so sure Milt is going to be as excited about the tickets," Jack said.

"Come on, Jack, let's make the rounds and give out the rest of the tickets."

Everyone seemed to be most appreciative of receiving the Broadway tickets. The party was a very happy gathering. Jack's mother finally caught up with him, and they had a long talk about his career and also some dialog about the status of Peggy's annulment. Mrs. Schmidt was very disappointed to find out the church had not yet approved the annulment. She promised her son she would put a little extra effort into her prayers and perhaps things would change soon.

As midnight drew near, the guests called for Jack and Peggy to lead them in some singing. There was no piano in the house, so Peggy thought she could start things with a little bit of stage theatrics. But before she had a chance, there was Jean's brother, Bill, standing on a chair in the center of the room directing people to their places and then positioning Jack and Peggy so they faced the others.

"Here we go," Bill called out as he started the group off with a German song and led them much like an orchestra leader. Jack and Peggy took over from there, and the entire group sang songs right up to midnight when they concluded with the singing of "Auld Lang Sine".

On New Year's Day, Peggy and Jack were going back over the events of the party.

"Jean's brother is something else, Jack. He had the party guests laughing until their eyes were watering. I should talk to him about considering doing a little vaudeville."

"He is definitely a funny guy and most certainly he must be the life of the party wherever he goes. And his German is so fluent. What kind of work does he do?"

"All I know is Jean told me he works for Dunn and Bradstreet."

"Peggy, I didn't tell you last night, but your singing was just wonderful. You really put your heart and soul into those songs we were singing."

"Well, Jack, I just love being with your family. They all seem to accept me as a family member and there are no pretenses. I think that and a few of those mixed drinks got me so into the singing. I really, really enjoyed myself especially after we returned back here to our little love nest."

"Yeah, me too. Last night was just perfect. Now what would you like to do today?"

"I think I would like to just put my feet up and relax. Do we have plenty of food in the ice box?"

"We do."

"Okay, Jack, but first I need to talk just a little bit of business. Remember when your agent asked for a name of someone in the movie business. Well, I've been giving it a lot of thought and want to try this on you for size. Suppose we put our agents in touch with one another. Your agent can get the contacts he wants, but more importantly, we can ask both of them to coordinate our bookings, so we can maximize our time together. Kind of like when we first met in Chicago. What do you think?"

"I like it." Then Jack scoops Peggy out of her chair, kissing her before placing her over his shoulder and heading for the bedroom. "Business is now closed. It is time to start our relaxing."

Nineteen hundred and twenty six started out as a very promising year for both Jack and Peggy. But then a rather strange event altered their lives forever. There was another threat of a Broadway Actors' Strike. Peggy's agent foresaw little advantage in awaiting settlement of another strike and began searching to book Peggy elsewhere. He found an opportunity for stage actress bookings in London. Peggy was soon off to London and became a sensation in *Kippers and Kings* at the Savoy Theater on the outskirts of London.

Jack was saddened by Peggy's departure. His recording sales, however, were doing well. "Gimme A Lil' Kiss, Will Ya, Huh?", released in March, had moved right up the charts to become a number one hit. "When the Red, Red Robin Comes Bob-Bob-Bobbin Along" followed in April and had moved up to number nine. Many of the other releases were also performing very well.

Jack and Peggy kept in touch. Both were extremely busy with their successes, and therefore able to accept the separation between them. The best thing that they had done was to put both of their agents in touch with one another. Stan told Jack he was working on a booking that would take him to London and Berlin in the early part of the summer.

Two days before his birthday in May, Jack received a small package from London. Upon opening it, he found a short, mechanical lead pencil. The engraving on the outer case read, Jack From Bam-Bam MAY 31, 1926. There was a small card that read:

> Happy Birthday, love.
> I miss you like crazy.
> Use the pencil for autographs.
> I found it saves a lot of ink stains.

It was a sobering moment for Jack. He realized how much he really missed Peggy. Jack vowed to first fire off a telegram to Peggy thanking her from the bottom of his heart for the birthday present and also informing her that he hoped to be in London next month. Secondly, he made a mental note to call Stan and nail down the arrangements for his performances in London and Berlin. Jack contacted Stan a short time later, and before he could ask about the London booking, Stan was already into relating the details about the up and coming trip. He would tour the south of England with the majority of his performances in London. At the end of the London booking, there would be approximately a one-week break before he was to perform in Berlin. Following his time in Berlin, he would return to London to perform with the Blue Skies Theater Company. The agency was already working on his travel arrangements. Jack interjected that he wanted his transit to Berlin to be by way of Paris with a two or three night stay in Paris.

"Okay, Jack, we'll work that in for you. What do you have in mind for Paris?"

"I just want to return to revisit some of my war experiences. I'll contact Janet and give her the name of the village near Paris that I want to visit. Thanks for working this trip out for me, Stan. I should be able to hook up with Peggy O'Neil in London."

"Good, Jack, we'll be in touch with you as we get the details of your travel worked out."

The next month went very fast. Jack was booked for passage on Cunard Line's *RMS Mauretania*. The ocean liner had been converted from coal to oil fired burners a few years earlier, with numerous improvements to the onboard accommodations. Janet told Jack that this liner was reported to be one of the most comfortable ships for travel abroad. Janet had his travel itinerary all set up with his side trip to Paris, and she had obtained instructions for him to obtain transport to the village of Saint Aubin Fosse Louvain.

The next step was to tell his mother. Stan would handle the radio broadcasting schedule. Jack called his mother and invited her to go to the club with him on Saturday evening. She was thrilled and asked what the occasion was. Jack responded by telling her that it looked like he would be having some changes in his work schedule. He closed by saying he had not seen her for a while and he also wanted to catch up on what's going on in the family.

"Good, Jack. Come by anytime on Saturday."

"Okay, Mom. See you then. I have to run now."

Well, let's see what else I need to be thinking about to get ready. Wardrobe, the English have a reputation for being very formal, so I better take at least two tuxedos along with plenty of shirts and ties. I wonder if I'll be able to get a few rounds of golf in? I should be able to stay with Peggy when I first arrive, but who will handle the lodging arrangements when traveling in other parts of England? I'll check with Janet next week. What am I going to do on the ocean liner without Peggy being along? I guess it will be a good time to catch up on my reading. That's another question for Janet. Is there a good library onboard the ship or should I bring along some of my own books? What should I do with the Chalmers? I don't want to just leave it parked for eight or ten weeks. I think I'll ask Milt to use the car while I'm gone. He loves that car, and I know he will take good care of it.

Jack headed down to the reception desk to put together a telegram. The clerk gave Jack a form to fill out. Now let's see, Jack thought, *It's to the Park Lane Hotel in London, England, for Miss Peggy O'Neil. Now for the message:*

> Thanks for gift. Love it – stop. Will arrive London mid June – stop. Plan to stay with you early on tour – stop. After

> approx four weeks tour moves to Berlin – stop. After Berlin back to London. Hope to spend time together – stop. Jack

Jack told the clerk to charge the message to his account and returned to his apartment for a quick lunch, and then it was time to head to the station for his broadcast. He liked broadcasting and was going to miss it, but there is nothing like performing in front of an audience to keep your entertaining skills sharp.

When Saturday arrived, Jack decided to go to his mother's house early in the afternoon. His nephew Charles was now living with Mom, but would probably not be there on a Saturday afternoon. Jack thought it might be best to bring his mom up-to-date on his pending travel in the privacy of her home rather than in the country club dining room.

"You're early, son. Come on into the kitchen. I was just fixing a cup of tea. Will you join me?"

"Sounds good, Mom. Make mine black with just a touch of sugar."

Jack went on to tell his mother about his coming travel. She was thrilled for him and very excited about Jack going to Berlin.

"We lived for many years about one hundred miles from Berlin. You will love it, Jack. Berlin is a beautiful city surrounded by many lakes. It is just a marvelous place in the spring and summer. Will you have any free time?"

"I have some days off in between my performances in England and Berlin. I've asked the agency to set me up with a few days in Paris, so I can visit some of the war sites and the soldiers' cemetery. Mom, how are Milt and Jean doing? I'm thinking about leaving my car with Milt. What do you think?"

"That will be wonderful. They are doing fine, but that old car that Milt drives scares me a little. I'm sure he will appreciate the use of your car, and I know he will take very good care of it."

"And how are you getting along with young Charles living in the house?"

"Oh, he's fine, Jack. He's very considerate and will do anything for me. He is a little on the quiet side, but we get along just fine."

"Well, how about we drive down the street to Milt and Jean's for a short visit. If Milt is home, I'll ask him about taking the Chalmers for a while."

Milt and Jean were both at home, along with Jean's mother. Jack and his mother had a nice visit. It seemed like a good time to tell them about his coming trip to Europe, so Jack went into some of the details as he knew them. Milt was thrilled about getting a chance to use the Chalmers for several months. Jean was very excited for Jack. She had received several letters from Peggy, and brought Jack up to date on how Peggy was thoroughly enjoying England. She asked Jack if he could deliver a small package to Peggy.

"If it will fit into the suitcase, I'll certainly do it."

"It's a pair of foot warming socks that can be worn as slippers. My mother makes them. Peggy says that sometimes the weather is bone-chilling damp there in London. Mom thought these would at least help keep her feet warm."

"I'll be sure she gets them, Jean. It is very considerate of you and your mother to have done this. Now, Mom and I should get going to the country club. Milt, the day before my sailing I'll call you about the car. I think the simplest way to handle it is for you to drive your car over and park in my spot. I'll set things up with the people at the apartment."

With that, Jack and his mother were off to the country club. During their dinner, his mother told him how proud she was of his accomplishments. She was still very concerned about Peggy O'Neil's annulment case, and thought maybe the two of them could investigate further with the church in England. Jack told her they would consider doing so, while also reminding his mother that Catholics were in the minority in England. They both enjoyed a hearty meal while reminiscing about past times and events. When parting that evening, Jack promised to keep his mother informed by sending letters.

ENGLAND

Crossing the Atlantic on the *RMS Mauretania* was a welcome experience for Jack. In comparison to his earlier crossings aboard troop ships, Jack found his days onboard to be very relaxing and vacation-like. No one seemed to know of his celebrity status. Jack worked to keep it that way. The ship had an excellent library where he caught up on the post war changes in France. His thoughts wandered to the war nurse, Cecilia. Jack had brought along an extra "Cecilia" record, thinking that it would be a nice gift should he locate her. He remembered how attractive Cecilia was, and thought if she had survived the war she most likely has married by now. He opened his billfold and took out the card Cecilia had left him on their last night together and began to read it one more time.

> Cecilia Lefebvre from the village of Saint Aubin Fosse Louvain.
> North and East of Paris along the border of Normandie.
> I will never forget you and your music.

After seven days on the Atlantic, the *RMS Mauretania* docked at Liverpool. Jack reviewed the details about how to forward his baggage to the Park Lane Hotel and what train to take to London. Upon departing the ship at the end of the gangway, there was a gentleman dressed in a chauffeur's uniform holding a sign that read, "Whispering Jack Smith". Jack approached the gentleman and identified himself as Jack Smith.

"Please come along with me, sir. I have an automobile ready to transport you to London."

"Okay, but hold on for a few minutes. I have to arrange for transport of my luggage."

"That has already been taken care of, sir."

Jack walked to the end of the pier with the gentleman, and as they approached the end, he caught a glimpse of a woman that looked like Peggy O'Neil waving her arms in the air. Within seconds, they were embracing and passionately kissing each other.

"Jack, I am so glad to see you. I couldn't stand waiting at the hotel for you to arrive, so I asked Graham if we could just drive to the pier and pick you up. Jack, meet Graham, he is the best driver in all of England."

Jack shook hands and thanked Graham for his assistance. The limousine was a Rolls Royce with a privacy window and curtain between the chauffeur and passengers. Graham opened the limousine doors for Jack and Peggy to enter, and they were soon on their way to London.

"Sit back and relax, love. We have about one hundred and seventy-five miles to go. I want you to tell me about everything that is happening in New York. We'll stop for lunch along the way, and if you care to see a castle up close and personal, Graham will take us to one where we can easily explore the inside."

"I don't know where to start. It seems like time flew after you left New York. Stan has kept me very busy promoting my records. I hit number one on the charts with 'Gimme A Lil' Kiss, Will Ya, Huh?' And several of my others are in the top ten. The only problem with all the success is the never ending demand for personal appearances and autographs. Thank you again for the pocket size lead pencil. It is perfect for autographs and as you said, ink can sometimes be messy."

Jack went on to tell Peggy how everyone in the family was doing and that they had all asked about her. In response to Peggy asking about the outcome of the threat of a Broadway actor's strike, Jack didn't know a lot, but thought things were pretty much back to normal. Peggy filled Jack in about her part in *Paddy the Next Best Thing*.

"I just love performing here in England. The audiences are just fabulous. Sometimes the weather is not the best, but being from Buffalo, I am used to cold weather. Jack, you are going to love London. There are so many things to do, and my hotel is located right on Piccadilly overlooking the Green Park in Mayfair. The underground transit is just a hop, skip, and jump from the hotel and it is very easy to use. We are going to have a great time together. When do you start work?"

"I'm not quite sure. In a day or two, I think. I have a number to call once I get settled in and I will need to send a telegram to Stan. How have you been?"

"I'm fine, Jack, a little lonely at times, but now you're here to take care of that."

They embraced and kissed for a moment and then settled back to enjoy the ride. The Rolls Royce was an exquisite automobile with a surprisingly smooth ride. It wasn't long before Jack dozed off with his head on Peggy's shoulder. He drifted into a dream about his wartime experiences in France and startled Peggy by moving his arms to a position much like one holding a rifle.

"Jack, are you all right?"

"Oh, I'm sorry. I was back in the war again. I haven't had one of those dreams for a long time. Maybe it's because I did a lot of reading on the ship about post war France."

"That's okay, Jack. Put your head back on my shoulder. We'll be stopping in another half hour or so for a bite to eat."

Jack dozed off again, and this time dreamed about Cecilia. He was back at the field hospital, and Cecilia had just locked them into the room with the piano. She opened the piano bench and gathered the blankets and linen to spread on the floor as a makeshift bed. This time, the room was much brighter. Jack just stared at the beauty of Cecilia's face and figure. He knelt next to her as they each helped the other unbutton and remove their clothes. There was no talk with a mutual understanding of what was going to happen.

He gently wrapped his arms around her as their lips met. Next, he moved his hands to feel the fullness of her breasts when suddenly he was being shaken awake.

"Jack, I didn't want to interrupt your dream, but we are stopping for a bite of lunch. I hope the dream was about me. I can't wait until we're alone in the hotel tonight."

Graham pulled up in front of a rather classy-looking English pub. Peggy and Jack were seated at a table, while Graham moved over to the bar. The menu was quite different for Jack, so Peggy ordered for both of them. They continued their conversation about New York and London. As Jack listened to Peggy, he got the feeling that she was not at all anxious to return to New York. He had hoped that their agents were arranging more bookings where they would both be performing in close proximity of one another. Jack made a mental note to have a more detailed discussion before he parted England. Jack found the food to be not very appetizing. He ate some and told Peggy it was good because she had ordered it for him. Then he begged off finishing with an explanation about the very large breakfast he had aboard ship. They were soon on their way again. Graham wanted to know if they were still interested in stopping at a castle. Peggy, realizing that Jack was somewhat tired, told the chauffeur they would save the castle visit for another day and to head straight for the Park Lane Hotel.

The Park Lane Hotel was every bit as exquisite as Peggy had described it. Jack marveled at the large crystal chandeliers, the ornate furniture, the marble floors, the large paintings, and the colorful tapestries decorating the walls of the lobby. It was obvious that Peggy was a celebrity guest. The doorman and elevator operator addressed her as Miss O'Neil. At Peggy's floor, arrangements were made to have Jack's luggage brought to the suite. Inside, Jack was again impressed with the opulence of the suite. There was even a fireplace in the sitting room.

"What do you think, Jack?"

"I'm impressed. Maybe I should let your agent handle my affairs."

"It has been a long day, love. I'm going to run a nice hot bath. Please come and join me when I call. It is a very large tub."

From the bathroom, they wrapped towels around each other and moved to the bedroom. It had been a long time since they had been together like this. It brought back so many memories. They kissed and laughed and made love to each other for a very long time until Peggy finally exclaimed, "Jack, I think we should take a break. Let's get dressed and see a little of London after dark."

London was a very impressive city. They walked around the area of Piccadilly Circus. As they strolled along, Jack noticed that so many people were purposely moving in all directions.

"Peggy, where are all these people going at this time of night?"

"Well, Jack, London is a lot like New York City. This city never seems to go to sleep. Many of the people are headed for the underground transit. Others are going to and from their jobs and of course, many in this area are simply out for an evening of entertainment, food, and fun."

They stopped and read most of the posted billings for entertainers. Jack didn't recognize any familiar names. Peggy pointed out those that she knew about and gave Jack a brief description of each. When a double-decked bus passed, Jack commented, "I thought they only had those things for movies."

They found a nice, quaint restaurant and decided to go in for diner. Again, the menu was a little strange to Jack. Peggy told him that one of the most popular dishes in the city was sausage with mashed potatoes and gravy. She suggested a nonalcoholic drink, Elderflower, which was made from flowers and berries. Jack took Peggy's advice. After the meals arrived, Jack commented that the food was pretty good. They both ordered bread pudding along with tea to finish off the meal.

"Peggy, how long is your booking here in London?"

"I am currently in a two-month booking. Usually, my agent will not book for longer than one month. We made an exception this time simply because the money was so good."

"Do you have plans to return to New York?"

"Nothing definite yet, Jack. I know I will be doing a return performance of *Mercenary Mary* in Buffalo, but it may not be until next year. Why do you ask?"

"Oh, just because I miss you so much when you're over here and I'm in the States."

"I know, love, but you're here now, so let's just enjoy our time together. I promise I'll try to get my agent to set up something for New York."

Jack accepted Peggy's answer, but remained a little skeptical about her true desires to return to the States. He thought, *She is right about being together now, and we should make the most of this time.* They returned to the hotel and truly made the most of the rest of the evening.

The next day, Peggy introduced Jack to the underground transit system. First, they traveled to the Tower Bridge. Jack was surprised to learn that it was located so close to a castle. The Tower of London Castle was open for tours, so they joined in on one. Jack was amazed at how the structure was made to last forever. The tour guide espoused a lot of facts about who had occupied the castle during various periods of time, dating back centuries. For the most part, the information passed into one ear and out the other. Jack was more occupied with Peggy. She just looked radiant in the light of the castle. Jack's thoughts went back to how they first met. *What a lucky guy I am,* he thought. *There is really no other way that I would have ended up dating a star like Sweet Peggy O'Neil except for the odd events that transpired back there in Chicago.* They were at the tail end of the touring group, so he moved in close to Peggy, grasped her hand, and spun her toward him. He quickly embraced her and kissed her very passionately.

"Wow! What was that for?"

"That was because you are so beautiful and irresistible. And because I am so lucky to be here with you now."

"Well, thank you, love, but we better catch up with the group or we may be lost in here forever."

They spent the rest of the day taking in the sights and sounds of London on a beautiful, clear day. Jack was impressed with the precision of the military during the changing of the guard ceremony in front of Buckingham Palace. He told Peggy he was sorry he had not brought his movie camera from home and would certainly bring it the next time.

Back at the Park Lane Hotel, Jack thanked Peggy for a wonderful day and asked if he might use her phone to call his London contact about his performance schedule. He was to start the following day. Two of the theaters were in London. The third was not and would require staying outside of London for several nights. There also was to be a special performance for the Prince of Wales and his entourage. Peggy was very excited when Jack filled her in.

"The Prince of Wales, Jack. I am so jealous. What kind of songs are you going to sing?"

"Well, I know most of the Rogers and Hart's along with just about all of Gershwin's, so unless I get some special requests, I'll probably stick with them. You know me. I'm pretty good at improvising."

The London audiences that had a reputation of sometimes being boisterous took to Jack like icing on a cake. The audiences were brought to a complete hush during his performances. His smooth vocalization, exceptionally clear diction, and the way he rolled his *R*s had a most appealing quality. Like Peggy, he became a favorite with the English audiences almost overnight. By the beginning of the second week in July, the first part of Jack's European tour was over. He was going to visit France for the best part of a week and then move on to Germany for his performances at the Palast Theater in Berlin. Jack was very fluent in German, and had practiced singing some of his numbers in German.

On their last evening together, Jack and Peggy had one of their very rare spats. Jack had been very forthright with Peggy about his future work schedule and his intent to return to Europe. Peggy was evasive in discussing her intentions to accept bookings in the States.

"Peggy, my current tour here will be over sometime in September. Can I plan on seeing you back in New York for the Christmas Holiday?"

"I don't really know. I would like to see everyone in New York again, and I know it will get lonely here around the holidays."

"Why don't you just plan a vacation trip to the States? I'll take some time off and we can even visit Buffalo if you want."

"Jack, I can't just leave. I love performing here in England. And the trip across the Atlantic is not very pleasurable. I was seasick for three days coming over here."

"Well, when do you think we might be together again?"

"Please, Jack, don't put pressure on me. You have been the only man in my life since we first met and I truly love you, but I feel married to the English stage. Please be patient with me, Jack."

"Married to the English stage. What happened to married to Jack Smith?"

"I tried, Jack. You know I tried. The church is not going to give us permission to marry, so we need to move on with our lives."

"Well, I'll be moving on to Berlin in the morning. Right now I need to finish packing."

They remained distanced from each other that evening, and Peggy slept in as Jack prepared to depart early the next morning. He left the package containing the handmade foot warmers in the sitting room with an unsigned note that read: These were made for you by Jean's mother. Some people in New York still love you.

FRANCE AND GERMANY

The trip to Paris was uneventful. Jack couldn't stop thinking about his argument with Peggy, and the more he thought about the note left with the foot warmers, the more he realized he should have used less combative words. *Oh well*, he thought, *what's done is done.* I'll see how things go when I return to England. Maybe it is time for me to move on with my life.

Jack checked his baggage at the Paris Train Station, and then reviewed his instructions to find transportation to the village of Saint Aubin Fosse Louvain. It would be a short train ride and the trains left every two hours. Jack purchased a ticket and learned that the next train would be leaving in about twenty minutes. The train was not crowded, so he found a window seat. The scenery was just beautiful, much like he remembered France when he first arrived during the Great War. Wondering if he would really find Cecilia, Jack took her card from his pocket and looked at it again. Her last name was Lefebvre. *Let's see, how long ago was that? Wow, eight years. She has probably remarried by now or maybe she never made it through the war.* He settled back and took in the scenery. It wasn't long before the conductor tapped Jack's arm to indicate the next stop was his.

The village was small, much like the one near the field hospital that he and Francis Kelly had walked to. Here too, there was a market set up in the center of the village square. Jack approached one vendor after another asking if they knew of Cecilia Lefebvre. None did, so he stopped some of the shoppers asking the same question. Again, no one knew of Cecilia. He decided maybe the vendors and the shoppers he had asked were not from the village and therefore would not know of Cecilia. Jack changed his approach and first asked if the person he was talking to was in fact from the Village of Saint Aubin Fosse Louvain. Again, no one seemed to know of Cecilia. *Well,* he thought, *perhaps she was killed near the end of the war.* Jack said a little prayer for her and moved to the café on the side of the square. He sat at an outside table, just as he and Francis had done during the war. Soon the waiter arrived. Jack ordered coffee. When the waiter returned, Jack asked how long he had been in the village.

"I have been here for many years, monsieur. My father before me owned this café."

This man's English was very good, so Jack proceeded to ask if he knew of Cecilia Lefebvre. He did not. Jack went on to tell the café proprietor about his having been in France during the Great War and a little about the nurse who helped him regain his voice after being gassed. As he talked, Jack retrieved the card from his pocket. The proprietor asked if he might look at the card. Jack passed the card.

"Monsieur, you have been pronouncing the name badly. Yes, I know of Cecilia. Her last name sounds as LeFay. This is why no one seemed to know her. She is very famous now. She is a doctor in the Institute Nationale des Invalides hospital located in Paris. Cecilia seldom comes to our village anymore. If you go to the hospital, I am sure someone will put you in touch with her."

"Thank you so much, sir. For a while there I was afraid she did not make it through the war."

Jack returned to the train station and after a short wait boarded a train back to the main station in Paris. He retrieved a "Cecilia" record from his luggage and looked for a taxi to transport him to the Institute Nationale des Invalides. The taxi driver told him there were hotels near the hospital where he could get overnight lodging. Jack decided to first enter the hospital and see if someone could put him in touch with Cecilia. He had written "Dr. Cecilia Lefebvre, Institute Nationale des Invalides" on the reverse side of the card.

At the reception desk, Jack displayed the card and asked how he might contact the doctor. The receptionist asked for his name. He responded, "Jack Schmidt," because he knew Cecilia would only know him by Schmidt not Smith. The receptionist asked Jack to take a seat and she would try to find Doctor Lefebvre.

As he sat there, Jack observed the patients coming and going. Many were on crutches or in wheelchairs, obviously because of missing limbs. Most were close to Jack's age. He assumed that the patients had been wounded during the Great War. It all made sense now. This is exactly what he would have expected of Cecilia. She was continuing to help all the brave souls from the war years.

"Jack, I don't believe it!"

There she was, wearing a doctor's robe and every bit as beautiful as he had remembered her. Jack stood and they hugged for a long moment.

"Well, Doctor, you look as pretty as ever."

"Oh, Jack, I am so happy to see you. How long will you be here?"

"For several days, Cecilia. I was in England and I'm on my way to Berlin. I just wanted to see if you made it through the war okay and maybe visit the soldiers' cemetery here in France.

"Do you have a place to stay yet?"

"No, but the taxi driver told me there are hotels nearby."

"I will not hear of that. There is plenty of room at my place. You just make yourself comfortable here for a while longer while I take care of some things. I'll be back, and we are going to celebrate. Oh, I'm so excited to see you."

When Cecilia returned, she asked Jack when he had last eaten. She then told him there was a great café just around the corner from her apartment and everything was an easy walk away.

The café was very cozy and nice.

"Now, Jack, you must tell me what you have been doing with your life."

"Well, it's kind of a long story, so let me start with this."

Jack passed the "Cecilia" record across the table. He watched as Cecilia withdrew the record from the plain jacket. Her eyes glistened as she read the label. Cecilia moved to Jack's side of the table and gave him a big, long kiss.

"You have been successful with your music and you have made a record for me. Oh, Jack, this is wonderful. I can't wait to hear it. We will play it at my apartment as soon as we enter. But now you must continue. Are you married?"

The waiter arrived with their food. Cecilia moved back to the opposite side of the table as Jack gave her a very condensed version of his life since departing France in 1918. She was delighted to hear that he was not married, and so pleased to learn that he was something of a celebrity in America. Cecilia, in turn, described the events at end of the Great War and how she had a calling to work with the war's injured, much the same as a man having a calling from God to become a priest. She said it was a natural progression, but a lot of hard work to go from being a nurse to becoming a doctor. She still wore her wedding band from her first marriage, and told Jack there was little time in her life for romance and marriage.

"Jack, there are only two men I dream about. One is my husband as he was before being killed in the war; the other is you, bringing joyous music to us at that terrible time in the war.

I am so glad you took the time to find me."

After finishing their meal, Cecilia led Jack around the corner. They walked about half a block and then entered the rather exquisite lobby of Cecilia's apartment building. There was a lift that took them to the tenth floor. Entering her place, Cecilia immediately took the record to her player and placed it on the turntable.

"How I wish I had a piano. I would have you play and sing those old Irish songs all night long."

When "Cecilia" began to play, she went to Jack and began to dance with him.

"Oh, Jack, I love the song. I can't believe you made this for me. Thank you, Jack."

When the record stopped, she returned to the player and set it to play again. This time, they sat on the sofa next to one another. Cecilia asked if she could get Jack something to drink. Jack declined and they went on to talk about some of the people they remembered from the field hospital. Jack passed the card Cecilia had written on some eight years ago and told her how he almost gave up his search for her because he had been pronouncing her last name wrong. He then told Cecilia about how he had written bits of information about some of the people from those war years and deposited the written information into an old cigar box. He told her about the leather portfolio he had found in one of the trenches and then how back in the States he found the soldier that it had belonged to. He went on to tell about his trip to California and visiting with his old squad leader. Cecilia was impressed.

"Yes, Jack, war does things to us that are very hard to explain, and only those of us that have experienced the ravages of war really understand why. Now listen, tomorrow is a very big day for us here in France. It is the Bastille Day Holiday marking the fourteenth of July from 1789 when angry crowds stormed the Bastille prison in Paris at the start of the French Revolution. There will be a grand military parade down Paris' famed Champs Elysees Avenue with airplanes flying overhead and festivities everywhere. We will go, no?"

"We will go, yes," Jack replied.

"Now excuse me, Jack, I am going to run a hot tub of water for you, so you may clean up after your long day of travel."

Shortly thereafter, Cecilia called to tell Jack his bath was ready. Jack undressed and gently slid into the tub. The water temperature was just right and felt really good. Just as he started to lather some soap, Cecilia appeared in a robe.

"Jack, there is only enough hot water to fill the tub once. I am going to join you in your bath. Otherwise, I will have to wait another hour for the water to heat up."

She slipped out of her robe and carefully slid into the tub from the end opposite of Jack. Jack thought, *She is even more beautiful than I remembered.* Within minutes, they were passionately kissing each other. The bath was short. They quickly dried each other with towels and then ran to the bedroom.

"Oh! Jack, this is my dream come true."

When Jack awoke the next morning, Cecilia was playing her new record and preparing breakfast. As soon as she spotted Jack, she rushed to give him a big hug and kiss.

"Thank you for last night, darling. It was just perfect. Now, please sit at the table. Breakfast is almost ready."

Cecilia was so easy to talk to. It was like Jack had known her all of her life. She had planned their attendance at the Bastille Day Parade and talked to Jack about where the soldiers' cemeteries were located. Cecilia had time off coming to her at the hospital and made Jack aware that she was free to be with him as long as he could stay. *Wow*, he thought, *I'm going to stay as long as I possibly can.*

"I will need to stop by the train station to get some fresh clothes from my bag and to check the train schedule to Berlin. Then we will know how long I can stay."

"Wonderful. We can pass by the train station on our return from the parade. I hope we will be able to share more evenings just like last evening."

The Bastille Day ceremonies were fantastic. There were all kinds of military vehicles including tanks in the parade with a very large number of marching soldiers and sailors. Airplanes were flying in formation directly overhead. The crowds were very enthused and very festive. Jack wished he had brought along his movie camera. This would have really been something to show to everyone back in New York.

After a couple of hours near the parade, Jack and Cecilia found a café off a side street that was not jammed with people. They had a nice lunch. Jack thought, *French food is so much better than the food served in England.* Next, they went to the train station, where Jack first checked the train schedule to Berlin and then once again accessed his luggage for several changes of clothes. Cecilia inquired about trains to and from the Village of Romagne Sous Montfaucon, which was close to the American Cemetery. They decided to walk from the train station back to Cecilia's apartment where they deposited Jacks clothes and freshened up. Cecilia was anxious to show Jack through the buildings where she worked. She referred to the complex simply as Les Invalides. Jack was surprised to learn that besides the hospital there was a museum, a veterans' retirement home, a burial site for some of France's war heroes including Napoleon Bonaparte and numerous monuments. Again he was disappointed that he had not brought along his movie camera. Cecilia told Jack that on their return to the apartment, they would stop at the market. She wanted to make his dinner and stay at home because they would have a somewhat long journey the following day traveling to the Meuse Argonne American Cemetery.

The evening was much like the previous night. They shared a bath and then spent several passionate hours in the bedroom. As they laid back from each other for a breather, Jack thought, *This is exactly what I needed. Until now, I haven't thought even once about Peggy.* But then a feeling of guilt came over him. Cecilia sensed the change in Jack's mood.

"Jack, is there something bothering you?"

"I told you I'm not married and really I am not. But up to a few days ago, I had a long relationship with a woman. She is an entertainer now performing in London."

Jack went on to tell Cecilia all about Peggy O'Neil, how they met, Peggy's divorce, the Catholic Church's denial of her request for an annulment, and the spat they had just before Jack left London.

"I am so sorry you are having trouble with your lady friend. Is she the 'Sweet' Peggy O'Neil from the song?"

"Yes she is. And had things worked out with the church, we would most likely have married. Now I'm not sure if I'll ever see her again."

"You are returning to London again after Berlin, so don't be stubborn. You should go see her and apologize for leaving without waking her. If she truly loves you, Jack, she will welcome you back with open arms and the two of you will eventually work a solution to your problems. If that doesn't work, you come right back here to Paris, so I can spend more time with you. Seriously, Jack, I can understand Peggy O'Neil's feelings about being married to the stage. I, myself, have the same feelings about being married to my work at Les Invalides. It is natural for us women as we advance in age and have no real family or children. We need to feel attached to something. Now promise me you will go see her when you return to London."

"I promise, Cecilia, and I thank you from the bottom of my heart for taking such good care of me, first to recover from being gassed, and now to recover from the problems in my romance."

"Believe me, Jack, it has been very much my pleasure. I needed a break from the hospital. You have made me feel like a woman again just as you did that last night we were together in the war."

The following day, they traveled by train and then a local taxi to Meuse Argonne American Cemetery and Memorial. It took almost half of the day to get there, but it was well worth the time. The taxi driver left them at the entrance and agreed to return in two hours to take them back to the train station. The driver would not accept any payment until they were back at the station. The cemetery was immaculate with long orderly rows of white crosses above individual graves. The grounds were kept nicely, even better than those at the exclusive golf courses Jack had played.

"Is there a name you are looking for?"

"Not really. I probably spent time with some of the soldiers buried here, but I was only in the lines for a few days before I got gassed."

As they walked past the grave markers, Jack read the names. He stopped at one for a few minutes. There was something familiar about the name, Capt. William Hopkins.

"Did you know that soldier, Jack?"

"Maybe, I'm not sure. There was a captain that I helped with translation during the interrogation of prisoners. He never told me his name. Maybe I saw it someplace in the bunker. I don't know. I hope it wasn't him. He seemed like a fine officer and a gentleman."

They examined the monuments with names engraved in the stone. As they moved around, Jack asked Cecilia if she was in the front lines on the day the Armistice was signed. She was. He asked what time of the day they learned of the Armistice. Cecilia didn't know for sure, but thought it was early evening. Jack went on to tell Cecilia that the Armistice was actually signed at five in the morning. The document was signed on the eleventh day of the eleventh month and called for a cease fire at eleven o'clock. The French general in charge of the allied forces immediately passed the information on to the allied commanding officers including General Pershing. The American general relayed the information to his field commanders, but gave no specific orders. Unfortunately, many of the young field officers viewed the information as a last chance to make a name for themselves. They ordered the men under them to attack the Germans rather than to stand fast until the eleventh hour when they could have simply marched forward without bloodshed. The French general, however, gave specific orders to his French troops. His hate for the Germans influenced him to order an unrelenting attack on the Germans to inflict maximum punishment. There was to be no cease fire until the eleventh hour.

"Cecilia, the book I read had an estimate of three thousand five hundred American casualties because of the actions of the American officers on the day of the Armistice. I don't recall what the French casualties were, but I know the number was high. Continuing the battle was really senseless at a time like that. Back in the States, there was a congressional investigation concerning these actions, but nothing ever came from it."

"I never knew this, Jack. But you are right about the casualties. I remember there were very many wounded brought to our field hospital on that last day of the war. I am so ashamed of our leader's order."

It was time to return to the entrance and meet the taxi. On the ride back to the train station, the driver asked if Jack had served in the war. When Jack responded that he had, the driver thanked him and stated that he too had served with the French Army. Jack informed the driver that Cecilia had been a field hospital nurse during the war. He thanked Cecilia.

"Many of my friends owe their lives to the splendid work done at the field hospitals."

At the train station, the driver refused to accept a tip, stating that it was the least he could do for two veterans of the Great War. The ride back to Paris was pleasant but rather boring. Cecelia was tired and rested her head on Jack's shoulder. Within minutes, she was sound asleep.

Jack let his mind wander. Should he take Cecilia's advice and visit Peggy upon his return to London? If Peggy would only give in a little, they could still have a wonderful life together. But if she insists on staying in England, there is really no point in continuing their relationship. Jack liked what he had seen of England and France, but he knew that his bread and butter came from his work in the States. He envisioned traveling back and forth between the continents each year, but it was going to have to be a two-way street. Well, maybe he would return to see Peggy, but his mind was made up. She was going to have to do her part to keep their relationship alive.

Back in Paris, Cecilia and Jack spent one more wonderful evening together. Her nap on the train completely rejuvenated her. Cecilia must have been eight or ten years older than Jack, but before the evening was over, Jack was completely worn out, and Cecilia still wanted to engage in more lovemaking. In the morning, they went to the train station together where their good-byes were said. It was a tearful parting, but also a happy one. Jack promised to keep in touch and to let Cecilia know the outcome of his return visit with Peggy.

"I will always dream about you, Jack. Thank you for coming to see me."

The train ride from Paris to Berlin was pleasant and uneventful. The scenic countryside was very much like the landscape back in New York and Pennsylvania. Jack realized why so many of the German immigrants decided to settle in that region. As the train approached the city of Berlin, Jack could see it was every bit as beautiful as his mother had said. Once again he stored his baggage at the train station and then got a taxi to the Palast Theatre. He was to contact a Mr. Wilhelm Stuttgart at the theatre.

Mr. Stuttgart's office was attached to the theatre. After a short conversation with the receptionist, Jack was shown into the office. It was rather small, but very clean and orderly. Mr. Stuttgart spoke in English with some difficulty. After a minute or so of exchanging pleasantries in English, Jack, speaking German, asked Mr. Stuttgart if he would prefer conversing in German. Mr. Stuttgart showed great surprise as a big smile crept across his face. He indicated that he very much would prefer using German. Jack sensed that he had instantly made a new friend. A suite of rooms was already reserved in a nearby hotel. Arrangements would be made to have his luggage brought to his suite, and Jack was informed that rehearsals would start at nine the following morning. Jack was surprised to learn that he would be performing with a full orchestra. The rehearsals would definitely be needed.

That evening after settling in his suite of rooms, Jack decided to go for a walk outside of the hotel and find a place to eat. It was so much better being able to read all of the signs and to converse in German. Some of the restaurant menus were posted in the windows. *Now this is more like it*, Jack thought. All of his favorite dishes from New York were here. There was weinerschnitzle, bratwurst or corned beef with sauerkraut, homemade sausage with deep fried fritters, and even bread pudding for desert. I'm probably going to put on a few pounds before I get out of Berlin. He dined in a restaurant close to the hotel and then walked several blocks in each direction to get a feel for his new surroundings. He was definitely impressed with Berlin.

The next morning, Mr. Stuttgart walked Jack through the Palast and introduced him to the orchestra leader, Hans Gerhardt. Stan had already sent all of Jack's recordings along with quite a bit of sheet music. From Jack's conversation with Hans, it was obvious that the orchestra had been practicing for Jack's arrival. Hans walked around introducing Jack to each of the orchestra members. All seemed pleased that Jack was fluent in German. Jack sensed that there may have been difficulties in the past playing with people who did not understand German.

The practice started with simple melodies and progressed to somewhat more difficult songs. Jack was impressed with the orchestra. There was a piano player, so Jack would be on stage in front of the orchestra. He felt comfortable doing so, but was not sure how the interaction would be with a predominately German audience. Hans made a minimum number of changes to the venue, and by noon they were in pretty good shape. Hans declared a lunch break, requesting that everyone return in two hours.

Hans invited Jack to come along with him for lunch. The piano player and the clarinet player also joined them. They had a favorite spot just a block away. Jack settled for bratwurst with sauerkraut and a mug of soda. The Germans all had mugs of beer with their orders. Jack told them he had been in England for several weeks and then spent a few days in Paris with an old friend before continuing his journey to Berlin. The piano player asked if he had been in the Great War. Jack acknowledged that he had and very briefly described how he was gassed. The piano player had fought with the German Army in the northern parts of France. He had been wounded twice and returned to the line each time. Both Jack and the piano player were glad that the war was behind them. Hans was very much interested in Jack's radio broadcasting experiences in New York. It seemed he had an interest in getting his orchestra started in some radio work. The two hours went fast. Hans was a bit of a disciplinarian and marshaled the group, so they would be back at the theatre on time. They practiced for about two more hours before Hans felt comfortable with everyone's performances, and then he dismissed all until one o'clock the next day. They would have a dress rehearsal and then the performance would start at seven that same evening.

Hans introduced Jack to the audience.

"Heute abend sind wir priviligiertes die radio voice of America mit uns. Geehrte Damen und Herren, Ich prasentiere 'Whispering' Jack Smith." (Translation: This evening we are privileged to have the radio voice of America with us. Ladies and gentlemen, I present "Whispering" Jack Smith.)

The performance started off smooth with the audience responding with typical rounds of applause, but all rather docile. Jack had prearranged a little stage gimmick with Hans to liven things up. After the first forty-five minutes of performance, the orchestra stopped playing and the musicians all started to move back stage. Jack shrugged and moved to center stage with microphone in hand and addressed the audience in German.

"Die Union veriangt in regelmaBigen Abstanden eine Pause. Ich bin nicht teil der Europaischen Union, wenn sie gestattet, werde ich Klavier spielen und singen einige bis sie zuruck." (Translation: Their Union requires a break periodically. I am not part of the Union, so if you will allow me I will play some piano and sing some until they return.)

The audience came to life. The applause was long and loud with most of the people standing and shouts that meant, "Yes! Yes! We don't need them anyway". Jack had the result he wanted. He continued to engage the audience in German, asking if they would like to hear some of the favorite American songs and then he would sing to them in both English and German. Jack talked to the audience much the way he handled his radio broadcasts. He named the song writers and filled in with facts about where and when the songs originated. He asked for specific requests and was able to respond to almost all. He told them his parents came from Warnemunde where he hoped to visit before returning to New York. At that point, the orchestra members started to return to their positions. The audience booed and shouted for them to go away. Jack made a big ceremonious departure from the piano bench as he turned it over to the piano player. Now there was laughter. Moving again to center stage, Jack continued the performance as it had started. He had the audience where he wanted them. They continued to show their appreciation throughout the remainder of the performance with standing ovations and cheers.

Jack gave five performances a week for four weeks at the Palast. His audiences loved him, and most applauded so loudly after his closing song that he had to return to the stage for one or two additional numbers. He made many friends in Berlin and did travel to Warnemunde on one of the weekends with an orchestra member who had been born and raised in that city. Jack was impressed with the beach at Warnemunde. It was every bit as nice as those along the New Jersey shore. Some of the orchestra member's family worked at the shipbuilding yards near the city. They arranged a tour of the shipyards for Jack. Again Jack was very impressed with how industrious the Germans were. However, even with all of the special treatment that Jack received, he was starting to miss his mother and family back in New York City. He couldn't seem to get Peggy out of his mind and kept reviewing the events of their last evening together. *Maybe*, he thought, *I was to blame for the way we left each other*. He thought about the advice Cecilia had given him about returning to Peggy, but he could not quite envision just showing up at her place in London. Jack decided he would check into a London hotel and then take a little time to decide how to contact Peggy. Maybe he would just show up at one of her performances.

BACK TO LONDON

The train ride to the northern coast of France was again enjoyable for Jack. The towns and the countryside were just beautiful. Along the way, he retrieved the card Cecilia had left for him some eight years earlier at the field hospital in France. He looked at it for a long time as memories of his time with Cecilia flashed before his eyes, and then he reluctantly pulled out the pencil that Peggy had given to him and drew a large 'X' on each side of the card. *The end of another chapter in my life*, he thought. When I get back to New York this one goes back into the cigar box. He smiled. This was a happy closure. Cecilia had made it through the war and better yet she had done something very constructive with her life. He made a mental note that each time he cut a new recording, he would have one copy sent to Cecilia.

There was about a two-hour wait to board the cross channel ferry. Jack had a cup of coffee and a baguette and just spent the time people watching. It was obvious from the dress of some individuals they were either fishermen or dock laborers. Others appeared to be business men most likely traveling between France and England. He saw no military, which was so different from his time in France during the war. The ferry was quite large. Jack had envisioned one more the size of those crossing the Hudson between New York City and Bayonne, New Jersey. The channel was a little choppy, but the ferry rode the swells very well. He spent some time at the railing. It brought back memories of his return to the States at the end of the Great War. He went inside and before long the ferry was moving into the dock. He decided he would collect his bags and get a taxi to take him to a hotel close to the Park Lane Hotel.

The ferry pulled in at the King George the Fifth Dock in the Port of London. The dock had been completed in 1921 and was very clean and modern-looking. Jack arranged for a baggage handler to transport his luggage on a cart. As he and the baggage handler moved across the dock, Jack heard his name being called. When they reached the dock gate, Jack spotted Graham in his chauffeur uniform standing just off to the side of the gate. Graham approached Jack and the baggage handler as they passed through the gate. Peggy was nowhere in sight.

"Mr. Smith, I'm here to transport you to the Park Lane Hotel."

"Hello, Graham. Is Ms. O'Neil here?"

"No, sir. She has a rehearsal and asked if I would meet you."

As they transferred the luggage to the limousine, Jack wondered how Peggy knew where and when he was returning to England. She must have either contacted Stan or had her agent get the information from Stan. No one else knew. Graham opened the rear door for Jack, but Jack hesitated and asked if it would be all right to ride up front.

"Yes, if you like, sir."

"And Graham, please call me Jack. I feel like an old man when you address me as sir."

From that point on, Graham dropped the formalities of his position as he and Jack enjoyed a friendly conversation. Eventually, Jack asked how Peggy was doing.

"She is fine, but I do think she really missed you."

"Well, I missed her too, Graham. It was fun to see parts of France and but after a while you long to return to your real friends."

Graham parked the limo in front of the Park Lane Hotel lobby and told Jack he would arrange to have the luggage delivered to Ms. O'Neil's suite. He passed Jack the suite key and said Ms. O'Neil would return after rehearsal, which she estimated at around seven. Just outside of the lobby there was a flower stand. Jack thanked Graham and walked over to the stand. He thought flowers might be a good peace offering. With bouquet of flowers in hand, Jack took the elevator up to Peggy's suite and unlocked the door. No one was home, but there was a note on the table that read:

> Welcome back, love. I'm sorry I couldn't meet you at the ferry, but some of us have to work. I'm so sorry for the way I behaved before you left. I miss you like crazy and can't wait to hold you in my arms again. Please make yourself at home.
>
> Love, Bam-Bam.

Jack was touched, especially by Peggy signing the note as Bam-Bam. He started to feel guilty about the time he spent with Cecilia. Well, I certainly can't tell Peggy about my time in Paris. He decided to simply tell her he watched the Bastille Day ceremonies and spent a full day visiting the Meuse Argonne American Cemetery. He would try to talk mostly about his time in Germany. He was glad that Peggy wanted him back, but Jack still had the same unanswered question about Peggy not ever returning to the States. *Oh well*, he thought, *let's take it one step at a time. If Cecilia is right, we will come up with a way for us to share our lives together.*

Jack bathed and shaved. He dressed casually, and even though it was still August, he put on a sweater to keep warm. He settled into a soft armchair with a copy of the *London Times* to read when the door burst open. Peggy ran to Jack and jumped on him before he had a chance to stand up. She was hugging and kissing Jack while in between she would squeeze in phrases about how much she missed him and how sorry she was for the way she had acted. Jack finally managed to rise from the chair. He pulled Peggy close to him and whispered in her ear.

"I'm sorry too, Bam-Bam. I think I love you more now than before. Now stand back, so I can see what you look like." After a minute, "You are just as beautiful as I remembered."

"Jack, I am starving. Would you mind if we go to the hotel restaurant and get a bite to eat. You can tell me all about your performances in Berlin. I heard you knocked them dead."

Over dinner, Jack filled Peggy in about his time in France and Germany. As planned, he talked mostly about his time in Germany. Jack felt that way there was less of a chance that he would slip up and mention something connected to Cecilia. Peggy knew that Jack could speak German, but she was totally surprised to hear that Jack had sung so many of his songs in German to the Berlin audiences. Peggy ate faster than usual.

"Come on, Jack, finish up. I've been thinking all day about spending this evening in bed with you."

In bed that evening, Jack realized that there was no greater feeling in the world than to make love to the woman you truly love.

It wasn't until the next morning that Peggy discovered the flowers.

"Where did these lovely flowers come from?"

"I brought them when I first arrived. They're kind of a peace offering."

"Well, Jack, you can tell where my mind was last night, which by the way was really wonderful. I never even noticed the flowers. And I forgot to tell you how much I appreciate the foot warmers that you brought from New York. It does get damp and cold here sometimes, and I found the foot warmers to be very comforting. Thank you. I have already written to Jean asking that she thank her mother for me."

"You're very welcome. Listen, I'm going down to the lobby for a while. I want to get a telegram off to Stan. I need to let him know where I am and find out if there are any changes in my schedule."

Because of the difference in the time zones between London and New York, Jack did not get a reply from Stan until late afternoon. His schedule was pretty much as anticipated. He would be touring England with the Blue Skies Theater Company singing Gershwin along with Rogers and Hart songs. He would start in Manchester, but the tour would take him into or near to London on some of the stops, so he should have plenty of time to see Peggy. He was to meet his contact in two days to start the tour. Peggy was a little disappointed in that Jack would be traveling outside of London, but also happy that they would be able to see one another occasionally.

Peggy was off that evening, so they decided to tour some of London and eat out. It was still August, but fog rolled in along with the accompanying dampness. Jack and Peggy were seated in a very nice restaurant when Jack began to shiver almost uncontrollably with the chills. Peggy asked what was wrong and Jack simply replied that he could not get warm.

"Jack, I'm going to have the waiter bring you a glass of brandy. It will warm you up."

"Is it alcohol?'

"I know you don't drink, Jack. And yes, it contains some alcohol, but the people here in England drink brandy every day to chase away the chills."

"Okay, I'll try anything to stop shivering."

Jack sipped the brandy, and within minutes, he felt a warming sensation throughout his body and the shivering stopped.

"Peggy, I'm twenty-eight-years-old and that's the first alcoholic drink I ever had. You're right, it was almost like medicine chasing the chills."

Jack and Peggy thoroughly enjoyed their time together and then he was off to Manchester.

SURPRISE IN MANCHESTER

Working with the Blue Skies Theater Company was great. The performers were very professional and a good bunch of people to travel with. It was also nice to get breaks throughout the performances when other entertainers were on stage. Jack's reviews were excellent and the audiences loved his performances. As he had told Peggy, most of his songs were from Gershwin along with some from Rogers and Hart. He did mix in a few others and honored requests from the audience. They had just finished the first week of the tour when Jack was asked to report to the Blue Skies Theater Company manager. The manager had a telegram stating that "Whispering" Jack Smith was to be replaced immediately by a new all girls singing trio, the Hamilton Sisters and Fordyce. The manager had no other information, and told Jack that his performances were some of the best that he had ever experienced. He wished Jack luck and suggested that his agent might have more information for him.

Jack returned to the hotel to contemplate his next step. He would get a telegram off to Stan, but because of the difference in time zones Jack decided to have Stan reply to Peggy's suite at the Park Lane Hotel. He then placed a call to the Park Lane Hotel to tell Peggy what was going on. The desk could not reach her, so Jack simply left a message for Peggy stating that he was returning to London and would reach her hotel sometime that evening. It didn't take long to pack and then he grabbed a taxi to the train station. Trains between

Manchester and London ran pretty frequently. With a little luck, he would be at the Park Lane Hotel well before midnight.

Once aboard the train, Jack couldn't stop thinking about what had just happened. Could there be problems at home? *No*, he thought, *something like that would have come from Stan.* He knew his stage performances were every bit as good as any he had ever given. There was no conflict with any of the other entertainers. What could possibly have caused his sudden dismissal? *Well, Stan would certainly find out. But more importantly what was he to do next? Maybe I'll be returning to New York. Let's see, I would only have had three more weeks in England. He wondered how long it would take to finalize booking on a ship. If at all possible, I'm going to spend all of my time with Peggy.*

Peggy was waiting in the lobby for Jack when he arrived at the hotel. She had a message in her hand.

"Jack, what happened? I received this message from Stan, but it doesn't make any sense."

"I don't really know. The manager didn't have any information other than what was in the telegram he received, which simply stated that 'Whispering' Jack Smith was to be replaced immediately with a trio of women singers. Let me see Stan's message."

They sat on a couch in the hotel lobby and both looked at the message. One thing was clear. Jack would be returning to the States as soon as transportation arrangements could be made.

"See what I mean, Jack, it just doesn't make much sense other than you are going to be leaving."

"Now, I think I get it. See this line where Stan talks about when I first signed with him and we discussed my name change. Well, he couldn't come right out and say it in the message, but when I changed my last name from Schmidt to Smith it was because there was considerable anti-German sentiment following the war. I guess it is pretty much the same here in England, and probably my singing in the German language has somehow upset somebody here in England."

"What are you going to do?"

"Well, Peggy, my love, I am going to hang out with you as long as I possibly can. Now let's head upstairs, so I can show you how much I missed you this past week."

It took a full week before Stan's agency nailed down a steamship booking to New York for Jack. He would be leaving from the Liverpool Port. Peggy thought she might ride to the port with Jack, and if she could not arrange enough time off she would have Graham drive Jack to Liverpool.

"Well, this is pretty good. I'll be sailing on the *RMS Mauretania* directly to New York. It's the same ship I came over on. I don't know if I told you, Peggy, but the ship was recently converted to oil fired burners and the interior had a lot of renovations. It was a very comfortable ship to travel on."

"Maybe I'll try to book the same ship in December."

"Did you just tell me you'll be home for the holidays?"

"Yes, Jack, I've been waiting for an opportune time to tell you. I'm not just coming back for the holidays. I'll be performing in both Buffalo and New York. So you're going to have to put up with me for a while. Do you know a place where I might stay?"

"Baby, I know the perfect place and I'll have it all cleaned up just the way you like it. Oh! This is so great, Peggy. We are going to have a wonderful Christmas this year. I can hardly wait."

Early the next morning, Peggy and Jack said their good-byes. Graham had already placed most of the luggage in the limo. Jack told Graham he would like to start the ride at the back of the limo, so he might catch a little sleep and then later he would move to the front with Graham. He was thinking about Cecilia and what she had predicted. She was absolutely right. Things did work out. He would have to write at least one letter to Cecilia thanking her for her hospitality and telling her how things turned out with Peggy. He would have plenty of time to write once onboard the ship. Jack closed his eyes and within minutes, he was asleep.

This time he dreamed about his mother and pictured her in the house playing the piano. For an instant, his father was in the dream. His father accused Jack of drinking alcohol. Jack responded saying he only did it to keep warm.

"I told you what would happen to you if you partake of alcoholic drink."

Jack's mother came to his rescue telling him it was all right to take a drink for medicinal purposes.

Next, his dream changed to his golf game. Why can't I hit the ball out of sand traps? He pictured all of the bad shots that he had encountered in England. The English are so much better at hitting out of sand. He was back on the course in Manchester. His shot barely got the ball out of the bunker. But his next shot traveled close to two hundred yards and stopped just three inches away from the pin. The other players all congratulated him. As he walked up to the green, the crowd cheered. He tapped the ball into the cup and was escorted to the winners' circle where the King of England presented him with a trophy.

From the golf game, his dream took him back to France during the war. He could hear the screams from those dying and wounded. Cecilia appeared in a spotless, white uniform and led him away from all of the agony, and then the dream ended.

Jack opened his eyes and gazed upon the passing countryside. England was certainly a beautiful place when the weather was clear. He thought about his dreams. Is there a message in my dreams that I need to pay attention to? Then dismissing the thoughts from his mind, Jack asked Graham to pull over when convenient so that he could move to the front seat.

Onboard the *RMS Mauretania* that evening, Jack was invited to dine at the captain's table. It seemed that is was customary to have celebrities dine with either the captain or one of his senior officers. Jack was surprised when introduced to Mary Anderson, an American stage and screen actress who had been well received by the English. During their conversation, Jack was also surprised that they knew so many of the same people. She had worked for Emory Johnson, the movie director that Jack played golf with. She also knew Knute Erickson, the star in *The Non Stop Flight* movie. She reveled when Jack told her about how he and Emory teamed up against Knute and another actor and beat them by a good margin. Mary knew Peggy and had played some of the same stage roles. She even knew that Jack and Peggy were sweethearts. Jack looked forward to the evening dinner times and always tried to sit next to Mary.

On the third evening, the captain asked if he might impose upon Mary and Jack to team up to play and sing a few songs for the guests. How could they refuse? When Mary and Jack finished eating, they moved to the piano near the dance floor. The captain came forward and introduced them.

"Ladies and Gentlemen, this evening I am honored to introduce the famous Mary Anderson and the famous "Whispering" Jack Smith. After a little arm twisting, they have agreed to do a few songs for us."

There was a round of applause, during which, Jack asked Mary what songs she would like to do. Mary simply said for Jack to start the songs and she would join in. Her approach was perfect. Jack started with Gershwin songs that were very popular. Mary immediately joined in and they sounded very good as a duo. Soon guests were on the dance floor, and after several songs, Jack asked if there were any requests. When the requests were heard, Jack would look at Mary for a sign of approval and then start the playing and singing. They continued performing for a good forty-five minutes. At that point, the captain once again came forward and addressed the guests, while he thanked Mary and Jack for their performance. There was a standing ovation as Mary and Jack returned to the captain's table.

"Jack, I really enjoyed singing with you."

"Thank you, Mary, I enjoyed it also. I can't wait to tell Peggy that I sang duos with the famous Mary Anderson."

Mary and Jack became very good friends during the ocean crossing and promised to keep in touch. Mary made a note of Jack's agent for future considerations.

It took eight days to cross the Atlantic. Jack arranged to have his luggage delivered to the Chelsea Arms. He found a public phone near to the pier and stopped to call his mother. She was surprised to hear Jack was already in New York. He promised to stop at her house in the afternoon. Next, he called his agent. Janet put him right through to Stan.

"Jack, I'm glad you called. I have some great news for you. Can you come over to my office today?"

"I just got off the ship, but yes I can be there in an hour or so."

"Good, kid. I'll go over your latest contract offer and explain more about your being cut short in England."

"Okay, Stan, see you in about an hour."

Jack picked up a bouquet of flowers from a street vendor for Janet and headed for the subway. It felt good to be back in the city. He thought London, Paris, and Berlin are all great cities to visit, but there is no place quite like New York City. He took in the sounds and the smells as he walked along. *God, how I love this place.* At the agency, Jack presented the flowers to Janet, telling her they were a token of his appreciation for handling all of his accommodations. She was thrilled and gave Jack a big hug. Stan saw Jack from his office and waved him in.

"Come in, Jack, and please close the door. You are not going to believe the offer I have for you. How does a long-term contract with the National Broadcasting Company sound?"

"NBC, Stan, you really mean you've opened the door to true national radio broadcasting for me?"

"Yeah, kid, and wait until you see the dollar figures and the fringe benefits."

Stan briefed Jack about the pending contract. There was more money than Jack had ever imagined possible, and even though it was a multiyear-contract, there would only be seven months of work throughout any given calendar year. Jack thought it could be perfect for him spending time with Peggy. Stan then broached the subject of Jack's dismissal in England.

"I pretty much figured it out from the hint you put in the telegram. It's hard to swallow. I fought against the Germans in the war. Was I wrong to sing those songs in German?"

"No, Jack, actually your performance in Berlin can only enhance your career. I found out who was involved in your dismissal. They were a couple of two bit promoters who seized an unscrupulous opportunity to get their girls a chance to sing with the Blue Skies Group. We agents have friends even on the other side of the ocean, and I guarantee you, those guys will not get any more bookings."

"Thanks, Stan. I was kind of worried about the whole incident. I've never been dismissed from anything before. I feel a little better now."

"What are your plans now?"

"Well, I'm going over to visit my mother, and if I'm lucky, she will invite me to stay for some home cooked food."

"Good for you, Jack. I would like you to come in around the middle of next week, so we can finalize the NBC contract and go over your own personal accounts and investments. Give Janet a call, so she can set something up. It's good to see you back in New York."

They shook hands and Jack was off to see his mother. There's nothing like returning home after being away for a while.

THE GE MONITOR

After dining with his mother and being brought up to date on all of the family members, Jack walked down to visit with Jean and Milt. Because Jean corresponded with Peggy, she pretty much knew about Jack's adventures in Europe.

"Milt, how is the Chalmers doing?"

"It is one great car. I hate to give it back, but if you like I'll drive you to the Chelsea Arms and we can switch cars."

"Is your old jalopy ready to drive?"

"Yeah, Jack, I've been over a few times to start it up and kick the tires. It'll be fine."

On the way over to Jack's apartment, they talked mostly about the golf courses that Jack had played in England. Milt was doing well in his job with the Chilton Company and had attained permanent union status. Milt's old Ford started right up. He pulled out of the reserved space and waved as he headed back home. Jack looked over the Chalmers before heading into the Chelsea Arms. It looked better than new. Knowing Milt's attention to car care, he assumed that there were one or more coats of polish on the car.

The doorman and desk clerk made a big fuss over Jack's return claiming that they had missed him. Inside his apartment, Jack looked around and decided that maybe it wasn't as big and fancy as Peggy's suite in London, but it certainly had all of the comforts of home and best of all, it was warm. He checked the ice box and found it to be stocked with fresh milk, butter, eggs, and bacon. Now who did that? It was probably Janet. I am really getting to be spoiled. Tuning in the radio, he found a news broadcast. *Well, this is living. I think I'll just stay home, fix myself some bacon and eggs and relax. The only thing I really have to do is go down to the desk and send a telegram to Peggy.*

Jack slept in late the next morning. After downing a cup of fresh brewed coffee, he called the desk to find out if his luggage had been delivered. It had, so Jack asked that it be brought up to his apartment. As he unpacked, Jack sorted the clothes that needed to be cleaned and pressed.

In an inside pocket of one of the bags he had placed the card with Cecilia's Paris address and phone number. He copied the name and address on fresh stationery, and then took the card to his bedroom where he retrieved the cigar box he used to store old addresses and remembrances. The card now had a large 'X' drawn across each side. Well, that was a very pleasant closure. I am so glad that Cecilia survived the war. I will give her name and address to Janet and ask that each time I have a new record released one copy be sent to Cecilia. Jack thought for a moment and then returned to his desk. He copied Peggy's London address and phone number onto a five-by-eight card. Back in the bedroom, he first placed the cards into the cigar box and then put the cigar box back on the closet shelf.

Wednesday came quickly. Jack's meeting with Stan was for ten o'clock. At the agency, Jack gave Janet the paper with Cecilia's Paris address and instructions to mail one copy of each new release to her. Janet began to tease Jack, saying that she now knew what he was doing in Paris.

Jack simply responded that she was the nurse that helped him recover from the gas attack during the war.

Stan had a lot of papers spread out over his desk.

"Jack, bring a chair around to my side of the desk. I want to go over a lot of these documents with you."

"Judging from the number of papers and books you have spread out, this looks like it might be a little complicated."

"It is, Jack, but it is also beautiful. You are going to be sitting pretty once we get the contract signed. Now we have three big players: RCA, GE, and NBC."

Stan went on with some background history and information about how the three companies were involved. It all boiled down to the merging of stations WEAF and WJZ. The new station would have a Red Network and a Blue Network. Jack would be broadcasting with the Red Network. This network would specialize in commercially sponsored music and entertainment. The Blue Network would broadcast non-sponsored news and cultural programs. The money was very attractive, and best of all, Jack would only be responsible for broadcasting seven months out of each year. Jack especially liked that as he envisioned his availability to spend more time with Peggy. Stan talked about fifteen-minute serial format broadcasts and told Jack that one serial called the *Amos 'n' Andy Show* had already been reviewed and was soon to be broadcast on a weekly basis.

"Okay, Stan, I'm sold. Where do you want me to sign?"

"I want you to go home and sleep on this one, Jack. This will be a multiyear-contract so you need to give it some thought. Janet has a packet of papers for you to look through at home. And now I have some bonus information for you. I want to put some of the money from your account into GE stock. They are branching out into everything, Jack, and well on their way to becoming a giant corporation. One of their latest products is a home refrigerator to replace all those old ice boxes. It's called the Monitor. On the top of the square-like refrigerator there is a round turret-shaped enclosure that houses most of the working mechanisms. The people at GE selected the name Monitor because it resembles the turret that was on the old iron sided Civil War ship."

"Okay, I'm sold again. Pick up some stock for my portfolio."

"Here's the best part, Jack. Stockholders will be given the opportunity to purchase up to five of these refrigerators at roughly half price before they are placed on sale in retail stores. GE wants to have some already in peoples' homes before they start their advertising. Janet will give you a GE brochure to take home. It's a great deal. Let me know how many you want to buy."

"Will we get them before Christmas?"

"I think so, Jack. And I'm going to set you up to resume broadcasting next Monday."

"Okay, am I still at the WJZ studio?"

"Yes, eventually you'll be moving to the new NBC studio on Seven Eleven Fifth Avenue."

Back at his apartment, Jack reviewed the packet of papers Janet had given him. He was excited to think all of his broadcasts would be on national radio. In the past, some of his were sent to different parts of the country, but to know he would be singing and talking to people all over the country was just mind-boggling. Well, I'm going to do whatever Stan recommends. He has treated me like an ace since day one. Jack moved on to the GE material. So General Electric is into more than just electric motors and generators. He recalled that the tugs used to position ships going through the Panama Canal were manufactured by GE. The material about the Monitor refrigerator was very interesting. All that was required was an electric outlet to plug in the refrigerator. People are going to love not having to deal with the delivery of ice. Jack thought about the coming holidays. His mother would certainly love to have a home refrigerator and maybe his brother? Jean and Milt could certainly use one also. Well, counting his own apartment, he would need to order four. Jack started to do some quick math in his head and then shrugged and thought to himself, *I have more money than I know what to do with. I'll order four of the Monitors as long as they can promise delivery before Christmas directly to the addresses I provide.* He went to the desk and wrote all four addresses on a sheet of paper. *I'll pass this to Janet next week and most of my Christmas shopping will be finished.*

When Monday arrived, Jack was up early and very anxious to return to radio broadcasting. He had decided to flavor his music selections with a little dialog about his experiences in Europe. It felt good to be back on the airways. Broadcasting was quite different from entertaining on the stage. It was much more one way, thereby giving Jack almost complete control. Jack started out slowly injecting a little dialog here and there about where he had played and sung various selections in England. He talked about meeting the famous "Sweet" Peggy O'Neil in London, about performing for the British Royalty, and how he teamed up with Mary Anderson on his return Atlantic crossing to entertain others onboard. The engineer at the radio station continued to give Jack the thumbs-up signal indicating that his broadcasting performance was going well.

Jack felt good when he wrapped up for the day. When he returned to his apartment, there was a call from Stan.

"Great broadcast today, Jack. I listened to most of it. Try to continue in the same format tomorrow while I get some feedback about how the radio audience liked your show. I think we may be in a position to negotiate a very favorable contract. Did you look through the material Janet gave you?"

"I did, Stan. Let me just say I didn't see anything troublesome. I'm not that good with contractual language. That's why I put my trust in you, Stan. I know you have my best interests at heart, so just go ahead with what you think works best."

"Okay, kid. I'll put together a proposal. It may get modified a little after I meet with the station people. Why don't you give Janet a call about the middle of next week to schedule a sit down with me? We'll go through the paperwork page by page and I'll explain the meanings and impact of the proposed contract."

"Thanks, Stan. It felt good to be back at the station today. I hope everything works out."

"It will, kid. I'll see you next week and think about some tunes that you would like to record. We want to get you back on the market pretty soon."

"Okay, Stan. I'll see you next week."

That evening, Jack spent a good amount of time at the piano in his apartment. He wanted to come up with six or so songs that he felt good about recording. Many of the songs had romantic lyrics. His mind kept flashing back to times spent with Peggy. *Wow, I really miss that woman*, he thought. Jack got up and moved to the kitchen. There was a bottle of brandy on the shelf. He thought why not have a glass? It will ease the pain I feel for Peggy. One glass led to a second, but then he began to feel better. He returned to the piano and belted out a few more melodies.

He stopped for a moment and then remembered the list of twelve songs he had previously prepared as good songs to record. Jack stood, opened the top of the piano bench, and there was the listing. He crossed out those that had already been recorded and added "When Autumn Leaves are Falling". *There*, he thought, *I am familiar with all of these and I remember Janet telling me most were very good selections.* To celebrate, he returned to the kitchen for one last glass of brandy before turning in.

The next several months flew by for Jack. Between recording sessions, personal appearances, and the additional time spent at the broadcasting station to accommodate the pending move to the new NBC Studio, Jack had little time for himself. In a way, it was good because it kept him from thinking about Peggy. Suddenly, December was upon him. The GE Monitor refrigerators were reported ready for delivery and Jack needed to arrange for the installation of each. The one slated for his brother in Valley Stream was relatively easy. Jane was now a fulltime housewife, and it simply meant that she needed to be home for the refrigerator to be installed and the ice box to be removed. Jack felt that either he or his nephew, Charles, needed to be at his mother's house for that installation. It turned out that Charles would be able to handle it. The hardest one was at Milt and Jean's house because they both worked and Jean did not think her mother would be capable of handling the situation. Jack volunteered to be available so that all GE Monitors would be installed before Christmas. After the installers hooked up the refrigerator in his apartment, he would go with them to Milt and Jean's until the installation was finished. Everyone was thrilled with the new refrigerators. They were true marvels and what a convenience to no longer have to have ice delivered.

PEGGY RETURNS

Peggy returned to New York just four days before Christmas. The ocean crossing had been tiring for her, but at least she did not get seasick. Jack met her at the pier and then escorted her to his apartment. He made a big fuss about getting her set in bed and then excused himself to go off to the radio station. He was now broadcasting from the new NBC Studio on Seven Eleven Fifth Avenue. During his broadcast, Jack announced that Peggy O'Neil had just returned from London and he hoped to have her on the air tomorrow to share some of her experiences abroad. When Jack returned to the apartment early that evening, he found Peggy to be in much better spirits. He first kissed her passionately and then escorted her to sit near the radio. Jack tuned in the new NBC station for Peggy and then moved to the kitchen to prepare a nice home cooked meal. Having been an ocean crossing passenger, Jack knew how nice it felt to just sit and relax for a while in the comforts of home.

They enjoyed a candlelight dinner. Jack poured a glass of wine for Peggy and a glass of brandy for himself. He proposed a toast, "May our time together like this last forever."

"Here, here, and thank you, Jack. It feels so good to be off that ship and to just relax."

"That's exactly how I felt when I returned to New York. Have you been listening to my new broadcasting station? What do you think of the programming?"

"I'm impressed, Jack. I loved the short "Amos 'n' Andy Show". I'll try to listen to your broadcast tomorrow."

"Better yet, babe, I want you to come to the new studio with me. I would even like to put you on the air for a few minutes. It will be like free advertising for you."

"I'd love to see the new studio, but I don't know about talking on the air."

"Just leave it to me. I'll ask you a few questions and you answer anyway you please. It'll be fun. But right now let's pile the dishes in the sink and head back to the bedroom for a little different kind of fun."

The next day, Peggy did go along with Jack to the new NBC Studio. She was recognized within minutes and from that point on, treated like royalty. After some introductions, Jack asked that a guest chair and second microphone be setup at his broadcasting position. In no time at all, everything was set for Peggy to join in on the broadcast. The chair for Peggy was placed just to the right of Jack's piano bench with a microphone extending from a holder situated on top of the piano.

Jack started with "When Autumn Leaves are Falling" and then mentioned to his audience that today he had a special guest who had just returned from England. He played a few notes of "Sweet Peggy O'Neil" before continuing: "You guessed it, Ladies and Gentlemen, the renowned actress we all love, Miss. Peggy O'Neil. Well, Peggy, how does it feel to back in New York?"

"It feels wonderful, Jack. You don't realize how many New York City things you miss until you're away for a while."

"Peggy, tell us a little about your theater performances in London."

And so the dialog went for almost ten minutes until Jack asked her what song she would like him to sing. Her response was "Me and My Shadow". After Jack sang, the dialog interspersed with a variety of piano melodies and songs continued for almost forty-five minutes. At that point, Jack asked Peggy to join him in singing "Blue Skies" before the break for news.

Stan called Jack the next morning to compliment him on his broadcast.

"Yesterday's broadcast was just beautiful, Jack. And the timing could not have been better. I am going to wrap up the final draft of your contract today. Keep up the good work. I'll give you a call when everything is ready for your review and signature."

When Peggy rolled out of bed, she too complimented Jack.

"Honey, I just want to tell you I really enjoyed being on the radio with you. You are so smooth, Jack. I don't think I could handle that kind of performance every day. My stage routines are much more regimented."

"Well, first of all, you were just superb on the radio. You give a great interview and you have a wonderful singing voice. How about marrying me?"

"Oh, Jack, how I wish I could."

"I know, babe, just remember we're doing pretty well without exchanging rings. In fact, I forgot to tell you that Jean called yesterday. We are invited to their house for a family Christmas celebration. So you see, everyone already thinks of you as being part of the family."

"Oh! That's wonderful. I can't wait to see everybody, but I don't have any gifts."

"That's all been taken care of. The cards accompanying the Monitor refrigerators had both of our names on them."

"Thank you, Jack. That's great, but I'm still going shopping today to pick up a few incidental items."

Peggy went along with Jack on his way to the NBC Studio, but this time kissed him good-bye at the studio entrance and continued on to do some serious Christmas shopping. When she could not carry any more merchandise, Peggy headed back to the apartment and spent the rest of the day wrapping gifts. She made a list of everyone she expected to be at Milt and Jean's house and then sorted the gifts while she wrote little brief messages on cards she later attached to the packages.

Jack was very impressed when he returned to the apartment. He told Peggy to take a break and freshen up. He had arranged for dinner at the country club and promised a big surprise. They left in kind of a hurry because the surprise was to meet someone at the club. Peggy could not imagine who was going to meet them.

"I know it's going to be your mom. I always enjoy spending time with her."

Jack was noncommittal and would not answer affirmatively or negatively.

"Well, if not your mom, it's probably Stan."

Again Jack was noncommittal. After three or four more guesses, Peggy gave up and resigned herself to the fact that she would just have to wait until they arrived at the club.

At the club, the hostess greeted Jack and made a fuss over Peggy and then ushered them to one of the premier tables overlooking the eighteenth fairway of the golf course. As they drew closer to the table, Peggy realized that someone was already seated at the table.

"Oh! My God! Mary Anderson, I can't believe it."

Mary and Peggy hugged and then settled in at the table. There was a lot of stage talk about various plays and performances, so Jack didn't get a chance to join in the conversation much, but he did readily see that both Mary and Peggy were very appreciative of his arranging the evening's surprise meeting. Mary and Jack eventually did tell Peggy about their time at the captain's table aboard ship and how he coaxed them to perform for the other passengers. As dinner came to a close, Mary and Peggy arranged to meet the next day for lunch and some last-minute shopping.

In the Chalmers and on the way back to the apartment, Peggy snuggled up close to Jack putting her arm around him.

"You are such a devil, Jack. Why didn't you tell me we were to dine with Mary?"

"Well, had I told you ahead of time, you would still be back in the apartment trying on different outfits and fussing with your makeup."

"You're right, Jack. It was really a wonderful surprise. Thank you so much."

The next day, Jack and Peggy went their separate ways. There was sort of a Christmas party at the radio station, so Jack was later than usual returning to the apartment. Peggy was tired from a long day of shopping with Mary Anderson. They decided to turn in early and get a nice fresh start on Christmas and that they did. Jack was up early fixing a good solid breakfast consisting of bacon, eggs, toast, and coffee. At the breakfast table, they exchanged gifts. Peggy's was diamond earrings; Jack's, diamond cuff links. Both were thrilled, and they joked about the way the diamonds sparkled as they moved the jewelry about.

After bathing and dressing, they headed for Jack's mother's house. Mrs. Schmidt was always up early, so there was no need to worry about what time they arrived. Jack's mother was thrilled when they arrived. She ushered Peggy straight into the kitchen and had her sit while she fixed fresh coffee for them. Mrs. Schmidt wanted to hear all about Peggy's time in England. Jack felt somewhat left out, but happy that Mom and Peggy got along so well. Eventually, the ladies invited Jack to join them for a cup of coffee. Jack's nephew Charles was still asleep, so they tried to keep things quiet. Mrs. Schmidt was thrilled with the new Monitor refrigerator and told them she was the envy of the neighborhood. She thanked both Jack and Peggy, at which point Peggy excused herself and returned within minutes with a small package carefully decorated with Christmas wrappings and placed it in front of Jack's mother.

"Another present? Well thank you, Peggy."

The package contained a beautiful broach shaped like a butterfly with brightly colored wings. Peggy knew that Mrs. Schmidt often wore pins on her coat. The gift was an immediate hit, greatly overshadowing the more expensive Monitor. Of course, it was all because the gift was from the famous actress, Peggy O'Neil. Again, Jack was just happy that Peggy and his mother got along so well.

Jack's nephew joined them and sat to have some breakfast. He too was very much interested in Peggy's tales about London. At least Charles would periodically ask Jack about his experiences abroad.

"Are you coming with us to Milt's?"

"No, Uncle Jack, I'm going to pick up Mamie and then join you at Milt's."

"Mom, what time do you think we should show up at Milt's?"

"Oh, we can go whenever you want. I talked to Milt a little while ago and they are all ready for us."

"Do they have a tree?"

"Yes, son, I think it's a blue spruce that reaches almost to the ceiling and it's completely decorated."

Milt and Jean's house was completely decorated both inside and out. They were excited to see company arriving, and of course, Peggy was the guest of honor. Jean marshaled Peggy into the kitchen to catch up on events since they last corresponded. Milt and Jack sat in the living room near to the Christmas tree.

"That's a beauty of a tree, Milt. How did you get it here?"

"It was kind of fun. We headed out to a farm on the Island that George Ransom had told us about. The tree was cheap enough. The problem was we had to cut it and transport it. Jean and I had a tough time keeping it on the roof of the car and we had to drive pretty slow making the drivers behind us kind of mad, but it was all worth it."

"How's the job going?"

"We are doing just great. I'm responsible for the layout of a lot of pages now. I like the work and I feel like I'm pretty good at it. Jean is doing well in the business office and Jean's mom is a real plus here at home. She does almost all of the cleaning, cooking and laundry. Jean and I are really getting spoiled."

"Well good for you, kid. You had your share of some tough times, so you deserve a break."

They went on to talk about who was coming and how Jack's brother was doing. Before long, more guests started to arrive and the house slowly became as busy as a beehive. It was a joyous gathering with Jean's brother, Bill, entertaining just about everyone with his stories and jokes. Peggy's little gifts were a big hit. Jack spent some time catching up with his brother and Jane. After dinner, drinks were served. Jack surprised some of those close to him by taking a glass of brandy. He explained that he had not had an alcoholic beverage until one cold and damp evening in London when at dinner he couldn't stop shaking. Peggy suggested a glass of brandy and within minutes, he felt warm and was free of the shakes.

When Peggy and Jack returned to the apartment that evening, he first offered Peggy a drink and then poured another brandy for himself. By the time they went to bed, Jack silently counted the amount of brandy he had consumed. He came to the conclusion it was at least a half a dozen glasses. *Wow*, he thought, *it wouldn't be hard to get hooked on this stuff*!

THE WOW YEAR

Nineteen hundred and twenty seven started as a fantastic year for both Peggy and Jack. Peggy's agent had her booked to do *Mercenary Mary* in Buffalo. She would be there for about one month. The play was to be at Shea's Court Street Theatre. Peggy was ecstatic. She would get to visit with her aunt and some old friends. Jack would be able to come up on the train for three or four days. After the performance in Buffalo, Peggy would return to New York City and be able to spend more time with Jack before returning to England.

Jack's new broadcast was an immediate hit. He still had trouble coming to grips with the fact he was now a true celebrity. Several new records were soon to be released and he would be making guest appearances to promote the sales. He often thought about the war years and all of the individuals who had helped him along the way on his road to success. Jack decided to make a list of those who helped him, and then attempt to visit or at least contact each individual so as to show some appreciation for their efforts. And so, he started to think back to the events that had been most helpful. The first job as a song plugger was definitely one. Moving to play in O'Malley's Piano Bar was mostly a good experience and led to him meeting both Lorie and Stan. Of course, meeting Peggy, and in turn her friends and business associates certainly impacted his career moves. And the most important of all was his mother's insistence that he practice on the piano. He started to write some names and annotate comments nearby.

Cecilia – now a doctor in Paris who encouraged me to make up with Peggy
Francis Kelly – sang the Irish songs over in France when my voice was gone
Father Dougherty – started me playing piano in church over the Christmas Season
Frank Murphy – the parishioner who gave me a steer to the song plugger job
General Goethals – made me proud of my time in the war and info about the Panama Canal
Arthur Kennedy – the Irving Berlin Publishing Company executive who became my mentor
Katie – the music store manager who taught me a lot about sheet music
Pat O'Malley – who let me develop my song deliveries in his piano bar
Lorie Bradford – a wonderful sponsor but now married and not as involved in my career
Stan Schuman – an outstanding agent to whom I will forever be indebted for his care and advice
Janet – the girl making all travel, lodging and many other arrangements for my comfort
Mom and Peggy–?????

Jack looked the list over, trying to decide how to best show his appreciation to each individual. He thought about Cecilia and decided to write a letter telling her about the outcome of his relationship with Peggy and thanking her for a wonderful time in Paris. He didn't know how to reach Francis Kelly, so that one would have to be put on hold. Jack thought perhaps a bundle of his records packaged with a nice check to be used however the Reverend desired might be appropriate for Father Dougherty. He would discuss this one with his mother. Perhaps a bundle of records for Frank Murphy would be good. This would be another one to discuss with his mother. General Goethals was a tough one, so he decided this one would best be determined by talking it over with his mother. For Arthur Kennedy, he would either arrange to take him to lunch or dinner. Maybe Katie could come along with Arthur Kennedy, thereby finishing two off the list at one time. The more he thought about it, the more he realized it would be better to handle each separately. So Katie would be for dinner someday after she closed the music store. He would visit Pat O'Malley and perhaps bring along a bundle of records. He thought about Lorie for a while and decided the best approach would be to keep his distance and perhaps send a gift of some kind. He would have to give this one more thought. Stan was a tough one. The only thing Jack could come up with was to do something related to movies because of Stan's fascination with the movie business. He would probably take Janet to either lunch or dinner and maybe give her a tour of the radio station. She would probably appreciate that. And above all, what could he possibly do for his mother? Again he thought, *I'll give this one some time. Maybe I can take her to see Peggy perform? I know she would like that. And Peggy, if only we could marry.* He folded the paper and placed it in his cigar box.

A few days later, Peggy departed for her scheduled performance in Buffalo. Jack was kept busy with his new broadcasting schedule and other promotional events. The hardest time was late in the evenings. He really missed Peggy. On occasion, Jack was able to talk over the phone lines with Peggy, but then he would only miss her more. He found that a glass or two of brandy late in the evening helped him fall asleep. Time passed quickly, and before long, Jack was on the train to Buffalo. He couldn't wait to hold Peggy in his arms again. Their three days together were just perfect. Peggy was so full of life and endless energy. Jack attended one of her evening performances and just marveled at how she was so alive on stage with the audience totally under her spell. Peggy was thrilled to have Jack in her company and always introduced him as "Whispering" Jack Smith her, very good friend. Most people knew of "Whispering" Jack Smith from his national radio broadcasts; some also knew that he and Peggy were sweethearts.

The last night in Buffalo with Peggy was extremely hard for Jack. He just wanted to stay with her forever. After they made very passionate love, Peggy began to wipe tears from her cheeks.

"Oh, Jack, you make me so happy and also so sad. I so look forward to seeing you and making love with you, and before I know it, you are gone. I sometimes dream that we are married and living in a cute little house with a white picket fence around it. I know it will never happen, and it saddens me to think this is as good as our relationship is going to be."

"I know exactly what you mean, love. But my dream is just a little different. I dream that we will be working together at the radio station and making personal appearances together as we travel around the globe. We will have almost every evening together just like this one. My dream may not come true, but I think there is a chance it can come close."

When Peggy returned to New York City, Jack felt as if he was starting to live his dream, but then she was off again for a lengthy engagement in London. However, this time their agents along with Mary Anderson's were coordinating with one another to try to book Jack, Peggy, and Mary in the same locations throughout Europe. Jack felt good about the planned effort and anticipated he would be in Europe by late spring or early summer. The trick now was to stay busy, so he didn't have time to think about Peggy not being near. He started working on the list of names he had put away in the cigar box. His first evening at home, he wrote a long and thoughtful letter to Cecelia. He thanked her from the bottom of his heart and explained how he and Peggy had reunited. When finished, Jack felt good and retired to bed, falling to sleep almost instantly, and enjoying a very restful night. The next evening at home, he didn't feel like working on anything and simply listened to the radio for a while. When he turned in, Jack was unable to sleep. He got out of bed and went to the kitchen to drink several glasses of brandy. He did fall asleep, but experienced a rather restless night. Up early the next morning, Jack vowed to work at keeping occupied and to stay away from the brandy before bedtime.

Keeping busy seemed to work. He thought about Peggy, but she was not dominating his thoughts. Jack spent time with his mother going over his list and nailing down methods to reward those who had helped him. During the next several weeks, he had records delivered to the rectory for both Father Dougherty and Frank Murphy. He arranged to take both Katie and Janet to dinner, and left each with an open invitation to come to the radio studio for a guided tour. Jack was feeling much better about himself, and his communications with Peggy indicated everything was going well in London. He was anxious for Stan to inform him about his spring or summer schedule overseas. It was hard to be patient, but he stuck to his plan and stayed away from the brandy bottle. He visited with Pat O'Malley and had dinner and lunch with Arthur Kennedy on two separate occasions. Jack contacted Emory Johnson, the movie director in California, and arranged for Stan to spend the best part of a week on the movie set with Emory to learn something about the movie business. Stan could not believe that Jack had arranged time on the movie set for him. He couldn't stop thanking Jack. It was definitely one of the best things he could ever have done for Stan. Jack's only condition was that Stan had to have his own European tour finalized before traveling to California. The strategy worked. Jack was scheduled for various performances in England, Scotland, Denmark, and Germany starting near the end of April and early May. He would be working in close proximity to both Peggy O'Neil and Mary Anderson. *Wow!* Jack thought, *this is going to be great*!

And great it was. When Jack arrived in England, he went directly to Cambridge to meet up with Peggy. She and her cast were performing at the New Theater in the stage show, *The Flying Squad*. The cast and supporting staff were great to be around. There was always a lot of joking around and good clean fun. Some of the group enjoyed playing golf, so Jack managed to get some time out on the links. Mary Anderson was also in the area. She and Peggy spent time together shopping and sightseeing. Jack had his Bell and Howell movie camera on this trip to Europe and spent little time in getting started shooting. *The Flying Squad* actors were very cooperative and even went out of their way to clown around, so Jack could capture some home movie footage. Cambridge was impressive. The university buildings were spectacular and everything was kept immaculately clean. Jack shot several reels of film. He remembered what Emory Johnson had told him about never having too much on film because it was very easy to cut unwanted material from the final reel.

The New Theatre, Cambridge, England. Frame from Jack Smith's 16mm home movies

Poster in front of New Theatre. Frame from
Jack Smith's 16mm home movies

There were only three performances remaining at the New Theatre. After that, most of the cast was traveling to Edinburgh, Scotland, where veteran silent film director Herbert Brenen was setting up to do a film of *The Flying Squad*. Some of the stage cast had hopes of landing a part in the film. Mary Anderson was also being considered for the lead role. Peggy had no interest as she and Jack were booked to perform in Amsterdam at Tivoli Park. Peggy and Jack had free time before going to Amsterdam, so they decided to travel along with those going to Edinburgh. Once again, Jack had the opportunity to get some great film shots. The initial gathering was at an airstrip where a bi-wing airplane was made available for use in the movie. Additionally, the director had an agreement with the airstrip operator to use the airport ambulance and fire truck in some of the scenes. When the film crew was doing live shots of the airplane moving about on the ground with the ambulance and fire truck approaching, Jack was just off to the side of the cameramen shooting his home movie footage. Later, he got permission to film

Peggy climbing in and out of the airplane cockpit wearing parts of an aviatrix outfit, including goggles around her neck. Jack had a feeling that Director Brenen would have loved to have Peggy for his movie in the lead role.

Peggy next to Biplane

Three days later, they were in Tivoli Park. Except for one, all of *The Flying Squad* cast had come along, making it much easier to put on the play without recruiting replacements. Jack was booked in the Park as "Whispering" Jack Smith, the Radio and Recording Artist from America. That evening in the hotel, Jack commented to Peggy, "Now this is living. We've been together almost nonstop for the past week and I've loved every minute of it."

"It has been great, Jack, and I've loved every minute of our time together too."

"Well, babe, we're booked through the end of June and then I return to New York. But if all goes as planned, I'll be back around the end of August and we're off on our vacation down to Venice, Italy."

"I can't wait, Jack. I've heard so much about Venice and Lido Beach. It's just going to be great to get away for a while and relax without signing autographs and providing comments to reporters."

The time went so fast when Jack and Peggy were together. In the middle of June, Jack received a message from Stan advising him that a recording studio in Hayes, Middlesex, England, was interested in recording some songs. Stan had it worked out so that Jack could do the recordings just before returning to New York. Jack mulled it over, thinking that he would be sacrificing a few days with Peggy, but he would be returning to Europe in late August, so it was really something he should do. Jack fired off a one liner telegraph: "Okay with Middlesex. Send specifics."

Jack made recordings of "It All Depends On You", "Blue Skies", and "The Birth Of The Blues" before returning to New York. He found working in an English recording studio to be much more formal than back in New York. However, the recording sessions were comparatively simple because he played his own piano.

The return sailing was pretty routine with one exception. There was a jewelry shop onboard the ship with deeply discounted prices attributed to being special purchases that were all tax-free. Jack purchased a necklace for his mother and then began to look at the diamond rings. He had no need for another ring, but thought it might be a nice gift for his nephew. Milt had done a great job chauffeuring Jack around New York, and he knew Milt would have the Chalmers all cleaned up and running like a clock when he got to New York, so why not reward him. They both had about the same size hands, and the shipboard sales representative said it would be a minor matter for a jeweler to change the size if needed. The only sticking point was whether to pay in English pounds or American dollars.

Jack always felt great returning to New York. There was something special about the city that was really lacking in other parts of the world. His ship tied in to the pier early in the morning, so Jack decided to arrange for his luggage to be delivered to the apartment, giving him the freedom to go directly to the Star Agency and check in with Janet and Stan. Janet and Stan were thrilled to see him.

"Come on in the office, Jack. It's a slow morning for me, so if you have an hour or two to give me there are some things I would like to go over with you."

"Well, no one knows I'm back in the city yet, Stan, so I'll be glad to stay provided Janet can get me a nice cup of coffee."

Stan called for Janet to bring in some coffee and then he pulled Jack's file from his desk drawer.

"Jack, you have been doing great, in fact, better than great. I went through your portfolio last week and found a couple of things that need your attention. The income from your recordings has been much higher than we anticipated, and now you will be getting even more from the records you made over in England. The bad news is that you have too much money just sitting around not doing much for you. I want you to buy more stock. I'm still high on Coca Cola and it wouldn't be a bad idea to pick up some shares of NBC."

"Stan, you know I trust your judgment. My only concern is how much money is available to be spent? You know Peggy and I have planned a vacation for late August and early September that will take us through Europe and down into Italy."

"You have plenty, Jack. I had Janet do some preliminary planning for you and Peggy. She has come up with some very attractive deals for the both of you and everything is first-class."

"Thanks, Stan. That's all I need to know. Go ahead and add some more stock to the portfolio. And now I would like to hear about your visit with Emory Johnson."

Stan went on to tell Jack that the trip to California was just fabulous. Emory had treated him like a king. They played golf and Emory introduced him to so many movie stars that Stan had trouble remembering their names, which is highly unusual for him. He told Jack there was gold in the movie business and he was looking at getting a piece of the action on the east coast.

"I'm going to keep you in mind, kid. Emory told me they are very close to revolutionizing the industry with talking movies. Someday, Jack, you're going to be singing in front of cameras instead of in the recording studios."

Jack returned to England in the third week of August. Stan had him booked in London for one week, and then he and Peggy were to be off on their European vacation. Peggy was very excited. Being something of a workaholic, she seldom took time away from the stage. They started their trip in late August. Janet had them booked in a really classy hotel in Paris with tickets for a show and dinner at the Moulin Rouge. Following their short stay in Paris, they traveled by rail to Vienna. The weather was just perfect, and again Jack had his movie camera along to capture pictures of the beautiful countryside and historic buildings. Peggy wanted some of the footage to include shots of Jack, so she had Jack show her how to operate the Bell and Howell camera. Jack was amazed at how quickly she picked up running the camera, and he anticipated that many of her shots would be rather good. From Vienna, they again traveled by rail to Venice, Italy. Their hotel was right on Lido Beach. It was just the perfect place to be. The hotel suite was near the top of the building with a balcony facing the beach and water. Directly below their suite, there was a beach cabana that was for their exclusive use. It was so relaxing to be on the beach and just be with each other.

Jack and Peggy on Lido Beach

In the evenings, they would take a water taxi to Saint Mark's Square where there was always fine dining and music. Of course, a gondola ride following dinner was also a very romantic experience. On their second gondola ride, both Peggy and Jack joined in singing with the gondolier. Back in their suite later in the evening, they made love and told each other how wonderful life was when they were together.

"Jack, I will forever be indebted to you for talking me into taking this trip. Up to now, everything has been just perfect. There is one thing I want to do before we leave and I don't want you to laugh at me for doing it. Okay?"

"Okay, babe, I promise not to laugh. What is it?"

"I want to go to Saint Mark's Square during daylight hours and feed the pigeons, so they land on my outstretched arms and my shoulders. And I want you to capture me on film doing it."

"We can do that and maybe I'll also feed the pigeons with you running the camera."

They took a water taxi to Saint Mark's Square the next day just before noon. On the ride to the Square, the driver asked if they knew about the Regatta. Neither Jack nor Peggy knew much, so he went on to describe the event as a spectacular flotilla on the canal not to be missed.

"It is held on the first weekend of September every year. Every boat for miles around will be in the canals of Venice. There will be races and water hose events. If you have an interest in seeing the Regatta, I can take you in my boat to a dock just across from the salt storage building. We will tie to the dock and you will have one of the best vantage points to see everything and to take pictures if you so choose."

"It sounds good to me, Antonio. What do you say Peggy?"

Peggy was all for it, so they agreed on a price and set a time early on Saturday to meet Antonio.

At Saint Mark's Square, they headed straight for the center of the piazza where Jack practiced shooting some movie shots of the pigeons. It was common for visitors to buy some feed and then have the pigeons swarm around them as they continued to hand out the feed. Jack purchased a small bag of feed.

"Okay, babe, you're on. Here is your bag of feed. Remember to save some for me."

Jack stood back with his camera pointed at Peggy and told her to start feeding the pigeons whenever she was ready. People in the square were very considerate about not walking between anyone with a camera and their subject matter. Peggy started feeding a few of the pigeons, and within seconds, the birds were all around her and landing on her outstretched arms and head just as she had wanted. Jack caught it all on film and told Peggy so. She was anxious to rid herself of the pigeons and quickly passed the feed bag to Jack. He gave her a few last minute instructions about the camera and then moved into position to start feeding the birds. Peggy was ready with the camera and the same scene was repeated, but this time, with Jack covered by pigeons. They both laughed and quickly moved away from the birds. Jack passed what feed was left to a bystander and they moved further on down the square laughing about their experience.

Peggy feeding pigeons in St Mark's Square

Jack feeding pigeons in St Mark's Square

That afternoon, they found the line to enter Saint Mark's Cathedral to be very short, so they decided to tour the inside of the Cathedral. It was impressive and spiritually moving. They both prayed, first to thank God for all their blessings, and then to ask for a small miracle to somehow approve Peggy's request for annulment of her marriage. Next, they went to the Doges' Palace for a guided tour. It was amazing to envision how people lived and were governed so differently many years ago. When told about how the prisoners had their last look out through a window on the Bridge of Sighs between the palace and the dungeons before they were incarcerated, both Jack and Peggy expressed their thankfulness for living in more civilized times. They were tempted to climb the steps of the tower, but when hearing how many there were, changed their minds and decided to simply walk along the canals and pass the shops until Peggy tired of shopping.

The next morning, they were up early to have a hearty breakfast and then meet Antonio at the boat dock. It was a beautiful day and crowds were already starting to form. Antonio quickly ushered them onto the boat and then hightailed it over toward Saint Mark's Square. The salt storage building was just a short distance past the square. Antonio headed straight for the salt storage building and then made a sweeping left turn, dodging in and out between varieties of watercraft before miraculously coming to a stop at a dock on the opposite side of the canal. Once Antonio had the boat secured, he helped Peggy up and onto the dock, showing her where to stand so her view of the passing regatta would not be impaired. In no time at all, the canal was filled with boats seemingly traveling every which way. Jack commented to Peggy that it looked as if one could walk across the canal simply by going from boat to boat. Antonio narrated the proceedings, telling both Jack and Peggy which events to watch with a description of the event. Some were races; others were simply passing pageantry. All were as spectacular as Antonio had promised. After a period of time, streams of water could be seen shooting up skyward. Antonio explained that this was the time for the water hoses. It is a display without intent to get any of the people in the boats wet; however, many would get soaked. Next, came what reminded Jack and Peggy of a parade down Broadway except this parade was being performed on water. All of the boats were propelled by oars. All were decorated and those onboard were in a variety of colorful costumes. One large double hulled watercraft passed with a gold-colored seat set up rather high. There was a canopy above the seat and the woman riding under the canopy was dressed as an Egyptian Queen. Everyone applauded as she passed by, tossing flowers from her perch above the oarsmen.

Peggy was thrilled with the events and became a movie director, telling Jack where to aim the movie camera as he tried to capture much of the regatta on film. Slowly, the boats began to thin out as darkness approached. Antonio signaled that it was time to return to Lido Beach. Jack and Peggy thanked Antonio at the Lido dock and handsomely rewarded him for taking such good care of them. They had a light dinner in the hotel dining room, and then decided to go to their private beach cabana to sit and gaze at the beauty of the starlit night sky. Jack pushed the two beach chairs together and reclined the backs. Before long, they were kissing and embracing. Jack began to loosen Peggy's blouse as he kissed her very passionately.

"Jack, we should go to our room."

"Don't you feel the excitement with the night sky and the water rolling onto the beach? I want to make love to you right here and right now, babe."

Jack continued to unbutton Peggy's blouse. She did feel the excitement of the moment and helped Jack remove her upper garments and then loosened his belt and pants. In the heat of their passion, they were soon both half undressed and sharing their bodies.

"Oh Jack, I wish we could stay like this forever."

At that very point, the beach chair they had rolled onto gave way crashing to the sandy floor. Once they assured each other there were no injuries, they laughed, dressed halfheartedly and hurried to their bedroom to finish what would forever be engraved in their memories as a perfect day.

Three days later, they were back in England once again saying their good-byes. Jack was returning to New York and Peggy to the stage, but this time, Peggy had taken the initiative to make arrangements for her return to New York over the holiday season. Jack was ecstatic. He knew their love for one another was to be forever. It was so much easier to depart knowing that in several months they would again be together.

The trip across the Atlantic Ocean was somewhat boring. Jack caught up on his reading and bought some jewelry for his mother and Jean. When the ship docked early in the morning, this time Jack sent his luggage on to the apartment and took a cab straight to his mother's house. He knew she would be up and he had a yearning to catch up with family news.

And news there was. His nephew Charles was to marry in the coming spring. Milt and Jean had announced they were expecting a child to be born early next year. His mother had decided to stop giving piano lessons and instead would take over the responsibility for the choir and piano music at church.

"Well, Mom, a lot of things happened while I was away. Is Charles going to be leaving you after he and Mamie marry?"

"Not right away. They want to stay with me for a while until they build up a little nest egg and find a place of their own."

Jack felt somewhat relieved. He did not want to see his mother living by herself. They went on to discuss changes in the neighborhood, and talked about Jack's brother and how things were going out in Valley Stream. It sounded like his brother and Jane were getting along fine and he was doing great in his job at Madison Square Garden. Charles had a brand-new Buick that according to his mother was just a marvelous car. Jack was pleased that everyone was doing well. Of course, his mother asked about Peggy and wanted to know all about their trip through Europe. Jack filled her in without a lot of detail and promised to give a full account along with a picture show as soon as he was able to get his movie film developed.

"When you have the film, how about I make dinner for the family and after dinner you can show us the movies?"

"That's a great idea, Mom. See if you can arrange things for a Sunday in about two weeks. I'll drop the film off today to get it developed. And don't skimp on anything. It'll all be my treat."

Jack called Stan from his mother's house and learned that he was due back on radio the next day. He peeled off some bills from his money clip and passed them to his mother.

"Here is some money to buy food for the Sunday dinner. I have to run. Stan has me back on the radio tomorrow afternoon. Don't forget to tune in. Bye, Mom, love you."

When Jack was busy he seldom thought about Peggy, but as soon as things slowed down his mind always returned to thoughts about her and their times together. As he rode along on the trolley back to his apartment, he was daydreaming about their time together in Venice and almost missed his stop. He thought, *I wish I had a little more time to prepare for my return to the station.* At the apartment, he went through his baggage, pulling out the movie reels and the clothes that needed cleaning. He dropped the clothes at the desk with instructions as to how he liked his laundry and then headed uptown with the movie reels. He was almost sure two weeks would be adequate time to have the film developed, but wanted a little reassurance from the clerk at the Kodak Store. The clerk promised the film to be done within ten days. On the way back to his apartment, Jack picked up a bag of groceries. The thought crossed his mind that he really didn't have much need for his automobile, so he wouldn't worry about getting Milt to bring the Chalmers over for at least a few more days.

After fixing a bite to eat, he moved to the piano and began to play. It was like joining up with an old friend. There was no hesitation. He hit the keys as if he had not been away from the piano at all. Soon he was singing and the lyrics just flowed along with the music. It felt great. Jack made some pencil notes charting what he would do upon his return to the radio station and then ran through each song. One time through and he felt confident that he was ready for his return to broadcasting.

That next afternoon, Jack gave one of his best radio performances ever. He flavored the show with comments about his time overseas. He mentioned Peggy O'Neil and how on this trip he had been privileged to take movies of the many people he had met and the places he had been. He closed the broadcast with his number one hit, "Me and My Shadow", and drew a sincere round of applause from the station employees.

Stan called the following morning and congratulated Jack on his return broadcast.

"Great job yesterday, kid. I want you to keep me in mind when you get those movie reels developed. I would love to see them."

"We are going to show them at my mother's house two Sundays from now. A lot of our family will be there, but you know most of them. Consider yourself invited for dinner and a show. I'll get back to you with the time."

"Great, Jack, I'm looking forward to it. Let me know what I can bring."

Time flew by and before Jack realized it was almost time for dinner at his mother's. He decided to give the Kodak Store a call and make sure the reels of film were back. They were, and he arranged to pick them up on the way to the studio. That evening, Jack setup his projector and movie screen to preview his film. Jack was impressed. The shots were very clear for the most part. He had remembered Emory's advice and kept the sun over his shoulder, thereby eliminating shadowy sequences. It took some thinking to recall the names of all of the actors in *The Flying Squad* and the facts about some of the historic buildings. Jack decided to make a few notes just in case. He really wanted to impress his family and other guests. Jack figured he had about thirty minutes of movies. He would need a little time to change reels and probably answer questions, so a good estimate was the need for about one and a half hours. *That should work,* Jack thought. Any more than that and people will lose interest.

The next day he called his mother and set dinner time for four o'clock on Sunday. They both felt sure that by the time dinner was over, the skies would be dark and they would be able to easily darken a room for the movies. Jack told his mother about inviting Stan. Mrs. Schmidt liked Stan and was happy to hear he was coming.

"Stan wanted to know what he can bring, Mom."

"That's not necessary. We have everything we need."

"Well, if we don't tell him anything, I know Stan will still show up with something. So this way you get a chance to get something useful."

"Okay, then just suggest a bottle of wine."

"Good, Mom. See you Sunday. I'll probably go to your nine o'clock Mass and then come right over to the house. Bye, Mom."

Dinner on Sunday was just great. Stan showed up with not one bottle of wine, but three. There was one red, one white, and one from the Champagne family. The biggest surprise for Jack was to learn that Jean was expecting. It seems everyone else knew, but neglected to tell Jack. He found out halfway through dinner when his brother, Charles, proposed a toast for the expectant baby. When Jean moved from the dinner table, Jack took a good look at her and didn't think she looked pregnant at all. Later he chatted with Jean and congratulated her. The baby was due in either February or March. Jean and Milt were both very excited and happy. They had started to look for a larger house somewhere close by in the Bronx.

"Well, I'm happy for both of you, but this will make me a Great Uncle and that's going to make me feel kind of old."

"You are thirty now aren't you, Jack?" Milt commented, rubbing a little salt in to his Uncle's wounded pride.

"Just remember you never changed your name to Smith, so any claims that we are related will be denied."

And so the afternoon passed with everyone enjoying the gathering. The sky darkened early as anticipated. Jack enlisted Milt and young Charles to help setup the dining room something like a theater, with all of the chairs facing one wall where Jack would place a special movie screen. Once the room was set, Jack and his nephews went out to the car to bring in the projector, the movie screen, and several reels of film. With the movie screen extended from the cylinder and properly attached to the stand, Jack moved to the end of the dining room table and started to set up the projector. Milt was very much interested and watched intently as Jack plugged in the projector, turned on the lamp, and adjusted the white picture area to fit the movie screen. Charles quickly lost interest and moved on to another room. Milt continued to be fascinated with watching how the movie film was threaded through a series of sprockets and wheels and then attached to an empty reel at the bottom of the projector. Jack explained to Milt how important it was to properly thread the film, stating that if it was not done right, the outcome would most likely be broken film.

"Okay, Milt, I think we are all set. You go over to the light switch and when I say *off*, turn the lights out. I'm going to run for a minute or so to make sure we are good and then reverse the film to the starting point. When I turn the projector off, you turn the lights on, okay?"

"I'm ready, Jack. Roll 'em."

The first minute of the movie showed a billboard outside of an English theater with pictures of Peggy O'Neil and some other actors in a play entitled *The Flying Squad.*

"Wow, Jack. That's amazing. Everything is so clear it's almost like I'm standing right there."

"Okay, Milt, turn the lights back on. Wait until we go a little further into this first reel and you're going to see some nice shots of an airplane that is going to be used in *The Flying Squad* movie. But first let's round up our guests and get them seated and ready to watch."

Once everyone was situated so they could see the movie screen, Jack called for Milt to switch the lights out. The room was very quiet as Jack turned on the projector and interjected a narrative explaining where the movies had been taken and who the people were. Almost everyone in the room immediately recognized Peggy O'Neil, with some commenting how wonderful she looked. The footage with the airplane in motion was a big hit. Milt asked Jack if he could run it again.

Biplane used in filming of *The Flying Squad*

Jack obliged before changing to the next reel. When the movies came to a close in Venice, Jean and several of the other women asked Jack to rerun the Venice footage. Again he obliged and finally called for lights *on*.

Canal Regatta in Venice

There was a spontaneous round of applause as if Jack had just finished a vocal. Jack thanked everyone for coming, and went on to answer individual questions as the gathering started to disperse to other parts of the house.

Back in his apartment that evening, Jack's thoughts wandered to Peggy. She did look beautiful in the movies and would certainly have been proud of how the movie film turned out. He couldn't wait until she arrived back in the States. *Let's see*, he thought. *Peggy should be here in less than five weeks*. Jack didn't like to write letters, but he decided this was the perfect time to put his thoughts down on paper and get a letter on the way to London before Peggy was actually on her way to New York. He wrote a lengthy letter about his broadcasting activity and the family gathering. He made sure to include that he had learned Jean was pregnant. *Actually*, he thought, *Peggy may already know because she and Jean are always exchanging letters*. He devoted one full sheet to a description of how the home movies were presented and wrapped up with a comment about how he was planning a private showing for Peggy in the darkest room of the apartment, which just happened to be the bedroom. After addressing and sealing the envelope, he immediately took it to the desk clerk and explained that the letter needed to be forwarded as early as possible. The clerk assured Jack that it would be on its way in the morning.

Back in his apartment, Jack moved to the piano and began to randomly play love songs. This evening he could not stop thinking about Peggy. He decided to try a glass of brandy. One led to another and before long, he was feeling rather melancholy. *Well*, he thought, *I didn't want to do this but at least I'll be able to sleep tonight.*

Peggy's ship arrived in New York early in the morning five days before Christmas. Jack was at the pier to meet Peggy. After a very long embrace and passionate kiss, Jack excused himself long enough to arrange for her travel trunks to be delivered to his apartment. Then they grabbed a taxi and headed straight to the apartment. The transatlantic crossing had taken its toll on Peggy. She didn't get seasick, but for some reason, ocean travel seem to drain her energy. It was a work day for Jack, so when they reached his apartment, he escorted Peggy to the bedroom, drew a nice hot tub of water in the bathroom, and put some hot water on for tea in the kitchen.

"Okay, babe, your bath is all set for you. When you finish, put my robe on and come join me for a cup of tea in the kitchen. Then you are going to catch up on your sleep while I go to do my broadcast. I'll tune the radio, so all you have to do is raise the volume should you choose to listen to yours truly singing all of those passionate love songs to you."

"Oh, Jack, you are always so considerate. Give me a quick kiss. I promise I'll reward you handsomely tonight."

Peggy bathed, but never made it into the kitchen. When Jack went to check he found her sound asleep on the bed. He gently covered her and then went to tune the radio before heading off to the broadcasting studio.

The Kodak Store was within walking distance of the radio studio, so Jack decided to stop by after concluding his broadcast. He wanted to find out about getting duplicate reels of film made. Jack thought it would be an ideal Christmas present for Peggy. It would also be nice to pick up a projector, but it would have to be lighter and much more portable than his. Jack explained his situation to the clerk. The store clerk said they could easily make duplicate reels of film and by splicing the smaller fifty-foot reels together six or seven could be placed on one seven inch reel, which worked on most projectors. Jack would have to leave his film for about one week at the store and mark the reels in the sequence he wanted the film to be shown. The clerk also recommended a light but very reliable sixteen millimeter Keystone projector. The machine was very easy to thread and there was a carrying case that could be purchased as an accessory. Jack told the clerk to order the Keystone projector and carrying case. The clerk assured Jack that everything except the duplicate reels of film would be in before Christmas, and he would even have the projector and case gift wrapped. Jack would bring the reels of film in after he had a chance to show the movies to Peggy. The important thing was to get them back before she returned to England.

The next stop was the corner deli, which was just one block away. Peggy loved corned beef on rye sandwiches with a dill pickle right out of the deli barrel. Jack knew Peggy would be perfectly content to remain at the apartment for the evening and eat in. He planned on sharing a quiet dinner together as they caught up on each other's activities and then running the movies of their time together in Europe, followed by some piano music and songs. *The rest,* he thought *should just come naturally.*

Of course, Jack was wrong. Upon entering the apartment, Jack immediately noticed that Peggy's travel trunks had arrived.

"Is that you, Jack? I'll be right there."

"I brought you some corned beef and a dill pickle right out of the deli barrel."

Peggy came from the bathroom doing a little shuffle dance right into Jack's arms. They embraced and kissed for several minutes, and then Peggy took the deli bag from Jack and placed it in the Monitor refrigerator. Jack couldn't take his eyes off her. She was dressed in a beautiful form fitting, white, silk nightgown with a long slit up one side and a very revealing neckline. *My God*, Jack thought, *she is so beautiful*. Returning to Jack's side, Peggy took Jack by the hand and led him into the bedroom. The bed was perfectly made with the top sheet turned down and the pillows fluffed up.

"Jack, I've been dreaming about this moment all day. Come over here and let me help you out of your suit. We have some catching up to do."

About two hours later, they returned to the kitchen for the corned beef and pickle. Then Peggy led Jack to the piano bench and sat down next to him.

"Now, lover, sing some of those beautiful songs I've missed so much."

It was just a perfect evening for two people very much in love with one another. The movies would have to wait for another day.

The next day, Peggy was off to do Christmas shopping. She told Jack that some gifts she had acquired in London were in her steamer trunk and for him to stay out of the trunk. Jack was curious, but patient enough to wait until Christmas to see what she had brought for him. Peggy spent most of her shopping time looking for presents to give to Milt and Jean for their soon to arrive baby. It was hard not knowing if the baby was going to be a boy or a girl. She decided on diapers along with a package of diaper pins, bibs, linen for the crib, and a baby blanket. She arranged to have the items gift wrapped and sent to Jack's apartment before continuing on to buy some gifts for Jack's mother and her aunt in Buffalo. By the time Peggy was finished, it was past lunch time.

Knowing Jack was already on his way to the radio studio, she hailed a taxi and made a surprise visit to the studio. When Jack arrived at the studio, Peggy was already sitting by his broadcasting booth.

"Well, what a nice surprise. Who let you in?"

"I have influence around here, Jack. The director even ushered me right to your broadcasting booth and brought me coffee."

"Great, babe, do you want to do some air time?"

"Sure, as long as you don't ask me any embarrassing questions."

The broadcast was one of Jack's best. Radio listeners loved when guest celebrities were on the air. Peggy was extra special because she could talk about things over in London and other parts of Europe as compared to here in the States. They sang a few impromptu duets with a lot of feeling. Their performance was later described as breathtaking.

Christmas was upon them before they knew it. They exchanged gifts Christmas morning. Peggy brought Jack a leather travel dressing case from Finnigans on Bond Street in London. Jack presented Peggy with a Keystone projector and promised that he not only would have the reels of film from their European vacation ready for her to take back to England, but also would make a duplicate reel of everything in the future for her film library. Both were thrilled with their presents. Each couldn't wait to try out their gift. Jack decided to use the shaving cream, the lather brush, and the Gillette safety razor from the case. Peggy started to read the instruction manual that came with the Keystone projector and asked Jack if they could show the movie reels on her projector later in the evening. It was the beginning of a beautiful Christmas.

Leather Travel Case from Finnigans in London

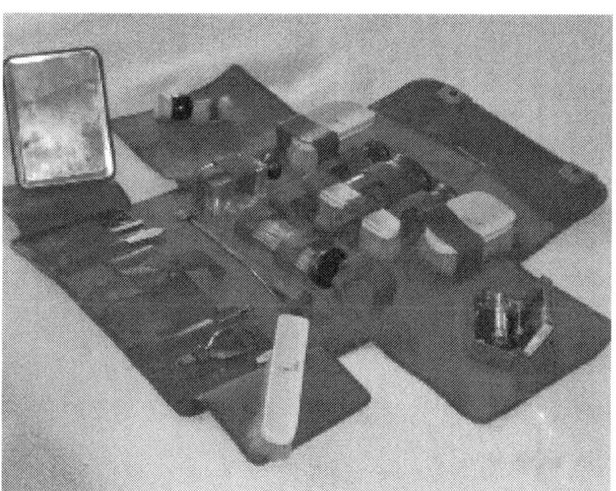

Travel Case displayed open

The "Jack" engraved into the case was copied from his signature on a letter to Peggy O'Neil. Notice most items are engraved or embossed with Jack's signature. The closure flap in the upper right of the picture reads *FINNIGANS BOND ST, LONDON*

Early Keystone 16mm Home Movie Projector

They attended Mass at Jack's mother's church and spent most of Christmas moving among the Schmidt family residences. Peggy was thrilled to see Jean and Milt. Peggy loved babies and expressed a sincere desire to remain in the States until after the baby was born. Jack's brother, Charles, was doing well at Madison Square Garden and was sporting a new Buick as a result of his success. He and his second wife, Jane, seemed to be getting along just fine. Everyone was healthy with the exception of General Goethals. No one seemed to know the details about the General's sickness, but some did know that he was unable to continue his work with the Port Authority.

They wrapped up their day receiving an invitation to spend New Year's Eve at Jack's brother's house out on Long Island. It sounded like the whole family along with other guests would be there. Peggy and Jack responded they would definitely be there, said their round of good-byes and headed back to the apartment. There was still time to set up the movie projector and run the movies. Peggy had heard so much about the movies from those who had already seen them that she couldn't wait any longer. The Keystone projector was really easy to thread, focus, and change reels. Jack picked out an almost white wall to be the screen. Peggy didn't pay much attention to the running of the projector. She just wanted to see the movies and she was thrilled with them, making Jack show various sequences over and over. Finally, Jack called it quits and carried her off to the bedroom. As they embraced, Peggy whispered, "Thank you for another wonderful Christmas."

The New Year's Eve party was at Jack's brother's house out in Valley Stream, Long Island. Jack and Peggy had decided to stay overnight, so they were late arrivals. There must have been sixty or more people in attendance. A few were Charlie's neighbors. A good number were people he worked with. Jack remembered meeting a few of them in the past, including one of Jack's bosses who successfully persuaded Charles to change his last name from Schmidt to Smith. It was a great celebration with plenty of alcohol available in spite of prohibition. For Jack, it really didn't matter. When he was with Peggy he had no desire to drink.

In the early hours of the morning, Jack and Peggy retired to the guest bedroom.

"That was one hell of a party, babe, and last year was one wow of a year. I hope and pray this New Year will be every bit as good."

"Amen to that, Jack. It will be, love. I have a good feeling about it."

1928

The year started out as expected. Peggy was off to Buffalo for a visit with her aunt and friends. Stan had Jack lined up to promote three of his new recordings, "My Blue Heaven", "The Song is Ended, But the Melody Lingers On", and "Miss Annabelle Lee". All had been recorded in England and required copyright approval prior to their release in January. Stan anticipated that two more recorded in England, "Sunshine" and "Whispering" would be approved for release in March. The plan was for Jack to work the first three releases into his broadcasts and simply mention two more would soon be released.

Peggy returned to New York City on the sixteenth of January. On the eighteenth, Jack received a call from his mother telling him that George Goethals had died. It was hard for Jack to believe. The general had always seemed to be so healthy and strong. He was glad Peggy had returned from Buffalo to accompany him through this tough time.

"Jack, it's a shame the Goethals Bridge is not yet finished. Will the dedication of the bridge still be to General Goethals?"

"I'm sure it will, babe. At least the general knew the bridge was going to be named in his honor."

"Tell me again how General Goethals is related to your family."

"Well, the general was Charlie's first wife's brother. Catherine and the general were just two of thirteen siblings. Now, you remember George Ransom. Well, he is also married to one of the Goethals siblings, Elizabeth. As for the rest of the thirteen, I think I've met all of them over time, but I sure don't remember all of their names. We are taking Mom to the funeral and I'm pretty sure she knows all of the Goethals, so we'll just follow her lead."

"Wow, thirteen brothers and sisters. Now that is a big family."

It was a very large funeral with many dignitaries representing both the military and all levels of government in attendance. General Goethals was praised by all who spoke. Peggy was impressed and began to feel somewhat small and unimportant in comparison to this great man's accomplishments. Jack sensed Peggy's emotions and questioned her mood. Once he understood Peggy's feelings, Jack told her she should never feel small, as she actually stood as a giant in her own field of entertainment.

On the fourth of February, Jean gave birth to a beautiful nine-pound baby boy. Peggy was thrilled that she was still in the States and would be able to visit Jean and see the baby. She thought to herself, *God takes from us and then gives to us*. Maybe this baby will someday be as famous as General Goethals. Jack and Peggy visited at the hospital that evening. Milt was proud as a peacock and giving out cigars to all of the men who came by. Peggy was happy and jealous all at the same time. She held the baby for a long time as she talked to Jean and Milt. The baby was to be named Robert Milton. Jack took Milt by the arm and moved him a little away from the bedside.

"Come out to the hallway for a few minutes. There is something I want to ask you."

"Okay, What is it, Jack?"

"It's about your past troubles with the church, Milt. I just want to make sure this baby is going to be properly baptized."

"Don't worry, Jack, in spite of my disagreements with the church, I vowed to raise my children in the Catholic faith and so I will. In fact, I've already asked Charles and Mamie to be the godparents."

"Good, kid. I'm proud of you. Now I'll be able to sleep better tonight. Let's go back in and join the others."

Peggy visited with Jean and the baby over the next five days that Jean was in the hospital, and then it was time for her return trip to England. Jack was sad to see her go, but knew that Stan was lining him up for travel to England, Germany, and several other European countries, so he and Peggy would soon have time together again. He concentrated on his recordings, his radio broadcasting and various personal appearances that Stan set up. When evenings arrived, there was little time to think about Peggy and no need for a drink of alcohol to facilitate sleep.

"Sunshine" and "Whispering" were released in the first week of March. Jack's recordings were selling well and the income from his personal appearances continued to grow. Stan called for Jack to come into the office to review his contracts and financial status.

"In a nutshell, Jack, you have way too much idle money."

Stan again recommended putting some of his money into stocks. Stan's recommendations were for General Electric Company and Coca Cola. Jack gave Stan the *okay*, with the proviso that several thousand dollars would be used to purchase Coca Cola stock in his nephew's name, Milton Edward Schmidt. Jack went on to tell Stan about the birth of Milt and Jean's son and the fact that Milt was reluctant to accept any money from Jack even when he drove as Jack's chauffeur.

"I'll pass the stock certificates along as a present for the new baby's future."

"Okay, Jack, I can do that and should Coca Cola declare dividends over time, the money will be sent directly to your nephew. It's nice of you to do that for Milt."

"Thanks, Stan, and don't forget to send me a preliminary schedule for my European tour. I want to give Peggy some idea of when I'll be over there."

Several weeks later, Jack received the preliminary European tour schedule. It seemed exciting. The first stop was Berlin where he would be both performing and recording. *Well*, Jack thought, *I'm going to have to talk Peggy into visiting Germany*. Following Germany, there was a short week in Paris. This one could be trouble. *I'll just have to stay away from Cecilia.* After Paris, Jack was to go to England where he would again be on tour and also doing some recordings at Hayes, Middlesex. It looked like he would be departing New York City in April and returning sometime early in the summer. *Good*, he thought, *I won't have to be in that damp weather in England.* That evening, he wired Peggy with tentative schedule and asked if she would like to see Germany. The following day, Jack received a wire from Peggy saying that she would love to visit Berlin and had sent a wire to her agent to arrange a week or so off for her. *Things are looking good*, Jack thought as he prepared for his afternoon broadcast.

April was upon Jack before he knew it. He made his rounds in New York City saying his good-byes and once again was on an ocean liner headed across the Atlantic. To his surprise, the arrival port was to be Warnemunde, the city where his parents had lived prior to emigrating to the United States. Jack decided he would take at least some time to explore a little more of the city prior to boarding a train to Berlin. He had been to Warnemunde with one of the German band members on his previous trip to Germany, but Jack thought it would be kind of exciting to look around a bit on his own.

The ocean liner docked early on a Sunday morning. Jack arranged to have his baggage sent to the train station and then inquired as to where he might find a Catholic Church. There was one within walking distance, so he started off following the verbal directions he had received at the pier. This time he had his movie camera with him. He thought his mother would really enjoy seeing pictures of her old homeland. After approximately thirty minutes of walking, Jack felt like maybe he had made a wrong turn along the way and he should ask for further directions. The section of the city he had entered into was very picturesque with a high fortress type of wall running around the perimeter. Many of the buildings appeared to belong to either a college or university. There was a small group of young adults seated outside of a café. Jack stopped and asked for information about the Catholic Church. It so happened that two of the group were in fact about to go to the ten o'clock Mass. They invited Jack to come along.

The church was typically European with a high arched ceiling supported by columns around the inside walls. There was an abundance of statutes and considerable artwork painted on the ceiling. Jack knew that the lighting inside of the church was not good enough for movies, so he decided to wait until Mass ended and then get some footage of the building exterior. The Mass was in Latin and German, most of which Jack understood, but some of the proceedings were quite different from those found in New York City. Jack simply knelt, stood, and sat when the other churchgoers did so. When Mass was over, Jack asked the young men who had accompanied him if it would be all right to take some pictures of them in front of the church. They were thrilled to pose for movie pictures. Jack then showed one of the young men how he operated the movie camera and asked if he would take a minute or so of camera time showing Jack in front of the church. They conversed for a little while before Jack departed for the center of the city. The weather was just perfect with plenty of sunshine. Jack stayed on the side of the main road as his young friends had instructed and before long he was in a commercial zone with all kinds of shops and restaurants. Because it was Sunday, most were closed. He did find a small café open where he ordered coffee and a faschnaut, the German equivalent of a United States donut. The owner of the café told Jack that Schmidt was a rather common name in and around Warnemunde, so it would be rather difficult to find anyone who might have been related to his parents.

The owner gave Jack directions toward the center of the city. The train station was pretty far away, but the owner said there should be taxis available in the center of the city. Luckily, Jack had brought along German currency from his last trip. With all of the banks closed, it would have been hard to hire a taxi or even just pay at the café. He continued to enjoy his walk, stopping to shoot footage of interesting buildings and in one spot a statue. Maybe his mother would be familiar with some of the places. Soon he came upon a square with two parked taxis. Jack approached the first and asked what the fare would be to the train station. Immediately, the driver of the second got out of his taxi and moved next to Jack.

"Sir, I am about to go off duty and will be passing by the station. I will therefore take you there at half fare."

"It's a deal," Jack replied as he moved to the second taxi.

As they motored along, Jack expressed his concern that he had perhaps caused trouble between the two drivers. The driver's response was for Jack not to worry as the other driver was his cousin and they split their profits at the end of the week. Jack thought, *This system would never work back in New York City.*

At the train station he obtained a ticket for the train to Berlin. He was told the train would arrive within the hour. The train was on time and Jack was on his way. The ride would take a little over two hours, so he settled in for a nap and soon began to dream about Peggy. She had promised to be in Berlin several days after Jack arrived. He pictured her riding on the train. She was as beautiful as always and so outgoing and friendly with all of the nearby passengers. Jack loved her beauty and her mannerisms. He thought back to how they met in Chicago. *What a lucky guy I am*, he thought. In his dream Peggy was on the Palast Stage with him. They were singing duets and the audience loved their performance. When the theater closed, they first went to a nearby restaurant for a late evening dinner and then to the hotel. Peggy insisted on bathing before going to the bedroom. The dream had Jack filling the tub with hot water for Peggy, and once she was in the bathtub Jack entered the bathroom in his robe and explained that there was only enough hot water to fill the tub once. She signaled for him to discard his robe and enter the tub from the opposite end. They washed each other's back and then embraced, softly kissing. Then Peggy started tapping Jack on the shoulder. He brushed her hand away and said, "Why are you tapping me on the shoulder?"

"I'm sorry to disturb you, sir, but I must have your ticket," said the conductor.

Jack first folded his arms across his chest thinking he was still naked as in the dream and then sat up snapping awake and gave the conductor his ticket.

"We should be in Berlin in about ten minutes. Your baggage will be placed on the platform for you."

Another taxi ride brought Jack to the same hotel he had stayed in during his last visit. He thought Janet must have a good connection with the staff at this hotel as the rate is very reasonable and the service excellent. It had been a long and adventurous day. While thinking about his dream on the train, Jack filled the bathtub. Oh well, I guess I'll have to wash my own back this evening.

The next morning, he was off to meet Wilhelm Stuttgart and Hans Gerhardt. Both were expecting Jack and were awaiting his nine o'clock arrival in Mr. Stuttgart's small office. Jack arrived a few minutes ahead of time and was immediately shown into the office. Mr. Stuttgart and Hans, the orchestra leader, were truly pleased to see Jack. They conversed in German for fifteen minutes or so about Jack's last visit and the arrangements for Jack's performances. It was pretty much as it had been during Jack's previous visit, so Mr. Stuttgart sent Hans and Jack into the theater to discuss the positioning of the orchestra, the microphones, and a few of the other technical aspects of his stage appearance.

When they finished their discussion, Jack asked Hans if he knew anything about the recording studio in Berlin. Jack explained that during his visit he was to record a couple of songs.

"Will you be recording them in English?"

"Yes and no," Jack replied. "The songs are to be recorded mostly in German."

"In that case, let's try to work the songs into your stage performances, so you will be well-prepared for the recording session. I have been to the recording studio only once. It is top-notch with the very latest equipment and acoustical surroundings."

"I like your suggestion. The songs I know for sure I am to record are 'Ich Kusse Ihre Hand, Madame' ('I Kiss Your Hand, Madame') and 'Ramona'. The first I am going to sing in both English and

German. There was also some discussion about recording 'The Song is Ended but the Melody Lingers On'. I'll bring the sheet music with me tomorrow."

They wrapped up their discussion over lunch in the nearby cafe and then Jack was off to the train station to meet Peggy.

Peggy looked beautiful as ever when she stepped off the train. Jack found her almost immediately, and they stood in each other's arms for several minutes.

"You look wonderful, babe. Let's go make arrangements to have your baggage sent to the hotel and then we'll get a taxi."

"You look wonderful too. I never realize how much I miss you until you're back in my arms. I'm really hungry, Jack. Is there a place nearby where we can stop?"

"I'll ask the driver. If not, it is only a short ride to the hotel and we can get a nice meal there."

They did go straight to the hotel and then straight into the hotel dining room. It was great to catch up on the news from both England and New York. Peggy wanted to know all about Jean's baby boy. She said Jean writes to her, but it's so hard to imagine how that little baby looks and acts. Jack filled her in about the baby and then went on to talk about his planned recordings in Berlin and Hayes, Middlesex. Peggy wanted to know if he was going to sing in German and expressed some concern over what happened on his first trip when his tour was canceled in England.

"Yes, I am going to sing some songs on stage in German and record at least part of a couple in German. However, you need not be concerned about any backlash. Stan assures me we are past that point and that most of my listeners now know that I fought for the allies during the Great War. In fact, many know about my having been gassed during the war and even attribute my whispering style to the gassing."

"Good, Jack. I don't want you heading back to the States early like you did before."

"Not a chance. You're going to have to put up with me for a while, Peggy. Now let's talk show business. Remember how you visited with me at the broadcasting booth back in New York? Well, I thought you might like to join me on stage here at the Palast for a couple of sets. We can do duets kind of the way we did so in New York, only this time I will be singing some verses in German while you're singing them in English. What do you think?"

"I think I would rather be on the stage with you than just sitting and watching you perform. But I don't want to have to waste time rehearsing. I want to see some of Berlin."

"Great, babe, I'll fill the orchestra leader in tomorrow. I promise no practice or rehearsals. We're going to see a lot of this city while you are here. I'm so happy that you came to join me."

After they settled in the hotel room, Jack kept thinking about his dream on the train. He thought to himself, *Why not, maybe it was an omen*. So he went to the bathroom and filled the tub with hot water. Next he approached Peggy and pulled her up from where she was seated. He hugged her briefly, kissed her softly, and then whispered in her ear that the bathtub was full of hot water and waiting for her.

"Thank you, Jack. I was just thinking about a nice hot bath."

Once Peggy was in the bathroom, Jack quickly undressed and slipped into his robe. He thought she is either going to love me or hate me for this. He knocked lightly on the bathroom door and then entered. He delivered his line about how there was only enough hot water to fill the tub once. To his surprise, Peggy laughed long and hard before telling him to get out of his robe and into the tub. It seems that there was a scene in a French play that used the same line. It didn't matter because it turned out to be the most enjoyable bath Jack ever experienced.

Jack and Peggy spent two weeks in Germany. The performances at the Palest were sellouts. Peggy was not at all of the performances, but when she was the audiences especially loved her coming onto the stage and performing with Jack. When they had free time together they would tour throughout Berlin. Jack wanted to see the new Tempelhof Airport, which had just opened in 1927. It was a very impressive airport and even offered passenger flights to both Paris and London. Jack approached the *Deutsche Luft Hansa* counter and inquired about the passenger flight service. The airline operated German-built Dornier Merkur (Mercury) airplanes that were capable of carrying six passengers. The airline representative at the counter gave Jack pricing to Paris and also to England. At that point, Peggy moved to the counter. The representative then asked if both Peggy and Jack would be traveling. If so, the representative had the authority to reduce the fares. Jack moved Peggy to the side for a private conversation.

Dornier Mercury

"What do you think, babe, are you up to trying a flight back to England?"

"I'm willing to, but I wouldn't fly by myself."

"Can you continue on to Paris with me? I only have four stage nights there."

"I'll have to make sure with my agent."

"Okay, let's see what *Luft Hansa* can offer us."

Moving back to the counter, Jack asked if the airline flew from Paris to England. The answer was affirmative, so he went on to give the representative some tentative dates for departures from Berlin and Paris. There was some discussion about baggage with an agreement that should all six passenger seats on the airplane be filled and the baggage weigh too much, Luft Hansa would package a portion of the baggage contents to be shipped at a later date. Jack drew Peggy into the conversation, and when they were done they had arranged to fly first to Paris and then a week later from Paris to England.

On the ride back to the hotel, Peggy told Jack she was very excited about trying an airline flight and asked him if he thought the airlines would eventually fly back and forth across the ocean.

"I'm sure we'll see that someday. And by the way, how did you like my negotiating the price down?"

"You did fine, Jack. You can tell they are anxious to get business. How many people can really afford to fly even at the reduced fares that we got?"

Near the end of the two weeks in Berlin, Jack asked Peggy if she would like to accompany him to the recording studio. They were both impressed with the studio. Hans had told Jack earlier that the studio was equipped with the latest equipment, but Jack didn't expect to experience such modern technology. The recording session was very organized and the actual recordings went super smooth. Peggy was impressed with the whole operation.

"Have you ever considered making a few records?" Jack asked.

"I've thought about doing it a few times, but my agent is not really hooked up with anyone like Stan is with RCA Victor."

"Would you like me to ask Stan about it?"

"No, Jack, I am so busy now I don't really need to start into a new venture. But thanks anyway."

The next day, they were packing and on their way to Tempelhof Airport. The weather was beautiful. Jack kept his movie camera handy, so he could shoot some footage from the air. There was no problem with taking all of the baggage on the flight, so Peggy was greatly relieved. She had no idea as to what she would have left behind. The airline personnel were very professional and courteous. The pilot was already onboard the aircraft and greeted each passenger as they entered the airplane. There were three seats on each side of the fuselage with a narrow aisle running between the seats. Each seat had a window, and because the wing was mounted high above the fuselage, visibility down to the ground was excellent. Jack sensed that he was going to get some very nice aerial shots. There were only five passengers. Another couple was seated like Peggy and Jack across from one another and the fifth passenger was toward the back, seated behind Jack. The pilot moved to the cockpit, and within minutes the engine started and they began to move to the end of the runway. The pilot ran the engine at high speed for a minute or two to check it out and then they were moving down the runway. It was a little bouncy at first and then began to smooth out as the airplane lifted into the sky. Peggy was amazed. She had parts in the movies *Air Pockets* and *The Non-Stop Flight*. She had acted in *The Flying Squad* stage show and had even climbed in and out of the airplane that was to be used in the movie. But she had never envisioned how exciting and wonderful it would be to actually fly in the sky. The view of the landscape below was breathtaking. Jack was busy shooting movies. Because of the engine noise, it was difficult to talk, so Jack and Peggy resorted to hand signals to point out different things. Before long they were descending as they approached Le Bourget Airport. The engine noise subsided. Jack spotted the airport and told Peggy it was the airport at Paris where Charles Lindbergh had landed after flying across the Atlantic Ocean in 1927. The landing was smooth and in a very short time, they were inside of the terminal building waiting for their baggage. Once the luggage arrived, Jack engaged a baggage handler to move the bags out to the taxi stand and then they were on their way to the hotel.

On the ride, Jack asked Peggy if she knew much about Lindbergh's flight to Paris. She remembered reading about it, but she was not in New York when they celebrated his accomplishment. Jack then went on to tell Peggy what he remembered about the historic flight.

"He took off from Roosevelt Field out on Long Island and flew something like three thousand five hundred miles non-stop before landing here in Paris. There was a big cash prize for the first aviator to successfully complete the flight. A businessman, Raymond Orteig, had offered the prize in the amount of twenty-five thousand dollars for the first flight between New York and Paris. For a couple of years, several aviators tried, but all failed. Some died or were never heard from again in their attempts. Mr. Orteig extended the offer for several years until finally Lindbergh won the prize."

Jack's performances in Paris went well. On the second evening, Peggy joined him on stage. Peggy sang some lyrics in French completely surprising Jack. The audience loved it and applauded louder for Peggy than they did for Jack. Later that evening, Jack asked Peggy about her singing the lyrics in French.

"Well, Jack, there are some things you just don't know about me. Last year when you were so busy back in New York City, I performed here in Paris for one whole week."

"Why didn't you tell me?"

"I didn't think it to be very important. Traveling from London to Paris is faster than traveling from New York City to Buffalo."

"You always amaze me, babe. I guess that's why I love you so much."

At the end of the week they were back at the Le Bourget Airport ready for their flight to the Croydon Airport in London. A *Luft Hansa Merkur* airplane had arrived several hours earlier from Berlin and was being serviced with fuel for the flight across the

English Channel. Peggy was a little nervous about flying over the channel. Jack reassured her by relating what he had read about how far many airplanes were able to glide without power. The flight was very much like their flight from Berlin to Paris except the pilot flew the airplane at a much higher altitude. Jack thought it must have had something to do with gliding back to land should there be an engine problem. As they approached the coastline of England, the white cliffs of Dover came into view. The pilot throttled back the engine and started a slow descent. Flying without the roar of the engine was so much more enjoyable. It was a clear and bright day, so they were able to see Buckingham Palace, the Big Ben Clock Tower, and many of the other landmarks in and around London. Soon an airport came into view.

"See the airport, Peggy. That must be Croydon."

Thirty minutes later, they were on their way to Peggy's Park Lane Hotel. Jack couldn't wait to get settled in. He knew he had some free time coming, and with the weather looking so good, he figured to get a few rounds of golf in. Peggy would have to get back to the stage, but there would be plenty of time to share together. That evening, Jack sent a telegram to Stan reporting satisfactory completion of everything through Paris and asking for confirmation of his schedule in England.

Stan's message was delivered to Peggy's suite the following day. It looked like a relatively easy tour in and around London with recording sessions scheduled for Hayes, Middlesex close to the end of the tour. Jack was anxious to find out if any of the actors he had met on his last trip were still performing with Peggy. A couple of them were pretty good golfers, and he would love to play a few rounds with them again. Later in the afternoon, Jack went to Peggy's rehearsal for a quick visit, and sure enough, two of the actors were indeed the same guys he had the pleasure of playing golf with last year. When the rehearsal broke, Jack said his *hellos* and was surprised when the actors asked if he would have any time for a round of golf. They made some tentative arrangements and then Jack and Peggy were off to the restaurant.

"I'm pleased with my schedule, babe. We should both have time open during the day to see some of the castles we talked about and maybe even get to Bath and Stonehenge."

"I would love that, Jack. I think we are due for some rather nice weather, so when the weather looks good, we'll go. My chauffeur is very good. He tells me when we need to leave places so that I am back to the theater in plenty of time for my performances."

The next five weeks were close to perfect. Jack's performances were well received. His free time was spent either touring with Peggy or playing golf. He and Peggy did get to Bath and Stonehenge, staying overnight in a nearby village where Graham, the chauffeur, had grown up. When his tour was finished, Jack went to Hayes, Middlesex to record six songs and then back to the Park Lane to spend a few more days with Peggy.

"Tell me what songs you recorded, love, and how was the Hayes operation compared to your recording experience in Berlin?"

"The Hayes recording studio is not quite up to speed technically with the very modern Berlin studio, but working with the people at Hayes is so pleasurable. They are always so polite and their use of the English language is always so proper. I recorded: 'S'Wonderful', 'Crazy Rhythm', 'Funny Face', 'That's My Weakness Now', 'The Song I Love' and 'All By Youself in the Moonlight'. And I had a chorus working with me on 'All by Yourself in the Moonlight'. That was a lot of fun even though we had to do multiple takes. I think you'll like the chorus effect."

"When will the records be available to purchase in the music stores?"

"I'm really not sure. I know it can take several months for all of the copyright stuff to clear and then a little time for RCA Victor to make the stampings and get the production run going, so it will probably be around late October or sometime in November. Don't worry, babe, if you are still over here, I'll have Janet ship copies to you."

Advanced Copy Record of "S' Wonderful" from Jack Smith's collection.

Production Run Record of "S' Wonderful" from Jack Smith's collection.

The next day, Jack sent another message to Stan stating that he had successfully wrapped up everything through Middlesex and asking for booking details for his ocean liner trip back to New York. That evening, a message from Stan was received stating "Well done" and detailed the booking arrangements. Jack had a full three days to spend with Peggy and he planned to make good use of the time giving Peggy his full attention.

On their last evening together, they reminisced about all of the adventurous things they had done together. Peggy's favorites included Venice, the airplane ride, and their first trip together to the old World's Fair Museum in Chicago. Jack agreed with Venice and the airplane ride, but questioned the World's Fair Museum visit.

"Why was our trip to the Chicago museum one of your favorites?"

"Well, because you were somewhat of a mystery man then, and because I think that's when I really fell in love with you."

"You're right, babe. Now that I think about it, we did have a great day together. I remember when we first held hands and the very special feeling it gave me."

They kissed passionately and made love well into the early hours of the morning, and then it was once again time for Jack to depart.

As much as Jack enjoyed his time in Europe, he still loved returning to New York City and really looked forward to resuming his radio broadcasts. At the pier in New York, he made arrangements for his baggage to be delivered to his apartment and then took the subway to Stan's office. Janet was kind of expecting Jack to check in, but was still surprised when he arrived.

"Jack, you look wonderful. Europe must agree with you."

"It was a good trip, Janet, but I'm always happy to get home. Is Stan here?"

"Yes, he is. Let me tell him you are here."

Stan was glad to have Jack back in New York. He reviewed some of the potential bookings and asked for Jack's feedback. They put together a tentative schedule, and then Stan moved on to go over Jack's finances.

"You are doing just great, Jack, but in my opinion, you still have too much money in the bank. I think you should consider making purchases with some of that money. Let me ask you about Milt. Will he still be chauffeuring for you?"

"Yes he will, but not always because he also holds a full-time job. Sometimes I have to make other arrangements."

"Jack, I think it might be a good time to consider buying a new motor car. One that is sporty enough for you to drive when you want, but also big enough to provide the flexibility of being chauffeur driven to special performances. I should be able to write off some taxes for you as business expenses associated with the motor vehicle and the chauffeur."

"Well, Stan, I'll have to give that one some thought. I did like the Rolls Royce Motor Cars over in England, but I'm not sure I would want to drive one on my own."

"Also you might want to consider buying some real estate. Property investment is a good way to make money with little risk."

Jack promised to think about both the motor car and real estate. During the general conversation that followed, Stan's ears really perked up when Jack mentioned flying from Berlin to Paris and then from Paris to London. He wanted to hear all of the details, and Jack immediately knew that it would not be long before Stan was on an airplane ride. Jack parted with his broadcasting schedule in hand and decided to ride the trolley over to visit with his mother for a while. She would be anxious to hear about Germany, and of course, Peggy.

As Jack settled back into his broadcasting routine, he began to give thought to Stan's recommendations. He had discussed investing in real estate with his mother, and they were both of the opinion that Jack did not have the time to be looking after properties. His mother liked the idea of getting a new motor car and told Jack to be sure to get one with roll up windows.

Later that week, Jack called his old friend Arthur Kennedy and invited him out to lunch, so they might discuss automobiles. He knew Art would jump at the opportunity to talk about motor cars, and Jack also respected Art's knowledge of the subject. When they met, Jack and Art caught up on how each had been doing and then began a discussion about automobiles. The key element boiled down to Jack wanting a motor car that he would sometimes drive and sometimes the motor car would be chauffeur driven.

"Okay, Jack, I think I know exactly the car for you. It'll be expensive and you will probably have to order one and wait for delivery. It's the Cord Phaeton. I've seen pictures of it. All of the Cords are very sporty-looking, and yes, it has the roll up windows your mother talked about. The only negative I can think of is it has been reported to be a little underpowered and probably won't be as snappy as your Chalmers Six. Let me find out where one can be seen. I would love to go along with you."

"I won't mind if the Cord isn't as fast as the Chalmers. I seldom get out on the open road these days, and when I do, a chauffeur is driving. And I would very much like you to tag along with me to go see one."

They parted with Art promising to call as soon as he located a Cord Phaeton they could go see and maybe even drive.

It was almost a month before Art nailed down the location of a Cord Phaeton they could both go to see. The motor car was reasonably close by in Newark, New Jersey. He called Jack.

"Jack, I've finally located a Cord Phaeton we can go to see and drive. The problem has been the car is really not in full production yet. The one over in Newark is what they call a pre- production model, but the people I talked with told me it looks identical to those that will be coming off the assembly line. This young guy, E.L. Cord, took over the Auburn Automobile Company out in Indiana and is making some revolutionary changes in the designs of the motor cars they are making. The car goes for about three thousand, so if that's too steep for you, just say so, and I'll cancel out with the Newark people."

"I think I'm okay with three thousand dollars. And maybe I'll be able to trade in the Chalmers reducing the price further." If you can set something up for a morning around nine or ten, we can drive over to Newark in the Chalmers."

Two weeks later, Jack and Art were in New Jersey parked at the brand-new Newark Metropolitan Airport waiting for Art's contact to drive up in the Cord.

"Well, Art, it was worth the drive just to see this airport. I figure we drove about fifteen miles. This is exactly what New York City needs."

Jack went on to tell Art about his experiences flying from Berlin to Paris and then from Paris to London. While they were parked in the lot, an airplane that looked something like the *Luft Hansa Mercury Transport* that Jack and Peggy had flown in taxied up to the end of the runway. When the engine revved up, Jack explained to Art how the pilot was checking out the engine before taking off. They were both so preoccupied watching the airplane that they didn't see the Cord drive up until it was parked next to them. Art immediately got out and moved over to greet his contact. Jack also got out of the Chalmers and walked slowly around the Cord before stopping next to Art and the driver.

"Jack, this is Fred Siegel. He's here to show us this beautiful motor car and answer any questions we might have about the new L-29 Cord Phaeton."

With that, Mr. Siegel stepped out of the Cord and walked to the front of the motor car. He then opened the hood, all the while describing what he was doing and citing technical terms about the car and its engine. By the time they got completely around the automobile, Jack had made up his mind that this motor car was meant for him. He asked Mr. Siegel if he might drive the Cord for a short distance.

"You certainly may, Mr. Smith. We can drive around the perimeter of the airport and we'll end up right back here."

As they drove along with Art in the back seat, Mr. Siegel pointed out different features of the motor car and described how to work the accessories. He asked Jack if he could feel the difference in the way the front-wheel drive responded compared to the Chalmers rear-wheel drive.

"It is very smooth and much quieter than my Chalmers. I would feel quite comfortable driving this machine and it certainly is an eye catcher."

L29 Cord Phaeton

Back at the parking lot, there was a lot of discussion about how to order the motor car. Mr. Siegel and Art were both very helpful in reducing Jack's preferences to writing. Jack made out a check for a five hundred dollar deposit and signed the order sheet. They shook hands all around and then Jack and Art were back in the Chalmers and on their return trip to Manhattan.

"I wish I had brought my movie camera, Art. What a beautiful automobile. How did it ride in the back?"

"It's very smooth and comfortable. And because the drive wheels are up front, there is no drive shaft, so the floor really is perfectly flat. You're going to love it, Jack."

"Well, it'll be worth the two-month wait. I should have it by January."

That evening, Jack sent a telegram to Peggy telling her about ordering the new car and asking if she was coming to New York around the holidays. The following day, Jack received a response from Peggy stating she would definitely be in New York to get a ride in his new car. Later that same day, Janet called Jack to inform him that sales of the two recordings made in Berlin were doing well and both were moving up on the charts. Additionally, five of the six recordings made in Middlesex were now in the stores. The sixth recording, "All by Yourself in the Moonlight", had not yet been cleared for release, but Stan expected it to be released around

Christmas time. Stan also suggested that Jack sing all of the new recordings during his broadcasts and mention that most were now available in the stores.

Jack reflected on the happenings of the past year for a few minutes and then whispered to himself, "It's been quite a year. I can't wait until Peggy gets here."

THE YEAR OF THE CRASH

Christmas and New Year's came and went fast. Peggy had arrived shortly before Christmas and as in previous years she shared all of the holiday events with Jack and his family. Peggy was planning a trip up to Buffalo when Jack got word that his new L-29 Cord Phaeton was in Newark and would be ready for Jack to take possession in just two days.

"Babe, how would you like to ride up to Buffalo in my new motor car?"

"I would love to, Jack."

"Let me see what I can get Stan to set up. If I can't get enough time off, maybe you can return to New York City by train."

"Whatever works, love, I'm game."

The following week, they were on the road to upstate New York. After about two hours on the road, they pulled into a roadside restaurant for a bite to eat.

"Jack, that car is so comfortable. I don't feel the least bit tired."

"It's smooth to drive, babe. Would you like to give it a try?"

"No, I would not. I would however like to ride in the backseat if you'll wear the chauffeur hat that I gave you for Christmas. Did you bring it along?"

"I sure did. I keep it on the little shelf under the dashboard."

"Okay when we return to the motor car, you put the hat on and I'll try out the backseat. If it is as comfortable as the front, maybe

I'll order a Cord for my use over in England. Do you think one can be sent overseas?"

"Anything is possible today, babe. All it takes is a lot of money. The main reason I bought this new motor car is because Stan said I had too much money in the bank."

"Jack, my agent is telling me the same thing. He wants me to invest in some construction firm here in the States. What do you think I should do?"

"I'm really not the right person to ask. Stan wanted me to consider investing in real estate, but I decided against doing so because it would take a lot of time and worry on my part. The other thing for you to consider is that you will be over in England a good portion of the year and therefore not in a good position to watch what is being done with your money. It's really up to you, babe. I think it all boils down to how much confidence you have in your manager's abilities with the handling of money."

When they returned to the Cord, Jack put on the chauffeur hat and then opened the rear passenger door for Peggy.

"You look so cute in that hat. Would you like to come to London and work for me?"

"No, thank you, my lady. I prefer the weather here in New York."

After driving for fifteen minutes or so, Jack found Peggy was no longer talking. He glanced in the rearview mirror and saw her sleeping with a nice smile on her face. *How I love this woman*, he thought. *I'll just let her sleep right on through to Buffalo*. Jack drove straight through to the hotel and once parked, he moved to the rear of the motor car and gently shook Peggy. To his surprise, she simply put both arms around him and whispered for him to please not make her get out of bed yet.

"Peggy, we're in Buffalo and you're still in the motor car. It's going to get a little cold in here soon, so I suggest coming along with me to our nice comfortable bed."

"Oh! Okay, Jack. I can't believe we are already here. Help me up a little and then please wait until I fix my makeup."

Standing alongside of the motor car with his chauffeur hat on Jack mumbled, "The things a chauffeur has to do!"

"I heard that, Mr. Smith. Now give me that silly hat and help me out of here."

Peggy was still very tired when they got to the room, so Jack suggested ordering room service and simply relaxing for the rest of the evening.

"Oh, that sounds wonderful. I don't know why I'm so tired."

"Sometimes everything just catches up with you, Peggy. It happens to me sometimes. You know we are on the go a lot and don't get regular sleep like the bankers do. So once in a while you just have to crash."

"After we finish eating, will you do something for me?"

"Just name it, babe."

"Run a nice tub full of hot water for me and then come and join me in the water."

"My pleasure for sure, love."

That night they made love long into the evening, sometimes dozing off and then reengaging with renewed energy.

The next morning, Peggy was up rather early and was as fresh as a daisy.

"Come on, sleepyhead. We have lots to do today and all of your action last night has made me as hungry as a horse. Let's go down and get some breakfast. We can plan our day as we eat."

Jack knew for sure they would be visiting her old church and of course stopping at her Aunt's. Peggy still had a lot of friends in the Buffalo area, some of which she corresponded with much the way she did with Jean. Jack wondered where she found the time and energy to do so. Jack only had the one day to be with Peggy and her friends before he had to hit the road again for the long drive back to New York City, so they planned a full schedule with Jack sometimes wearing the chauffeur hat and sometimes not. It was going to be a fun day.

On Jack's return trip to New York City, he kept visualizing the events of the previous day. *It's truly amazing*, he thought, *how much everyone loves Peggy and how she cares for each and every one of her friends.* She always has some sort of present or souvenir to give to each and delights in the reactions of those receiving the gifts. *What a wonderful woman*, he thought. Then his thoughts turned to the new motor car. He was driving on a smooth open stretch of highway and felt tempted to see how fast the Cord would really go. But then he recalled some of the things Art had told him about breaking in the engine. So instead of revving the engine up to maximum speed, Jack alternated his speeds, and when in the mountainous stretches of road, he practiced down shifting to save the brakes on steep down slopes. The Cord was definitely a pleasure to drive, and everyone that had seen the motor car had complimented the beauty and styling of the automobile. He couldn't wait to show his nephew Milt the car and ask him if he would continue chauffeuring whenever he had availability.

There were still a few hours of daylight remaining when Jack drove into New York City, so he decided to stop by Milt and Jean's house for a visit. Maybe Milt would get home from work while there was still daylight so he could get a good look at the Cord. Jean was home with their baby.

"Hello, Jack. What a pleasant surprise! Please come in."

"I'm just on my way back from Buffalo, and thought I would stop by and see how you, Milt, and the baby are doing. When will Milt get home?"

"He should be here in about an hour. Can I get you a cup of coffee or tea?"

"Coffee sounds great, thanks, Jean."

When Jean returned with two cups of coffee, they talked about Jack's trip to Buffalo and his new motor car. Jack asked about the baby and Jean's mother. Both were doing well and Jean stated the baby would be celebrating his first birthday in February. Jean knew some things about Jack and Peggy's travel in Europe from his holiday visit and from Peggy's letters, and decided to take advantage of their one-on-one time together to get more information from Jack. Jack rather enjoyed answering her questions and tried his best to vividly describe their experiences. After a long discussion, Jean respectfully suggested that Jack should try to include some of the information in his radio broadcasts.

"Most people know little or nothing about flying in an airplane, and Jack, you describe the experience so beautifully. I can almost imagine myself in the airplane with you. I think your listeners would love to hear about such experiences."

"Well, thank you. I'll give it some thought."

At that point, Milt entered the house very excitedly.

"I just knew the motor car outside was yours. Come on out for a minute, Jean, and get a look at this beauty before it gets dark."

"You and Jack go out. I just want to check on the baby and I'll be right there."

Soon the three of them were examining the new Cord. They sat inside of the motor car and marveled at the exquisite appointments and luxurious trim. Milt wanted to know if Jack had put down the top yet. In answer to Jack's question as to whether or not he would be able to chauffeur for Jack, Milt responded that he most certainly would. They reentered the house for a few minutes where Milt and Jack made plans to meet after Sunday Mass, so Milt could try driving the Cord. Then Jack departed for his apartment.

Back at his apartment, Jack reflected on his good fortune. He went to the closet and retrieved the cigar box that held his mementoes. He thumbed through the notes, souvenirs, and pieces of paper from the box, stopping momentarily with each in hand and then depositing them in one of two piles on the bed. One pile was considered to be closed, the other open. In a short while, he came to the folded sheet of paper. Unfolding the paper, Jack thought, *This is what I need to work on.* It was hard for him to believe that he had written the names and comments almost two years earlier. Time was flying by. As he began to read through the list, he pictured each individual and paused as memories flashed through his head. The first name was Cecilia. Jack moved to the desk in living room and sat down to make some annotations. Next to Cecilia's name, Jack marked closed. The second name was Francis Kelly. For this one, he marked open. When he got to General Goethals, Jack stopped and said a few prayers. It was still hard to believe that the general was no longer with them. There were thirteen names on the list. When he finished, six names were annotated closed. He put a question mark next to Lorie Bradford and then decided that Arthur Kennedy, Mom, Peggy, Stan Schuman, and Janet would all remain kind of open. He simply marked a dash next to each. *Well,* he thought, *I've made some progress.* Maybe I can reward Arthur for his help in getting the Cord by letting him have the motor car for a day.

Jack had trouble sleeping that night. It was probably because Peggy was not with him. He got up and walked around the apartment for a while, but refrained from drinking any brandy.

The next day, he was back at the broadcasting studio. Jack thoroughly enjoyed broadcasting. About halfway through the show, he decided to sing one of the songs he had recorded in Berlin and then give a little dialog about his first flight in an airplane from Berlin to Paris. He then sang a tune he had recorded in Middlesex.

"Now how do you think I got from France to England?" Answering his own question, Jack exclaimed, "You're right. I climbed right back into an airplane almost identical to the one that brought me to Paris. The difference this time is that we were going over water, a whole lot of water." He went on to describe his anxiety while flying over the English Channel and the comforting feeling that came over him once the White Cliffs of Dover were in sight.

Stan called the next day and told Jack his broadcast yesterday was spectacular.

"Where did you come up with the idea to describe your flying experiences? I've been getting calls from coast to coast this morning requesting your availability to perform on stage."

"Well, Stan, the idea really came from Jean. I was describing my flying experience to her and she suggested I should share the experience with my radio audience. I'm glad it was well received."

"Listen, Jack, one of the calls was from a vaudeville manager down in Galveston, Texas. He really wants you in his lineup and is talking some serious money. What do you think?"

"I'm game, Stan. Peggy will be returning to England in about two weeks, so any time after that should work for me. It's warmer down there, so maybe I'll be able to get some golf in."

Three days later, Peggy returned from Buffalo. The next ten days with Peggy were just perfect. On two occasions, Jack and Peggy drove to and parked the Cord at Jean's house in the morning. Peggy stayed with Jean and her baby while Jack took the trolley to the broadcasting studio. Peggy adored the baby and just loved spending time with Jean. During their last evening together, Peggy told Jack it had been one of the best vacations she had ever experienced.

"I won't ever be able to repay you for allowing me to be part of your family. Everyone just treats me so nice and without any pretense. I truly feel like I belong. And best of all, Jack, I love every minute we spend together. I really don't feel like returning to London, but a contract is a contract and once I get back on stage I'll be all right. You just make sure Stan gets you set up with a nice long European tour this year."

"I will, babe. I'll be in London before you know it."

The next day, Peggy was on the ocean liner to England and Jack was in Stan's office reviewing bookings for the next several months. It looked like he would be in Galveston in early March.

Galveston was much warmer than New York. The people were quite different, but very friendly. Most of the men wore cowboy hats and many of the women wore boots. There was a railway that ran right down the center of the main road. Work trains were continually moving up and down the middle of the street. The vaudeville theater where Jack was booked to perform was within walking distance of a golf course. Jack thought, *I should certainly enjoy my time here*. After checking in with the vaudeville manager, Jack walked over to the golf course, introduced himself in the Pro Shop and asked if it would be possible to get some golf lessons while he was in town. Almost immediately, the course pro grabbed a bag full of clubs and had Jack follow him to the practice range.

"Don't worry about your pants, Mr. Smith. They will get a little dusty. We'll brush them clean when we're done. I'm going to hand you different clubs and ask you to hit the practice balls down range. After you've hit a dozen or so, we'll talk about where I think you can improve your game."

They spent about twenty minutes with the pro passing clubs to Jack and setting balls up for him to hit.

"Not bad, not bad at all, Mr. Smith. I think you can use a little work on your short irons. Can you come by tomorrow for about an hour?"

"I should be able to, Mr. Richey."

"Well good. Let's walk back to the Pro Shop and see what we can schedule. And by the way, just call me Leonard."

"Okay, Leonard, and please call me Jack."

For the next three days, Jack walked over to the Pro Shop each morning for a lesson with Leonard. On the third day, Leonard told Jack his swing was good and he would like to see him out on the course.

"I'm scheduled for a round of golf with two club members tomorrow morning at nine. Would you like to join us, Jack? You need not worry about golf attire. Just wear pants, shirt, and sweater if it is cool. I'll get you set up with a pair of shoes from the Pro Shop."

"Well, thank you, Leonard. Yes, I can make nine o'clock and I think I'll enjoy playing on the course with you and your friends. Is there going to be any wagering of bets?"

"Yes, but no big money. You'll be my partner. I think we'll do okay together."

When Jack arrived the next morning and met the other golfers, he felt a little out of place as everyone except Jack was dressed in golfing knickers, white shirts under short sleeve sweaters, and white golf caps. The club members were a little older, probably in their early fifties. They were introduced simply as Bob and Tom. Both were very friendly and made Jack feel welcome. Jack had brought his movie camera along and asked the others if they would mind if he shot some movie footage. They were all receptive. In fact, Bob had a movie camera at home, so he volunteered to help Jack in shooting the film.

When the round was finished, Leonard and Jack were ahead in points and collected twenty- two dollars from their opponents. Jack quietly told the pro to keep all of the winnings. He knew that was how most pros made their living. Jack then got an address from Bob, so he could send a copy of the golfing film to him.

Jack played golf every other day for the remainder of his two weeks in Galveston. His evening shows were all sellouts and he thoroughly enjoyed performing for the Texan audiences, but there was still no place like New York City.

Jack Smith pictured in 16mm movies with two of the caddies

Jack Smith's putting stroke

Easter Sunday was on the last day of March. Jack was back in time to return to the broadcasting studio the week before Easter. He had fun with some of the Easter melodies and told a few stories about his experiences in Galveston. Storytelling was becoming a trademark of his blended radio broadcast. That week he received two letters from Peggy. Jack loved to receive Peggy's letters. He would sit and read the letters three or four times and then later in the evening read them once more before going to bed. She was doing well, but very anxious to know when Jack was coming to London.

The next morning, Jack called and talked with Janet at the agency. She and Stan had a lot of the arrangements made for his up coming European tour. The bookings for Germany and Denmark were completed, but some of the contracts for appearances in England needed work. Janet assured Jack that the tour was coming together nicely, and he could expect to depart from the States in mid June.

The trip went very smoothly. Jack started the tour in Germany and worked back to Tivoli Park in Copenhagen and then on to London. Peggy was also very much engaged in her stage schedule and unable to join Jack in either Germany or Denmark. They did keep in touch by telegraph and grew more excited as the time approached when they would be reunited. Jack and Peggy spent a good amount of time together in London during the summer. It was truly a delightful time. They made plans for Peggy's return to the States and talked about sailing together back to Europe just after the Christmas Holidays. Jack spent some time recording at Hayes, and then once again it was time for their good-byes and Jack's return to New York. They were on top of the world and time was flying by.

Then a strange and uncontrollable event happened. On Thursday, the twenty-fourth of October, the New York Stock Exchange share prices abruptly fell. There was a lot of concern and excitement at the radio broadcasting station. Jack's program was interrupted multiple times for news flashes. Things settled a little as financiers put a lot of money into the market attempting to stabilize share prices. Then on Tuesday, October 29, sixteen million shares were traded and the market lost 12 percent of its value. The two dates became known as Black Thursday and Black Tuesday. Bank runs the following week led to the failure of over four thousand banks.

Stan called Jack and told him he was watching the situation closely, and with the exception of some bank money, Jack's portfolio was pretty much intact. He advised Jack that once he got a handle on all of the financial information, Jack would be called to come into the agency for a briefing. That same day, Jack received a telegram from Peggy expressing a lot of concern over the financial situation, and a line in the message that hinted, she might not be returning to New York as they had planned. She too was working closely with her agent.

As the Thanksgiving holiday approached, it became obvious that there was not going to be a quick recovery of the financial markets or banks. Milt's bank was one that had failed. Milt and Jean were devastated. The bank failure had wiped out their entire savings. The only good news was that Milt still held a job. Stan finally called and suggested that Jack come to the office, so they could go over his portfolio and assess the impact on his major holdings. He was to meet with Stan on the day before Thanksgiving.

Jack arrived at the agency around nine. The office was busy with people. Jack stopped at Janet's desk and greeted her.

"Oh! Hello, Mr. Smith. I am going to have to ask you to take a seat for a short while. As you can see, we are quite busy."

After thirty minutes or so, Janet approached Jack and asked him to follow her. She led him to an office that he had never been in.

"Stan will be with you soon. If you care to, you may look through the files on the desk. All are related to your portfolio."

Jack sat in one of the chairs by the desk and started to thumb through the folders. There was a folder marked, "Jack Smith Stocks". As he browsed through the file, many of the company names were familiar to him, but Jack never really followed his holdings. Over the years, he had simply put his trust in Stan to do what was best. At that point, Stan entered the room.

"Jack, it has been hell the past few weeks trying to keep up with the New York Exchange and guess what's going to happen next. I did go through your portfolio and I think you're going to come out of this thing okay. All of your major holdings, GE, AT&T, Coca Cola, and RCA are pretty solid. The value of your shares has dropped, but these companies are not going to go under. Now your bank accounts are a different story. As you know, you have accounts in two different banks. One bank has failed and all of the money in those accounts is gone. Luckily, it was the bank we took money out of earlier this year to buy the new automobile. The other bank is solid, and I don't think it can possibly go under. So what I'm recommending is that you just sit tight for a while. You've lost some value and some money, but believe me, Jack, you're in much better shape than most investors. Now the best news is that your broadcasting contract is solid and the two movie contracts I've been working on with Hollywood are going to be okay. Your record contract with RCA will also continue without any problems. In a nutshell, you are still going to have considerable income. Our problem is going to be what to do with the proceeds to keep the money safe. Now, do you have any questions?"

"Thanks for bringing me up-to-date, Stan. You're doing a great job just as you always have. I do have one concern. Is this financial situation impacting things over in England? I ask because Peggy is still in London and from her messages, she seems to be having some problems."

"Yes, the impact is going to spread far and wide. There most probably will be a worldwide depression. Hopefully, it will only last a year or two. Okay, Jack, I've got to run. Some of those people waiting outside of the office have real problems. Stage productions have been dropped and contracts were cancelled, leaving many unemployed with no place to go. I only hope I can help some of them. Keep your chin up Jack. You should come through this okay."

Jack spent Thanksgiving with the family. Dinner was at his mother's and everyone came. The conversations were almost all about the Wall Street crash and the people who had been affected by it. Jack already knew that Jean and Milt had lost all of their savings in a bank failure. Jack's brother, Charles, had also lost some money due to a bank failure. But all in all, the family had weathered the crash pretty well. All were still working and none had serious financial shortcomings. So as Jack's mother led them in saying grace before their dinner, she thanked the Lord for what they had and asked the Lord to help those now suffering so much.

On the morning after Thanksgiving, Jack received a telegram from Peggy stating she would not be returning to the States for the holiday and that more information would be forwarded in a letter. Jack was devastated. This was the time of the year when he so looked forward to spending the holidays with Peggy. He tried to envision what was keeping her in England. Stan had said the financial crisis was spreading worldwide. It could be problems with the ocean liners. Or worse yet, maybe Peggy suffered a lot of financial loss and just doesn't have the money. *If she needs money*, he thought, *I can wire some to her.* Finally, Jack decided he would just have to wait for the letter to arrive. In the meantime, he would visit with his mother this morning and help her clean up a little. While there, he would tell her about Peggy's telegram.

Jack's mother advised him to just sit tight until the letter arrived. She assured him that Peggy was very level-headed intelligent woman and she would either work through whatever the problem was or seek Jack's help. She tried to stress the importance of being patient. *Easier said than done*, Jack thought. He was okay as long as he was busy. He had a Thanksgiving party to entertain on Saturday evening. Sunday would be kind of tough because he was off. Then probably another seven to ten days before any mail from England would arrive. He would just have to not think about Peggy. The evenings at the apartment were the hardest. Jack managed to stay away from the brandy, but it was hard.

Peggy's letter arrived on Friday, the thirteenth of December. Being somewhat superstitious, Jack was tempted to wait until the next day to open the envelope. Of course, waiting another day would not change what was written in the letter and the suspense had been eating at him for days. So he carefully opened the envelope and sat down at the kitchen table to read it.

> My Dearest Jack,
>
> It pains me dearly to write this letter. I had so planned on spending time with you over the holiday, but the problems with the financial markets have impacted so many things. From what has been reported in the newsprint, I'm not sure if I could even have booked passage. But the real problem is with my contracts. My agent has told me he cannot really get me any bookings in the States and even if he could, the money would not be good at all. He doesn't want me to take a break from the London Stage for more than one week. He says as long as I continue to perform under my existing agreements, my compensation will be unchanged; however, should I change things my compensation will go down. My

agent says when I travel to the States in effect he has to negotiate changes to my contracts. I don't understand it all, Jack, but my agent has done well by me over the years, and so I trust and believe in him.

Jack, love, I had so many plans for us. I had a dream not long ago about you in New York City with your family. In the dream, Jean told me she has a second child in her womb. I was so jealous. I just love visiting with Jean and holding her baby. But the best part of the dream was when you and I were sailing back to Europe just after the Holidays. One night you proposed that we get married right then and there onboard by the ship's captain. We had a long discussion about the church and decided it would really not consider the wedding to be valid so why not. And we were married. I was so happy, Jack. It gave me such a feeling of a togetherness that would last forever.

Then a few days later, I wake up to find that everything has been turned upside down in this world. From what I have read, I guess I should be thankful for what I have. My finances are good, Jack, as I hope yours are also. Thank God we both have good agents.

Well I don't know where we go from here. My agent says I should expect to sit tight for at least a year until the markets return to normal. Jack, I can't imagine a whole year without you in my arms. I'll be praying for us and all those who are now in trouble. Please write often and tell me what your situation is. I am hoping that you will still be coming to Europe.

I miss you so much, darling.
With all my love,
Bam-Bam

Jack read the letter over and over again. Finally, he moved to the kitchen cupboard and brought out the bottle of brandy. *Well, this definitely calls for a drink*. He thought for a minute and then without pouring any, he returned the brandy to the cupboard. I'm not going to start that again. Next, he paced back and forth. He moved to the radio and tuned in some news. Most of the news was bad. People were actually committing suicide by jumping off buildings because they had lost everything. *How sad*, he thought as he turned the radio off and moved to sit down at the table again. Once more, he read Peggy's letter. Next, he moved to the piano and played many of the melodies he had recorded over in England. After a while, Jack finally tired. He bathed and went directly to bed. To his surprise, he had no trouble sleeping that night and didn't awaken until almost eight the next morning. Maybe just knowing that Peggy was okay is all he needed to settle himself.

LIFE GOES ON

There is an old saying, "Life goes on". And that pretty much is what happened to Jack and Peggy after the New York Stock Exchange crashed. Jack went through the routine of spending the Christmas and New Year Holidays with his family, but it was just not the same without Peggy by his side. He wrote to her almost every day at first, but then found communicating across the ocean was somewhat difficult because it took so long to get a response. On some occasions, when there was special news, he would send a telegram. When Jean announced that she was in fact pregnant, he sent the news immediately to Peggy and commented about how accurate her dream was.

In the first week of February 1930, Stan called Jack to come to the office and go over two contracts for his appearance in Hollywood movies. Jack was in Stan's office the next morning.

"Hello, Jack. Have a seat next to me here by the desk. I've got some very nice news for you. The producers in Hollywood are ready to sign you for parts in three different movies. I think we can handle the shooting for scenes in two of the movies with just one trip to Hollywood. The third movie will be a little later in the year and will require a separate trip."

"What can you tell me about the parts?"

"Here is a portion of the script for the first movie. The title will be *Happy Days* and a lot of the filming will be on sets of a Mississippi showboat and a Broadway theater. Your part will be that of the master of ceremonies over a very large and gala production cast. These are all talking movies, so in this one you will be both talking and singing. I'm going to give you the script to take home, so you can study the part. If you foresee problems in any of the roles, let me know right away so that I can negotiate changes for you."

"From what I see here, Stan, I would have no problems with performing as the MC."

"Now this script is for your part in a movie to be titled *Cheer up and Smile*. You will be playing yourself, 'Whispering' Jack Smith, a popular radio singer. You are knocked unconscious during a robbery, after which a squeaky-voiced college kid fills in for you and becomes an overnight sensation."

"Well, I'll have to look this one over closely. I don't know if I like the idea of being replaced by a squeaky-voiced kid."

"Believe me, Jack, it can do nothing but enhance your career. Spreading your name around is always going to return positive results. Now the third movie may not start shooting until the summer months. It is titled *The Big Party* and you will play the part of Billy Greer who entertains during the party with some pleasant tunes. This should be the easiest of the three."

"So when do you think I will be travelling to Hollywood and how long do you think I'll be out there?"

"I'm aiming for mid March and I want you to be out there for three to four weeks. Time is money in this case, so even if you are not busy for the full three to four weeks, your compensation will be based upon that amount of time. If the filming requires that you stay longer, I will have a clause in the contracts that requires additional compensation."

"Okay, Stan, it sounds pretty good to me. I'll go through these scripts and other papers tonight and try to let you know what I think by tomorrow."

"Good, it's important that we move fast before the people in Hollywood change their minds. I'll be here for your call tomorrow."

Jack went back to his apartment before going to his afternoon broadcast. He was excited about the movie roles. Jack knew about

Hollywood and wondered if it was like Edendale where he had met Emory Johnson, the director of one of Peggy's movies. Maybe he could somehow hook up with Emory again for a round or two of golf? The scripts looked simple enough. He read through some of his lines and then memorized a few, so he could walk around the apartment speaking the lines aloud. It was kind of fun. By accenting different words and phrases he could almost change the meaning of the lines. He thought, *This is going to be great.*

That evening, Jack wrote a nice long letter to Peggy detailing all of the information about his coming movie roles and reminiscing about their trip to Edendale when Peggy was making *The Non-Stop Flight* movie. In the closing of his letter, Jack wrote about how fast the marvels of this modern age were coming upon them. He cited the fact that Peggy's movie was silent and here four years later his would be complete with him both speaking and singing.

When Saturday rolled around, Jack decided to drive over to visit first with his mother and then with Milt and Jean. He was always amazed to find how well his mother adapted to the changing times. She had been very busy these past several months working with the church in getting the food cupboard well stocked and keeping the operation staffed, so they could meet the food needs of those who no longer had jobs. Jack visited the food cupboard room at church with his mother. As she explained the operation to Jack, it was obvious that she was very proud of her part in helping those in need. When a family member came to the cupboard, four days of food would be packaged according to the number of children and adults in that particular family. The family member simply signed for the food and carried it home with the knowledge that his or her family would not be eligible for additional supplies until four days had passed. The shelves appeared to be fairly well-stocked. Jack asked where the food came from, to which his mother replied that the parishioners were very generous. She explained some brought food items to the church while others donated money to be used for stocking the food cupboard. She said it was not necessary to be a member of the church or even of the Catholic faith to get food.

Jack gave his Mom a big hug, telling her how proud he was of her and that when they returned to her house, he would write a check to help in keeping the cupboard stocked.

After having lunch with his mother, Jack drove over to Milt and Jean's house. Milt was out front trying to show his son how to play step ball. Of course, young Robert was still a little too small, but they were having fun.

"Hello, Jack, what brings you here?"

Jack first said hello to young Robert and made a fuss over him. He then replied to Milt.

"I was over at church with your grandmother. She is very involved with the running of the church's food cupboard. I was quite impressed with what she showed me."

"I'm glad you're here. I was thinking about calling you for some fatherly advice. Are you free this afternoon?"

"Yes, I guess so. What's up Milt?"

Milt went on to explain that he and Jean had been thinking about moving to a larger house. With the new baby due in July and with Jean's mother living with them, it was really going to get crowded. He had heard about some new homes that were recently constructed in the Bronx up on East Two Hundred Fortieth Street. One of the guys at work had rented one for a song because after the Market Crash, the owner couldn't find anyone to either buy or rent the homes. Jack told Milt he would be glad to go along, but they had better go in Milt's car so the owner didn't get the wrong impression of their financial status.

Jean's mother would stay and watch young Robert, so Milt, Jack, and Jean were off to see the new homes. The homes were fairly close to the cemetery where Jack's father and Milt's mother were interned. There was a sample open with a sales person seated inside of the house.

"Good afternoon, folks. My name is Richard. I'm here to answer any questions you might have."

"Is it okay if we walk through?" Milt replied.

"You most certainly may. On this floor you'll find the dining room behind me followed by the kitchen and pantry. On the second floor, there are four bedrooms and the bathroom. There is also an attic and a full basement. Feel free to browse as you like."

Milt, Jack, and Jean were very impressed with the house. Richard told them one rental was available for immediate occupancy and gave them a key for house number 264 should they care to look it over. They did, and were every bit as impressed with the rental unit. Returning to the sample, Jack did a little negotiating and managed to get a rental figure that was less than Milt and Jean were currently paying. Jack had enough cash with him to cover a security deposit, so after Milt and Jean signed some rental agreement papers, they departed with a move-in date for the first of April. Needless to say, Milt and Jean were ecstatic. Jean insisted that Jack stay with them for dinner.

Over dinner, the conversation eventually got around to Peggy. Jean had been corresponding pretty consistently with Peggy and usually received a letter from Peggy every month or two. Jack filled them both in with Peggy's contractual situation and explained why she was kind of stuck in England for a while. Milt couldn't believe Peggy had a dream about Jean being pregnant even before they knew. The hard thing was Peggy being stuck in one country and Jack pretty much being stuck here in another. To bring things back to a happier note, Jack told both of them he would write and tell Peggy about their day together renting a house. They talked some more about the new rental with great anticipation and then Jack departed.

HOLLYWOOD

Jack stopped at the newsstand in the train station to pick up some reading material for his trip to California. One of the magazines he found was pretty much all about Hollywood and the movie star celebrities. He included it along with several newspapers and other magazines. Next he summoned a Red Cap to handle his luggage and moved to board the train. The sleeper car did not appear to be crowded. His room was found to be clean and well-equipped so Jack tipped the Red Cap and unpacked enough to make his trip as comfortable as possible.

Along the way, he found the dining car to be good. The food was okay and most of his fellow travelers were sociable. It was good to relax without any pressure to be someplace to perform. He wrote two letters to Peggy and one to his mother. Shortly after the train departed Chicago, Jack pulled out the magazine about Hollywood and began to read some of the articles and thumb through the pages looking at photographs. He became somewhat mesmerized with the content of the magazine. The women were amazingly beautiful and the men were all strikingly handsome. The homes and motor cars were all very luxurious-looking. The neon light district seemed to put Broadway to shame. There was a photo of the "Hollywoodland" sign located in the Hollywood Hills area. The caption stated it had been placed there in 1923 and was three hundred and fifty feet long with letters forty-five feet high. There were pictures of the movie studio lots. Compared to what Jack remembered about the studios in Edendale, these were incredibly big. The article accompanying the picture of the Hollywood sign gave a brief history about the development of Hollywood. Much of the area had simply been ranch land. There had been a good amount of planning put into developing Hollywood that was accelerated when the politicians on the East Coast put steep licensing fees and taxes on movie productions in New York and New Jersey. Many of the East Coast companies simply moved to California where there was plentiful real estate and a better climate in a tax-friendly environment. Jack thought, *There should be a lesson to be learned here by the New York City politicians.*

The train arrived at the Los Angeles station on a Tuesday afternoon. It was going to feel good to get off the train for a while. Janet had made Jack's hotel reservation, so he simply had his baggage sent to the Hollywood Plaza Hotel and then hired a taxi to take him on a scenic drive around Los Angeles ending at his hotel. Jack was impressed with the city and surrounding area. He liked the idea of being close to the ocean on one side of the city and close to the mountains on the other.

At the Hollywood Plaza, he was treated royally. His suite of rooms was plush and there was no indication of the bad economic conditions having affected anything he had yet experienced in California. He freshened up and headed to the hotel dining room for an early dinner. The menu was five pages long with rather attractive pricing. He thought how his mother would like this place.

The next day, Jack was up bright and early. He had slept well and didn't dwell on thinking about Peggy. *Maybe*, he thought, *Hollywood is going to be a good place for me to be at this time in my life.* After cleaning up and shaving, Jack returned to the hotel dining room for coffee and some breakfast. The restaurant was very busy and as he looked around, the clientele reminded him of the pictures in the *Hollywood Magazine*. The women were all very attractive, even his waitress. Jack settled for pancakes with bacon on the side and of course, coffee. When the waitress brought his order, she asked him if he was headed to the movie studio. Jack responded that as a matter of fact he was. The waitress asked Jack what his name was and upon hearing it, she immediately recognized him as the radio broadcasting singer.

"I have a lot of your records. I should have recognized you from your picture on some of the jackets. And you're a bachelor, aren't you Mr. Smith?

"Well, I'm glad you like my songs. And yes, I guess I am still a bachelor."

"If you need someone to show you around Hollywood, I would certainly consider it a privilege to be your escort. My name is Joann and I'm here serving all three meals almost every day."

"Thank you, Joann. I'll keep you in mind."

Then she was off to wait on other tables. *Wow*, Jack thought, *I never had a good-looking waitress in New York approach me like that.*

Jack finished his breakfast and then headed over to the Fox Studio. When the taxi arrived at the gate, a guard came out and asked for Jack's identification. The guard then checked his listing and as he returned, Jack's papers he told the taxi driver to go to studio B. At Studio B, Jack was ushered into a reception area and offered a cup of coffee. After a short wait, a pretty, well-dressed young lady approached Jack and asked him to please follow her. They went down a rather long hall and into a plushily furnished office.

"Please make yourself comfortable here, Mr. Smith. Mr. Hanson will be in directly."

And then she was gone. Jack sank into a soft leather chair and looked around the room. There was no window in the room and all of the walls were decorated with framed poster billboards from an assortment of movie pictures. Jack didn't know who Mr. Hanson was, but if he had something to do with all of these movies, he must be a pretty important man. It turned out that Mr. Hanson was nothing more than a scheduler. It seemed that getting everyone to the right place at the right time in the movie business was somewhat of an art. Jack left the office with a printed schedule and a diagram of the studio layout in hand. In addition, there was an invitation to a "Get to Know the *Happy Days* Cast Party". The party was to be held that evening in the Knickerbocker Hotel Ballroom, very close to where he was staying. There was nothing more for Jack to do until the time of the party. Mr. Hanson had made it clear that Jack was expected to attend the party.

By the time Jack got back to his hotel, it was time for lunch, so he headed straight to the dining room.

"Hello, Mr. Smith. I'm surprised to see you back here so soon. How did everything go?" It was Joann, the same waitress who had served his breakfast.

"Well, Joann, I'm not quite sure. Business here in Hollywood is conducted much differently than it is in New York City."

Joann passed Jack a menu and recommended two selections from the menu, which she claimed to be excellent choices. She then asked if he would like a cup of coffee and excused herself, commenting that she would be right back with the coffee and a glass of water. Jack looked around and noted there were only a few customers in the dining room. Again, it seemed quite different from New York City at lunch time. Joann returned with his coffee and water. She made a little small talk as she took his order and then scurried away. In a short time, Joann was back with his order. She placed his food on the table and then asked if Jack would mind if she sat at his table for a few minutes. Jack motioned affirmatively.

"Now, Mr. Smith, please tell me about your morning over at the studio. I might be able to settle your mind about how business is conducted here."

Jack saw no harm in describing his morning at the studio, so he told Joann pretty much how things had been done. She then asked to see the papers he had been given.

"Was the man's name, Hanson?"

"Well, yes it was."

"May I call you Jack?"

"Sure."

"Well, Jack, Hanson is no more than a troubleshooter. But his job is important because in the movie business, there are so many different people involved and they all have very different personalities. Many movies have been in trouble simply because the cast members could not get along with one another. Hanson tries to get everyone started out on a friendly basis and works to iron out any difficulties or conflicts as the shooting progresses.

"Now this evening's party is very important, especially for someone such as you, commonly known as an 'Out of Towner'."

"Joann, how do you know so much about the movie business?"

"I've been there, Jack. I never hit it big, but I've had some good supporting roles. It's a tough business, Jack. And it pays to know who the players are. My offer to be your escort still stands. I can keep you on the right track and maybe even get my own foot back in the door."

"Okay, Joann. I think I'll accept your offer."

Joann suggested what attire Jack should wear and they agreed to meet in the hotel lobby at eight o'clock.

Jack was in the lobby a few minutes before eight dressed in suit and tie and in his own opinion looking pretty good. At exactly eight o'clock, Joann entered the lobby. She was wearing a long, silky, silver colored evening gown that just flowed with her every movement as she walked across the lobby. Her hair was completely different from earlier and just beautiful. She held her hand out for Jack and commented.

"Perfect, Jack. You are dressed just as I had pictured you. Shall we go?"

Jack was speechless. He couldn't take his eyes off Joann and when the fragrance of her perfume reached him, he just melted. Recovering he said, "Joann, you look absolutely beautiful and yes, let's get going."

Earlier Jack had inquired at the desk as to where the Knickerbocker Hotel was located, so he knew it was only a few blocks away. He decided there was no way he was going to walk Joann several blocks in her flowing evening gown. He immediately hired a taxi and within minutes, they were at the Knickerbocker. The doorman was a rather colorful character who greeted Joann by name while helping her exit the taxi and asking for the name of her gentleman escort. In a very commanding voice, Joann introduced Jack as the famous radio singer, "Whispering" Jack

Smith. Jack noticed that some couples nearby immediately turned their attention to Joann and him. He thought, *I think it was a good decision to have Joann come along as an escort.* Upon entering the ballroom, the same scene was repeated with Joann commanding the attention of those nearby as she introduced this famous New York City radio personality, "Whispering" Jack Smith. *Wow*, Jack thought, *she is good.* As Joann guided Jack around the crowd in the ballroom, she intentionally picked and chose those who were to be bypassed and those who deserved introductions. She always included some phrase in the introductions that pointed out he was a radio personality from New York City. She was always by Jack's side, often with arms interlocked as if they had been long-time friends. When the band started to play, they were gliding across the dance floor. Joann was an excellent dancer, and as they danced she would offer bits of information about the people he had thus far met. Jack thought, *This lady should have been a talent agent.* He sensed an immediate trust in her judgment, much in the way he trusted Stan's. When the band took a break, they were at the punch and drink table. There was no sign of prohibition here. Jack settled for a glass of punch hoping there was not much alcohol in the mix. Waiters and waitresses continually stopped and offered assortments of hors d'oeuvres from large hand carried trays. Eventually, Joann guided Jack to a table with two open seats. Once more, she introduced Jack to the two couples already at the table and then asked if they might join them.

The two gentlemen at the table were considerably older than most of the guests. Jack guessed they were probably close to seventy. One was a producer and the other a director. Jack found the other couples very easy to talk to and thought, *This is really a nice party and a good way to start my time here in Hollywood.* Contrary to his initial feelings about attending the party, Jack found that he was actually enjoying it. During the table conversation, Jack mentioned to the director that he had spent some time playing golf with Emory Johnson who was directing a silent movie several years back. The director's eyes immediately lit up and Jack sensed that he might be in for a round or two of golf with this new crowd. Before Jack became more involved, Joann had him back on the dance floor feeding him bits of information about the two couples at the table. She added that Emory Johnson was no longer a big name in Hollywood. *Wow*, Jack thought, *Joann is really all business and all I was thinking about was lining up a round or two of golf.*

Shortly after midnight, the ballroom lights were brightened and then softened several times. Joann told Jack this meant that someone was about to speak to the attendees. A gentleman moved to the stage microphone and before he could utter a word, Joann had told Jack who the speaker was and what he was about to say. The speaker was actually some vice president in the Fox hierarchy who had some flowery words of praise for all who were in attendance and some hard line figures about the dollars involved in the undertaking and the necessity to avoid any cost overruns. A second Fox speaker was introduced. His message was all about which groups of people were to be where throughout the following day. This speaker closed by thanking all for attending and announcing that the band would continue to play for another hour.

As Jack and Joann said good-byes to their table companions, the director passed a folded note to Jack telling him to read it at his leisure. Jack simply slipped it into his pocket and then they departed the ballroom. Along the way, Joann asked Jack if she might ask for a favor.

"Of course you may, Joann. I am certainly indebted to you for all that you have done for me today."

"Well, Jack, I am scheduled to waitress rather early in the morning at the hotel and it would be so much easier if I could bunk in with you. I have a bag with my work uniform stored in the lobby. I can sleep in a chair or even on the floor."

"You are most welcome to. It sounded like I don't need to be at the movie lot until after lunch, so I can easily stay out of your way. And I won't hear of you sleeping on the floor. There is a large bed in the room and I've had some practice sleeping on my side of the bed without touching the person next to me."

"Okay, that sounds great, Jack, but no fooling around. I do need my sleep."

The next morning Joann was up, bathed, and dressed in her waitress attire before six o'clock. She kissed Jack gently on his cheek and told him to stop in for breakfast before going to the Fox movie lot. Jack acknowledged and fell right back to sleep. A few hours later, he was up thinking about what had happened in the past twenty-four hours. This is almost a replay of when Peggy and I first met. How many men sleep with a woman the first time they meet and never touch them? And Joann is certainly a good-looking woman. I couldn't help looking at her figure as she slipped into bed last night. And what was with the kiss on my cheek this morning? She did leave her gown and some toiletries here also, so does that mean we will have another night together? Oh, I almost forgot about the note the director handed me last night. Jack retrieved the note from his jacket pocket and unfolded it.

"Jack, I do see Emory on occasion at the golf club and thought we might be able to put together a foursome with you included. Please give my secretary a call if you are interested."

Well, Jack thought, *things are looking up*. He folded the note and placed it in his pants pocket and then finished dressing and grooming before setting off for breakfast, hoping Joann would be the one to serve him. Joann spotted Jack entering the dining room and motioned to a table for him to go to. She was almost at the table the same time as Jack.

"Let me get you some coffee and I'll be right back." She left a menu on the table and was back within minutes with a cup of delicious smelling coffee.

"I'll have to keep moving this morning with little time for real conversation, so what do you say we make a dinner date for this evening? You will most likely end your day at the studio with an invitation to an evening party and I would love to be your escort again."

"Sounds great, but I really don't know when I'll be back to the hotel."

"Eight o'clock should work, Jack. I'll meet you in the lobby again."

"Okay, eight o'clock it is."

Then Joann was off to the kitchen with his breakfast order. On one of her trips back to Jack's table she told him to dress casually in a sport shirt and sweater for their evening date. In hope of having a little more time to talk to Joann, Jack lingered at his table for a little while. It became obvious that was not going to happen, so he left a handsome tip on the table and headed for the street outside of the hotel lobby. Jack had some time to kill before going to the movie lot, and he loved to explore new territories. The street was very pristine, with small shops scattered along each side. There were several nearby restaurants, which appeared to be quite adequate for lunch or even an evening meal. Perhaps he would suggest one for dinner later with Joann.

He returned to his hotel room to freshen up and decided to head over to the movie lot. Jack liked to be a little early for his engagements to entertain. Doing so helped in getting a feeling for his surroundings and a chance to meet the other people involved. The routine from the previous day was repeated. The guard at the Fox gate checked Jack's identification and then screened his listing before giving the taxi driver directions as to where to take Mr. Smith. Once on the set, Jack found a lot of people milling around in what seemed to be a much disorganized fashion. Actually, most knew exactly what they were doing and where they were going as Jack was soon to learn. Eventually, one of the workers on the set asked Jack what his name was and then, checking a sheet on his clipboard much like the one the guard at the gate had, he asked Jack to follow along. Jack was introduced to a makeup specialist who evaluated his needs and then passed Jack along to a wardrobe specialist who took a lot of Jack's measurements. He was then instructed to sit in a small set of bleacher seats just off to the side and behind the set. Someone would eventually come to get him. Observing the action on the set was much more interesting than what Jack had experienced watching the silent filming of Peggy's. One big difference was that microphones were strategically placed to record the sound, but stay out of view. Some microphones were mobile in that they were raised and lowered or sometimes moved from side to side.

Jack had brought his script along and was busy studying his part when a young man asked him to follow along. The young man took Jack to the wardrobe tent. Two people immediately assisted Jack in changing into a tuxedo. A few quick modifications were made while the tuxedo was still on Jack. Next he was off to the makeup tent. A half dozen or so actors and actresses were seated in barbershop-like chairs having makeup applied. In the past, Jack had endured having makeup applied for photo shoots, but he never did like it, especially lipstick which he thought was better suited on women. Nonetheless, he sat like a good soldier throughout the process and even underwent a slight trimming of his hair.

Next, he was taken to the set for what was called a walk-through. The scene was to center on Jack with a young actress under his right arm and a young actor under his left. Jack had a few lines and would then begin to sing "Happy Days" to the young couple as he embraced them. The walk-through was rather direct and easy. There were spots marked on the floor where they were to start from and just a short distance away where they would finish the scene. The director asked if they knew their lines and were ready for the first take. Hearing three affirmative responses, the director stepped back behind the cameras and waited momentarily while a stagehand pinned a fresh carnation to Jack's lapel. Next Jack heard, "Ready on the set, lights, camera, action." Jack swallowed hard and by the time he had heard *action* he was relaxed and voicing his lines. He moved effortlessly into the "Happy Days" lyrics and continued to the end without interruption from the director.

"That was a good take, but I think we can do a little better. I want all three of you to show more movement. Look at each other and sway to the beat of the song. Okay, positions and camera, action, roll them."

The second take did seem better, and the director seemed to be satisfied.

"You people are finished for today. We'll look over the film later in the screening room and contact you if we need a retake."

Jack approached the scheduler with the clipboard and asked when he should return to the studio. The scheduler leafed through his clipboard papers, and finally told Jack he would not be needed until Wednesday or Thursday of the following week when the grand finale would be filmed with a cast of more than fifty. His only instruction was to check once or twice a day with his hotel clerk for any messages. Jack thanked the scheduler and made his way back to the tents to change clothes and scrub the makeup off. He was shown a locker in the tent, which was temporarily labeled "Jack Smith" and asked to keep his tuxedo and accessories in the locker. Upon opening the locker door, he found a large envelope addressed to "Whispering" Jack Smith. Inside was an invitation to a party that evening. Joann was right again.

Once again, Joann arrived at eight o'clock sharp in the hotel lobby. She was wearing a very colorful blouse that was not tucked in and covering a small portion of a well-tailored, pleated skirt. As Joann crossed the marble floor, Jack's eyes moved to a very high-heeled pair of shoes making a precision like clicking noise. He thought, *How do women manage to walk in those heels*?

"Well, Jack, where is the party?"

"You look fabulous, Joann," Jack commented as he handed the invitation to her. "I don't really know where the party is, but there is an address on the invitation."

As Joann looked over the invitation, Jack again detected a very pleasant and somewhat familiar fragrance, but different from last night's perfume.

"Is that Chanel No. 5 perfume that smells so nice?"

"Well finally, a man who knows and appreciates fine fragrances. Thank you, Jack. That was one of the nicest of compliments."

Wow, Jack thought. *I'm really not a connoisseur of perfumes. It's just that Peggy often wore the same perfume. I guess I had better not say any more on the subject.*

"If I'm not mistaken, the address in the invitation is Benjamin Stoloff's Estate. Ben is the director of your movie. We can easily verify that with the taxi driver. Jack, I know I said dinner date, but I'm really not very hungry. Would you be all right with a cup of coffee and a light snack? I'm sure there will be plenty of food at Ben's and we should kill a little time before going to Ben's."

"That will suit me fine. How about we just go to one of the little places out on the street?"

Joann agreed and they walked down the street to a nice small sized restaurant. Once settled at a corner table, Joann asked Jack to tell her about his day at Fox. Jack felt very comfortable talking with Joann. It seemed like he had known her for a very long time, when in fact they had just met yesterday. Jack described in detail pretty much what he had done that afternoon at the studio. When he finished, Joann reached across the table and took his hand in between both of hers as she told him that he was off to a wonderful start. She told him Benjamin Stoloff was a great director, but also known to be very demanding, and for Jack to have wrapped up his first scene with just two uninterrupted takes was marvelous.

"Now, Jack, I would like to hear more about you personally. I know about your being gassed in the war. Tell me something about it and how you got started in your broadcasting career."

Jack started with his experiences in France during the Great War. He intentionally left out some parts such as his time with Cecilia. Joann would occasionally interrupt with a question or comment. Before long, an hour had passed and it was time to get a taxi.

"You are an amazing man, Jack. I want to hear much more about you. Let's see if we can leave this party at an early hour and if you don't mind, I would love to stay with you again tonight. It will give us time for you to tell me more about your life."

The Stoloff estate was big and beautiful, containing all of the amenities associated with success in the movie business. As Jack looked around, it reminded him of Lorie Bradford's Estate along the Hudson River back in New York. There were the usual introductions as they made their way around. Director Stoloff remembered Jack and commented, "Very nice job today, young man." As they exchanged greetings. Shortly after shaking the director's hand, Joann guided Jack over to a table where several young actors were seated. Joann introduced Jack to all, and then as they moved on, she told Jack to remember the actor named John Wayne. That young man is destined to become a star. He has all of the attributes—voice, physical presence, athletic abilities, good looks, and even a little swagger. Jack asked what kind of movies he acted in and Joann replied that the movies were mostly cowboy movies, but she sensed he had the talent to do all kind of roles. They made a quick pass at a very long table filled with food and drink and then Joann locked arms with Jack and suggested they return to the hotel.

In Jack's suite, Joann went directly to the bed, kicked her shoes off, and stretched out. She patted the bedding along side of her, inviting Jack to come join her.

"Now, tell me more about yourself. You were discharged and eventually got a job playing piano in a sheet music store. What happened next?"

Jack removed his sweater and shoes. He then stretched out on his back beside Joann, folding his arms behind his head and continued his story. After a bit, Joann got up and dimmed the lights. Jack was at the point in his story where he met his agent at Mrs. Bradford's estate. When Joann returned to bed, she moved closer to Jack. She kissed him softly on the cheek and then whispered in his ear, "Did you sleep with the widow Bradford?"

"Well, Joann, I can't lie to you. Yes, I did sleep with her and she was a wonderful teacher."

Joann moved yet closer and pressed her lips to Jack's with a long passionate kiss. Jack gently wrapped his arms around Joann, and as he kissed her the strangest thought crossed his mind. He was saying, "Close your eyes, Peggy".

"Now, Jack, how do you think the widow would grade that kiss?"

"I think she would definitely give that an A plus."

And with that Jack completely surrendered. All thoughts of Peggy were gone from his mind as he and Joann removed their clothes and began to engage in passionate lovemaking.

The next morning, Joann was once again up early and ready for her waitress job before Jack even stirred. She moved next to Jack bending over to kiss his cheek and whispered in his ear, "The widow Bradford was indeed a very good teacher. I can't wait to see what happens next." And then she was gone.

When Jack finally got out of bed he thought, *What a night.* And then paused and apologized in his mind to Peggy. His thought process quickly changed once he realized that his day was free and just maybe there was a round of golf to be played. Jack retrieved the note about golf and placed a call to the number for Director Henderson's secretary. After a few minutes of the secretary talking to Director Henderson, Jack was asked if he could be at the Lakeside Golf Club between twelve and one o'clock that day. He was to simply go to the Pro Shop and give them his name. Someone would then see that he was properly equipped and led to the practice range where the other members of the foursome would meet him. Jack responded affirmatively, hung up, and began to select clothing that would be most suitable for a round of golf.

The hotel clerk advised Jack that the Lakeside Golf Course was about a thirty-minute taxi ride from the hotel. Jack decided to get an early start and hired a taxi for eleven o'clock. To his surprise, the Lakeside Club was more inland than the courses he had played with Emory Johnson. At the Lakeside Pro Shop Jack was treated royally. The course pro actually measured Jack before selecting a set of clubs for his use. He was fitted with shoes and a Lakeside Golf

Club shirt along with a club hat. Next, the Pro escorted Jack to the practice range.

"How long has it been since you last played a round, Mr. Smith?"

"Please call me Jack. I think it's close to one month now."

"Well, Jack, if you would like I'll watch you take a few practice shots. If you have picked up any bad habits, I'll try to help you straighten them out before your round today. Mr. Johnson tells me you are a very good golfer and he is very much looking forward to playing with you again. However, the pair you are playing against today are very competitive and will not cut you any breaks."

Jack thanked the pro and loosened up with a few iron shots down the range followed by six or eight drives. The pro complimented Jack and then suggested a slight change in his grip on the driver that might eliminate the slice on his drives. After a few more drives, the slice was all but gone. Before returning to the clubhouse, the pro told Jack he thought he was all set and to have a good round. Jack continued to leisurely hit practice balls until he heard a familiar voice.

"Save some of that energy for the course, partner."

It was Emory. They were truly happy to see each other. Emory eventually asked about Peggy, to which Jack simply responded that since the market crash she has been stuck over in England.

"Jack, this Henderson and his partner, Fred, are tough cookies, but if your game is as good as it was several years ago, I think we can take them. We'll have a friendly wager for the losers to pay for dinner and drinks after we finish. I just don't want to face the humiliation of losing to these two."

"Okay, Emory, I'll try my best. We did have a lot of fun the last time we played."

The eighteen holes of golf passed rather rapidly. Dave, Fred, Emory, and Jack all got along with one another fabulously. By the sixteenth hole, Jack and Emory pretty much had the match won. Later over dinner in the clubhouse, Emory made a big fuss over how sweet it was to enjoy a free meal and drinks. Of course, Dave and Fred wanted to get even so a rematch was set for the next day.

Emory offered Jack a ride back to his hotel as he was traveling in the same general direction. Jack accepted and again the conversation along the way turned to Peggy O'Neil. Jack mentioned Peggy's acting in *The Flying Squad* stage show at the New Theater in Cambridge, England, and how he and Peggy had travelled to Edinburgh, Scotland, to watch preparations for the making of *The Flying Squad* movie. When Jack talked about taking home movies at Edinburgh, Emory became very interested. Emory had in fact had a strong interest in directing that movie. Jack promised to get a copy of his home movie reel made and sent to Emory provided he would not be too critical of his camera work. At the hotel, Emory thanked Jack and confirmed he would pick him up at noon the next day.

That evening, Jack and Joann walked to a nearby restaurant and enjoyed a candle light dinner. This time it was Jack's turn to ask Joann about her career.

"Oh, Jack, it's easy for a pretty young local girl to get a small part in the movies, but then it took me almost a year before I moved up to speaking a few lines. Of course along the way, a girl has to put up with a lot of men trying to hit on her. I dated some, never any that were married. I got to meet a lot of key people in the industry along the way. The money was good when I had a part and nonexistent when I didn't. So I settled into my flexible waitress routine and still keep looking for that big break. The problem is I'm not getting any younger."

"Do you mind telling me how old you are?"

"Not at all, Jack, I'm twenty-eight."

"Well, I personally think you are a very pretty young woman and you don't look a day over twenty-five."

"Thank you. You will be justly rewarded later."

Jack went on to tell Joann about the relationship he had with his talent agent. He mentioned reading a magazine on the train that used the term "Casting Agent".

"Now, Joann, I have to tell you that you were very good in handling my introductions and giving me advice these first few days.

It made things so much easier and enjoyable for me. You remind me very much of my own agent. And you probably realize that a lot of agents make more money than many actors and actresses. So what I'm trying to tell you is I think you should give some thought to becoming a 'Casting Agent'. If you would like me to call back to New York for a little advice along those lines, I'll be happy to do so. My agent is very good at helping people."

"Well, I don't know, Jack. I've never thought about being a casting agent. You really think I can do it?"

"I know you can. It's almost exactly what you did for me. I'll make the call tomorrow and see what my agent has to say."

"Thanks, honey. I think I am ready to give up waitressing, so I will give what you said some serious thought."

Their night together in Jack's suite was perfect. Joann was not only beautiful, but also a great lover with a wonderful sense of humor. Jack no longer thought of Peggy and thoroughly appreciated having a woman like Joann by his side. It wasn't the same kind of love he had for Peggy, but it was great. It was more a feeling of mutual respect and desire for one another with a kind of special fulfillment for each of them.

The next morning, Jack did call Stan and asked about advice for Joann. Stan simply said if she handled things that well for Jack, she probably did have the abilities to become a casting agent. They ended the call with Stan offering to talk directly with Joann the next day around three o'clock in the afternoon, New York time.

The next round of golf was very enjoyable even though Emory and Jack lost on the last hole. This time they paid for the food and drinks. Of course, being tied at one round each, called for another match. Dave Henderson had to be on his studio lot the following day, so they set the match for two days hence. Jack thought, *Perfect, I'll be able to be with Joann when she calls Stan tomorrow.*

That evening, Jack and Joann simply walked along the streets of Hollywood, occasionally stopping into a California version of a speakeasy for a drink. Jack limited himself to two glasses of brandy. Joann held her alcohol well and had a few more drinks than Jack. At the second speakeasy, Joann told Jack that after considerable thought, she really liked the idea of becoming a casting agent.

"Jack, I'm going to put my casting agent badge on for a few minutes. An agent should truly have the client's best interests at heart. Isn't that right?"

"Well, yes, that's the way I see it."

"There is something I neglected to tell you, Jack, and it may be rather important to you in terms of being properly compensated for your time here in California. Your movie is a William Fox production. Now Mr. Fox was a very dynamic, hands on business man until about a year ago when he was injured in an automobile accident. He is not the same since the accident, and I do hear from fairly reliable sources that there is a move on to take over Fox. Should that happen, a lot of business decisions could be made with the potential of directly hurting you. For example, suppose the new management team was to cancel the movies you are involved in. Would you still be paid in full or even paid at all?"

"Well, you certainly are thinking like a casting agent. When you talk to Stan Schuman tomorrow how about going over what you just told me. Stan will know if anything needs to be done at this point. Now take that casting agent badge off and open those bedroom eyes. Let's go back to my suite and continue your lessons."

At ten the next morning, Jack placed a call to the Star Agency. Stan answered and spoke briefly with Jack and then at length with Joann. When Joann finished, she was all smiles. She placed her arms around Jack and began to cry, but it was a happy cry.

"Well, tell me what Stan said."

"You won't believe it, Jack. Stan said when you return to New York, I should come with you. He has been thinking about hiring someone to help in the agency, so it will be a good opportunity for him to try out an additional employee and at the same time a good chance for me to learn something about running an agency. Oh!

Jack, I'm so excited. Will you help me find a place to stay and show me around the city?"

"Yes I will. In fact my place has two bedrooms and I will love showing you New York City. How long did Stan say you will be at the agency?"

"He thought two or three months would work."

"Well if the timing is right, we can ride the train together back to Hollywood when I return to play Billy Greer in *The Big Party*."

"I don't know how to thank you, Jack, but for starters get over here in bed with me."

The next two weeks flew by. Jack got quite a few rounds of golf in and he spent a lot of time with Joann. The final shoot for the movie was spectacular. It was done on a multitiered stage with sections that swung in and out. The cast exceeded fifty with chorus girls, dancers, and singers all in costumes and tuxedos. There were a couple of practice runs and then the final shooting was done without interruption. Director Stoloff congratulated the cast and all supporting staff for a job well done and asked everyone to stay in town one more day to allow for his final screening.

Two days later, Jack and Joann were on their way to New York City. They had a sleeper with upper and lower berths and a small bathroom. Both were avid readers, so the time on the train passed pleasantly between reading, passionate interludes, simply watching scenery pass by and of course, trips to the dining car for rather tasty meals and socializing with other travelers. As they departed Chicago, Jack told Joann the long train ride was the most pleasant he had ever experienced and suggested that they work very hard to make sure they returned to California together.

NEW YORK, NEW YORK

"I just love this city, Joann."

Jack and Joann were approaching Stan Schuman's Star Talent Agency.

"Now, Joann, I know both Janet and Stan are going to take good care of you. A short time after I introduce you, I am going to head over to the broadcasting station. Are you sure you're okay using the transit to get back to the apartment."

"Don't worry, Jack, I'll be fine. See you back at the apartment later. Thanks for looking after me, honey."

An hour later, Jack was in the radio studio. Everyone was glad to have him back. Jack had several hours to prepare for his broadcast, so he scratched some notes about his time in Hollywood anticipating that he might adlib some lines in between his songs to give his listeners an impression of how *movie land* works and plays. Once again, his broadcast was spectacular. His listeners had missed Jack's music style along with the dialogue he had become so well known for. Jack was having fun. *This*, Jack thought, *is where I belong*. Being in the movies and associating with the celebrities in Hollywood was a good experience, but broadcasting is my true love.

When Jack returned to the apartment that evening, Joann was already bathed and dressed for bed. She looked tired.

"How did your day at the agency go?"

"It was great, Jack, but there is so much to learn and there are so many people out of work who need help. I completely understand why Mr. Schuman wants to hire more help. I only hope I don't slow him and Janet down too much when they are showing me things."

"Don't worry, Stan is a straightforward guy and if he feels you are holding him back, he will tell you so. Have you had something to eat?"

"Yes, I'm good, and if you don't mind I think I'll go to bed now."

"I don't mind. Get a good night's sleep and if you wake up with your nightgown on backwards, don't be concerned. It will probably be just from me fooling around."

Joann kissed Jack and told him not to worry, she would set aside a night strictly for him.

The time passed fast with both Jack and Joann being very busy and involved in their respective ventures. Jack had been to visit his mother and told her just a little about Joann and how she was kind of serving an apprenticeship with Janet and Stan before returning to Hollywood to start her own business. He likened his relationship to his with Mrs. Bradford when she had chosen to sponsor Jack's career development.

"This young lady helped me so much in understanding the way things worked in Hollywood. It really makes me feel good to be able to kind of sponsor her in getting started as a casting agent. Stan thinks she has what it takes, so I hope it works out. If you would like to meet her, Mom, maybe we can go out to dinner sometime this weekend."

"I would love to meet Joann. Why don't you bring her here Sunday afternoon for some home cooking and I'll see if Milt and Jean can come over."

"Okay, great, Mom. I just hope Stan and Janet don't give her a lot of homework."

When Sunday arrived, Jack tried to coax Joann to ride in the rear seat of the Cord on their ride over to his mother's, but she would have none of it.

"Riding back there will get you used to being chauffeur driven, so when you are successful back in Hollywood it won't have to be a new experience."

"Thanks, but no thanks, Jack. If and when the time comes for me to have a chauffeur, I'm sure I'll be able to handle it."

Joann loved the Cord and told Jack so. Jack drove a little out of the way, so he could point out things of interest. He pointed out some of the mansions in Manhattan and told Joann a little about the owners and how they reportedly obtained such wealth. When they passed Madison Square Garden, Jack commented that his brother was a big shot in running the maintenance of the complex.

"Okay, now we are going up to East Two Hundred Fortieth Street in the Bronx. I'll show you where my chauffeur lives. Actually, he's my nephew, but I'm just five years older, so we kind of grew up like brothers. Let's see now, look for house number 264."

"There it is, Jack."

Jack pulled up and parked in front of the house.

"Come on up to the house with me. We are going to give Milt and Jean a lift over to my mother's."

Of course, Milt and Jean were expecting Jack because he had telephoned earlier in the week. Introductions were made and then Jean was anxious to show her guests through the house. It was obvious Milt and Jean had put a lot of effort into furnishing and decorating their home and they were very proud of the results. Jack kidded Jean about having a big belly with her second pregnancy. Milt wanted to hear all about Hollywood. Joann seemed to fit right in, just as if she had known Milt and Jean for a long time. She helped Jack with his descriptions of various events and places back in Hollywood and told Milt and Jean about what a marvelous job Jack had done in his movie roles.

When it was time to head over to Jack's mother's house, it was decided that Milt would chauffeur with the two ladies seated at the back and Jack in the front passenger seat. They had a good time as Joann told about how Jack tried to get her to ride alone in the rear seat. Joann's demeanor was always very proper and there was never a hint of any kind of romantic involvement between her and Jack.

Dinner was pork roast with all of the trimmings, followed by chocolate cake and coffee. Mrs. Schmidt was very much interested in hearing about Hollywood and was very much engaged in conversation with Joann. Jack was carrying dishes to the kitchen where Jean had started to wash them.

"Have you heard from Peggy, Jack?"

"Not for some time now. I think the last letter came before I went to Hollywood."

"She still writes to me, Jack. She seems to be doing very well. In the last letter she told me she was the first person ever interviewed on television. I didn't even know what television was. Somehow both a picture and sound can be sent out like a radio broadcast. Anyway, Peggy appeared on an experimental televisor at a Home Exhibition in Southampton. It was a very big deal over in England."

"Well good for her. Does she know I was out in Hollywood doing some movies?"

"Yes, she always asks about you, Jack."

"Well, I'll try to get a letter off to her tonight or tomorrow. It's tough because she wants to know when I'm coming back to England and Stan doesn't really have any prospects for me to go."

"Jack, can I ask you a personal question?"

"Sure, what is it?"

"Joann is such a pretty woman. Is there anything going on between you two?"

"Jean, remember Mrs. Bradford and how she helped me get started in my career? Well, this is kind of the same thing. It's time for me to reach out and help someone. Joann helped me in Hollywood and never asked for a dime, so I'm kind of returning the favor to help her get started in her own business."

"Thanks, Jack, I didn't mean to pry. But you know, Milt thinks of you as a brother and he'll have a thousand questions for me later tonight."

Later in the evening, when Jack and Joann were in bed, Jack thanked Joann for the way she blended with his family without revealing their romantic involvement.

"When I was in the kitchen, Jean came right out and asked me if there was anything going on between us. Remember when I told you some things about my career I mentioned Peggy O'Neil?

Well, Peggy knows everyone in my family and everyone knows Peggy and I were lovers. But right now Peggy is stuck over in England and I'm kind of stuck here in the States."

Joann placed her finger over Jack's lips indicating to shush.

"Jack, I know this is a 'one night stand'. I only hope it is a very long 'one night stand' and that when over, it will become a lifelong friendship. Now, I reserved this night to share our pleasures in passionate lovemaking, so no more serious talk. Just let me have your lips."

Jack did write to Peggy. He told her about Hollywood and playing golf with Emory Johnson. He mentioned Emory's interest in the making of *The Flying Squad* into a movie and that he had sent a copy of his home movies from Edinburgh to Emory. He told Peggy how much he thought about her every day and how much he missed her. He congratulated Peggy for her television interview. He then finished by stating that Stan was still searching for any opportunity for a booking in England or Germany. He mentioned his contract to return to California and that it would be at least several months before there was any chance of getting back to England. Jack read through what he had just written several times and was tempted to tear up the letter and try writing another later. *No*, he thought, *I'll just keep putting it off, so I'm taking this to the desk and arranging to have it mailed.*

The weeks flew by with Jack and Joann essentially working different hours. Joann loved what she was doing, and from Jack's conversations with Stan, she was a natural. When they had time together, they thoroughly enjoyed each other's company. Jack took pride in showing Joann around New York City, including his broadcasting studio. At the studio, he actually had an on the air question and answer type of interview with Joann, who he had introduced as a movie casting agent from Hollywood. Joann performed flawlessly and the audience feedback was that they loved it. A few days later, Stan asked Jack to stop by the office for a quick sit down.

"Jack, there isn't much more we can show Joann. I feel it's time for her to head back to Hollywood and start into her new venture. Janet tells me you will be traveling to Hollywood next Saturday to finish the last movie on your contract. I think it will be smart for you two to travel together and when you arrive in Hollywood, perhaps you can provide some assistance to Joann in setting up her new business."

"I'll be glad to help in any way I can, but I'm not much of a businessman."

"You're a better businessman than you think, Jack. Janet has prepared a check list for you and Joann to work with. It all comes down to common sense and hard work. Joann has proven she is a hard worker, so all she needs is a little support and advice along the way from you as she makes some major decisions such as renting office space and hiring an assistant. Will you do it?"

"Sure, I'll help her, Stan. I'm the one who brought Joann to you. It feels kind of good to be a sponsor."

"Thanks, Jack. Janet and I both like Joann and we're only a phone call away if you get into anything over your head. And Jack, you used the word 'sponsor'. One of the things I need to go over with you has to do with your sponsor for many years. B and B Industries notified us they will no longer be supplementing your rent at the Chelsea Arms effective as of the first of next month."

"Stan, I didn't know Lorie was still involved in sponsoring me."

"She told me early on it was in return for a favor you did that preserved her marriage. Her company is experiencing hard times just now, so they had to rein in a lot of unnecessary expenses. The good news is that I have already talked to the Chelsea Arms manager and they will continue your rental for the amount you have been paying on top of the B and B money. As you probably have noticed, the rental business at the high rises is sliding downhill with this poor economy and the manager was just happy to be able to keep you as a tenant."

"Well, that's great. Thank you, Stan. I still can't believe she was doing that. I hope her company comes out okay."

"I'm sure it will, Jack. Lorie is a very smart business person. Check with Janet on the way out. I think she has train tickets for you and Joann. You may also want to tell Joann she'll be traveling with you."

"Thanks, Stan. I don't know what I would do without you."

Jack and Joann celebrated that evening, first with a five course dinner at the country club and then a long evening in the apartment where Jack played the piano and sang his favorites, sometimes with lyrics he just made up. Joann was sitting next to Jack on the piano bench. She excused herself for a moment and returned shortly thereafter wearing the sleepwear Jack most admired. Again she sat next to Jack on the piano bench, moving very close while placing one arm around Jack and beginning to gently rub his leg with the other. Jack smelled a slight trace of Chanel No. 5 perfume as Joann's lips moved ever so slowly across his cheek and up to his ear. Then she whispered very softly, "This is going to be a night you will never forget."

"I surrender," Jack exclaimed as he swept Joann off her feet and carried her into the bedroom. Several hours later, they feel asleep in each other's arms, each dreaming about what was in store for them in Hollywood.

THE THIRD AND FINAL FILM

Upon their return to Hollywood, Joann talked Jack into staying with her in the apartment she rented. Joann said it was only fitting as Jack had graciously provided her room and board in New York. It was a nice little one bedroom unit located on top of an appliance repair store. The location was okay, but without any of the Hollywood glamour. There were restaurants within easy walking distance, so Jack felt he would have a comfortable stay. And of course, Joann's companionship would be a definite bonus. Jack pretty much knew his way around and was also familiar with routine at the movie studio. He and Joann spent their first day together kind of reminiscing about Joann's time in New York City and planning how she would proceed in setting up her new business venture.

On the second day, Jack was off to the Fox movie lot. It took a little more effort to get a taxi to pick him up by the appliance repair store, so Jack made a mental note that he would have to allot a little more time for his taxi rides. On the Fox lot he found that the filming had been underway for over a week. The part for his character, Billy Greer, was pretty small. Jack had studied the script on the train and he was already familiar with the tunes he had to perform. Pretty much the same people handled him for his makeup and costume. The director's name was John G. Blystone, but everyone referred to him as either "JG" or "J.G. Blystone." His style was quite different from Director Stoloff's. The cast was much smaller, with most of the scenes inside of a swanky apartment suite. As Jack watched the filming with what seemed to be a litany of retakes for every segment of the movie, he decided that JG's method was required, at least in part, due to the small area in which the scene was being filmed. In any event, it made for boring days and frustrated actors and actresses. Jack's only accomplishment on his first day was to meet with the makeup and costume people.

Each day, Jack was required to be on the set and available for filming should the director so decide to shoot any scene in which the Billy Greer character might be involved, even if the Billy Greer character just sat kind of motionless or simply walked past other members of the cast as they performed. Jack soon realized that there would be little time for golf on this trip. *Maybe*, he thought, *I can get something lined up for the weekends*. When Jack talked to Joann that evening, she informed him that Emory Johnson was up in San Francisco working on a project and Ben Stoloff was deeply involved in a new movie he was directing and most likely would have little time for golf for the next few months. The good news was Joann had made considerable progress in starting her business venture. She told Jack all about her search for a small office and finding two that possibly would satisfy her needs. She wanted to know if Jack would be able to look at both with her on the coming Saturday.

"As long as I'm not required to be on the set, I'll be glad to go with you on Saturday."

"Thanks, Jack. You'll be free both Saturday and Sunday. It's kind of an unwritten rule William Fox has."

They sat next to one another. Joann put her arms around Jack and kissed him gently.

"It's been a rough week for both of us, honey. Let's get cleaned up and retire to bed early."

"Now you're talking. You know thinking about you and what is in store for me in the evening is what keeps me going all day on that set."

They both realized the clock was ticking and before long, Jack would be on his way back to New York City. Every evening was therefore filled with heated passion and occasionally a tear or two.

Joann was right again. When the cast was dismissed on Friday, instructions were to return to the set by eight o'clock Monday morning. Unlike Jack's previous two movie ventures, there was no open invitation to a weekend party. There appeared to be little cliques of groups who were going to have individual gatherings. Jack knew he was still considered an "Out of Towner" so being excluded did not bother him. In fact, it was better as he would have more time to help Joann.

Early the following morning, Joann and Jack set out to look at the office spaces. Joann was naturally very excited. Jack remembered how he negotiated a very nice rental amount for Milt and Jean. Before they reached the first office, Jack mentioned this to Joann. Joann agreed to let Jack negotiate. After all, Jack told Joann we can always return to the asking figure. When they arrived at the first office, the owner was there just unlocking the door.

"Come in, come in. I had hoped to get here ahead of you to make sure everything is in order."

"Mr. Copper, I would like you to meet Jack Smith. You may have heard him on the radio. Mr. Smith is both my sponsor and mentor."

"Yes, I've listened to your broadcasts many times. It is my pleasure to meet you, Mr. Smith."

"Please, just call me Jack."

"Well, Jack, you and Joann go right ahead and look around. If you have any questions, I'll be glad to answer them."

Jack and Joann moved away from the owner as Joann talked to Jack about how she thought the space could be set up. The only problem was if a secretary was to be hired, there was plenty of room, but no separation existed that would afford both the secretary and Joann the privacy they would sometimes need. Jack moved over to the owner and started some light conversation about the office space. He then enlightened the owner about the intent to also have a secretary working in the office and the need for a wall to separate the secretary and waiting clients from Joann. He went on to describe how a client entering the office would automatically come to the secretary's desk, which would be someplace near the entrance door. He described that nearby there would be chairs for up to four or five clients to sit and wait in. Jack then walked over to an area that would be walled off as Joann's office. He demonstrated where a doorway into Joann's office should be located so that when the door was open Joann could see her secretary, but the clients would not be able to see into her office.

"Now, Mr. Cooper, Joann needs to open for business within a week. I consider the rental fee you are asking to be reasonable, provided that you can modify this space as I have indicated and have it ready for occupancy one week from today. If you cannot, we have several other spaces to look at today, so we will not take any more of your time."

"Well, I really would like to rent this place. It has been vacant for over a year. Can we sketch out what you described?"

"Sure, if you have some paper, I'll step off some rough measurements with my feet and we'll draw up a sketch that should work with any contractor. And we will pay you one month's rent in advance to cover the cost of building the wall."

"I don't plan on using a contractor. My brother-in-law is out of work now and I'm sure he'll be glad to do this."

After Jack and Mr. Cooper finished the sketch, Jack added a series of notes below the sketch to provide a good understanding of what was needed. He then wrote a check for the first month's rent and told Mr. Cooper they would sign the lease on the following Saturday after inspecting the finished modifications. Everyone shook hands and they departed.

"I can't believe it, Jack. You were marvelous, darling. Where did you learn all about office layouts?"

"Let's stop in the Café just up at the next corner and I'll explain everything."

Over their cups of coffee, Jack explained that all he really did was describe and then sketch Stan's office back in New York City. Joann started to picture the layout in her mind and then reached across the table with both hands holding Jack's cheeks as she planted a big kiss on his lips. She told Jack how smart he was and how excited she was.

"What do we do next, Jack?"

"We go furniture shopping. Do you know any places where we can get some good used furniture?"

The rest of the day was spent looking through various places. Joann definitely knew her way around. Near the end of their searching, they returned to one store that had almost everything that was needed. Jack negotiated a very favorable price, including delivery the following Saturday, and placed a deposit to complete the transaction.

"Darling, I'm bushed. I can't believe we got almost everything done. Let's go back to my apartment, get cleaned up, take a nap together, get dressed and then find a nice quaint restaurant for a romantic dinner."

"Perfect, but will we pass any stores along the way where we can look at window curtains. If you noticed, the layout of your office will give you a nice sized window. To impress your clients you should have some attractive and pricey looking curtains."

"I don't think we pass any stores that sell curtains, but don't worry, Jack, I know exactly what you mean and I can handle getting the curtains next week. I'll call Mr. Cooper on Monday for the window measurements. Besides I'm kind of anxious to get into bed with you for a little pre nap exercise."

The rest of the evening was perfect. On Sunday, Jack was up early and off to church. When he returned to Joann's, she had breakfast ready. They spent the rest of the morning making sketches of how the office would look with the wall modifications and with the furniture they had purchased. Joann suggested she pack a lunch and they just go to the nearby park for the afternoon. In the park, they pretty much relaxed except for a discussion about getting business cards made. Joann would get everything set and just wait until she had a business phone number before ordering the cards. Monday rolled around and Jack was back to his same boring routine at the movie set.

The next two weeks passed lightning fast. The wall modification in Joann's office turned out just right. The furniture was delivered on that Saturday afternoon. Jack and Joann set everything in place and went about cleaning and polishing the desks and chairs. Joann had purchased curtains for all of the windows in the office. The curtains for the window in her office were rather special and expensive-looking. When they hung the curtains, Jack told Joann she had done an excellent job in getting set for business. Joann had a friend who would sit in as her secretary for the first few weeks while Joann went out beating the bushes to drum up clients. Before heading off to the movie set on Monday of the second week, Jack wished Joann luck. By Thursday of that same week, Jack did not see Joann until almost midnight. When she arrived at the apartment, she was all smiles, still full of energy and talking non-stop to Jack about how many clients she had lined up and how the movie executives were excited about using her services. *Well*, Jack thought, *there was no need to wish this young lady luck.* She definitely has what it takes, and before long she will be so busy in her business she won't even miss old "Whispering" Jack.

Another week passed and the filming of *The Big Party* was finished This time, Sue Carol, one of the lead actresses, personally asked Jack to come to a party she was having Saturday evening at her residence. When Joann found out, she was more than excited.

"Sue Carol is my favorite actress! You are going to take me to the party, aren't you Jack?"

"Well, I was going to ask you, but I guess I already know the answer."

With that, Joann jumped into Jack's arms, kissing him, and telling him how much she loved him and how she would never be able to repay him for all that he had done for her. Jack picked her up and carried her to the bedroom where they made love for several hours. Jack's time in Hollywood was coming to an end and they both knew it.

On Monday, Jack was on the train heading back to New York City.

THE DAIRY FARM

The train ride back to New York was not at all pleasant for Jack. He felt depressed and couldn't stop thinking about the women in his life. He thought, *Why does it always end with permanent separation?* Peggy was back in his thoughts and dreams. His time with Joann was a blessing in disguise because when with her, he seldom thought about Peggy, but now he couldn't stop thinking about Peggy. He found that a drink or two in the dining car before going to bed did help him get some sleep. The third day on the train, he decided to write to Peggy. He wrote about the movie he had just finished and then emptied his heart out about how much he loved and missed her. The letter never once mentioned Joann, as Jack knew doing so would only be upsetting to Peggy. He promised to work especially hard with Stan to find something he could handle in Europe, so they would at least get to see one another again.

After folding the letter, he placed it in his travel case. Inside of the travel case was a dozen of Joann's new business cards. Jack took out just one and then drew an 'X' across the face of the card from corner to corner. On the back, he annotated the date with a brief comment, "She will do just fine." *This*, he thought, *will go into the cigar box when I get home*. The rest of the cards will be for Stan and Janet.

Back in the city, Jack fell into his routine of broadcasting with occasional personal appearances booked by Stan to keep Jack fresh and also to earn additional income. Jack spent a good bit of his free time with his family, especially his mother and his nephew's family. Jean had her second baby and he was named after Jack. Jack was quite proud and the best part was the baby's name was actually Jack, not John. Milt asked Jack to be godfather at the coming baptism. Of course, Jack was honored and told Milt he would be more than happy to do so.

Jack's problem was with the free time he had by himself. He continued to think about Peggy. He was worried about her. Jean had not received any mail from Peggy in over two months. Jack's letter that he had written on the train should have reached Peggy weeks ago. Why didn't she respond? He thought about sending a telegram, but decided doing so would not really get him the answers he wanted. The only thing that seemed to help was a glass or two of brandy, especially around bed time.

Time just seemed to go by. There was little to look forward to. Jack did receive one letter from Peggy, but it was so empty of any emotions he began to feel she no longer loved him. The two glasses of brandy before bed became three. Then while doing one of his personal performances, Jack was asked by one of the guests if he would like a drink brought to the piano. Jack started to refuse, but then said if there was any brandy, he would certainly appreciate a glass. Before the night's entertainment was over, Jack had finished off four glasses of brandy. Back at his apartment that same evening, he had two more glasses of brandy before going to bed. The amazing thing was that he slept pretty well without dreaming about Peggy and he hardly had any hangover the next morning.

The holiday season was soon upon Jack, and even though prohibition was still in effect, alcoholic drinks were readily available just about everywhere in New York City. Jack just kind of fell into the mode of letting the good times roll. He was always alert and sharp for his broadcasts, but frequently drank at his personal appearances and performances. Jack never got drunk to the point where he couldn't walk a straight line, but he did get a little melancholy and sometimes couldn't remember the details of the previous evening.

On New Year's Eve, he ended up taking a woman he had just met back to his apartment and was surprised when he woke up on New Year's Day with a strange woman in bed. He couldn't even remember her name or if anything had happened between them. He sometimes had a drink of brandy with his breakfast.

In the last week of January 1931, Janet contacted Jack and asked him to come to the office for a meeting with Stan. She didn't mention a subject, so Jack started to think that maybe Stan had him lined up for something in Europe. When Jack arrived at the office, he was immediately shown into Stan's office.

"Please close the door, Jack. I have some unpleasant business to discuss with you."

"Darn, Stan, I had hopes you were going to tell me you had something for me in Europe."

"Jack, I don't have anything in Europe. In fact, I am having a hard time getting you booked here in New York. Jack, I've been in this business a long time and I've seen a lot of successful people go through what you are now experiencing. I think you are going to have to put Peggy behind you. But more importantly, you need to get a handle on your drinking habits. Let me ask you this, do you ever take a drink first thing in the morning?"

"Well, yes, I do sometimes, but it never interferes with my broadcasting."

"Okay, Jack, here's the bottom line. I see this having the potential of becoming a career ending problem that will totally destroy your livelihood. But if you're willing to cooperate, I think we can nip this problem in the bud. I've taken the liberty to set you up for a three-week stay on a dairy farm over in New Jersey. The people there will dry you out and get you back on a healthy diet. I've also talked to your nephew Milt, and he has agreed to drive you to the farm and come visit you each weekend. The radio station will only know that you are on vacation. Now, Jack, you have always trusted my decisions in the past. Are you going to trust me with this one?"

"Wow, my father used to preach about staying away from alcohol. I know I have been drinking more than I should, but I didn't realize it was so obvious to others."

"Well, Jack, when the stories get back to me, it is obvious that others are watching what you do and because you are a famous entertainer, people in the press will be watching you all the more closely."

"All right, Stan, you set it up with Milt and I'll have a suitcase packed and ready to go."

Huber's Dairy Farm was located not far from Fort Dix in the farmlands of New Jersey. On the ride to the farm, Jack apologized to Milt for letting his personal life get so messed up. He thanked Milt for driving him to the farm and then they talked mostly about Milt's two boys. Jack did ask if Jean had received any information from Peggy. The answer was no and they quickly changed the subject. At the farm, Milt accompanied Jack as they checked in. The farm looked very clean and well-cared for. Jack's room was on the second floor of the main house. There was a fairly large dining room with an attached kitchen on the first floor. There also was a good-sized library and a sitting room with a radio in it.

Mrs. Huber was an immigrant from Germany. She was about sixty years of age, dressed very plainly and spoke good English, but with a German accent. After showing the two of them to Jack's room where they deposited the suitcase, Mrs. Huber invited them to come along on a short tour of the farm. The front porch of the main house was very large and furnished with a variety of rocking chairs and a glider. She first led them to the barn where the cows were milked every day and then on past several chicken coops. Next, they went to a second barn, which housed hay, along with various tractors and farming tools. Just beyond the second barn there was a rather large pond. Mrs. Huber stated that there were fish in the pond and guests were allowed to fish there provided anything caught was either thrown back or brought to the kitchen. Speaking in German, Jack complimented Mrs. Huber for having such a nice farm. She immediately smiled and replied to Jack in German. At that point, Milt knew Jack was in good hands and felt that he would be well-cared for. Milt said his good-bye to Mrs. Huber and while walking to the automobile with Jack, he gave him a few words of encouragement.

"Jack, compared to the hell you went through over in France during the war, this should be a piece of cake. There's not a drop of booze around here for miles, so there will be no temptation. Get a lot of rest and get back to eating healthy meals. You're going to feel a lot better by the end of the week. I'll be back to see you next weekend. I have Mrs. Huber's phone number, so I'll call next Friday to see if there is anything I need to bring along."

They shook hands and Milt was on his way back to New York.

The first week on the farm was very hard. Jack's stomach contracted at times with so much pain he thought he was truly having a medical problem and not just withdrawal pains. He did a lot of reading and listened to the radio broadcasts, particularly from his NBC station. Milt and Jean came for a short visit on the weekend. They brought their older son, Robert. He had a great time looking at the cows and chickens. Jean didn't wait for Jack to ask about Peggy. She simply told Jack there was no news from England and then moved on to talk about Jack's mother and other things. Milt told Jack he had polished the Cord and it looked brand-new. Both Milt and Jean were trying to talk about things that would give Jack incentive to get back to New York. Then it was time to leave. They left a small bag of toiletries that Jack had asked for and were gone.

Jack really felt all alone once Milt's automobile passed out of sight. *Well,* he thought, *no news from England is better than bad news.* They had not talked about Stan. He wondered if Stan would call Milt to find out how he was doing. *Now, what am I going to do for the rest of the day*? Jack decided to walk down the long driveway leading from the farm house to the main road. It felt good to walk.

He wished he had his golf clubs along. He made a mental note to get Milt to bring his clubs and a lot of golf balls the following weekend. As long as there was no snow, the pasture would serve as a fairway for his practice. This week he would try to get his body in better shape by walking a lot and practicing some of the old exercises he had done while in the army.

The next weekend, Milt arrived with not only Jack's golf clubs, but also his own. They spent several hours together trying to best one another with golf shots on the pasture. Milt was impressed with the progress Jack had made.

"Jack, I think next week will be your last here. You look great and sound so much better than when I brought you here. Do you think you'll be able to stay away from the booze?"

"I know I don't want to go through this again so, yes, I think I'll be okay."

After the third week, Jack was on his way back to the city. Milt drove directly to Jack's mother's house. Within the family, they had all decided to try to keep Jack occupied and avoid having him spend a lot of lonely hours in his apartment.

THE EARLY THIRTIES

Jack's lifestyle changed when he returned from the dairy farm. Several weeks after he returned to the city, he decided to give up his apartment at the Chelsea Arms. Most nights Jack had been staying at his mother's and she encouraged him to move back in. The major problem was his piano. Jack finally negotiated with the Chelsea Arms management to leave the piano in the apartment in exchange for his last monthly payment, which was two weeks overdue. He sold the GE Monitor refrigerator to one of the technicians at the broadcasting studio and made arrangements to rent a garage for his Cord within a block of his mother's house. He felt good about his change. The temptation to drink was almost nonexistent.

The entertainment industry was very slow in the early thirties. Some of the movies were doing well, but because of the high unemployment rate, the general populace could not afford the price of admission. Most of the movie theaters did not have adequate finances to purchase and install the equipment required to show wide screen movies such as the *Happy Days* movie Jack had recently finished. So Jack did not get much recognition for his work in the movies. His broadcasting role was fairly stable, but because of the changing style in the music world his was not as popular as it had been. There was little demand for his recordings and no new ones were made. Basically, Jack was treading water in an industry that thirsted for the new and the different. Stan knew that Jack's star was waning, but there was little he could do except wait for a break to come along.

Jack plugged along still pretty much enjoying his time at the broadcasting studio. He felt much closer to his family ties now, especially his mother and his favorite nephew Milt. He dropped his membership in the country club, but he and Milt often played a round of golf on the weekends at one of the nearby public courses. He no longer wrote to Peggy and really did not thirst for knowledge about her. He knew Jean still corresponded with Peggy, and every once in a while, Jean would tell him something about Peggy. It was usually about what stage play she was now performing in or something along those lines. Jack had taken Stan's advice and pretty much put Peggy out of his mind. He still thought about her on occasion, but it was more like remembering a good time they had experienced together rather than some thought about the future. Most of his free time was spent with his family members. Jack was proud of the fact that he had not taken a drink since returning from the dairy farm.

In 1932, Jean delivered a third son. He was initially named Gerald, but by the time of the new baby's baptism, his name was changed to Eugene Gerald. The story was that Jean always wanted a girl and at least naming the baby Eugene or Gene for short was kind of like naming the baby after her. In January of 1933, Milt was informed at work that a new plant was being set up in Philadelphia, and if he wanted to retain employment with the Chilton Company, he would have to move to the Philadelphia plant. Jack took the news badly. It seemed to him like every time he got close to anyone, a separation would follow. By the end of February, Milt and his family were living in a very nice row house in the western section of Philadelphia.

On March 22, 1933, President Franklin Roosevelt signed into law an amendment to the Volstead Act known as the Cullen-Harrison Act. In effect, prohibition was over. There was a lot of celebrating in New York City. Jack was tempted to join in the celebration but managed to stay away from drinking any alcohol. He was quite proud of his own will power and his mother praised his resolve.

Stan asked Jack to meet with him shortly after the signing of the Cullen-Harrison Act.

"Jack, you've come through your rehabilitation with flying colors. I'm glad you agreed to staying at the dairy farm and proud of how you handled it. Now, I have both good and bad news for you. The good news is that the ending of prohibition is opening up more opportunities for entertainers such as you. Because you can work individually or with an orchestra, we can book you for weekends and evenings throughout most of the year. I need to know what your preferences are before we go further with your schedule."

"Thanks, Stan. Because Milt and his family have moved to Philadelphia, I think I would prefer weekend bookings over evenings. However, I can do either. You mentioned bad news. What's the bad news?"

"The bad news is that we are negotiating a new contract for you with NBC and it looks like your compensation is going to decrease significantly. I'm still negotiating, but because the network now has so many options to fill their broadcasting schedule, we are at a disadvantage. Some stations are now simply playing records instead of providing live broadcasts. I think between getting you more bookings outside of the radio broadcasting and keeping you as active as possible with NBC we will go forward with a fair amount of income for you."

"Well, Stan, as you know, I've made quite a few adjustments to my lifestyle, and I now get along pretty well on a limited amount of income."

"Hang in there, Jack. I'll keep you posted if anything changes."

Jack felt a little depressed as he left Stan. Janet saw him leaving and asked that he wait just a minute as she had something to show him.

"Here's a letter we received from Joann last week. She is doing just great, Jack. I thought you should see the letter as you did so much to help her get started."

Jack sat and read the letter. Joann sounded very happy, very positive, and very busy. She repeatedly thanked both Janet and Stan for their teachings and asked that they pass a word of thanks on to "Whispering" Jack who helped her so much both in New York and Hollywood.

"Well, that's very nice. I'm glad she is doing so well. Thank you for sharing the letter with me, Janet."

Jack felt a little better after reading Joann's letter. She was definitely on her way to becoming something special out there in movie land. Jack wondered if he would again ascend to stardom or was his time at the top over. *It all happens so fast*, he thought. *One day you're sitting on top of the world and the next everything is upside down. Wow! It was a great ride. I just hope I can get back onboard again.*

On December 5, 1933, ratification of the Twenty-first Amendment to the Constitution repealed the Eighteenth Amendment (Volstead Act). Prohibition was officially dead, along with many of the speakeasy clubs that thrived under the Act.

Jack was busy over the holiday season, appearing on stage every weekend. He enjoyed his performances and felt good. He stayed away from the booze and made his drink of choice ginger ale. Life felt good again. During one of his performances a rather attractive, well-dressed woman approached his piano as he was performing and placed a folded piece of paper on the end of his piano bench. Requests were not unusual, but there seemed to be something special about this lady. Jack lost sight of her as she returned to the audience. At the next break, Jack unfolded the note and read the request. It was for "To Be in Love". The note went on to say "I have all of your recordings and think this one is the best." It was simply signed Marie. Jack acknowledged the request at the beginning of the next session and added a comment that it was one of his favorite recordings. He finished the evening of entertainment without again laying eyes on Marie. Jack thought it was a shame because he was seldom attracted to women since Peggy and Joann were out of his life, but there just seemed to be something very different about this lady.

In June, Jack and his mother took a train to Philadelphia to stay overnight with Milt and his family. Milt met them at Thirtieth Street Station and drove to Fifty Sixth and Chestnut Street on the way to his home, so he could show his grandmother and Jack the new Chilton Company printing plant. Milt walked them through the plant on a short tour. They were both impressed with Milt's knowledge of the printing operations, but more interested in getting to Milt's home to see Jean and the boys. Milt sensed what his grandmother and Jack really wanted and wasted little time in concluding the tour. The West Philadelphia brick row home was big and beautiful. There was a large front porch and the rooms inside were very spacious with plenty of natural light from the windows.

Jack commented, "I think this place is bigger than the one you left in the Bronx."

"It is bigger and much closer to work. On nice days, I sometimes walk to work."

Milt's grandmother was delighted to see her three great grandsons and she enjoyed conversing in German with Jean's mother. It was like old times back in the Bronx. Jean's mother prepared dinner while the others caught up on the changes in their lives since Milt and Jean moved to Philadelphia. One of the surprising changes was that Jack had sold the Cord.

"Well, Milt, since moving in with Mom, I seldom drove. It just seemed a whole lot easier to jump on the trolley rather than go over to the garage I had rented. And then one day I got a call from my old friend, Arthur Kennedy, asking if I would be interested in selling the Cord. He had an associate who wanted one, and the L-29 is rather rare and hard to find. The buyer was willing to pay top dollar, so I let it go."

Milt responded, "I'm still driving the old Ford, but Jean and I figure when I get my next pay raise, we'll be in a position to get a new car. Financing is easy to get provided that you are employed in a stable job."

Jean's mother finally called everyone to the dinner table and then brought out a covered platter of deep fried blueberry pancakes. This was an old German favorite that they all loved. Once the thick, blueberry filled pancakes were placed on the individual dinner plates, a coating of powdered sugar was shaken over the plate and a large slab of soft butter was centered at the top of the dish. Jack was delighted. He had forgotten how good this dish was. Within a short time the covered serving platter was empty. Jean's mother moved to the kitchen and within minutes returned with another covered platter. They all applauded. It was an evening of fun and storytelling.

On Sunday morning, they all went to Mass except Milt and Jean's mother. Jean's mother was Protestant and did not understand the Catholic Mass, especially as it was said in Latin. Milt still had not forgiven the church for what he was put through before permission was given for him to marry Jean. Jean and her mother prepared a late breakfast and then Milt drove his grandmother and Jack back to the station to catch their afternoon train. Some tears were shed by all three at the station as they said their good-byes.

Back at Milt and Jean's and after the kids were in bed, they talked about the visit.

"Milt, do you get the impression that Jack is having financial difficulties?"

"I sure do. He loved that automobile and I still can't believe he sold it. I'm going to talk to my grandmother about it the next time we make our long distance call to New York. In the meantime, do you remember what we did with those stock certificates he gave us for shares in the Coca Cola Company? I might write to Stan and see what can be done to return them to Jack."

In 1934, Labor Day fell on Monday, the third of September. Jack was performing with an orchestra over the three-day weekend. He rather enjoyed working with an orchestra. Doing so gave him opportunities to be spotted singing sometimes standing in front of his fellow musicians and other times while he played at the piano. During the Sunday afternoon performance, a rather attractive lady came forward while Jack was playing and placed a folded note on the piano bench. Jack only had a glance at the lady and thought she looked very familiar. When an opportunity to unfold and read the note finally came along, Jack was quite surprised. It simply read, "Please sing my favorite, if you remember it from my last request. Marie." Jack immediately made the connection. He thought that was why she looked so familiar when she brought the note to his piano bench. Jack knew "To Be in Love" was the song, but wasn't sure if the orchestra was okay playing the melody. He would wait for their break and check with the leader.

The orchestra leader said they could easily follow Jack's lead on the piano, so after their break, Jack returned to the piano and announced the next song as "To Be in Love". He went on to say it was a request from a lady named Marie and then asked if Marie would please stand. No one stood, so he simply went into the melody and then the lyrics. While performing, Jack thought this lady is becoming somewhat of a mystery. Maybe she left during their break. If so, I hope she returns tomorrow. I think I would like to get to know this mystery lady.

Jack looked forward with anticipation to meeting the mystery lady during the Labor Day performance; however, there was no indication that she was in the audience. He took a shot in the dark and announced the next selection as "To Be in Love" and again asked Marie to please stand. To his amazement, the mystery lady stood for a few seconds by a table at the back. She gave a quick wave and then sat back down. Jack couldn't really see her when she was sitting, but from the few seconds when she stood, he was almost positive it was the same Marie who had twice given him the song request. Jack made a mental note of the table location with the intent to seek out this Marie on their next break.

When the break came, Jack wasted little time in getting a tall glass of ginger ale and then heading in the general location of the mystery lady's table. She was nowhere in sight. Jack asked a few of the people nearby if they knew Marie. One couple told Jack that the lady who stood to acknowledge the song request had departed just before the break. Jack thanked them and headed back to the stage. *Well,* Jack thought, *I'll have to be a little smarter if and when she comes to any more of my performances. The next time I won't let her get away.*

It wasn't until Thanksgiving weekend before Jack once again encountered the mystery lady. This time he was playing and singing at a popular New York City piano bar. This establishment was much smaller in size than those he performed in earlier when Marie passed Jack notes requesting he sing "To Be in Love". This time there was no note. Marie simply approached Jack at the piano and asked if he would sing her favorite song.

"It will be my pleasure, Marie, but only if you'll promise to stay around until my break. I want to talk to you."

"Okay, but I can't stay much longer than that."

When the break came, Jack went directly to the table where Marie was sitting with two other mature, but very attractive women. Introductions were quickly made, and then Jack asked the other two if they would excuse him and Marie for a few minutes as he offered his hand to Marie and then led her over toward the bar.

"Marie, you have been such a mystery to me. I only have a few more minutes before I have to return to the stage. I would very much like to get to know you better. Would you consider going out to dinner with me sometime?"

"Yes, I would like that very much, but I'm going to be out of town for the next two weeks. Here is my business card. My home phone number is on the back. Please give me a call after two weeks and we'll work something out. Okay?"

"Okay, but you're not just pulling my leg to get rid of me, are you?"

"Absolutely not, Jack. I will anxiously be awaiting your call. Now I really must get back to my guests."

With that, they parted. Jack returned to the stage and Marie to her guests.

That evening, Jack studied Marie's business card. It seemed that she was a buyer of women's apparel for Macy's Department Store. Jack guessed that she was going to be out of town for two weeks on work related business and that her two guests that evening had something to do with her business relationships. *Wow*, he thought, *she is still a mystery. I can't wait until we can sit down over dinner and become better acquainted. Now, shall I put this card in the cigar box? I guess so, but first let me copy her home phone number and put it in my billfold. I hope the next two weeks fly by very fast.*

It was only a few weeks until Christmas when Jack made his call to Marie. To his surprise, she answered on the second ring.

"Hello."

"Well, hello, Marie. This is Jack Smith. Did you have a nice trip?"

"Hello, Jack. Yes, it was pretty good. But this is such a busy time of the year for me I don't really have any free time to sightsee."

"From your business card I assume you are a purchasing agent for Macy's."

"I am, Jack."

"Well after having two weeks to think it over, do you still want to have dinner with me?"

"You bet I do. While I was away, I kept thinking is he really going to call me or is he one of those celebrities who simply collect phone numbers for their black book?"

"I don't have a black book, Marie. But I do keep a few very special names and addresses in a cigar box, and guess what? Your business card is in that cigar box right now. I would love to tell you about it. I'm booked over in New Jersey for Friday and Saturday evenings this week, but free all of the others. What will work for you?"

"Can we make it early Sunday evening?"

"Yes, we can."

Their conversation continued while Jack made note of Marie's address, set a time to meet and discussed a few dining options. Jack was impressed. Marie sounded so positive in such a nice way.

Well, Stan had suggested I forget about Peggy and going back to England. Maybe this is exactly what I need.

Each day that week, Jack dedicated the song "To Be in Love" to someone in his audience named Marie. When Sunday finally arrived, Jack was quite excited. At breakfast after Mass, his mother sensed the change in him.

"You certainly are happy today. Is there something going on I should know about?"

"You read me like a book, Mom. Yes, I have a dinner date this evening."

"Is her name Marie?"

"How did you know?"

"I listen to you on the radio, son. Every day this past week you dedicated a love song to someone named Marie."

Jack went on to tell his mother about Marie's requests over the past several months for him to sing "To Be in Love" and that this would be his first chance to really talk with this lady.

"Well, son, you know how much I like Peggy, but I'm glad you're venturing out on a date. After all this time, it's obvious that Peggy intends to remain in England. Jean still corresponds with her, and from what Jean tells me, Peggy is doing okay. But Jack, I don't like what's happening in Europe and I worry about Peggy getting caught up in another war. I still pray for her every night. I hope you enjoy the company of your new lady friend and I would be most happy to meet her sometime in the future should the two of you become close friends."

"Thanks, Mom. I'll tell you more about Marie after our dinner date."

It wasn't until Jack paid close attention to the address where he was going to pick up Marie that he realized it was only one block away from his old apartment in the Chelsea Arms. *Well, nice neighborhood*, he thought. She must be paid pretty well by Macy's. Upon arrival at Marie's building, he found it to be quite similar to the Chelsea building. Jack signed in as a visitor at the desk, after which, the clerk rang Marie's apartment. Marie soon arrived in the lobby and they were off to dinner. Marie used the subway just as Jack did, so there was no need for a taxi. On the subway, Jack mentioned the Chelsea Arms. Marie knew he had resided there some time ago and just assumed that he left to take better care of his mother. Their stop was at Madison Square Garden. They had settled on dining in Jack Dempsey's Restaurant, which was located at Eighth Avenue and Fiftieth Street, just opposite of Madison Square Garden.

Dempsey's was divided into two sections. The entrance took them past the first, which was a rather magnificent Broadway bar and cocktail lounge. Somehow, Marie also knew about Jack's earlier problem with alcohol. She commented on the beauty of the bar and lounge, but just kept walking along toward the restaurant section. The hostess knew Jack and greeted him by name as she ushered them to a table.

"I come here on occasion with my brother. The restaurant that was here before was the Aqua Delight. I think when Jack Dempsey purchased the old Aqua Delight he had most of it demolished. It actually had a very large fish tank above the bar where a couple of women dressed in mermaid suits swam from side to side. Charlie has a management position over in the garden, so it is convenient for us to get together at this location once in a while."

"Where does your brother live?"

"Charlie used to live just a block down from Mom in the Bronx, but after his wife passed away, he eventually remarried and now lives in a beautiful house out in Valley Stream on the Island. Maybe someday, I can get him to give you a tour of Madison Square Garden."

"I would love that, Jack. But you have to promise to come along."

They enjoyed very light and pleasant conversation as they made their dinner choices. The nice thing about Dempsey's was the menu offered both simple and elegant selections. Jack liked the simple selections and it turned out that Marie also ordered from the simple meals. Jack wasn't sure if it was her real preference or was she doing so to please him. In any event, he was definitely impressed with this lady. She was very attractive, immaculately dressed, very smart and above all, pleasant to be with. They actually found they had a lot of things in common. They talked about Marie's apartment building and compared the operation of her building to that of Jack's old Chelsea Arms. The other amazing thing was Marie knew so much about Jack's career and about all of his recordings. She even knew that he had been gassed in the Great War. Realizing that he knew so little about Marie, Jack began to ask subtle questions. Marie was very open and soon he learned that Marie shared her apartment with her younger sister. Her sister was also employed at Macy's and managed the Women's Clothing Department. Marie cited this as being a tremendous advantage for both of them because they constantly exchanged information and ideas about their business at Macy's to the betterment of all. Her parents were both deceased. Jack didn't ask outright, but it seemed Marie was of Italian descent. She was a practicing Catholic and spoke very highly about her parish.

The time seemed to fly by as they soon finished dinner. Both enjoyed coffee, so they stayed to have a cup of coffee, but no dessert. It was still early, so Jack asked Marie if she would like to go over to his broadcasting studio for a short tour. Jack knew there would not be much going on as it was Sunday. Marie was delighted with Jack's asking and responded she would love to visit as long as she could return to her apartment reasonably early because she had a big day scheduled for Monday and needed to go over some things before retiring for sleep.

On the way to the studio, Marie asked Jack to tell her more about his cigar box. Jack started and as he talked about the items in the box that were from his time in the Great War, Marie, very gently, reached for his hand and held on as they walked along. To Jack it instantly reminded him of his time with Peggy in the Chicago World's Fair Museum. *Well*, Jack thought, *I didn't believe I could ever feel this way with a woman again*. At the studio, Marie was very interested and quite impressed with the operations of radio broadcasting. They held hands on the way to the subway and on the subway. In the lobby of her apartment, they set a date to meet for lunch on Wednesday at a café close to Macy's. Before leaving the lobby, Jack reached to hold both of Marie's hands and turned her to face him; he then said good night and kissed her gently on the lips. When they released their hands, Jack turned for the lobby doors and walked out while Marie simply stood and watched until she could no longer see him.

On the day of their luncheon date, Jack and Marie decided to attend Christmas Mass together at Marie's church. Marie came to the piano bar where Jack was entertaining on New Years' Eve. They celebrated the start of 1935 together and wished each other a long and happy friendship. Each week, as long as they were both in New York City, they met once or twice for lunch. It was such a welcome break in their work routines. Their kisses and embraces had become much more passionate and they definitely missed each other when they were separated for any length of time. They were obviously in love. Jack tried to rationalize his feelings for Marie to those he had held for Peggy. It made no sense. Eventually, he confided in his mother. Her answer was so simple and direct.

"Son, love comes from your heart. It doesn't mean that you no longer love and care for Peggy. It simply means events in your life have kind of bumped Peggy aside and now Marie has filled that void in your heart. Your only concern should be does Marie truly deserve the place she now holds in your heart?"

During the summer of 1935, Milt and his family arrived in a brand-new Ford sedan. They stayed out in Valley Stream with Jack's brother for three nights. Jack decided it was time for the family to meet Marie. He called his brother Charlie and discussed his intention. Charlie offered to pick Jack, Marie and Mom up on that Sunday following Mass and take them to his Valley Stream home. There was plenty of room, and with the nice weather they were experiencing Charlie would arrange for a catered outdoor meal. When Jack and Marie arrived, almost everyone was surprised to find out Jack had a new lady friend. Marie just blended right in as introductions were made. It was like old times with the adults making a big fuss over Milt and Jean's children. Jean's brother, William, and his wife, Eloise, arrived later in the afternoon, along with Milt's brother, Charles, and his wife, Mamie. Of course, William was once again the life of the party with his never ending stories and jokes.

Milt took Jack away from the gathering, supposedly to show him the new 1935 Ford Sedan.

"Jack, one of the pressmen from work came to the Philadelphia plant the same time that I did. He's a real nice guy by the name of Ralph Weeks. He doesn't have any kids, so he spends a lot of time with his hobby of restoring old cars. About every other weekend or so, he drives one of his antiques over to our place and sometimes gives the kids a ride. Ralph has *The New York Times* newspaper delivered to him in Philadelphia. He saves the papers for me and usually brings them to the house on his visits. The reason I'm telling you this is because last week Ralph left a batch of papers, and when Jean was reading through them, she found this article about Peggy. Maybe you have already seen it. If not, here it is. You can look it over later. It seems Peggy has serious financial problems and she vacated her London hotel with a process server searching for her. We just thought you should know."

"Thanks, Milt. I'll look it over later when I'm alone. Things between Peggy and me have been over for some time now, but I still care about her and maybe there is something I can do to help her. Nice automobile, can we lift the hood panels? I've read a little about the "V Eight" engine and how much power it has."

They walked around the car chatting for a while and then returned to the group in the yard. Jack's brother and his wife Jane were talking with Marie when they rejoined the group.

"Jack, Charles has offered to show me through Madison Square Garden next Sunday after Mass. Will you be available to come along?"

"I'm almost sure my schedule is clear. I'll double check with Janet in the morning."

"Jane also told me she used to be one of the mermaids that swam at the old Aqua Delight."

"I guess Marie told you we had dinner at Dempsey's. I told her a little about the old Aqua Delight, but Jane, I swear I never revealed your identity as one of the mermaids."

"I know you didn't, Jack. When I look back on my mermaid years, I think they were some of the best years of my life. And to top it all off, I would not have met your brother if it hadn't been for the Aqua Delight. I'm quite proud of being a mermaid and love to tell people about it."

At that point, Charles Junior and Mamie joined the conversation, indicating they were heading back to Manhattan and offering to give Marie and Jack a ride. Jack thanked his nephew and asked him to give them a few minutes to say their good-byes. The few minutes turned into about half an hour and then they were on their way. During the ride, Marie learned that Mamie was employed as a sales person in her sister's department at Macy's. They dropped Marie off first and then took Jack and Anna home.

"Good night, Grandma. And Uncle Jack, it was a real pleasure to meet Marie. She is a real nice lady. We hope to see you both soon. Good night."

"Thanks, Charlie. Good night."

The next day, Jack and Marie met for lunch.

"Jack, I must tell you I love your family. And Jean's brother, Bill, he is something else. I haven't laughed so much in months. And your brother's wife, Jane, why didn't you tell me she had been a mermaid at the Aqua Delight? I felt kind of embarrassed when she was telling me about swimming in the tank and all."

"Well, I guess I didn't tell you because Milt and I used to refer to her as the 'Fish'. Yeah, it was an unusual occupation and I can see you being embarrassed hearing about it. I'm sorry. It will never happen again."

They had a good laugh and hurriedly committed to a time for their next date later in the week. Then both were off to their jobs.

THE SPANISH MANSION

In the summer of 1936, Stan called Jack to discuss a booking in the Philadelphia area.

"Hello, Jack. I received a kind of strange call from Philadelphia to book both you and Peggy O'Neil for a private party in the Philly area. It seems that you and Peggy were on stage eight or ten years ago in Atlantic City and a number of big-time gangsters were seated in front of the stage and close to a couple who were on their honeymoon. I assume the couple was Milt and Jean. Do you remember any names of the gangsters that were there?"

"Wow, yeah, I remember Lucky Luciano because he was a New York City guy. And the Atlantic City boss, Nucky Johnson, was there. There were others seated at several nearby tables who appeared to be with the gangsters. I met some, but don't recall any names. They actually treated us very nice because Milt and Jean were on their honeymoon. Who called you?"

"That's the thing, Jack, he was very elusive about giving out his name and said to ask for 'Lefty' when I call back. I explained to him about Peggy being over in England, that she was really handled by a different agent, and that it would be nearly impossible to get her to come to Philadelphia for a one-night performance. He seemed to accept that, but is still insisting on having you perform for his party. Somewhere during our conversation, there was kind of a threat thrown in with a comment something like, I hope it won't be necessary for me to have one of my friends in New York come visit you. He's offing a lot of money for you to come to Philly and entertain at his party. What do you think, Jack?"

"I think I remember another name. There was a Philadelphia boss named Mikey or Mickey Duffy. Maybe he's the guy who called you?"

"Jack, I did a little research before calling you and there was a Mickey Duffy who was into bootlegging and running numbers in Philadelphia. But he was killed several years ago by a hit man while asleep in his room at the Atlantic City Ambassador Hotel. The guy I had doing some checking for me thinks whoever called is probably the gangster that took over after Duffy was killed."

"Well, how dangerous do you think the booking is?"

"I don't think it will be dangerous at all. In fact, from what my contact tells me, the private residence where you will be performing is a Spanish-style mansion just outside of Philadelphia that Duffy had constructed like a fort. He says the walls and doors are reinforced with steel plates, there is a very elaborate security system, and guards are on duty around the clock. In his opinion, if anyone wanted to make a hit, they would simply wait like they did to get Duffy when he was away from the mansion."

"Well, I guess I can do it."

"There is more, Jack. Now this Lefty guy thinks you are super rich, so he was giving me instructions for you to have your limo driver to go to the south gate and give the guard there a password phrase. The phrase is 'Jack jumped over the candlestick'. I gave all of this some thought and came up with the idea that maybe we can arrange to have Milt put on his old chauffeur uniform and drive you to and from the mansion. Didn't you tell me he recently bought a new car?"

"He did, but it is a basic 1935 Ford, four-door Sedan."

"Actually that may just be perfect. Because of the 'V Eight' engine in the newer Ford automobiles they are very fast, so both the police and the gangsters are buying them, and it is not uncommon for a gangster or a police chief to be chauffeured in one of those cars. Do you think Milt will do it for you? The party is to start around noon on Saturday the twenty-second of August. You and Milt will probably be there until the early hours of Sunday morning."

"I'll give him a call. I think he'll do it as long as Jean doesn't know what's really going on. I'll call you back right after I talk to Milt."

Jack talked it over with Milt that evening. Milt was kind of excited about doing the chauffeuring as long as Jean didn't know what it was all about. His only concern was what he would do with all of the time he was at the mansion. Jack called Stan the following day and gave him the okay to set everything up. Stan thanked him and told Jack it would be a relief to get the gangsters off his back. Janet would prepare a package for Jack containing round-trip train tickets and specific instructions for entering and exiting the Spanish mansion.

When the twenty-second arrived, Jack was on an early train to the Philadelphia Thirtieth Street Station. Milt was to meet him in the main lobby of the station near the Information Booth. The train was on schedule and arrived at nine forty-five. Both Jack and Milt were glad there were no glitches. There is something about having to please gangsters that makes you try to do everything on time and as ordered. They drove partway to the Spanish mansion, which was located at 1505 City Line Avenue in Montgomery County and pulled into a diner for an early lunch.

"Milt, I want to thank you for giving me that article about Peggy. Tell Jean I did some checking and she was in trouble, but it has been pretty much taken care of now. Peggy had financial investments in some stage productions over in England that folded. Additionally, her agent here in the States had her invested in some construction projects that went belly up. So you might say she went bankrupt, but she is working on stage and will be okay. Also tell Jean to wait until Peggy sends her a new address before trying to correspond. I don't know if you want to alarm Jean with this, but your grandmother and I worry about what is going on over in Europe these days. Hitler is arming Germany again and there is a lot going on in Spain. We worry that another Great War is coming and Peggy will be stuck in the middle of it."

"If there is another war, do you think you'll be called up?"

"I don't think Uncle Sam will want me anymore, and because you now have a family you should be safe also."

"I hope you're right, Jack. I also wanted to tell you I figured out what to do with some of my time at the mansion. I brought along some auto polish and rags. The car needs a good shine and that's what chauffeurs do when they aren't driving. What do you think?"

"I think that's great. Now all you need to do is cover the time after darkness."

"Maybe I'll be able to get a nap in."

When Milt turned into the south gate at the Spanish mansion, they were immediately met by two guards. Jack was riding in the back seat of the Ford. One guard opened the back door for Jack and asked him to step out. Jack offered the "Jack jumped over the candlestick" password, to which the guard thanked him and motioned for the second guard to have Milt shut off the car and step out. One guard escorted both Milt and Jack to the gate house while the other searched the car. After ten or so minutes, the searching guard motioned for them to return to the car. He asked Milt to unlock the trunk and after looking inside instructed Milt where to drive to discharge Mr. Smith. Milt was told the people at the entrance to the mansion would give instructions for parking the car.

"Wow, Jack, they don't fool around here."

"That was Stan's point. He said this place is so well fortified no one in their right mind would attempt anything here. When I get a break, Milt, I'll try to get out to see you."

With that, Jack was ushered inside. He was introduced to a handler and started to familiarize himself to his surroundings. The handler advised Jack there would also be a "Songbird" to work with him. Jack thought that might complicate his performance, but he knew better than to argue with gangsters. Milt moved the car about the length of a football field away from the house and parked on a well-mowed field of grass. He was met in the field and shown to a building with bathroom facilities and a lounge. Milt asked if it would be all right to hang out by the automobile as he was expected to polish it in his free time. He was given permission to do so and he was also informed that food and drink would be made available to the chauffeurs in the lounge. And so their day at the Spanish mansion began.

It seemed that everyone was identified by first name or nickname only. When Jack was introduced he was "Whispering" Jack. His "Songbird" was Ella. It turned out that Ella was also from New York City and had worked at the Apollo Theater, the Harlem Opera House, and the Savoy Ballroom. She appeared to be only about nineteen or twenty years of age, but seemed to know music. The musicians were from the Chick Webb Orchestra out of New York City. Ella had done some work with the musicians, so that was a plus. Chick Webb and some other members of his orchestra did not come along. Around noon, they all huddled together and talked over their approach. It seemed everyone had improvisational abilities, so it was decided that "Whispering" Jack would announce a selection and simply start playing the piano and singing. The musicians would join in and Ella would sometimes join Jack and sometimes take the vocal lead.

Jack was amazed at how smoothly things went. Ella was just outstanding. She and Jack sang with impeccable diction. The guests were kind of mesmerized with their performances, so much so that there were literally no conversations at the tables. Everyone was locked onto the entertainers and remained so until there was a break. Just before the second break, Ella thanked the guests for their applause and introduced each musician, but only by first name. It was a very enjoyable night for Jack. Jack was enjoying himself as were the other entertainers.

At the break around midnight, Jack realized he had forgotten about Milt and asked one of the men who was obviously a bodyguard if it would all right if he went to check on his chauffeur. The bodyguard told Jack to wait where he was for a few minutes until he got clearance. The bodyguard soon returned and stated he would escort Jack. They walked to the lounge being used by the chauffeurs and guards, but Milt was not there. The bodyguard asked Jack what kind of automobile he had and then they proceeded out to the parking area. And there he was sound asleep in the front seat. The bodyguard knocked on the window. Milt quickly scampered to an upright position, put his chauffeur's hat on, and opened the door to get out of the Ford.

"We didn't mean to startle you, Milt. I just wanted to check to see if you had eaten and to tell you it looks like I'll be inside for several more hours."

Keeping up his chauffeur act, Milt responded, "I'm fine, Mr. Smith. There was plenty of food for us in the lounge and I did manage to finish waxing the automobile."

"Good, Milt. I'll be back as soon as we finish up inside."

As the bodyguard escorted Jack back to the main entrance of the Spanish mansion, he commented that it was nice of him to take time to check on his chauffeur.

The music continued until almost two o'clock in the morning. At that point, a rather tall, well-dressed gentleman moved next to the piano where Jack was seated and asked everyone for his attention. The room came to an immediate hush as the gentleman spoke.

"I want to personally thank 'Whispering' Jack, Ella, and all of these fine musicians for an unforgettable evening of great songs and music. Let's show our appreciation with a Philadelphia round of applause."

There was a long and loud response, and as it died down, the tall gentleman asked Ella and Jack to come along with him. Two bodyguards quickly moved in as they walked down a corridor and into a very plush office. There was a photographer already inside of the office.

"I want to thank you two again. I take pride in throwing the best parties here on the Main Line and you two were certainly outstanding performers. Now if you don't mind, come over here along side of me, so I can get a couple of photographs of us together."

After the photographer flashed several shots, the tall gentleman removed two envelopes from his inside jacket pocket. Passing one envelope to Ella and the other to Jack he said, "Here is a personal token of my appreciation for the effort you put forth this evening." He then exited the office with one bodyguard following behind. The second bodyguard waited a few minutes and then escorted Ella and Jack back to the main room.

"Well, Ella, did you notice he passed the envelopes to us with his left hand. My guess is we just met Lefty. Before we leave, I want to say you were just great, kid. I thoroughly enjoyed working with you and look forward to maybe doing it again sometime. One of the musicians told me you all came down on a bus together, so have a safe journey back to New York. I'm staying over with some family in the area, but should be back on the broadcast by Monday afternoon."

"Good-bye, Jack. I enjoyed working with you also. I enjoy listening to you on the radio whenever I get a chance. And maybe we will be able to work together again. I would like that."

Jack found Milt still napping in the Ford. They went directly to Milt's house and then straight to bed.

The Catholic Church was just a short walk away, so Jack attended Sunday Mass by himself. When he returned to the house, Jean had a nice breakfast waiting. Milt joined them just as Jean was asking about their experience at the Spanish mansion. Both said it was rather routine and kind of boring. Milt also boasted that he did have enough daylight to get a good coat of wax on the Ford. Later, Milt took Jack to the Thirtieth Street Train Station. During the ride, they talked about the gangsters and bodyguards, having a few good laughs along the way. At the train station, Jack took half of the money Lefty had given him out of the envelope and passed the open envelope with the remaining money in it to

Milt. Upon exiting the Ford, he reached over to shake hands and thanked Milt for helping out.

"Thanks, Jack. It was kind of fun. I only wish I could tell Jean more about our time at the Spanish mansion, maybe someday. Good-bye. Keep in touch."

THE FINAL GOOD-BYE

Nineteen hundred and thirty seven began as a good year for Jack and Marie. They were very much in love and both were doing well in their work. They occasionally discussed marriage, but it always came down to the same two problems. Marie did not want to leave her younger sister to fend for herself and Jack still felt responsible for his mother. Then out of the blue and very much to Marie's surprise, her sister announced she was getting married. The wedding was to be in June. Jack and Marie put their heads together and once again considered their options for a married life living together. Marie liked living in her Manhattan apartment and was reluctant to consider living in Mrs. Schmidt's house. But over time, Marie eventually conceded and agreed to move in with Mrs. Schmidt.

Marie's sister's wedding was rather small but very nice. Jack played and sang at the reception. He told Marie it was the kind of wedding he would like when they married and when she agreed, Jack knelt down on one knee while taking a ring box from his pocket and asked Marie for her hand in marriage. In tears, Marie exclaimed, "Oh yes, Jack, I will. I have dreamed of this day for so long. I can't believe this is happening!"

Jack guided Marie back to the piano he had been playing and asked for everyone's attention.

"I think Marie has an announcement to make."

"Jack just asked me to marry him and I accepted his proposal."

She then held up her left hand displaying the diamond ring that had just been placed on her finger. The guests surrounded Jack and

Marie, offering their congratulations with hugs and handshakes. It was a very happy scene. The small and relatively calm reception became a very lively and happy celebration.

The next day, Jack took Marie to his mother's house to announce their engagement. Anna was so happy for them. She talked to Marie about how she worried who would take care of her son when she was gone. During the conversation, Marie learned Jack was the youngest of six children and that all of his brothers and sisters except Charles had passed away before Jack was even born. Marie didn't quite know how to respond and simply told Mrs. Schmidt to no longer worry about Jack as she would take very good care of him.

Three weeks later, Jack called Marie to tell her his mother had been taken to the Lebanon Hospital in the Bronx. Marie met Jack at the hospital that evening. Jack's mother had suffered a heart attack and the prognosis was not favorable. Jack and Marie went to the chapel in the hospital and prayed. Before the night was over, a doctor came to inform them that Mrs. Schmidt had passed away. She was seventy-two years of age.

Over the next few days, Jack and Charles made funeral arrangements for burial of their mother with her husband, Charles Henry, and her four deceased children, Josephine, Adam, Elsie, and Gertrude in Saint Raymond's Cemetery in the Bronx. All of the Schmidt family was there on the day of the funeral. It was a difficult time for Marie, as she had not seen many of the family members and they were offering condolences to Jack and then offering congratulations for her engagement.

Just before his mother's casket was lowered into the grave, Jack placed a flower on the top of the casket while quietly saying, "Thanks for looking after me all these years, Mom. I will never forget what you have done for me. This is my last good-bye, Mother."

As things settled over the next several weeks, Jack and Marie started to talk more seriously about wedding plans. It was decided that Jack would move into Marie's Manhattan apartment. They would arrange to have a piano moved from Jack's mother's house to the apartment, along with a few choice pieces of furniture and some of the china and cookware. The remaining items in the house would be offered to family members and whatever was still left would be sold or given to charity.

TYING THE KNOT

Jack and Marie were married in September. It was a small wedding with family and only a few selected friends in attendance. Rather than a reception, there was a simple gathering at Jack's brother's house out in Valley Stream. The wedding and the gathering at Charles's house was just what both Marie and Jack wanted. The newspaper carried a rather small article entitled, *Radio Broadcaster takes a Bride*. Again both were happy with the small amount of publicity. Jack had reached that point in life where a certain amount of privacy was important and Marie never really wanted to be in the public eye. The only person unhappy was Jack's agent. Stan believed that good publicity was priceless and necessary to keep a celebrity in the limelight. Nevertheless, Stan respected Jack and Marie's desires and wished them both a long and happy marriage.

It was truly a happy marriage. They were both busy with their careers. On occasion, Stan and Janet were able to arrange a booking for Jack in locations where Marie would be traveling to on business for Macy's. The money was not ever enticing, but Jack and Marie had settled into a very reasonable lifestyle, so money was not as important to Jack as it once was. What was important was to be with Marie and enjoy their surroundings. They also enjoyed their life in Manhattan. The apartment was in the ideal location for both of them. Once or twice a year they would travel by train to Philadelphia to spend a few days with Milt and his family. Whenever Milt and Jean came to visit in New York, Jack made every effort to spend some time together with them.

In late 1939 and 1940 Jack made something of a comeback in his career. He was recording again and two of his recordings, "I'm Knee-Deep in Daisies and Head Over Heels in Love" and "A Faded Photograph", became very popular. When he sang the first selection Jack had visions of Marie in his mind. When he sang "A Faded Photograph", he thought of Peggy O'Neil. His thoughts about Peggy were not romantic in nature, but rather worrisome in that she was still in England. Jack had his taste of war and could not imagine Peggy going through the devastation that was spreading throughout Europe. The fight for France was over. The beaten British and French soldiers were evacuated from Dunkirk. The French officially surrendered to Germany on June 22, 1940. Germany now ruled most of central Europe along with Denmark and Norway. England refused to surrender, so in mid August, Hitler ordered the Luftwaffe to launch an aerial assault on Great Britain with the intent to bomb them into submission. As the air war progressed, London and its civilian population became a prime target for the German bombers. In New York City, the newspapers and newsreels showed the heartbreaking devastation in London resulting from the air raids. Jack prayed for Peggy's safety every day.

THE USO AND BEYOND

Jean still occasionally received mail from Peggy. She knew of Jack's concern and discreetly passed information from the letters to Jack. Peggy was actually rather upbeat and had volunteered to entertain the allied troops. Upon learning this, Jack decided it was time for him to become involved in the war effort. He asked Stan to find out where volunteers gathered in the city to entertain the troops. Several days passed before Stan got back in touch. From what Stan had learned, there was no real organization or any specific group handling entertainment for our soldiers and sailors. There were occasional gatherings sponsored by the Salvation Army and the Young Men's Christian Association, but there was no schedule of events, so it would be very difficult for Jack to volunteer his services. Stan did find out that the White House was concerned with the situation and President Franklin D. Roosevelt would soon be requesting something be done to provide morale and recreation services to the uniformed military personnel. Stan suggested that Jack sit tight for a month or two and give the organizations in New York City a chance to respond to the President's request.

On February 4, 1941, the United Services Organizations (USO) was founded and incorporated in New York. Six civilian agencies united in support of the military troops. Stan followed the proceedings closely and coordinated volunteering Jack's time and services as an entertainer. Big name entertainers like Bing Crosby, James Cagney, Fred Astaire, Glenn Miller, Martha Raye, and the Andrew Sisters were involved nationally. Stan admired Jack for his interest in helping with the morale of the troops. Of course, Jack's exposure might even help boost his popularity.

Jack had asked Jean if she might mention to Peggy in her next letter that he was entertaining military personnel on a volunteer basis here in New York City. Jean now became the "go between" to pass information from Jack to Peggy and vice versa. She didn't at all mind doing so. If anything it gave her letters to Peggy some information of interest. It seemed that both Jack and Peggy were rather busy entertaining the troops up to the end of World War II.

For almost a year before the war in Europe ended, Jean did not receive any letters from Peggy. Her fear was that something bad had happened to Peggy. She had just about run out of excuses in answering Jack about news from England when a letter did arrive. It was a rather sad letter. Peggy had been arrested for stealing a chocolate bar from a vendor in London. She was not sure as to an address where Jean could reach her, but promised to send one soon. Peggy always drew a little smiley face next to her signature on the letters. This letter had a sad face. It was the last letter Jean ever received from Peggy O'Neil. Jean simply told Jack she had received another letter from Peggy and she was all right.

Jack's popularity on a national basis had seriously declined. He still had bookings throughout New York City and sometimes in New Jersey. His radio work had also declined and sometimes it simply consisted of singing commercials. The decline in Jack's career, however, did not at all dampen the happiness in Jack and Marie's marriage. Marie's career was solid. They had no real financial problems. And most of all, they truly loved one another and enjoyed their time together. They enjoyed family gatherings and events such as anniversaries, birthdays, and graduations.

Jean and Milt's youngest son was to graduate from high school in June 1949. Jack and Marie had been to the graduation of both older sons and would not miss this one. When the invitation came, something struck Jack as being different. The two older sons, Bob and Jack, had graduated from Upper Darby High School. This invitation was for a graduation from Clifton Heights High School. Jack remembered Milt talking about moving, but thought the move would be to another home in the same township. He decided to look at some of the old notes and clippings he kept in his cigar box. Oops! The cigar box was missing from the closet shelf.

"Marie, have you seen my old cigar box?"

"Yes, Jack. Let me think for a minute. I know I didn't throw it away. I just moved it to make room for the blankets on the closet shelf."

Within minutes, Marie had located the cigar box and brought it to Jack.

"What is so important about the contents of this old box? I looked inside once and it looked like a lot of old junk in there."

"Well, come along with me to the kitchen table and I'll show what's in the box and explain the importance of each item."

They sat side by side at the table and Jack started to remove individual items from the box. He kind of arranged a lot of the cards, envelopes, and scraps of paper in a chronological sequence.

"Yes, this is the one I'm looking for. 'It reads Francis Kelly, Clifton Heights, Pennsylvania'."

Jack went on to tell Marie about his time in World War I with Francis Kelly and how Francis sang the lyrics as Jack played an old piano in a church that had been set up as a field hospital in Sainte-Menehould, France. He explained that his voice was so weak from being gassed that he could barely whisper.

"Now, Marie, the invitation we just received for young Gene's graduation is for a high school in Clifton Heights. When Bob and Jack graduated, it was from a high school in Upper Darby. So maybe, just maybe, this Francis Kelly will still be in Clifton Heights when we visit with Jean and Milt. Many years ago, I vowed I would try to catch up with Kelly."

Jack picked up an old envelope and told Marie about how he had found a mud caked billfold in a trench during the war. The billfold contained a letter that he traced to a soldier named Glenn Raney.

On one of his trips to Illinois, he took a side trip and met the soldier that had lost not only the billfold but also an arm over in France. He told her about JJ, the squad leader, who probably saved his life or at least his voice during the war by telling him exactly what to do after his gas mask malfunctioned. He mentioned meeting up with JJ and his wife out in California and buying dinner for them. He intentionally left Peggy out of the story. As he explained the significance of each item, Jack displayed where he would draw an X across the card or paper, indicating closure.

Marie picked up what looked like a commemorative pin from the table. The pin was attached to a white card the about the size of a typical business card. And there was the X marked across the card from corner to corner.

"What's the significance of this pin? It's dated from way back in 1893, before you were even born."

World Columbian Exposition Pin

Jack took the pin from Marie's hand and held it, so both could read the inscription.

"See what it says, 'World Columbian Exposition Chicago'. And see how in the center there is Christopher Columbus's Santa Maria sailing ship positioned on top of two globes. Each globe depicts the geography from one half of our earth and the numbers fourteen and ninety-two represent the year Columbus discovered America.

So this exposition was in commemoration of the four hundredth anniversary of Columbus discovering America. Today, we refer to it as The Chicago World's Fair. My mother and father were both there and brought back this pin along with magnificent stories about electricity and other early inventions. So, when I was performing in Chicago during the twenties, I had the opportunity to tour the museum on the site of the fairgrounds. You may not understand this, but doing so brought me a feeling of closure."

"I think I understand, Jack. And how about this rather short mechanical pencil?"

Jack took the pencil from Marie and rotated it in the light so she could read the inscription.

"There, can you read the engraving?"

"Yes. It says, 'To Jack from Bam-Bam. May 30, 1928'."

"This was a birthday present from Peggy O'Neil on my thirtieth birthday. See how it retracts to about three inches. It was very easy to carry in my pocket, and in those days when we signed lots of autographs there was no messy ink to worry about."

They went through the listing of names Jack had written with comments about how they helped him get started in his career and how he tried to show his appreciation by doing something for each of them. Jack told a little story about each entry. Marie was impressed. Jack could see Marie was tiring, so he picked up the business card Marie had given him when they first met.

"This, my love, is my most favorite of all. And without the phone number you wrote on the back of this card, we might not be here together now."

With that, Jack rose from his chair and pulling Marie from hers in a sweeping motion, carried her into the bedroom.

"Now you have to pay for all of the information I just gave you."

They made love and then just lingered in their bed for hours reminiscing about all of the good times they had experienced together.

Milt had to be at work the day Jack and Marie were to arrive at the Philadelphia Thirtieth Street Station so Jack, the second oldest of the three sons, met them at the station.

"Hello, Uncle Jack. Hello, Aunt Marie. How was the train ride?"

They embraced and shook hands exchanging pleasantries. Young Jack took their luggage and led them to the car parked nearby. It was the same 1935 Ford that Milt had used to chauffeur Jack to the Spanish mansion.

"I see your Dad still has the old Ford."

"Actually, I bought this car from Dad and he is now using my brother Bob's Chevrolet Fleetwood until Bob returns from the army."

"He's not overseas is he?" Marie asked.

"Well, Bob is overseas, but he lucked out and got to go to Germany."

"And how about you, will you be drafted soon?"

"Not for a while, Aunt Marie. I've been deferred because the company where I work manufactures instrumentation for our military aircraft."

"Well, we are looking forward to seeing your new home."

"It was pretty neat to move into a brand-new house. Mom just loves it."

The drive from the station to Clifton Heights took about twenty-five minutes. Young Jack pulled up almost in front of the brick row house in a community named Westbrook Park. He told his aunt and uncle that parking spaces on the street were sometimes limited, but they could always go around to the back alley and park either in the garage or on the driveway.

Jean was watching from the front door for their arrival and immediately came out of the house to greet Marie and Jack. Once inside, Jean took great pleasure in showing them through the house. She had young Jack take the suitcase upstairs to the bedroom that Marie and Jack were to use. Shortly thereafter, Marie and Jack went upstairs to freshen up and settle in for their short stay. Jean busied herself between the kitchen and dining room with the preparations for their evening meal.

Soon Milt arrived from work and Gene from his baseball practice. They all gathered in the living room and caught up on what had happened over the past year. There was quite a bit of talk about the ten-inch RCA television set in the room and about sometimes receiving New York channels, giving them a total of six channels to choose from. Jean periodically went to the kitchen to attend to preparation of the meal. On one occasion, Jack slipped into the kitchen, and in a soft voice, asked if there was any news from England. The answer was negative and Jack just shook his head before turning to return to the group.

"When you go back out there, please tell the baseball player he has ten minutes to get cleaned up for dinner."

After a fine dinner, the two boys asked to be excused and were off to spend time with their friends. Jack asked Milt to tell them how they came about selecting their new home.

"Well, Jack, it wasn't easy. When the veterans started to return from World War II, many of the rental properties were put up for sale. A veteran could buy a house with no money down, so the real estate market went from renting to selling. Our entire neighborhood of twin houses in Upper Darby was put on the market. The homes were already forty years old with coal burning furnaces and stucco exteriors that were in disrepair. We had to either buy or move. For us to buy anything we would have to come up with a 10 percent down payment. So we started looking around and soon found that getting the 10 percent plus closing costs together for houses priced between eight and ten thousand dollars was a formidable task.

"Jean and I talked it over, and then one night after dinner, we asked the boys to join us at the dining room table for a serious discussion. We put the facts and figures on a sheet of tablet paper and passed it to each of the boys. Jean explained with the money they had saved from their various part-time jobs, we could pool the money together and maybe have enough to meet the down payment for a new home. We are blessed with good kids. They didn't hesitate a minute. They brought their bank books and war bonds to the table and we started adding numbers. It didn't quite seem fair for the older sons to chip in all of their savings, but it was necessary. We never had one complaint. In fact, I think they were proud to be able to help out."

"Well, you should be proud of your boys. That's a pretty amazing story. Now I want to tell you a little story about my time in World War I and then ask you a question. As you know, I was gassed and spent some time recovering in a hospital over in France. Well, we had a company runner by the name of Francis Kelly. He and I were in the hospital at the same time, and we spent a good bit of time together. He told me he came from Clifton Heights, a small community just outside of Philadelphia. I would sure like to see him again. Do you per chance know him or is there some way we can look up his name?"

Jean responds, "Our Jack is dating a pretty young receptionist where he works. Her name is Nancy Kelly and she was born and raised here in Clifton Heights. When Jack comes back, I'll ask him to find out about this Francis Kelly for you."

The next morning at breakfast, Jean told Jack that Francis Kelly was in fact Nancy's father.

"Mr. Kelly very much remembers the 'Piano Player' from over in France and is looking forward to meeting up with you later today. Our Jack is going to take you to Mr. Kelly's house after the graduation ceremony."

"Wow, that's wonderful, Jean. I wonder what he looks like today. He used to be able to run like the wind. Thanks, Jean."

Francis Kelly looked pretty much the same, just thirty years older. He still had a very slim build and looked like he might still be able to run like the wind. Jack and Francis first embraced and then stood apart to look at each other.

"I knew you were going to be a great entertainer, Jack. I used to tell my kids how we spent some time together during the war, but I don't think they really believed me."

"Well, if you have a piano nearby we'll play and sing some of the songs just as we did over in France. Maybe then they will believe you."

"We don't have a piano, but my neighbor does, and I'm sure he won't mind us using it for a bit."

A bit turned into the rest of the afternoon and part of the evening hours. It seemed like half of the neighborhood turned out. Most of the songs were Irish and Francis knew the lyrics just as he had known them in France. Others in the crowd joined in. It was just a great time for all. Francis had dispatched young Jack hours ago, so as darkness set in, he told Jack he would walk with him back to Milt's house. It was only about a fifteen-minute walk and it gave them a little time to themselves. Jack was shocked to learn Francis had eight kids. And Francis was surprised to learn about Jack's romance with "Sweet" Peggy O'Neil. They both could not understand how she kind of disappeared over in England. Francis told Jack he would get his address from young Jack, so they could at least exchange Christmas cards. They embraced again and then Francis turned and walked away as Jack moved to enter Milt's house.

Marie, Jean, and Milt were watching the Ed Sullivan Show. Jack simply told them he had a great time and then joined in giving his attention to the performers on the television screen.

THE ED SULLIVAN SHOW

In the spring of 1950, Stan called Jack with a lot of excitement in his voice.

"Jack, you won't believe it. I got a call from one of the TV guys handling the Ed Sullivan Show. They want you make an appearance on the show and sing one or two numbers. This is big, Jack. You make a good showing and we'll have bookings all over New York City and possibly across the country, maybe even some new records. What do you think, kid?"

"I think that's great, Stan. How much time will I have to prepare for the show?"

"We're looking at the last week in May. And, they have suggested two numbers, 'Me and My Shadow' and 'A Faded Photograph'. They want a short audition sometime during the first week of May."

"I'll send my tux out to the cleaners and start practicing right away. Thanks, Stan, I can't wait to tell Marie."

"Okay, but make sure you and Marie keep it under your hats. The TV guys like to keep the schedule for Sullivan's show very hushed up."

"Thanks again, Stan. Let me know when you get more details."

Marie was ecstatic when she heard the news from Jack. They decided to celebrate by going out to dinner that evening.

Over the next few days, Jack started his preparation by first listening over and over to the recordings he had made of "Me and My Shadow" and "A Faded Photograph". Next he moved on to playing the piano along with the recordings. Once he felt confident, Jack turned off the record player and played the piano without any sheet music. He felt good about these two songs. Soon he was singing the lyrics as he played. By the time the third day rolled around, Jack felt he was ready for a command performance.

That evening, he tried out his performance with Marie.

"Oh, Jack, that was just beautiful. You're going to knock them dead on the show."

On the following Monday, Stan called to tell Jack he was scheduled for his audition on Wednesday. Jack was prepared and told Stan so. He continued to practice, but for the first time in many years, a nervous feeling crept in. He had trouble sleeping. He imagined missing a key on the piano or a word in the lyrics while performing. Marie sensed his uneasiness and tried to calm Jack by reassuring him that his playing and singing were even better than when she first met him.

The day for the audition arrived. Jack was to meet Stan at his office and then they would both go to the audition together. Jack was late getting to Stan's.

"Janet, have you heard from Jack? He should have been here by now."

Before Janet could respond, Jack entered.

"Sorry I'm late. I guess I'm a little out of practice."

Stan and Jack immediately left for the Ed Sullivan Studios.

"Are you all right, kid?"

"Yeah, I'm just a little nervous. You know, Stan, Peggy O'Neil was the first person ever interviewed on television, and here I am some twenty years later about to appear on television for my very first time. It's a little different from movies where should you make a mistake they just do another shoot."

The atmosphere at the studio was very informal. There was a small orchestra for accompaniment. Jack went over a few things with the orchestra leader and then took his position at the piano. A specialist approached Jack and informed him she was going to apply some makeup while he was on camera. Once the specialist and the camera operator were satisfied with the television picture, they were cleared to proceed on the director's signal. Again Jack was nervous, but after striking the first cord he kind of calmed down and gave a very good performance. The director then approach Jack and gave him some guidance on how to exit from the piano bench and move over to a spot on the stage where Ed Sullivan would be during the show.

"Mr. Sullivan may ask you a few simple questions. Your answers should be concise and then you will exit behind the curtain just off to your left. Is there anything you would like to ask?"

"No, sir, I think I've got it."

"Good, Jack, I want you here at least three hours before show time. Good luck."

On the way out of the studio, Stan told Jack his performance was excellent, but to continue to practice. Then they departed in different directions.

Jack religiously practiced back at the apartment. He even ventured away from "Me and My Shadow" and "A Faded Photograph" and played some of his old-time favorites. The lyrics came back to him as if it were just yesterday since he last sang the songs. He was feeling very confident and called for Marie to come and listen to a few of the songs. It was Saturday morning on the thirteenth of May. Jack's schedule for the Ed Sullivan Show was firmly set for Saturday evening the twenty-seventh of May, just two weeks away. Marie came into the room and sat across from the piano.

He started to play her favorite, "To Be in Love".

"Oh, Jack, that is so beautiful."

Then, suddenly, Jack stopped playing and slumped to one side on the piano bench.

"Jack! What's wrong?"

Marie quickly moved to his side and helped him get to a prone position on the floor. She then called for an ambulance. Jack had suffered a massive heart attack. He died before reaching the hospital.

There was a small funeral attended by family along with some of Jack's old contacts and friends from the music and broadcasting world. In accordance with his wishes, Jack Smith is buried next to his mother at Saint Raymond's Cemetery in the Bronx. His grave is unmarked.

Several months after Jack's passing, Marie asked Milt to come to New York and take much of Jack's memorabilia, some of which has been either cited or pictured throughout this text.

Almost ten years later, an obituary for ex-stage star Peggy O'Neil was published in *The New York Times*. She died in London on January 7, 1960. The last four lines of the obituary read, "arthritis afflicted her so badly that she was unable to walk. Twelve years ago she was confined to a wheelchair."

EPILOGUE

Jack's wife, Marie, passed away just a few years after Jack. Her death was reportedly a result of receiving the wrong blood type during a transfusion.

Jack's brother, Charles, moved to Toms River, New Jersey following his retirement. After a lifelong commitment to owning and driving Buick automobiles, his last car was a Nash. He passed away in 1963.

Milt and Jean remained in the home they had purchased in Clifton Heights until the time of their deaths. Milt died in 1981; Jean in 1991.

Jean's brother, William VonderLieth, was employed by Dunn and Bradstreet his entire working days. He received a gold watch upon his retirement for completing fifty years of service. In all probability, he will be the only person to do so in the company as they have a mandatory retirement at age 65. He died one year after retiring.

Milt and Jean's oldest son, Bob, went on to become a structural design engineer. He was involved in the building of skyscrapers worldwide. Bob passed away in 2010.

Milt and Jean's second oldest son, Jack, married Nancy Kelly after completion of his tour in the army. As of this writing, he remains active in the management of a manufacturing company.

When Nancy's father, Francis Kelly, became a widower, he moved to live out his final years with his daughter and young Jack.

Milt and Jean's youngest son, Gene, enlisted in the USAF and served twenty-eight years of active and reserve duty. Along the way, he graduated from college and later earned an MBA degree. His career was in aviation operations and logistics. Gene is currently retired. The past two years of his retirement have been devoted to writing the novel, *Whispering Jack and Peggy 'O'.*

"WHISPERING" JACK SMITH'S RECORDINGS

A Faded Photograph
Afraid of You
All by Yourself in the Moonlight
Are You Sorry
Baby Face
Birth of the Blues
Blue Skies
Cecilia, Does Your Mother Know You're Out?
Clap Yo' Hands
Crazy Rhythm
Don't Be a Fool, You Fool
Feeling Kind o' Blue
From Sunrise to Sunset
Funny Face
Gimme A Lil' Kiss, Will Ya, Huh?
Glad Rag Doll
Half a Moon
Heartbreaker
I Care For Her and She Cares For Me
I Don't Believe It-But Say It Again
I Faw Down and Go Boom
I Kiss Your Hand, Madame
I Never Dream't
I Wanna Go Where You Go, Then I'll Be Happy
I Wish I Knew How to Tell You
I'd Climb the Highest Mountain If I Knew I'd Find You

If I Didn't Know Your Husband and You Didn't Know My Wife
If I Had You
I'll Be Lonely
I'm Crazy Over You
I'm Knee-Deep in Daises, and Head Over Heels In Love
I'm On My Way Home
I'm Tellin' The Birds-Tellin' The Bees
It All Depends On You
I've Built My Hopes
Little Girl
Me and My Shadow
Miss Annabelle Lee
My Blue Heaven
My One and Only
My Sunday Girl
No One but You Knows How to Love
OO! Golly Ain't She Cute?
Peace of Mind
Play-Ground In the Sky
Poor Papa
Precious
Ramona
Rosy Cheeks
S' Wonderful
Sally of My Dreams
She's a New Kind of Old-Fashioned Girl
So Will I
Sunshine
Sweet Forget-Me-Not
That's a Good Girl
That's My Weakness Now
The Birth of the Blues
The Song I Love
The Song Is Ended, but the Melody Lingers On
Then I'll Be Happy
There Ain't No "Maybe" in My Baby's Eyes
There Must Be Somebody Else
To Be In Love, Espesh'lly with You

To-Night's My Night with Baby
When Autumn Leaves are Falling
When Day Is Done
When the Red, Red Robin Comes Bob-Bob-Bobbin' Along
Where Can You Be
Whispering
You May Not Like It
You Won't See Me, If I See You with Anyone

Artist's drawing from Jack Smith's files